# Media Audiences in Ireland
## Power and Cultural Identity

# MEDIA AUDIENCES IN IRELAND

## Power and Cultural Identity

edited by

MARY J. KELLY
BARBARA O'CONNOR

University College Dublin Press
Preas Choláiste Ollscoile Bhaile Átha Cliath

First published 1997 by University College Dublin Press,
Newman House, St Stephen's Green, Dublin 2, Ireland

© The several authors, each in respect of the chapter submitted, 1997
Introduction © Mary J. Kelly and Barbara O'Connor 1997

ISBN 1 900621 09 6

Cataloguing in publication data available from the British Library

Printed in Ireland by Betaprint, Dublin
Typeset in 10/12 Ehrhardt by Seton Music Graphics, Bantry, Ireland
Index by Helen Litton

# Contents

# Introduction

*Mary J. Kelly and Barbara O'Connor*

The typical media consumer, according to some recent thinking in the sociology of postmodernity, is the 'grazer' and the 'zapper', a product of the 'three minute culture' created as a consequence of the ever increasing flow of images across time and space. Within this scenario the impression is created of infinite choice and free flows among this kaleidoscope of cultures, subcultures and meaning systems. As we move in and through these systems cultural identities are formed and changed, adopted and rejected, imposed or struggled over. What escapes attention, however, in the postmodern debate, is the fact that access to and mode of participation in these cultures are structured and limited by social class, by gender, by ethnicity, by location in space, and by generation. This book examines the role of the media and their audiences in this struggle over meaning, identity and power and it places this examination within the social and cultural context of an unequally structured society.

Central to an understanding of the role of the media in society is an analysis of how audiences engage with and respond to media texts. Contributors to this volume investigate how particular audiences engage with and read a range of media including television drama, current affairs and documentaries, educational and children's programmes, radio magazine and chat shows, as well as film. The researchers explore the range of subcultural meaning systems which specific audiences bring to their media consumption. They also address the question of media power and the extent to which media consumption is used in the struggle for status and in the formation and negotiation of social identities.

An analysis of how media organisations construct audiences and how they address them is also crucial to our understanding of audiences. Is the audience addressed as citizen or consumer? What is the range of voices heard? How do the media form tastes and pleasures, and what is the relationship between these and the maintenance of power?

## Audience Research in Ireland

The book's main focus on broadcast media reflects both the centrality of these media in people's everyday lives as well as the 'state of the art' of audience research in Ireland. To date there has been little published research on Irish audiences and even less from a sociological or cultural studies perspective.[1] There have been occasional once off pieces of research which, although undertaken within established international scholarly perspectives, have not generated subsequent Irish research within this tradition. One of the best known pieces of early research is Grant Noble's (1975) study of the television viewing patterns of a group of teenage boys in Dublin. This social psychological investigation was undertaken within the very prevalent uses and gratifications audience research tradition of the time. In the late 1970s, research on the political influence of television was undertaken by Kelly (1983, 1984). This was part of a comparative nine-nation survey of the television coverage of the first European elections in 1979 which found that heavy viewing of the television coverage helped to mobilise voter turnout especially among the otherwise uninterested.

One might wonder at the relative absence of audience research within a sociological and cultural studies framework but when one considers the historical trajectory of these areas it is not quite as surprising. At both a theoretical and methodological level a sociology of culture (with the exception of some work on religious and political cultures) would have found it difficult to fit into the concerns of mainstream sociology. Historically one of the major influences on the shaping of Irish sociology in the South was the Catholic church whose agenda was social problem oriented and focused on issues such as work and unemployment, education, health and social welfare. In addition, many of the 'founding fathers', lay or clerical, in an effort to establish sociology as a professional and independent scientific discipline, worked almost exclusively with quantitative methodologies especially the social survey. The predominant methodologies were therefore not the most appropriate for the qualitative and interpretative approaches required for the analysis of cultural phenomena.

While the emergence of media and cultural studies in the early 1980s had generated an interest in media analysis, the initial focus tended to be almost exclusively on the examination of media texts with some linking of this textual analysis to an examination of production and cultural practices (see McLoone and MacMahon, 1984; Sheehan, 1987; Rockett, Gibbons and Hill, 1987; Dillon, 1993). Many of the young academics entering the developing fields of communication and film studies came from a literary, film studies or philosophical background in which textual analysis was predominant. And in conjunction with the disciplinary background of individual scholars, the theoretical hegemony of the *Screen* journal served to drive cultural analyses even further in a textual direction.

The contributions to this volume on media audiences are an indication of the present growing and lively interest in interpretative perspectives in sociology, cultural studies, and media studies. Now that these areas have begun to inform and enrich each other, research on media audiences in both Northern Ireland and the Republic has begun to accumulate and yet most remains unpublished. It is one of the main purposes of this book to rectify this. We have collected the existing qualitative research on audiences in one volume and are thus making available research findings which explore the rich cultural terrain at the interface between media, power and the subcultural discourses and identities of a wide range of audiences.

Three of the key issues which are central to this volume and which have occupied scholars of media consumption and audiences over the years are the media's power relative to that of the audience, how media texts and meanings are interpreted in the light of the different cultural identities of various audience groups, and, given what we know about audience reception of media texts, what the responsibilities of the media to its audience are within the democratic public sphere in which it operates. Each of these will be discussed in turn below, but we will first address some of the methodological issues which have influenced the qualitative audience research presented in this volume.

## Qualitative Research and Audience Studies

All the contributors use a qualitative research methodology consisting mainly of in-depth interviews and group discussions. This has come to be known as the interpretative approach to audience research and has become increasingly influential since the early 1980s when Morley (1980) undertook focus group research on the BBC television programme *Nationwide* and investigated the very different interpretative resources which various groups brought to their reading and discussion of this text. Detailed analysis of the discussions enabled the researchers to identify systematic differences between groups in their interpretations of the text due to the differing class, educational, occupational and subcultural position of various groups. Feminist researchers also turned to this approach seeking not only to explore women's interpretations of media texts, but also the pleasures of the text. Thus Ang (1985) analysed the tragic structure of feeling and melodramatic imagination which women brought to their engagement with and reading of *Dallas*. At the same time in Ireland, O'Connor (1987) was researching the responses of women in different social classes to Irish television drama (see Chapter 3 below) and later researched the gendered and class-based responses to both domestic and imported soaps (O'Connor, 1990).

*NB* ⸛

Qualitative research requires in-depth analysis of the responses of (usually) a small number of individuals or groups to media texts, and an interpretation of these responses in the light of the socially situated culture or lifeworld of the viewer. It is an attempt to 'sympathetically understand' the symbolic meaning of the text for viewers, and to begin to tease out the linkages between this symbolic meaning and their social world. As noted by Stevenson (1995:77) skilled use of this method '. . . is not governed by the author's cleverness, but by his or her ability to take the reader to the 'heart' of symbolically produced common meanings.'

In listening to, recording and analysing groups and individuals talking about their responses to the media, the researcher is interested not only in sympathetically understanding each group's interpretation of the text, but in identifying similarities in patterns of response across groups, and in particular how these may vary according to their social location. Typically, both in international research and in the research reported in this volume, interpretations tend to be influenced by the socially located interpretative frameworks viewers bring to their reading of the text. Viewers' class, gender, ethnicity and generation particularly influence these interpretative frameworks.

Although one of the limitations of this approach is the care needed in generalising findings to the population in general, the advantage is the access it offers to the local and everyday cultures and frames of reference which ordinary people bring to their reading of media texts. These rich linguistic and symbolic resources often remain hidden in other forms of audience research. This is history from below, and draws on Geertz's (1973:5) semiotic concept of culture as 'webs of significance', the analysis of which requires 'not an experimental science in search of law but an interpretative one in search of meaning'.

Qualitative audience research, frequently using focus groups, has become a highly reputable and systematic form of research. Some critics of this approach argue that viewers do not typically consume or talk about the media in a focus group setting. While this is so, there is ample evidence that audiences do talk to friends and neighbours, at school, at work and elsewhere, particularly about television, and use it to establish relationships and to test out and negotiate identities (see for example Gillespie, 1995). A focus group method simulates this while acknowledging that an ethnographic approach would be the ideal. Ethnographic research, however, involves considerable difficulty in negotiating access to what are private settings, as well as being very expensive and time consuming – a major difficulty particularly in Southern Ireland where the underfunding of social scientific research is well documented (O'Dowd, 1988).

## Media Power

One of the key issues which is central to this volume and which has occupied scholars of media consumption and audiences over the years is that of power.

Three distinct but related dimensions of power which are addressed in the contributions below are: the relative power of audiences in their everyday engagement with media; the power of media producers in selecting and defining content; and the role of powerful groups in influencing media definitions of events and indeed in defining media institutions themselves. The relative power of each group has generally been debated within the 'dominant ideology' versus the 'active audience' paradigm with proponents of the former claiming a powerful role for the media in influencing people's ideas and attitudes, while the latter school claim that audiences are active and selective in their media use.

The dominant ideology thesis argues that the media is one of the major ideological institutions in capitalist patriarchal societies, along with educational and religious institutions. This perspective, when elaborated in a European context, frequently draws on a Gramscian and Marxist perspective (see Hall, 1982, and Glasgow University Media Group, 1976, 1980), in the US on a media imperialism thesis (see Schiller, 1970), while feminists draw on a critique of patriarchy (see Tuchman, 1978). Ideology here is used to mean 'The ways in which meaning may serve, in specific socio-historical contexts, to sustain relations of domination' (Thompson, 1988:370). The media may also be seen to have more general 'symbolic power', meaning 'the way in which symbolic forms are use to influence and shape the course of events (Thompson, 1995:268). Ideological and symbolic power are best analysed within the context of other forms of power – economic, political and coercive. Thus this perspective – at its best – emphasises an analysis of the political economy of the media, or who owns and controls the media; an analysis of the symbolic forms of media texts; followed through with an analysis of audience reception. However, while those operating within this perspective make broad claims with regard to the ideological and symbolic power of the media, they have not always carried out the last phase, or research into audience reception, which might clearly and empirically demonstrate this.

This was particularly the case until the mid-1980s, but was rectified somewhat by the audience research of the Glasgow University Media Group (see Philo, 1991). They investigated audience response to the 1985 media coverage of the miners' strike, particularly their response to the media portrayal of violence by miners on the picket line. They found that while subcultural repertoires and other alternative sources of information did enable some to reject this media construction, those who had few alternative sources were particularly vulnerable to accepting the media portrayal. Furthermore the media portrayal in some instances was sufficiently powerful to 'overwhelm' subcultural perspectives.

The active audience perspective on the other hand has rejected the dominant ideology view of audiences. Research within the interpretative tradition has consistently highlighted that audiences use media forms selectively and that they bring cultural resources from the socially situated interpretative communities of their everyday lives and thus actively interpret media texts. They are not 'cultural dopes' as Fiske (1987) pointed out, or a *tabula rasa* on which dominant ideological images might be imprinted. Audiences may accept, negotiate or reject the 'preferred' or ideological reading encoded in the text by producers in the light of the cultural resources they bring to it.[2] There thus exists, according to Fiske, an open and semiotic democracy, rather than ideological domination. However while contributions to this volume confirm the importance of socially situated meanings in the readings of texts, particularly those of class, gender and ethnicity (see Kelly, O'Connor, R.Watson) none would argue for the extreme active audience perspective of Fiske. All would situate both the production of media texts and audience response within a broader societal context which is permeated by power relations.

Some of the research reported in this volume would support the thesis that the symbolic perspectives offered by the media are significant to the maintenance of power, not so much by bringing about widespread ideological conformity or unanimity, but by contributing to the symbolic confidence and perhaps unity of the privileged, while undermining the disempowered. For the powerful, the media's predominant emphasis on symbolic systems and perspectives, which support rather than fundamentally question the privileges and perspectives of the dominant, reaffirms their confidence and legitimates their power. It is of interest to note in this context the contribution of O'Neill to this volume. He examines the class based nature of the audience for the RTÉ radio programme, *The Arts Show*, in particular its attraction for the well educated middle class among its listeners, and analyses the cultural discourses articulated by 'elitist', 'middleground' and 'populist' listener groups. Drawing critically on the work of Bourdieu (1984) on social class and cultural capital, he uses his own findings to highlight the cultural confidence expressed by the middleground and middlebrow group as they pursue the arts as a source of identity.

Miller's contribution is also relevant in this regard. Some theorists of the dominant ideology argue that its power lies not only in integrating dominant groups but also in causing confusion and disintegration among the dominated (Poulantzas, 1975). Miller in his contribution would appear to offer supporting evidence for the latter claim. Miller looks at the role of the British state in the media misinformation regarding the shooting by the SAS of three members of the IRA in Gibraltar in 1988. He also looks at the extent to which audiences in England, Scotland and Northern Ireland, even some time after the event, still believed this misinformation. He finds that those audience groups that had few alternative sources of information except the media, in particular Scottish and English audience groups, did indeed continue to be misinformed. Yet this did not necessarily lead to wholesale support for the actions of the SAS among these groups but rather to some confusion and disquiet. He calls for further research that would explore in depth not only promotional strategies of dominant groups, and the extent to which these influence media production, content, and audiences' interpretations, but also the wider social, political and ideological outcomes of this process.

A further dimension to examining media power is to explore who selects and defines media content, not only in the more immediate terms of media producers, but also those who influence the media's definition of events and the structure of media institutions. The first of these questions is addressed in Devereux's chapter, which focuses on the way producers of *Glenroe* see its audience and more specifically on the way in which social issues such as poverty and groups such as Travellers are marginalised within the programme. He argues that the emphasis placed by producers on entertaining the audience and maintaining high ratings in their prime time Sunday evening slot, leads them to focus on character development rather than either dramatic plot or the exploration of social or class issues. The concern not to alienate a cross-class audience contributes to the production team's emphasis on 'safe' story lines, to privileging rural middle class characters, and to drawing on established ideological themes – in particular the dissolving of social and class differences in an ideology of familism and communitarianism. Within this frame, characters from deprived groups are not so much developed in their own right or in terms of their own subculture, but in relation to the dominant rural middle class characters, and social problems are resolved by the latter's kindness and philanthropy within the context of the Glenroe community.

Following through this theme of the construction of the audience, Iarfhlaith Watson looks at how the audience for Irish language programmes has been seen by broadcasting policy makers, including the state, broadcasting organisations and Irish language interest groups. He traces the development of changes in the policy regarding Irish language programming and highlights the current tensions between cultural and linguistic interests on the one hand and commercial considerations on the other in the establishment of Teilifís na Gaeilge (TnaG), the Irish language television station. Here broadcasting policy makers are not only attempting to guarantee the linguistic and media rights of Irish language speakers, but also to attract a potentially much wider audience with a range of programmes articulating a national and cultural distinctiveness. From the early planning stages, as this chapter shows, broadcasters were aware that both these ideals must be negotiated within a highly competitive national and international televisual market place. TnaG came on air on 31 October 1996. Initial indicators of audience levels show that, despite apparently attractive programming, TnaG faces a long haul to building audiences. It could be argued that the highly routinised nature of television viewing and programme selection in the home, in addition to linguistic and technical difficulties, presents TnaG with a particularly challenging task.

## Cultural Identity

The second major conceptual focus of this book is cultural identity. One of the central questions within cultural studies at the present time is the consequence of an increasingly internationalised media for the local, national and possibly global cultural identities of its audience. A second focuses on the pleasures of the text, on understanding – often using psychoanalytic theory – audiences' pleasurable engagement with the text, and from within a feminist perspective looking at the ambivalent and contradictory relationship between these pleasures and the possible patriarchal power of the text. Both approaches point to the complex, often contradictory, and multiple nature of identities in contemporary societies, and the ongoing and continuous processes of negotiating these identities.

Many cultural theorists (Hall, 1991; 1992; Featherstone, 1995; Gillespie, 1995) have raised the question of how increasingly globalised capital, labour markets and media may be related to shifting, multiple and hybrid identities. Have identities become increasingly fragmented as postmodernists argue? Is there increased dislocation of traditional local and national identities, or are groups successfully exploring and negotiating multiple identities. For instance Gillespie's (1995) research on young Asian adolescents in London found that they used a wide range of ethnic, local, national and global media in their exploration of complex and hybrid identities. She notes how this negotiation is characterised by a self-awareness and cosmopolitan openness.

Ireland offers an interesting exploratory context for questions regarding the media and identity. The questioning of the relationship between the extensive importation of media forms and its consequences for cultural identity has been recently raised in the larger European countries, especially France and Britain. Prior to the development of new media technologies (video, cable and satellite television) these countries imported few foreign programmes. On the contrary in Ireland, since RTÉ was established in 1960, not only has there been increasingly widespread access to British channels, but at least half the programmes on RTÉ itself have from the outset been imported. While home produced news and current affairs, chat shows and soaps remain highly popular, RTÉ retains nonetheless somewhat less than half of the total television audience. Furthermore Ireland's economy is very dependent on international capital and with a highly mobile population has experienced considerable cross-cultural contact. Thus one might expect, according to the postmodern hypothesis, an undermining of local, subcultural and national identities.

On the contrary, however, the research reported in this book indicates the enduring vitality of subcultural identities, in particular those of class, gender and ethnicity, although, as O'Neill's chapter shows, these identities are not rigid but can be negotiated and changed, and indeed the media may be used as a resource in negotiating these changes. The contributions also show how sub-cultural identities may intersect as groups draw on, for example, both class and gender discourses in their responses to television drama. O'Connor, in her contribution based on responses of selected groups of working and middle class groups of women and men to the television film the *Ballroom of Romance*, analyses the specific ways in which social class and gender-based discourses intersect to produce diverse responses to the film.

The importance of ethno-political identity in determining the construction of meaning around media messages is clearly indicated in Raymond Watson's chapter on responses of a small sample of nationalist and unionist families in Northern Ireland to a compiled television news bulletin. He identifies and describes their very different responses to the same news items, their selective attention and remembering, as well as their selective interpretation of images and texts. He relates these different interpretative strategies to their pre-existing ethno-political based value systems. Thus their news viewing operates in a way which tends to reaffirm social group interest and ethnic identity.

Nolan, in analysing responses to the programme *Orange, Green and Yellow* (one of a series made with the intention of improving relations between the two Northern communities), finds that despite these intentions, nationalists and unionists offer strongly opposed interpretations. However he also finds a strong congruence in one aspect of working-class responses – a mutual criticism of the programme makers for what is perceived as an absence of 'authentic' working-class voices in the programme and indeed their continued invisibility in programmes which purport to represent divided working-class communities and to give them a voice.

The two contributions that examine imported media focus on both the meaning and the pleasure of the media text: for children in the case of Gunning, and for women in the case of Byrne. The former draws on psychoanalytic theory, the latter on a feminist perspective. Byrne's piece is based on interviews with women who were regular cinema goers in Waterford during the 1940s and 1950s, and claims that the pleasures of cinema at the time performed a dual role for women, acting both as a 'utopian space' in which they could experience pleasure, excitement and a sense of liberation which contrasted with the sense of frugality, repression and control emanating from the social forces of family, church and work, and also as a socialising agent into 'modernity'. The pleasures of 'going to the pictures' for the women in Byrne's study were indeed multiple and varied and were related to the melodramatic narratives and characters such as romantic fantasies about the male stars and the emotional intensity associated with life's tragic situations. They were also related to the imitation of the fashion and hair styles of the female stars, and to the dis-cussion of the films with friends and work mates. Byrne views this 'utopian space' for women as essentially liberating.

The issue of the power-pleasure dynamic raised by Byrne's piece has been a dominant one in feminist writing on women's pleasure in popular cultural forms. The central question so frequently asked but so difficult to answer in any satisfactory way is the extent to which the pleasures such as romantic fantasies and the imitation of 'feminine' role models work to further reinforce patriarchy. Or alternatively, to what extent do they contribute to a sense of autonomy and independence? This echoes the ambivalence that O'Sullivan expresses in her piece about the possibilities for women's empowerment by participating in radio talk shows.

Gunning used a combination of psychoanalytic theory and focus group discussions to explore the pleasures of *Den TV* and *Baywatch*, favourite television programmes for two groups of Dublin schoolchildren, one of 8–9 year olds and one of 11–12 year olds. She examined both the texts themselves and the children's talk about the texts, finding that the most salient pleasure in *Den TV* was in the expression of the struggle between the Parent and Child selves, while the pleasures of *Baywatch* were mainly voyeuristic. These pleasures, she claims, were partially determined by the structure and mode of address of the programmes, but were also derived from extra-textual sources, specifically the stage of psychosexual development at which the children were operating. Using the critical powers at their disposal, both groups were actively engaged with the programmes and were able to deconstruct them in a variety of ways. She sees her findings as helping to dispel the idea, still so firmly held among many – educators and the general public alike – that children are passive and virtually powerless in the face of the omnipotent medium of television.

## The Public Sphere

As the previous discussion indicates there is no simple unilinear relationship between the media and its audiences. The research presented in this volume confirms Stevenson's (1995:180) conclusions that the media '. . . neither passively serve the interests of hegemonic formations nor are they economically, politically or culturally innocent . . . [They are] both dominatory and subject to the plural practices of audiences'. Thus the media confirm the ideological and symbolic power of some powerful and high status groups while weakening and disorganising those with little power. And yet it is possible for the latter to use the media creatively for their own psychological, pleasurable and cultural purposes. However, the pleasures of the text can be highly seductive and hide the symbolic power of the media to confirm the status quo, in particular perhaps by its ignoring of voices and cultures 'from below' and its non-articulation of alternative and radical perspectives.

The question of access to voices from below is addressed in two of the contributions. Nolan's and Kelly's chapters both deal with prosocial television programming. However the two programmes which they examine were produced in radically different ways. *Orange, Green and Yellow* was produced in accordance with an agenda sponsored by the British government and the Northern Ireland based Cultural Traditions Group, to promote better community relations. It was made by an independent professional production company working in accordance with their own established professional practices, and who appeared to pay scant attention to their intended audience. The programme articulated a middle-ground consensus that rejected sectarian and political extremism. As Nolan notes, to be outside this consensus was, by implication, to be against common sense. Working-class viewers forcefully rejected the programme, not least because of the exclusion of their perspectives.

The processes of production and reception regarding the *Right to Learn* programme on unemployment were very different as Kelly's chapter indicates. This series of programmes, although initiated and sponsored by RTÉ and the Audio Visual Centre in University College Dublin, directly involved twenty unemployed people in its production. The unemployed group selected programme themes, presented the programmes, interviewed the contributors, and wrote and played the drama sequences. The unemployed audience groups that viewed it responded to this participatory media production with interest, energy and enthusiasm. This did not mean that they were uncritical or that there was not a range of responses. But what it does show is that the media, by offering a diversity of voices and access to a wide range of opinion, can contribute to the establishment of a more encompassing and democratic public sphere.

O'Sullivan and Ryan also take up the potential for audience intervention in the public sphere. O'Sullivan addresses the issue in a chapter on listeners to the Gerry Ryan Show on RTÉ Radio 2. Her study of telephone callers to the show distinguishes callers by gender, topic and mode of discussion. In analysing the differences between types of callers in terms of the cultural competencies associated with each, she engages with the debate on the relationship between public and private spheres and the possibility of the media offering a forum that empowers the audience. She argues that the talk show is not part of a public sphere as defined by Habermas. That is, callers do not engage in rational critical debate where the force of the better argument wins. However the callers' use of the talk show for expressive purposes, for advice giving and receiving and for troubles-telling is, she suggests, potentially emancipatory especially for women. It allows for horizontal communication between listeners, and gives a public forum for the sharing of those emotional, relational and care-giving experiences that in the past have tended to be seen as the domain of women and confined to the private sphere. On the other hand, she points to the possibility that the airing of previously very private issues in public may lead to other forms of surveillance just as oppressive as that exercised by the church or the medical profession over women in the past. Furthermore, she notes that talk radio may remain at the level of individualised talk rather than social action, and thus in effect contribute to maintaining the status quo rather than changing it.

Ryan in his analysis of audience response to the televised coverage of the 1995 divorce referendum also raises the issue of the relationship between television and maintenance of the status quo. Having examined audience responses to clips from news, current affairs (*Prime Time*) and a studio-audience discussion (*Davis*) programme on the referendum, he discusses how a 'soundbite' television culture tends to confirm the already known, while social change requires more elaborate argument. As commercial, competitive and technological pressures increase, news, current affairs and studio discussions may well move to more fast-paced formats and styles, which, he argues, may both lessen television's contribution to informing citizens on public and complex issues as well as limiting its ability to offer forums in which new options for change may be explored in depth.

The fact that audiences are deeply divided by different class cultures is again evident from Ryan's research. Responses to the case histories of two working-class families presented in *Prime Time*, to the use of 'expert' knowledge and to programme pace were all class based. Working class voices were defined as 'inarticulate' by middle-class viewers, and lack of identification with them led to a concentration on the way that the message was communicated rather than its substance. Middle-class viewers preferred middle-class and 'expert' voices, which are indeed the dominant voices in the Irish media.

What then are the responsibilities of media institutions in relation to audiences in this complex world of not only multiple and crosscutting cultures, discourses and identities but also of power and money? Furthermore the media world is itself changing, becoming more complex and fragmented with the ongoing introduction of newer information and communication technologies and services. What is the role of public service broadcasting in these contexts? Public service broadcasting was introduced and continues to be defined in terms of civic and national responsibilities within a nation state. In the context of increased globalisation, is the nation state and sense of a nationally imagined community now dissolving in favour of locally based cultures on the one hand and globally based media and power on the other, as some have argued?

One of the clearest research findings presented in this volume is the continued vitality of subcultures based on class, gender and ethnicity. What is also clear is that there is a reflexivity and awareness within these subcultures, especially those less privileged and powerful, that their voices are not frequently heard in the media. Thus their legitimate aspiration to be heard and to be confirmed and respected is not seen by them as being honoured. Yet as already cautioned above, doing this needs considerable care to ensure that inclusion does not mean incorporation in terms of the voices and need of the dominant. It is the distinctive voice of the excluded and their cultural difference that needs to be heard.

Some theorists have persuasively argued that a major role which public service broadcasting has fulfilled in the past has been to ideological elaborate and legitimate the imagined community of the nation state (see Scannell and Cardiff, 1991, and Kelly and Rolston, 1995). It has also played a central role in confirming the authority of particular groups within the state, while also, it has been argued above, contributing to the disorganisation and continued marginalisation of others. However, with globalisation of economic and media forces, this central role in relation to the nation state, some would suggest, has been considerably weakened, as indeed has the nation state itself. Others have argued that globalisation has not weakened the state, and indeed that the economic forces powering globalisation need the state. They need it to ensure that social order is maintained, both ideologically and if necessary coercively, and to provide an educated and healthy workforce. Transnational corporations thus work in and through each individual nation state, and form a symbiotic relationship with it (see Hamelink, 1993: 386). Thus the role of national broadcasting systems, though not necessarily based on the public service broadcasting model, will continue to play a role even if not as predominantly as before.

The role of the media in relation to the public sphere refers to its relationship and responsibilities to its audiences, to the state and to the market. In the 1980s these relationships changed throughout Europe as commercial broadcasting and new media technologies (including increased satellite, cable and video services) threatened national broadcasting systems which in most European countries had been public service monopolies. The assumption of the prevailing neo-liberal ideology was that market forces would widen the range of broadcasting services and programming. This has not proved correct. On the contrary, monopolies developed, while for audiences it was, at best, more of the same on an increasing multiplicity of channels (see DeBens *et al.* 1992).

Public service broadcasting across Europe was significantly challenged as it competed for viewers with the entertainment oriented commercial channels. It has been argued that its ability to fulfil its public service remit has consequently been considerably weakened both by declining audiences and declining financial resources. This remit includes ensuring that citizens have access to that range of information which will enable them to know their rights, to discuss them rationally and to organise to pursue them, and to participate in political decision making and thus act as responsible citizens. It also includes ensuring that the cultural perspectives of all citizens receive adequate representation (see Curran, 1991; Murdock, 1992; also The Broadcasting Authority (Amendment) Act, 1975).

Ireland was no exception to the media changes being experienced across Europe. Although RTÉ had always faced strong competition from richer

British terrestrial channels, this was further intensified in the 1980s by satellite services and the extensive cabling of homes. The ability of RTÉ to fulfil its public service remit to citizens, and thus its contribution to maintaining a democratic and open society, cannot be divorced from an understanding of the highly competitive economic context in which it operates as it fights for audiences and advertising money. To fulfil its civic and cultural obligations it needs to understand its audiences and their cultures, and to understand how these interconnect with power, privilege and politics. To fulfil its public service obligations its financial basis needs to be protected, for it needs to work creatively to represent and develop these cultures and to promote the civic and democratic responsibilities of all citizens.

## Notes

[1]  Most audience research which has been conducted has tended to be market driven, for example undertaken by RTÉ or by newspapers mainly to serve their own needs and those of advertisers. Consequently it is not in the public arena for discussion. As far back as 1953 Radio Éireann initiated research on radio audiences and continues to commission the most substantial body of both radio and television research. While this rich source of data could be invaluable to academic researchers, and while RTÉ have been open to individual requests for audience data, there is as yet no formal relationship between them which would give access to bone fide researchers outside the national broadcasting institution. While acknowledging the commercial sensitivity of such data, a future consideration might be a policy of allowing access to data which is longer commercially sensitive. This would allow for a much more dynamic relationship between academic researchers and broadcast and other media institutions, which would enhance the quality of audience research generally and in particular it would make for the fruitful integration of the quantitative and the qualitative research traditions.

[2]  David Morley who originally introduced the concepts of audiences' acceptance, negotiation or rejection of the preferred reading of the text, subsequently criticised the oversimplified uses of these terms, as have others (see Morley, 1992).

## References

Ang, Ien (1985) *Watching 'Dallas': Soap Opera and the Melodramatic Imagination.* London: Methuen.

Bourdieu, Pierre (1984) *Distinction: A Social Critique of the Judgement of Taste.* London: Routledge.

Curran, James (1991) 'Mass Media and Democracy Revisited' in James Curran and Michael Gurevitch (eds) *Mass Media and Society*, London: Arnold.

De Bens, Els, Mary Kelly and Marit Bakke (1992) 'Television Content: Dallasification of Culture?' in Karen Siune and Wolfgang Truetzschler (eds), *Dynamics of Media Politics*, London: Sage.

Dillon, Michele (1993) *Debating Divorce: Moral Conflict in Ireland*, Lexington: University Press of Kentucky.

Featherstone, Mike (1995) *Undoing Culture, Globalization, Postmodernity and Identity.* London: Sage.

Fiske, John (1987) *Television Culture.* London: Methuen.

Geertz, Clifford (1973) *The Interpretation of Cultures: Selected Essays.* New York: Basic Books.

Gillespie, Marie (1995) *Television, Ethnicity and Cultural Change.* Oxford: Oxford University Press.

Glasgow University Media Group (1976) *Bad News.* London: Routledge.

Glasgow University Media Group (1980) *More Bad News.* London: Routledge.

Hall, Stuart (1982) 'The Rediscovery of 'Ideology': Return of the Repressed in Media Studies' in Michael Gurevitch, Tony Bennett, James Curran and Janet Woollacott (eds) *Culture, Society and Media.* London: Methuen.

Hall, Stuart (1991) 'Old and New Identities, Old and New Ethnicities' in A. King (ed.) *Culture, Globalization and the World System.* London: Methuen.

Hall, Stuart (1992) 'The Question of Cultural Identity' in S.Hall, D. Held and T. McGrew (eds) *Modernity and its Futures.* Cambridge: Polity Press.

Hamelink, Cees (1993) 'Globalism and National Sovereignty' in Kaarle Nordernstreng and Herbert Schiller (eds) *Beyond National Sovereignty: International Communication in the 1990s.* New Jersey: Ablex.

Kelly, Mary J.(1983) 'The Media View of the 1979 European Election Campaign' *Economic and Social Review*, 14(2).

Kelly, Mary J.(1984) ' Televised Elections as Ritual: The Case of the European Elections' in Chris Curtin, Mary Kelly and Liam O'Dowd (eds) *Culture and Ideology in Ireland.* Galway: Galway University Press.

Kelly, Mary J. and Bill Rolston (1995) 'Broadcasting in Ireland: Issues of National Identity and Censorship' in Patrick Clancy, Sheelagh Drudy, Kathleen Lynch and Liam O'Dowd (eds) *Irish Society: Sociological Perspectives.* Dublin: Institute of Public Administration.

McLoone, Martin and John McMahon (eds) (1984) *Television and Irish Society.* Dublin: RTÉ.

Morley, David (1980) *The Nationwide Audience.* London: British Film Institute.

Morley, David (1992) *Television, Audience and Cultural Studies.* London: Routledge.

Murdock, Graham (1992) 'Citizens, Consumers and Public Culture' in Kim Christian Schroder and Michael Skovand (eds) *Media Cultures.* London: Routledge.

Noble, Grant (1975) *Children in Front of the Small Screen.* London: Constable.

O'Connor, Barbara (1987) Women and the Media: Social and Cultural Influences on Women's Use of and Response to Television', unpublished PhD dissertation, University College Dublin.

O'Connor, Barbara (1990) *Soap and Sensibility: Audience Response to Dallas and Glenroe.* Dublin: RTÉ.

O'Dowd, Liam (1988) *The State of Social Science Research in Ireland.* Dublin: Royal Irish Academy.

Philo, Greg (1990) *Seeing and Believing: The Influence of Television.* London: Routledge.

Poulantzas, Nicos (1975) *Political Power and Social Classes.* London: New Left Books.

Rockett, Kevin, Luke Gibbons and John Hill (1987) *Cinema and Ireland.* Kent: Croom Helm.

Scannell, Paddy and Cardiff, David (1991) *A Social History of British Broadcasting, Vol. One, 1922–1939: Serving the Nation.* Oxford: Blackwell.

Schiller, Herbert I (1970) *Mass Communication and American Empire.* New York: M.E. Sharpe.

Sheehan, Helena (1987) *Irish Television Drama: A Society and its Stories.* Dublin: RTÉ.

Stevenson, Nick (1995) *Understanding Media Cultures.* London: Sage.

Thompson, John (1988) ' Mass Communication and Modern Culture: Contribution to a Critical Theory of Ideology', *Sociology*, 22 (3).
Thompson, John (1995) *The Media and Modernity, A Social Theory of the Media.* Cambridge: Polity.
Tuchman, Gaye (1978) *Hearth and Home: Images of Women and the Media.* New York: Oxford University Press.

# 1

# Participatory Media and Audience Response

*Mary J. Kelly*

Contemporary media have frequently been criticised for their non-democratic
and inegalitarian patterns of communication. Their control by a tiny minority
of high status, dominant and culturally acceptable groups leads to forms of
communication which is top-down and generally one-way. Many media
analysts have argued that these patterns have been intensified by increased
media privatisation, commercialisation and monopoly ownership. They argue
for greater media and cultural democracy and for the media to be more responsive to citizens and civil society, and especially to the marginalised and
excluded, rather than to the ideological, commercial and bureaucratic interests
of media owners, producers and professionals. They argue that there is a need
to explore further the meaning of cultural citizenship at the end of the twentieth
century, and to look at the implications of this for the media, especially in
terms of ensuring greater diversity and greater equality of access (see Golding,
1990; Garnham, 1990; Murdock, 1990).

Equality of access includes a range of rights as citizens: access to a diversity
of information and perspectives as well as the right to have one's own voice
heard. A media system informed by such rights, it is argued, would empower
and enrich citizens, local communities, cultures and subcultures, and thus contribute to maintaining and reinforcing democracy. These emancipatory processes
would liberate citizens and communities by raising questions regarding existing
power structures and their exclusionary and inegalitarian practices, offer a
language in which these might be discussed and analysed, and thus offer the
possibility of mobilising for change.

In an attempt to ensure a space for such democratic media forces, state
regulation of monopoly media control by commercial interests has been argued

for, as has continued state support for public service broadcasting. Within and alongside these however, a case has been made to support alternative and more participatory media forms (see Hamelink, 1983, 1994, 1995; Servaes, Jacobson and White, 1996; White, 1994; Downing, 1984; Dowmunt, 1993, Prehn, 1992). Both commercial and public service broadcasting need to become more responsive to the democratic interest, in particular to those groups excluded within society and from the media. They have a right to have their voices heard.

This chapter examines a case study of an attempt to provide access to television to one excluded and marginalised group, the unemployed, through facilitating a group of twenty unemployed people to produce a series of five programmes on unemployment, education and the media entitled the *Right To Learn*. The programmes were conceived, developed and transmitted within the remit of the Educational Programmes Department in RTÉ and the Audio Visual Centre in University College Dublin. They were produced in the Audio Visual Centre during 1993 and transmitted by RTÉ 1 twice during 1994, in late evening and daytime slots. It was envisaged that these programmes would draw upon and link back into the growing adult education sector, and especially unemployed groups within this sector. Thus not only were five programmes produced and transmitted, but these were edited into a 90-minute video, plus related workbook, for use in adult education settings.[1]

This chapter will focus not so much on the participatory mode of producing the series (see Kelly, 1996), but on the consequences of this for audiences. Audience response was explored through showing the first of the programmes to twelve mainly unemployed groups within the adult education sector, followed by a discussion. These focus group discussions were audio-taped and transcribed, and it is an analysis of these responses which constitutes the core of the chapter. The analysis is framed by drawing on the dialogic perspective offered by the Bakhtin Circle and by Paulo Freire.

## Dialogic Communication Perspectives: The Bakhtin Circle and Paulo Freire

The Russian linguistic theorists Bakhtin (1981, 1984) and Voloshinov (1973) have consistently emphasised the social nature of languages, texts and communication systems. Meaning for Bakhtin and Voloshinov is always social: the meaning of a word is 'locked into an intense relationship with the word of another', it is 'always addressed to another with a keen anticipation of response' – it is thus 'doubled voiced' (Gardiner, 1992:28–29). Hence the importance of a dialogic perspective in analysing language and sign systems. A dialogic perspective accepts that the word is addressed to another, words adapt and change according to the relationship between speaker and addressee, and the particular socio-cultural context of the interaction. Meaning is thus fluid, unstable and open to struggle, it is 'polysemous' or 'multiaccentuated'.

Authoritarian modes of communication attempt to limit this multiac-centuated nature of the word, to fix its meaning in the interests of maintaining power. For Voloshinov (1973:101), as for Gramsci, this occurs when meaning becomes 'a matter of dogmatic belief, something taken for granted and not subject to discussion'. The conditions which contribute to this authoritarian or monologic mode may include control by dominant groups over communication systems, the extent to which these dominant groups are seen to hold legitimate authority, the extent to which the message being communicated is seen as pivotal within the dominant ideology as a whole, and the extent to which various classes and groups in society are integrated or marginalised within the economic system. Alternatively, many different perspectives will exist when monopoly control of ideology and the media is weak, or when those who control it are widely criticised and without authority, and when classes and subcultures exist within society which are not integrated economically – for example, the unemployed.

Freire has also analysed and promoted the use of a dialogic mode, in this instance within educational systems. Rather than a 'banking system' of education in which educational knowledge is defined in an authoritarian manner by the educational system to be delivered by teachers to passive pupils, Freire would begin with the interests, common sense understandings and culture of the learners, who, through dialogue with others, explore and analyse this world. This analysis is fostered through examining how their everyday world is structured and influenced by the broader socio-economic, political and cultural contexts within which it exists. This analysis, particularly when undertaken by the marginalised, raises questions of cultural identity and subordination, of power and empowerment, of social change and democracy (see Freire, 1972, 1985; Shor and Freire, 1987).

Communications researchers have begun to explore the usefulness of Bakhtin's approach and continue to take up Freire in their analyses of alternative and participatory forms of communication (see Rahim, 1994; and Servaes, Jacobson and White, 1996). In this chapter emphasis is placed on examining the dialogic processes involved in how audiences responded to the *Right To Learn* programmes. Drawing on Bakhtin and his circle, an analysis will be offered of how these dialogic processes were influenced by the participants' subcultural discourses and by their immediate conditions of interaction as they discussed the programme. Reinforcing this interest in the dialogic process is Freire's emphasis on its emancipatory potential. The question will be raised of the extent to which the *Right To Learn* programmes encouraged among viewers critical discussion and analysis of unemployment, of the socio-economic and political contexts which maintain it, and of the possibility for change.

## Audience Research: Text, Reception and Response

In order to explore how the *Right To Learn* programmes were responded to by audiences, research with mainly unemployed groups – which were the target group for the programme – was carried out. Focus group discussions were completed with twelve groups, totalling 102 respondents. Having shown each group the first of the *Right To Learn* programmes, a 30–40 minute discussion on the programme and the issues it raised was facilitated and audiotaped. Each participant also completed a short questionnaire eliciting socio-demographic information and individual evaluations of the programme.

The programme, entitled 'Exploding Myths', questions some of the central and prevailing myths about unemployment and the unemployed. The introduction, linking pieces (including two short dramas) and interviewing are all presented by the unemployed co-producers of the series, thus clearly establishing their voice and perspective. After a brief self-introduction by three of the co-producers and an upbeat opening sequence cut to music, the programme begins with vox pop statements articulating such myths as: there are 'loads of jobs to be done out there', that the unemployed should 'get out there and go look for a job', that they are lazy. It then examines – with the objective of exploding – three major myths using the unemployed co-producers and presenters to interview selected 'experts' and provide linking pieces.

The first myth is entitled 'The Economic Myth'. One such myth discussed is the belief that the problem of unemployment can be solved by industrial growth. However, as is pointed out by two 'experts', it is not the responsibility of industry and business to solve unemployment, their business is to make a profit, which may mean getting rid of people rather than increasing the number at work.

The second myth is entitled 'The Wasters' Myth'. Here the assertion that the unemployed are wasters and lazy is examined by an 'expert' looking at research which indicated that the vast majority of the unemployed are looking for work, by talking to an officer of INOU (Irish National Organisation of the Unemployed) and also interviewing some unemployed who do unpaid voluntary work and who feel they have never worked harder. They are thus unwaged rather than unemployed. What is needed, it is claimed, is a voice for the unemployed themselves.

The third myth exploded is that training can get you a job. Here there is a double message: training cannot guarantee a job yet adult education is worthwhile in itself, in particular it builds self confidence. The myth that training can deliver a job is questioned in terms of the lack of jobs whether you are trained or not and the existence of many qualified people who are unemployed. Nevertheless adult education, especially that run by the community itself, is presented in a very positive light: it enables communities to take control of the educational system in their own area, to design relevant courses, to encourage participation, and it provides a context in which to examine fundamental social questions such as why some are rich and others poor, some have jobs and others do not.

In the discussion on adult education, a short drama, as well as interviews with working class women participating in adult education, pieces to the camera and voice-overs by the unemployed themselves are used. The drama, entitled 'the courses' drama' later in the chapter, presents a domestic family scene in which a husband sitting reading a newspaper questions his wife as she goes out the door to do 'another new course' down at the community centre. She replies that she is taking this course not necessarily to get a job but to become more confident, develop new skills and because it is something just for herself – something other than home and the kids. There is also a short 'training the trainers' drama, in which two tutors ironically send up the development of the biggest growth industry of all: training itself.

The programme ends with a six-minute drama again written and acted by the unemployed co-producers. In this, they hoped to examine two central themes: discrimination towards the marginalised and, to combat this, knowing your rights and insisting on these being honoured. The marginalised person in this instance is an unemployed Traveller. The drama is set in a social welfare office. Here four scenarios are enacted. In the first, a Traveller asks the officer at the counter to sign off the unemployment register as he is taking up a course. The officer makes derogatory comments to her colleague about a 'course for knackers' and tells him to come back another day, threatening police action when he protests. In the second scenario the Traveller returns with the course director. She explains the situation and because she is known to the officer she is not only treated politely but the request is fulfilled. The camera then pulls back so that the viewer can see that this is a drama being acted by the unemployed presenters. They discuss their dissatisfaction with the last scene, especially the fact that it is a settled person speaking on behalf of the Traveller. Instead they decide to show the unemployed traveller being accompanied by a Traveller – in this instance a well-known Traveller – to the welfare office. Because the latter is a well known actor in *Glenroe* there is no problem signing off. This scene is again found unsatisfactory, however, as they feel that ordinary Travellers should be able to insist on their rights. This is done in the fourth and final scene. When it appears that the traveller's request to sign off will again be rejected, the Traveller reinforces his claim by asking to see the supervisor and producing the Bill of Rights for the Unemployed. The officer signs him off.

All of the groups to whom the programme was shown were involved in adult education, either within the VEC [Vocational Education Committee] or in the voluntary adult education sector. It was from within this context that the groups were approached and focus group research completed. Seven groups were female and five male (for details see the appendix, p. xx). Half were Dublin based, the other half from a rural/small town area. Two thirds of the participants were working class, and the majority of all respondents were also at present unemployed. Just over half had left school at sixteen or less, while the average age was 37.

As Bakhtin and Voloshinov have argued, dialogic discourse is oriented to the 'other' and is to be differentiated from authoritarian and monologic discourse which attempts to dominate and normalise. Dialogic discourse is respectful of the autonomy and responsiveness of the other. Dialogue is thus best understood by contextualising it: examining how dialogue is structured to negotiate a relationship with the other. This relationship is structured not only by the immediate face-to-face situation, but *inter alia*, by its institutional context and the class, status and power relationships within which the face-to-face encounter occurs. Thus the fact that the focus groups were all conducted within an adult education context was highly material to the form and structure of the dialogue between participants. The established norm of interaction within the groups was that of openness, a willingness to listen to – but not necessarily to agree with – a range of opinions, while no one individual was allowed to dominate. This led to lively discussion with, in some instances, highly conflictual perspectives being aired. This was particularly true of those men's groups which were radical in socio-political orientation, although the heated nature of the discussion was undoubtedly over-emphasised by one participant as he temporarily left the room for a smoke commenting, 'They're f... killing one another in there'.

While all groups were open to the opinions of others, other aspects of discursive style varied quite widely. One major difference was between the majority of men's groups and women's groups. Men's groups, especially if well established and radical in orientation, were far more assertive, conflictual and argumentative in style than women's groups. Men in these groups more frequently raised new points, questioned and disagreed with each other. In women's groups there was more giving of support to one another, more interdependent elaboration of points as well as less disagreement. Tannen (1993:179), in her review of a wide range of research on gender and conversational interaction, reports similar patterns, while in the same volume James and Drakich (1993:302) note that women talk '. . . simply in order to keep the interaction flowing smoothly and to show good will towards others, and they . . . talk about personal feelings and other socio-emotional matters relevant to interpersonal relationships to a greater extent than men'. Coates (1993:203) has concluded from her sociolinguistic research that women's conversational style is based on solidarity while men's is based on power, a difference arising directly, she argues, from women's and men's membership of a patriarchal society and hence different patterns of socialisation and a male pattern of maintaining dominance through interaction.

A further gender difference which men and women brought to their reading of the *Right To Learn* text was a differential preference for the drama sections – in particular the Travellers' drama. Six of the seven women's groups liked the Traveller's drama and identified with the discrimination faced by the Traveller – often recounting similar experiences themselves. On the contrary, four of the five men's groups were critical of the Travellers' drama. They felt it was 'unrealistic', 'overdone', 'a bit overboard', and that the mixing of what they saw as two different issues, discrimination towards the unemployed in general, and discrimination towards Travellers, within the one drama, side-tracked from what they defined as the main issue – unemployment.

The finding of gender differences in responses to television drama is in line with other research both in Ireland and internationally (see O'Connor in this volume and Morley, 1992). The women's preference for the drama rather than the documentary sections of the programme led them to feel they were more likely to remember it and the issues it had addressed, than the prior discussion of myths about unemployment in the documentary section. For most men's groups, the Traveller's drama was a distraction from the 'real' issue – unemployment, which was better discussed in the documentary sections.

Not only did gender, the adult education context and the established norms of interaction influence the focus group discussions, so did the *Right To Learn* programme to which they were responding. All groups responded with a high level of engagement and interest – for some, critical interest – both while viewing the programme and in the subsequent discussion. Confirming Shor and Freire's (1987:97 seq.) argument, a major contributing factor here was that the programme, co-produced by people who were themselves unemployed, articulated a known world, a world which coincided with the respondents' everyday experiences and which thus confirmed, acknowledged and respected this world. Thus this audience, drawing on similar social experiences to the unemployed co-producers, responded with spontaneity and enthusiasm. This might be compared with the responses of six groups of second-year university students with whom this focus group research was initially piloted. None of the younger students spontaneously and enthusiastically engaged with the *Right To Learn* programme they had just seen, few seeing it as relating to their world, a world which for most of them was relatively privileged. The exception was one group of mature students some of whom had experiences of unemployment and marginalisation on which to draw and consequently responded with considerable enthusiasm to the programme.

It has been argued above that the groups' reception of and response to the programme were influenced by the adult educational institutional context in which the viewing took place, by gender differences, and by the enthusiastic dialogic response to a programme which confirmed and acknowledged their world.[2] Reception and response were also found to be substantially influenced by the socio-political orientation of the group. Three such orientations were identified as influential: a radical-critical perspective, a reformist-liberal perspective and a localist-familial perspective. These perspectives influenced how groups responded to the programme's treatment of the issues of unemployment and education. They influenced how the groups went on to discursively analyse the socio-economic position of the unemployed, and the extent to which they argued for social change. Each of these perspectives and how they influenced the discussions on unemployment and social change will be discussed in detail below.

## Radical-Critical Groups

Radical–critical groups were identifiable by their interest in and critical analysis of class and power structures and in particular how they contributed to maintaining unemployment. They also highlighted the need for radical change if the unemployment situation was to be improved.

Six groups were found to bring this perspective to bear when viewing the *Right To Learn* programme. They included the two Dublin men's groups, two of the three rural men's groups and two of the four Dublin women's groups. Two thirds of these respondents were working class. A socially structured factor which was strongly related to the holding of a radical perspective was extensive experiences of unemployment: two thirds had experienced at least three previous periods of unemployment, this being much higher than among those in reformist groups (33 per cent) or localist groups (13 per cent, see Appendix 1, p. xx).

The radical groups were highly critical of the unemployment situation and argued strongly for action by the unemployed. Four radical men's groups argued for political action by the unemployed united with the working class and trade unions, while the two radical women's groups argued for political action through community groups. All of these groups expressed deep and bitter criticism of the existing economic, political, class and power structures. An example from the discussion transcript of one radical group highlights this (see p. 269 for key to Transcription Symbols):

> . . . I think we have to look at the capitalist system [(chorus of 'mm' in agreement)] that does exist. Because the capitalist system is a major cause of unemployment and it's, it's the way in which the capitalist system is allowed to continue to develop and continue to draw on the most resources, financial resources to all of their dealing and wheeling, it's because of all that. All of that has to be questioned. But they have to be confronted, not just kind of talked about in little rooms like this or to a video [(mm)]. They have to be confronted directly, we're talking about direct action now [(mm)] because it really can't continue, particularly when we have so much hunger in the world [(mm)] we

have so much starvation, we have so much war. All of them questions have to be looked at. I know that we're looking at it in an Irish context here, I'm very aware of that. But there's connections, there's links and we have to take them, we have to look at it in the whole sense, you know, in a social analysis.
/ ( ) Purely and simply that profit comes before people.

(Radical Dublin women's group, G.6)

Radical men's groups agreed, and in their analysis of power began to specify who they felt held power:

. . . Like I reckon meself it's the government and the power blocs in the country that have created this system . . .

and later:

You're talking about ? (. . .)
/ Well I'm talking about big business. I'm talking about Tony O'Reilly, I'm talking about Tony Ryan. I'm talking about the whole lot of them.

(Radical rural men's group, G.9)

All agreed on the need to organise, to unite the unemployed and workers within the working class so that 'it's not the workers against the unemployed, it's the underprivileged against the privileged':

But what I'm talking about is the, like, we've seen [on the programme] the, your woman Hegarty from the INOU, right, like the problem with er, unemployed – stroke – working class people is that we've never historically and traditionally, we've never had a great lobbying group, but we've had trade unions and that, and guilds and that, but we've never had people who could stand up articulately and talk about issues that can be solved, rather than going off on tangents about things that can never be solved, like full employment – there'll never be full employment. You need people to stand up, looking at things from a 90s' perspective, and looking at things from a working class perspective and saying what can we do here, what can we change to make things better (. . .) but we haven't got enough lobbies, we haven't got enough there in the Dáil that are going, that are talking, look you've got to help us here, you've got to do this and that.

(Radical Dublin men's group, G.2)

All of the radical groups agreed with the programme's explosion of the myth that its the role of business to create jobs, rather its primary role is to make profit.

All groups also agreed with the programme's explosion of the myth of the unemployed being wasters, dismissing the suggestion that the unemployed do not want to look for work because they get a lot of money on the dole as 'a load of crap' (Radical rural men's group, G.13).

The government's policy of responding to unemployment by offering further training was bitterly criticised by radical groups, especially men's groups. They particularly criticised what they saw as compulsory government training and employment schemes, including those organised by FÁS [Training and Employment Authority] and Social Employment Schemes. These they saw as simply a manipulation of unemployment figures, as giving the unemployed crumbs to keep them relatively satisfied, as creating further unemployment, as an affront to a person's dignity, and lowering wages:

> This country would be better off getting rid of the FÁS courses and employers would have to take on people [(yeah)] give them a decent wage, there would be more money spent obviously and the more money the government is going to get in taxes and PRSI. ( )
> / That FÁS course is the greatest load of, of codswallop . . . horse manure. You're the employer and I walk in expecting £150, another feller walks in and he's going to work for £70, who would you employ?
>
> (Radical Dublin men's group, G.4)

The radical rural men's group agreed and concluded that the group benefiting most from this was:

> . . . the elites that are getting the work done cheaper all the time and that's why [(that's right . . . that's right)] it's a two-tiered society, it's a two-tiered society now.
>
> (Radical rural men's group, G.9)

These groups were much less critical of the VTOS [Vocational Training Opportunities Scheme] courses in which many of them were participating – its voluntary nature, and the fact that it gave a focus to their lives and offered a good education. They accepted the programme's analysis that it was a myth that training would get you a job – the jobs just were not there, but felt that courses voluntarily undertaken had a value in themselves, giving a sense of self-worth and dignity to participants.

Three radical groups raised the point that, within education, more emphasis should be placed on social and community analysis and on rights education:

> . . . I think that it is very important and I think everybody should be, learn about the value of life [(yeah)] the value of what it means to be within a society. What society is doing to you. What you can do to change society. Maybe it just needs a different way of educating people.
> / That's right, social analysis and social awareness [(yeah)] social awareness, social studies whatever you'd like to call it [(yeah, yeah)] . . .
> / That's probably what I'm trying to say. The way, the way the education system is going is, as far as I'm concerned, wrong. It's been coming out of books, it's been ordered by exams and there's still no kind of social awareness being taught.
> / Well, I was thinking that, if you broaden the definition of education you could link it to social life, people's social lives and their culture.
>
> (Radical Dublin women's group, G.6)

A radical Dublin men's group elaborated further:

> [What is needed is] more about rights . . . a rights' programme, or know your rights type of thing, because that's education, I keep coming back to education because that's the most important thing that we have, we haven't got now, but we should have. We should be educated.
>
> (Radical Dublin men's group, G.2)

Radical groups, especially four of them, also brought their critical faculties to bear in assessing the programme. In particular they questioned its potential to bring about the radical social change they perceived to be necessary if the employment situation was to improve. The programme in their view only showed what was already known about unemployment: there was nothing new in it; it did not go far enough and offered no solutions. Thus it did not get across the point that it is not the unemployed who were responsible for unemployment but '. . . the people in power that created the system'. (G.9). Twenty-five per cent of respondents in radical groups wrote in such evaluations on the individually completed questionnaires after the discussion. They also wondered why they – the unemployed – were perceived to be the appropriate audience for this programme: the unemployed knew all this already. Rather it was employers, politicians and those with power to whom it should be shown (11 per cent).

It was conceded nonetheless that the programme was:

> . . . a step in the right direction, but we seem to get programmes where people come on the screen and they're faceless and they say how . . . 'oh, it's terrible and no one listens' (. . .) You know, I'm unemployed and I'm bored by that . . . (G.4).

Overall, 64 per cent in radical groups wrote some negative comments about the programme on the questionnaire. Yet the programme was also judged to be more realistic and pointed than many current affairs programmes, particularly its highlighting of the economic, 'wasters' and training myths. Thus, while inadequate, it was 'a good start off . . . trying to change myths'. Furthermore, radical men's groups were more likely than those in any other category to assess the programme in terms of its potential to mobilise the unemployed through, for example, exploding myths, through showing unemployment centres, and through showing how the unemployed have a voice:

> The man [*Right To Learn* co-producer and presenter on the programme] is right, the unemployed have no voice, anywhere, the only place they have it is down in the dole office, or a protest down O'Connell Street – that's the only place, whereas the government, these committees on how to get jobs and all, they should have unemployed people, the IDA [Industrial Development Authority] should have unemployed people on their board, even if it's only one, even if it's only a token gesture, to have people like that, but no one ever comes to the unemployed and says, 'what would you like to do?'
> GF: But did that get across at all, like at the start of the programme, they had all these different people in their own communities, right, saying . . . this is what I do and we did that, do you think that came across?
> / It came across that people are taking power into their own hands and said 'right that's it, enough is enough'. Votes is power. If people learn how to use it properly that's where things are starting to change.
>
> (Radical Dublin men's group, G.2)

Radical women's groups looked particularly at the programme's potential to mobilise through its use in adult education:

> But you see showing, showing this to groups like I mean might actually make people y'know what I mean sit up and really want to do something about it. (. . .) But y'know what I mean, you sit down and you hear all this unemployed and you're unemployed yourself, you feel shit in yourself. [(yeah)] Like if you're sitting in a group and like I mean you're watching this video you say well Jaysus I'm not alone d'you know what I mean, there are other people like me . . .
> / That's right, I imagine it would give you a bit of a lift . . .
> / So let's get together, d'you know what I mean it might bring that effect. That could be positive y'know . . .
>
> (Radical Dublin women's group, G.3)

The adult education model used by *Right To Learn* of beginning with participants' own experiences and knowledge, and through discussion leading to further social analysis, was also commented on favourably:

> The role plays were important, yeah. But then even in terms of getting people as _____ [group member] says, having question and answer situations. [(yes)] Getting people to think. [(Generating . . .)] Yeah. It's generating interest, debate and awareness of the issues, that are important in one's life, or in one's community, or in one's family, or whatever. And then it goes on into the world. [(Yeah, that's right.)] You're, you're giving people, you're drawing from them their potential to think.
>
> (Radical Dublin women's group, G.6)

Both radical women's groups were from the voluntarily organised women's daytime adult education sector. This sector has been growing rapidly since the late 1980s, at which time they had almost 9000 women participating (Inglis, Bailey and Murray, 1993:59). What has made these groups unique, Inglis (1994: 56) has commented, is their voluntary, independent and locally based nature. He continues,

> Some groups appear to have grown spontaneously, of their own accord, through women responding to local changes in their area brought about by poverty, alienation, unemployment, and so on. Some have emerged within the shadow of existing institutions such as the local VEC [Vocational Educational Committee] or church. Others have grown within the context of community development initiatives. The prime movers in establishing groups tend to be local women who had previously been actively involved in the community, women's groups or adult education.

## Reformist–Liberal Groups

Reformist–liberal groups in responding to the programme articulated a more individualistic, psychological or social psychological perspective rather than the socially critical perspective of the radical groups. Thus in looking at unemployment, rather than examining it in terms of the economic and political power structure in society, they focused on discrimination towards the unemployed, especially as they had experienced it themselves, low levels of motivation among the unemployed and the consequences of unemployment on the family. Education was important for this group especially in terms of learning one's rights and hence tackling discrimination. The possibility of examining the structure of society as a whole, or changing it, was not addressed. Four groups articulated this discourse: two rural women's groups, one rural men's group and one Dublin women's group. When compared with the other two socio-political categories, reformists tended to have a higher standard of secondary education, two thirds having continued their education past sixteen years of age, and to be of a slightly higher social class – although the majority (55 per cent) were still working class.

The stigmatisation of the unemployed, exemplified in the *Right To Learn* by attitudes of the officers in the welfare office in the Traveller's drama, were particularly focused on by the reformist–liberal groups, as was the shame and guilt experienced by some when claiming welfare:

> I used to be embarrassed. I did, walking out. And you always knew people knew you were coming back from the Labour. There were always . . . a big, whole band of people, walkin' down. Y'know. (. . .)
> / I walked in there with my head up. You get embarrassed going in ?
> / I did. I used to get embarrassed.
> / I didn't. I started work when I was 17 years of age, and I walked in there because I paid tax for years. So I'm goin': 'well I'm entitled to that' . . . I wasn't going to make myself feel [(like shit)] just going in there . . .
> / I still, I hated going in there. It's one thing I hated.
> / Here we are [(making excuses for ourselves)] again. We're [(still)] making excuses for the fact that we were on the dole. And, we still feel bad and low about it. [(It's ridiculous)].
> / I don't anymore. I don't give a shit.
> (Reformist Dublin women's group, G.1)

A rural women's group expressed the same feelings of shame in being unemployed and how this was confirmed by the attitudes of the clerks in the employment office:

> And even though you're unemployed, like, you shouldn't be made little of.
> / No, you shouldn't. It's not your fault.
> / It's not your fault. It's not our fault that there's no jobs out there.
> / It [the programme drama] was typical of what goes on at the dole office, to be honest [(yes, it 'tis)] whether, no matter who you are . . . cut the nose off you . . .
> / Sure (. . .) if the jobs were there, you wouldn't be up, in signin' on, y'know what I mean to say . . . oh, yeah, they're quite snotty.
> (Reformist rural women's group, G.11)

In response to the wasters' myth, while the programme had attempted to explode this myth by stating that the unemployed did not lack motivation and indeed were frequently involved in unpaid voluntary work, reformist–liberal groups questioned this and sought social psychological explanations for this low motivation among the unemployed:

> [In the programme] one man said, ah, he wanted to explode the myth on motivation. But I would say that they have no motivation because it's destroyed by being unemployed [(yeah)]. They should bring that out more, how it eventually destroys you. We'd see people on the dole just being able to do the smallest of jobs. So I think that it was wrong. I disagree with that point. They don't have motivation. It's taken off them. I think they should deal with that more, bring it out, how it destroys you.
>
> (Reformist rural women's group, G.11)

Or again:

> The line about 'motivation' came across very strong. (. . .) They don't, people who . . . the producers don't understand that it's not that you lack motivation, it's that after a while, why the hell should you get up and move, 'cause every time you get a slap in the face it knocks you back like a year. So you may as well be on the dole all your life as far as this is to you . . . [(yeah, mm)].
> / Two steps back, one step forward . . .
> / . . . you get into such a rut. Y'know. So it's not that you lack motivation, or you lack intelligence, or you're not capable of doin' the job, it's just that you get slapped in the face so many times that you say, 'Ah, forget it, I'll never get anything now'.
>
> (Reformist Dublin women's group, G.1)

Reformist groups would have liked the programme to have shown more of the problems unemployment, low pay and social welfare create for families, young people and the individual. They did not offer a class, power or social analysis of unemployment as radical groups did but were however critical of politicians and government policies, in particular of the social welfare system and employment and training policies. They were also critical of FÁS training courses and felt that this did not come across strongly enough in the programme:

> But I think a lot of this trainin', an awful lot of this is just a shuffling of numbers, well the government, they do, they just shuffle us around and its numbers, they're just takin' us off the live register as they call it and all they're doin' is just coverin' it up [(yeah, that's all)] they're just coverin' it up, they ain't dealin' with the problem at all.
>
> (Reformist rural women's group, G.8)

Again, however, as with the radical groups, they felt that the VEC and VTOS courses that they were presently taking gave them increased confidence, motivation and self-esteem, and enabled them to escape from the stigma of being unemployed. They differed, however, as to whether the *Right To Learn* programme would have the desired effect of encouraging others to get involved in adult education. One, a reformist rural women's group was positive:

. . . for people that were watchin' that [ the courses' drama], they might say 'Jesus, I should be doing that, it's something to do, it's better than sittin' at home, I'm furthering my education, I'm getting better skills', and it might encourage people to actually go and do it. (. . .)
/ Isn't it very true to life [in the courses' drama] the way yer man was goin', knockin' her constantly, ye see any of the women especially the married women doin' a course, ye see their husbands goin' 'What are you goin' again for?' 'What are you goin' to get out of it?'

(Reformist rural women's group, G.8)

Another group however felt that some of the programme, especially the vox pop and the section 'training to be a trainer' drama exploding the myth that training could get you a job, would discourage potential adult education participants. In their eyes the programme should have more actively promoted taking adult education courses which, among other things, increased confidence:

I still think, the courses are very important. Because I find now since I've joined the course, that my confidence has come up an awful lot. I mean, when you're on the dole you've just no confidence (. . .) but I find since I've come on this course that my con', I feel sort of secure enough.
/ I don't think they spoke strongly enough about that in the programme though, to make people aware that courses are of benefit . . .
/ That courses are very important [(yeah)] . . .
/ It's not just education [(yeah, mm)] . . .
/ Yeah, they were a bit negative about the courses . . . [(yeah, mm)].
/ They should list it, where you go and find out about the courses. Maybe VTOS should be mentioned.

(Reformist Dublin women's group, G.1)

Reformist groups, in general, evaluated the programme in positive terms – 63 per cent writing in favourable comments on the questionnaires as to its high interest level, it being true to life, and liking the fact that it was made by unemployed people. A minority (33 per cent) felt that it did not go far enough and that for some viewers it might have a negative rather than a positive effect. They nonetheless favoured the *Right To Learn* programme over routine current affairs as the following quote shows:

It did cover a lot on it, anything they portrayed on it was true.
/ Yeah, it was good, it was very well put across.
/ Yeah but they should have put the school leaver into it, or maybe a family just even ten minutes of a family ye know, we'd say, young kids, a young woman there, a man about the house, how it can affect a marriage.
All: Family, poverty, yeah . . . (. . .)
GF: How do you feel about it compared to say other current affairs programmes?
/ Watchin' these television programmes there's an awful lot of these big words ye know, hi-tech.
/ (. . .) I wouldn't sit down and look at current affairs, the way I would a programme like that. Like I did two weeks ago when I seen the programme *Right To Learn* [on television] like I did, I sat down and looked at it like ye know and it

was interesting, like I wouldn't sit down and look at Today Tonight or current affairs or anything like that, 'cause to me it's all big nobs and they don't know what they talkin' about [(exactly)] anyone with a job doesn't know what they're talkin' about, they're patronising you, that's all . . . about how many in that . . . / Statistics, figures exactly, ye need a dictionary, ye probably won't know what they mean, when they're sayin' . . .

(Reformist rural women's group, G.8)

In terms of its potential usage in adult education, reformists, as well as those within other perspectives, agreed with the programme's emphasis on knowing your rights to counter discrimination:

GF: One of the things that (. . .) was brought out a bit in the drama, was the thing about knowing your rights, and that, that is in itself a lot of power.
/ An awful lot of power. Yeah.
/ Y'know it's true like. I only know a certain, like [(em)], the only reason I know some of my rights, is because I learnt it off other people. You don't even learn about it in school. Or you don't . . . There's no education, like, you just don't know. I might sit down with my father. He'd tell me certain things. If I . . . Or something on television, I might see, y'know . . .

(Reformist Dublin women's group, G.1)

## Localist–Familial Groups

Two women's groups, one Dublin and one rural, offered localist–familial responses. These groups consisted almost entirely of working class women working in the home. They had all left school at sixteen or less, were slightly older than other groups and had much less previous experience of adult education. Only a small minority had extensive experience of unemployment and in general expressed negative attitudes to the unemployed. They tended either to reject or misread the explosion of myths on unemployment as presented in the programme.

The two localist-familial groups discussed the unemployment situation in terms of divided and opposing groups within their local working-class community: those who were unemployed and dependent solely on the dole, versus those who claimed benefits but were also doing nixers and not paying tax or insurance, versus lower-paid workers receiving the same income as those on the dole but without the added benefits – especially a medical card. They also stated that while most unemployed wanted to work, others did not:

GF: Well if you look at the myths that were presented . . .
/ Like the unemployed being lazy, yeah lazy . . . Well I do think there's a certain element that don't want to work [(yeah)] . . . I do believe, agree about that in my heart, there are a lot of, now I'm not, probably about one out of ten, I mean as yer woman [on the programme] said, are ye waitin' for them [employers] to come knocking on your door? I mean if they did knock they still wouldn't take the job, they're just happy the way they are, goin' to the dole, collectin' there, I mean, I do believe that you know, it is a vast amount of people who want to work but . . .

/ An awful lot work, do earn money and are on the dole . . .
/ And as I said ( ) that's what I said.
/ I know many of them now and it bloody annoys me, and here's us payin' our tax and insurance.
/ That's what I'm sayin' . . .
/ That's what I said a few minutes ago . . .
/ That's what I'm sayin', the system is all wrong, the system is all wrong
/ But that's why they won't take work, unless they're allowed to sign on the labour as well [(yeah, yeah)]
/ They won't go down in the books, they want the money into their hands plus the labour.

(Localist Dublin women's group, G.5)

They thus concentrated on differences and problems within working-class communities themselves, fragmented and split by unemployment. They saw the interrelated system of wages, taxation and benefits as wrong and needing change. They offered no class analysis or proposals on how to bring about this change. Elements of the programme which suggested a class analysis were recognised although not discussed in any detail, the point of the unemployed being wasters being returned to:

The one [programme myth] about the industry where people think that industry is there to eh . . .
/ Create the jobs.
/ Create the jobs. It's, it's, yeah, they're there to make a profit. That was very good now. I never actually thought of it that way before [(yeah, yeah, yes)] until I seen it coming across there, you know.
/ That's definitely the way people think. They're there to create jobs, but I thought the laziness thing about the unemployed being lazy. In a lot of cases it's true, because people just don't want . . . they have it handy, they get up at ten or eleven o'clock in the morning, and go down and sign on, and go into the pubs for the evening after that.
/ Yeah, well particularly the youngsters, the youngsters nowadays. On a Thursdays you'd see them in _____.
/ They don't want to work . . .
/ They don't. They're going in there to the wall. They don't want to really work or they know the work isn't there for them, so they've given up . . .

(Localist rural women's group, G7)

Localist groups felt that the wasters' myth was true:

. . . I thought that it [the programme] was very true to life, that, the way things are today, unemployment, although I think there is work out there, if people would . . .
/ Yeah, well I think that too. I mean I never was unemployed. My husband was never unemployed but I'm sure if he was there's an awful lot of things he could go out there and do. There's people that doesn't want to work . . .
/ If they're willing to work, there's work like, you know.

(Localist rural women's group, G.7)

This was the only incidence of misreading – or not getting the producers' 'preferred reading' – which occurred within the group discussions. Few of those in localist groups had previously been involved in FÁS or other adult education courses and did not raise or discuss these in any detail. There was some limited and uncritical discussion of courses for young unemployed and approval of social employment schemes.

The voluntary women's group within the localist category discussed the development of community based and voluntary adult education by and for women and the consequences of this for the family, drawing positive examples from the programme:

> There was one [talking in the programme] about community education, and the way people in the community are taking things into their own hands [(yeah)]. (. . .) nowadays people are doin' it cause they want to educate themselves.
> / It's like the way the girl [in the courses' drama] when her husband was sittin' down readin' the paper, well I presume it was her husband, and she said she was goin' and he said about the courses she was takin' [(yeah)] he didn't seem impressed that she was takin' another course, but it was her way of gettin' out, I suppose and meetin' people [(yeah)] ye know she was probably sick of sittin' in and lookin' at the four walls, so she thought she'd get out . . .
> / I think a lot of women today now they're not prepared to sit in now and look after the kids as much as they ye know look after them alright, but . . . I just think they want to get out now and do something with their lives now ye know . . .
> / Women in the home are definitely changin' . . .
> / Well he resented that . . .
> / He resented that she was goin' out.
> / She turned around then and she thought maybe, well maybe you'd [the husband] come down with me ye know.
> / I think a lot of husbands can be jealous by all this.
> (Localist Dublin women's group, G.5)

The localist–familial groups were positive about the programme overall. In the questionnaire, 60 per cent wrote in positive comments. They perceived the programme as congruent with their reality, especially the drama sections and those which looked at women's issues and women in adult education:

> It was nice the way he [the producer] roped in those sort of people as well, yeah a mixture . . .
> / Yeah, different types [(yeah, well laid out, yeah)] and it pointed out what there is for women like and the kids being minded during in the day time and there was a crèche and that ye know, that was, that was alright that was, that they put that into it . . .
> / Some of her words were a little strong like ye know, just to a normal workin' class person, it mightn't catch the eye, inclined to drift away, I felt like that anyway did you ?
> / At the beginning yeah, yeah . . .
> / Ye know it was a bit heavy for us . . .
> / Yeah, it was a little bit, like some of it I didn't understand [(yeah)] but like ye know the real life situations [( ye know, yeah)] I could feel myself zoomin' in immediately.

And later:

> GF: With regard to the programme, you have all your current affairs programmes
> and everything every night like *Today Tonight*, *Prime Time*, whatever, talking
> about unemployment, what did you think of this compared to those programmes ?
> / I'd prefer that . . .
> / More down to earth. (. . .) It's different . . .
> / You'd relate to that better than you would *Prime Time* or something like that
> now . . .
> / Because it had the drama (. . .) I thought [it] really held your attention and
> they put their points over really well ye know through the drama . . .
> / And they were just ordinary people like there was nothin' . . . false about them
> . . . [(yeah)].
> / They were just ordinary everyday people ye know.
>
>                         (Localist Dublin women's group, G.5)

The second localist group concluded that given the programme's strong congruence with their sense of reality, viewing it would build self confidence and:

> . . . by looking at that you can identify with it, you know what I mean, and I'd
> say there'd be a lot of people who will identify with what is being said on the
> programme, you know.
>
>                         (Localist rural women's group, G.7)

## Discussion

Bakhtin and Voloshinov have argued that dialogic communication is oriented to
the other, it respects and anticipates the response of the other. It has been
argued that the *Right To Learn* project might be seen as an attempt to put into
practice, through participatory media production, a dialogic communication
process. This production by 20 unemployed co-producers and the Audio
Visual Centre, UCD, respected and acknowledged the voice of the
unemployed, the audience. And the audience responded enthusiastically to this.
All groups appreciated the involvement of unemployed people in the making
and presenting of the programme. They saw them as 'knowing what they are
telling about', and 'ordinary people' using an accessible language, unlike the
'hi-tech' and alienating language of some prime-time current affairs. The
articulation and confirmation of a known world and of their own experiences
led, as Bakhtin's and Freire's work would anticipate, to enthusiastic – but not
necessarily uncritically – engagement with it.

For the Bakhtin circle, dialogic communication is sensitive to the other and
to the social context in which the communication takes place. Communication
processes need to be examined in this light. In the *Right To Learn* research
three contextual factors were found to be of importance in how audience
groups responded to and discussed the programme. These included the adult
education context of the research which drew on established norms of respectful

interaction between adult education participants; secondly differential conversational patterns between men and women's groups as well as gendered stylistic preferences; and thirdly the socio-political perspectives which groups brought to their reading of the texts. These perspectives were themselves influenced by the extent to which members of the groups had experienced unemployment, with radical groups having had the most extensive unemployment experiences.

The unemployed working class, especially those from semi-skilled and unskilled sectors, represent one of the most structurally disadvantaged groups in Irish society. With industrialisation, jobs in this sector have rapidly declined. However semi-skilled and unskilled workers, or their children, have not been enabled to move into other expanding sectors of the labour market (see Breen and Whelan, 1996). Research has consistently shown the high levels of educational inequality experienced by those at the bottom of the social scale (see Steering Committee on the Future Development of Higher Education, 1995:133; Clancy, 1995).

Unemployment has also been concentrated here. As noted by Breen and Whelan (1996:140) 'unemployment among . . . unskilled workers has hardly fallen below 30 per cent since 1961, while that for the upper-middle class has only once exceeded 3 per cent'. The consequences in terms of poverty, health, education and well-being have been well documented (see Nolan and Callan, 1994). Their voice, however, is very rarely seen or heard on the media.

Due to increased monopoly control of media, media researchers point to the fact that despite an increasing number of media channels, diversity of content has decreased. Audiences have the right to hear a diversity of perspectives as well as the right to be heard themselves. Thus a strong argument in favour of greater access and participatory programming continues to be made, as has the argument for greater support for alternative media.

The ideals of alternative media are, firstly, to open up and democratise the access of citizens to a diversity of opinions and to media production. Secondly, to creatively develop new modes of representation and articulation for the voiceless. And thirdly, to inform, educate and create dialogue in order to bring about justice and solidarity. How successful was the *Right To Learn* in this regard?

While the *Right To Learn*, in comparison with other programmes, evidenced a strong movement in this direction, there were organisational limitations. In terms of audience access to a greater diversity of voices, the *Right To Learn* programmes themselves certainly offered this but transmission at off-peak hours certainly did not. The programme offered participation to a range of unemployed groups, but for some the voice of a radical and critical perspective was too muted. The fact that two established institutions – the Audio Visual Centre in UCD and the Educational Programmes Department in RTÉ – not the unemployed participants themselves, had ultimate responsibility for the programmes, perhaps contributed to this. Direct control – and responsibility – by specific unemployed groups for particular programmes would have contributed a more critical edge to programmes produced by radical groups, while other perspectives would also have their own programmes.

In relation to the second criterion of creatively developing new modes of representation and articulation with, and for, the voiceless, here again the *Right To Learn* began this process, particularly with its focus on participatory drama to which women especially responded with enthusiasm, identification and excitement.

Finally in relation to informing, educating and creating dialogue in order to bring about justice and solidarity, the *Right To Learn* project certainly aspired to this. Ultimately, however, linkages back into the communities from which the unemployed participants were drawn, and with whom it was originally hoped to introduce the *Right To Learn* video and thus start a multiplier effect, proved too weak. Downing (1984:355 seq), in his review of radical and alternative media internationally, has emphasised how groups who develop successful alternative media tend to have strong linkages to grassroots social movements. He also recognises that if these social movements are to contribute to radical change, they need to be open to the perspectives of other marginalised and oppressed groups. Thus through a holistic approach, through dialogue across different interests, these alternative media may come, he argues, to represent an autonomous public sphere – autonomous from state, economic and other powerful interests – and more democratically responsive to the interests of excluded groups.

# Appendix

| Characteristic | Radical | Reformist | Localist | Total |
|---|---|---|---|---|
| **Characteristics of Focus Groups Articulating Radical, Reformist and Localist Perspectives** | | | | |
| **No. of Groups** | 6 | 4 | 2 | 12 |
| **No. in Groups** | 53 | 34 | 15 | 102 |
| **Gender:**   Female | 2 | 3 | 2 | 7 |
| Male | 4 | 1 | 0 | 5 |
| **Location:**  Dublin | 4 | 1 | 1 | 6 |
| Rural | 2 | 3 | 2 | 6 |
| **Average age** | 37 | 35 | 41 | 37 |
| **Education:** | | | | |
| % left school aged 16 or less | 64% | 33% | 100% | 56% |
| **Adult Education:** | | | | |
| Course presently attending: | | | | |
| VTOS | 4 | 2 | – | 6 |
| Other VEC | – | 2 | 1 | 3 |
| Voluntary Women's Group | 2 | – | 1 | 3 |
| Had attended other AE courses (including FAS) | 58% | 51% | 13% | 50% |
| **Social Class:** | | | | |
| % Working Class* | 64% | 55% | 73% | 63% |
| **Present Work Situation:** | | | | |
| Unemployed/ VTOS | 83% | 81% | 7% | 72% |
| Work in the home | 11% | 11% | 87% | 23% |
| Employed | 4% | 7% | 7% | 5% |
| **Unemployment Experience:** | | | | |
| Three or more periods of unemployment | 62% | 33% | 13% | 46% |

*Social Class was categorised according to the respondent's present paid employment, previous employment if presently unemployed or working in the home, or job of partner if she/he had never been in paid employment. Working class was defined as including lower grade non manual (Census Classification 7) and manual work.

# Notes

1   This experimental project working with unemployed groups was funded by EUROFORM [European Community initiative concerning new qualifications, new skills and new employment opportunities], RTÉ and UCD. My research role was initially that of evaluator. There were three phases in this research: observation of the production process, audience research on programme reception, and a case study of the use and response by one adult education group of the *Right To Learn* video and workbook. For an account of each of these phases, see Kelly (1996).

2   It is of interest to note that subsequent research on the *Right To Learn* video and workbook (see Kelly, 1996) found that, when these were used within a structured adult education course over five sessions, they also encouraged dialogic discourse. This discourse, while initially grounded in the perceived reality of the students' lives, then moved on to explore these experiences by placing them within the context of socio-cultural and power relations and thus to begin to identify and analyse necessary change.

# References

Bakhtin, Mikhail (1981) *The Dialogic Imagination: Four Essays by M.M. Bakhtin.* Edited by Michael Holquist. Austin: University of Texas.

Bakhtin, Mikhail (1984) *Problems of Dostoevsky's Poetics.* Austin: University of Texas.

Breen, Richard and Whelan, Christopher (1996) *Social Mobility and Social Class in Ireland.* Dublin: Gill & Macmillan.

Clancy, Patrick (1995) *Access to Higher Education: A Third National Survey.* Dublin: Higher Education Authority.

Coates, Jennifer (1993) *Women, Men and Language*, Second Edition. London: Longman.

Dowmunt, Tony (ed.) (1993) *Channels of Resistance: Global Television and Local Empowerment.* London: BFI.

Downing, John (1984) *Radical Media.* Boston.

Freire, Paulo (1972) *Pedagogy of the Oppressed.* Harmonsworth: Penguin.

Freire, Paulo (1985) *Education for Critical Consciousness.* Harmondsworth: Penguin.

Gardiner, Michael (1992) *The Dialogics of Critique: M.M. Bakhtin and the Theory of Ideology.* London: Routledge.

Garnham, Nicholas (1990) *Capitalism and Communication.* London: Sage.

Golding, Peter (1990) 'Political Communication and Citizenship: the Media and Democracy in an Egalitarian Social Order', in M. Ferguson (ed.) *Public Communication: the New Imperatives.* London: Sage.

Hamelink, Cees (1983) *Cultural Autonomy in Global Communications.* New York: Longman.

Hamelink, Cees (1994) *Politics of World Communication: Human Rights Perspective.* London: Sage.

Hamelink, Cees (1995) *World Communication, Disempowerment and Self-Empowerment.* London: Zed.

Inglis, Tom, Kay Bailey and Christine Murray (1993) *Liberating Learning: A Report on Daytime Education Groups in Ireland.* Dublin: Aontas.

Inglis, Tom (1994) 'Women and the Struggle for Daytime Adult Education in Ireland', in *Studies in the Education of Adults*, 26 (1): 1994.

James, Deborah and Janice Drakich (1993) 'Understanding Gender Differences in Amount of Talk: A Critical Review of Research', in Deborah Tannen (ed.) *Gender and Conversational Interaction.* Oxford: Oxford University Press.

Kelly, Mary (1996) *Educational Television: Emancipatory Education and the Right To Learn Project*. Dublin: RTÉ.

Morley, David (1992) *Television Audiences and Cultural Studies*. London: Routledge.

Murdock, Graham (1990) 'Redrawing the Map of the Communications Industries: Concentration and Ownership in the Era of Privatization', in M. Ferguson (ed.) *Public Communication: The New Imperatives*. London: Sage.

Nolan, Brian and Tim Callan (eds) (1994) *Poverty and Policy in Ireland*. Dublin: Gill & Macmillan.

Prehn, Ole (1992) 'From Small Scale Utopianism to Large scale Pragmatism' in N. Jankowski, O. Prehn and J. Stapper (eds) *The People's Voice: Local Radio and Television in Europe*. London: Libbey.

Rahim, Syed (1994) 'Participatory Development Communication as a Dialogic Process', in Shirley White (ed.) *Participatory Communication, Working for Change and Development*. London: Sage.

Servaes, Jan, Thomas Jacobson and Shirley White (eds) (1996) *Participatory Communication for Social Change*. London: Sage.

Shor, Ira and Paulo Freire (1987) *A Pedagogy for Liberation, Dialogues on Transforming Education*. Mass: Bergin and Garvey.

Steering Committee on the Future Development of Higher Education (1995) *Interim Report of the Steering Committee's Technical Working Group*. Dublin: Higher Education Authority.

Tannen, Deborah (1993) 'The relativity of Linguistic Stragegies: Rethinking Power and Solidarity in Gender and Dominance', in Deborah Tannen (ed.) *Gender and Conversational Interaction*. Oxford: Oxford University Press.

Voloshinov, V.N. (1973) *Marxism and the Philosophy of Language*. New York: Seminar Press.

White, Shirley (ed.) (1994) *Participatory Communication: Working for Change and Development*. London: Sage.

# 2

# *The Arts Show* Audience: Cultural Confidence and Middlebrow Arts Consumption[1]

## *Brian O'Neill*

The arts constitute a form of cultural consumption that has been relatively neglected in recent academic discourse in comparison to the burgeoning literature of cultural studies dedicated to popular and mass-media forms of culture. This emphasis within cultural studies on popular genres over traditional forms of art – what has been labelled its 'cultural populism' (McGuigan, 1992) – systematically emphasises common, ordinary taste and resistant aesthetic strategies while denigrating 'high culture' as an elitist, middle-class leisure pursuit that has little relevance to most people (Willis, 1990). Going against this populist tide, this chapter argues that an examination of popular cultural consumption must crucially incorporate the category of the middlebrow within its analysis. The purpose of this chapter is to explore the middle ground of arts consumption in Ireland, an area of mainstream consensus which incorporates aspects of both popular and high culture. For the purposes of analysis, the middle ground of Irish arts consumption is represented by a study of audience responses to the popular radio arts review programme, *The Arts Show*, and in this analysis distinct discourses of the arts are identified which define and situate the meaning of middlebrow. *The Arts Show*'s popularisation of traditional forms of high culture provides a unique opportunity to study audience forms of identification with different types of cultural experience and while sometimes denounced as middlebrow, I want to argue that its successful appeal to mainstream aesthetic taste is a mark of the cultural confidence of the programme's largely middle-class audience. This characterisation should be set against the foregoing evaluation of the current dominance of 'cultural populism' within cultural thinking in general, and how this has resulted in a neglect of the social context for cultural consumption, in particular, the question of stratification and persistent inequalities in access to culture. Following this, the discussion turns to a consideration of some of the ways in which the work of Pierre Bourdieu has been applied to the analysis of culture in particular social situations. Of particular interest is the question, largely unexamined in the literature of cultural studies, of the relationship between the arts and social class. The claim that consumption of the arts in Ireland reveals a society that is becoming more culturally democratic is examined in the light of data about arts consumption presented by the Arts Council (Clancy *et al.*, 1994). While the revitalisation of the Irish arts sector and the high levels of reported attendance at arts events suggest a broadening of cultural participation, this is restricted in the main to middle-class participants and as in the case of *The Arts Show* provides evidence of the cultural aspirations and appeal for cultural legitimacy of that particular segment of the audience rather than characterising the cultural fabric of the society as a whole.

## Cultural Studies and Audiences for the Arts

At the heart of the cultural studies project, there is, as Jim McGuigan has observed, a populist sentiment towards culture (McGuigan, 1992: 13). In what he has influentially labelled the 'cultural populism' of much recent work within the cultural studies paradigm, there is the almost axiomatic assumption that 'the symbolic experiences and practices of ordinary people are more important analytically and politically than Culture with a capital C' (McGuigan, 1992: 4). This, it should be acknowledged, has both liberating and destructive consequences. From the time of Raymond Williams's assertion that 'culture is ordinary' (Williams, 1958, reprinted 1989) with its rebuttal of the elitist and hierarchical conception of culture represented by the tradition of Arnold and Leavis, to Paul Willis's eulogy for the 'grounded aesthetics' of young people's consumption practices (Willis, 1990), a tremendous impetus has been given to the validation of contemporary, ordinary and readily available cultural experience. The struggle for the popular, however, has been achieved with the abandonment of a range of cultural experience, traditionally denoted as high culture, and a relative silence on key questions of the sources of cultural authority, cultural value and the relation between social and cultural hierarchy. The assumption within cultural studies much of the time is, to echo Willis, that the arts and high cultural pursuits no longer possess any meaningful relation to audiences and are sustained merely by subsidy and patronage. Williams, among others, was, however, deeply ambivalent about the uncritical celebration of the sometimes exploitative, mass-produced and often undistinguished quality of popular cultural forms (see Williams, 1989). Within the paradigm of cultural studies itself, there has recently been a reaction against some of the populist excesses of audience and reception studies. Starting with McGuigan's own *Cultural Populism* (1992) which initiated a debate about the status of cultural studies there are now numerous works examining the origins of the discipline (Davies, 1995; Easthope, 1991; Storey, 1993; Strinati, 1995; Turner, 1990) and a number which attempt to reorient its direction (Blundell *et al.* 1993; Frow, 1995; Inglis, 1993).

One strand among the various attempts to reorient the direction of cultural studies research has been the call to reappraise the nature and role of high culture. In an article entitled 'High Culture Revisited' (1989), Jostein Gripsrud suggests that there is much in high cultural discourse that can be of use to the cultural studies theorist and that the sense of critical distance that is central to the aesthetic standpoint of high culture is precisely what is now lacking in cultural studies (Gripsrud, 1989). He voices the fear that the critical potential of cultural studies has been blunted by an inflexible orthodoxy in its conception of the popular and that its original mission of ideological critique of capitalist cultural forms, the 'total social critique' that was the ambition of the new intellectuals of the 1960s, has been lost by being too close to the objects of popular culture under scrutiny. Singled out for all the worst excesses of cultural populism, cultural critics such as John Fiske whose celebration of the 'semiotic democracy' that a polysemic media environment affords, are said to have 'sold out' in their fascination for contemporary (North American) cultural life (Fiske, 1987, 1989a, 1989b; but see Frow, 1995). It is claimed that populists' assertions of a cultural democracy in which all forms of culture are of equal value and equally accessible to all are simplistic and neglect the social facts of inequality in the distribution of economic and cultural value. Far from being defunct, the distinction and the gap between the culture of the ordinary and the culture of the elite is as real as ever, the denial of which is itself a ploy in the intellectuals' game of claiming authority for their interpretation of culture and their definition of the popular (see McGuigan, 1992:9).

A further critique of cultural studies is that by the standards of sociology, its empirical work has also been methodologically unsophisticated. Referring to the vogue for ethnographic studies of 'active audiences', Seaman criticises the generalisation from small numbers of cases to the characterisation of whole audience groups and the spurious claims that have been made from minimalist forms of ethnographic observation (Seaman, 1992). Even in the most celebrated of ethnographic readership studies such as Morley's *The 'Nationwide' Audience* (1980), Radway's *Reading the Romance* (1984) or Ang's *Watching Dallas* (1985), processes of data collection, the establishment of a sample and the attention to social factors like gender, age, class have by the standards of mainstream sociology been notably haphazard. For this reason, many commentators wishing to develop a more sociologically-informed cultural studies have turned to the work of Bourdieu (1984; 1990a; 1990b; 1993) as offering one of the most promising avenues of development for the study of culture (Garnham, 1990: 70; Moores, 1993: 10; Storey, 1993; Strinati, 1995: 259). For cultural theorists, the turn to

Bourdieu accomplishes a number of things: it offers a macro-sociological framework in which cultural tastes and preferences are tied to particular class interests; it conceptually unifies the field of culture and cultural consumption in a way that the binarism of cultural studies populism does not; it foregrounds key problems concerning cultural authority and cultural hierarchy which are effaced in cultural studies; and it also legitimates the use of a number of standard social science instruments including interview and survey research for the study of cultural practices. Bourdieu's major work *Distinction* (1984) offers a survey of class tastes in France *c.* 1968 and proposes that the making of aesthetic choices is based on a process of distinction from other social groups in an ordered hierarchy of taste ranging from the popular to the aristocratic. The significance of Bourdieu's work for sociologies of culture in different societies is not in the application of the highly culture-specific model offered in *Distinction* but rather in its particular mode of enquiry into the functions of cultural consumption.[2]

## Arts Consumption in Ireland

The place of the arts in Irish society has always represented something of a paradox: on the one hand, the reputation of the Irish literary and theatrical tradition and more recently Irish film and Irish music, both traditional and popular, gives the impression that the Irish are a profoundly artistic race. On the other hand, the philistinism of the Irish middle classes so bitterly referred to by Yeats in his diatribes from the stage of the Abbey Theatre, the low priority given to arts education in schools (Benson, 1979) and the perception that the Irish are 'indifferent and almost hostile to culture with a capital 'C' (Kennedy, 1990: 106) all make for a more sobering assessment of the state of the arts in Ireland. The issue of the relative health of the arts in Ireland really turns on the question of participation in artistic and cultural life and up to recently, this is an area of social science in Ireland that has been greatly under-researched.[3]

There are a number of reasons for believing that the arts in Ireland are now in a better position than at any time before in the history of the state. Over the course of a decade there appears to have been a remarkable cultural shift in terms of levels of participation in the arts. Attendance at arts events per annum went from 60 per cent of the population in 1982 to 78 per cent in 1994 – or even 83 per cent if an expanded definition of 'arts event' is taken into account.[4] This increase seems to be supported by public perceptions of the availability of the arts in that 84 per cent of people now believe that the arts have become more accessible in the past ten years. The arts are viewed positively not only for themselves but also in terms of their economic benefits: 89 per cent feel that arts activity helps to bring tourists to Ireland; 73 per cent think arts education is as important as science education and 60 per cent believe that the current level of spending on the arts should be maintained even in times of economic recession.

In economic terms, the arts sector had a gross revenue of some £450 million in 1993 (Durkan, 1994: 17); about 21,500 are employed directly in the arts sector accounting for 2.4 per cent of total employment and the sector is responsible for 1.6 per cent of GDP and exports worth £100 million.[5] Two areas in particular – music and film – account for 75 per cent of turnover and 80 per cent of employment.

This impressive level of activity has been accompanied by concerted political activity to develop the arts sector as an area of economic and cultural significance and to broaden access to the arts in general. Throughout the 1980s, the Arts Council has pursued a policy of regionalism, counterbalancing the centralisation of resources in national institutions located in the capital and developing a network of regional arts centres and arts officers in all county regions. In 1993 the first cabinet ministry of Arts and Culture with responsibility also for broadcasting was established. A major initiative was undertaken in relation to film with the re-establishment of the Irish Film Board to provide development money for indigenous Irish film and a package of tax incentives which has succeeded in revitalising the film production industry and attracting numerous international productions to Ireland. A task force has reported on the potential for employment in the music industry. An innovative Three Year Plan for the arts was agreed by government to develop regional centres of excellence in the arts, improve conditions of employment for artists and to campaign for a greater role for the arts in education (The Arts Council, 1995).

Official Irish arts policy as expressed by the Arts Council reflects this changing attitude. Ciarán Benson, chairman of the Arts Council, has described three successive phases in official arts policy: firstly, the period of Catholic and nationalist ideology which guided arts policy from the foundation of the state up to and including the foundation of the Arts Council in 1951; this gave way to a period of liberal elitism during the period 1960–1973 and is expressed most clearly in the Arts Council's enthusiastic support of modernism; and finally, the period in which cultural democracy began to exert influence and gain dominance in arts policy thinking from 1973 on (Benson, 1992; see also Kelly, 1989). An ideology of cultural democracy is now firmly established in official thinking about the arts and received explicit endorsement with the appointment of a new board to the Arts Council in 1993 and the adoption of a carefully balanced but essentially populist mission statement endorsing 'meaningful access to and participation in the arts' for all.[6]

*The Public and the Arts* (1994), only the second arts audience survey of its kind to be commissioned, provides some backing for the claim that access to the arts is now more widespread.[7] The rate of annual attendance at any arts event at 83 per cent compares favourably with most European countries. All social classes have increased their aggregate attendance since the last survey in 1981 but, as the following table of attendance at arts events by occupational class reveals, gaps between classes remain:[8]

Table 1 *Attendance at arts events by occupational class (in per cent)*

|  | All Respondents | Middle Class | Skilled Working Class | Semi & Unskilled Working Class | Farmers |
|---|---|---|---|---|---|
| Play | 37 | 58 | 35 | 20 | 31 |
| Classical Music | 14 | 30 | 10 | 6 | 7 |
| Popular Music | 39 | 53 | 40 | 33 | 22 |
| Visual Arts | 23 | 43 | 22 | 8 | 12 |
| Traditional Music | 24 | 26 | 26 | 20 | 27 |
| Ballet | 3 | 6 | 2 | 1 | 1 |
| Film | 55 | 71 | 60 | 47 | 30 |
| Attended any | 78 | 92 | 81 | 68 | 63 |

Source: *The Public and the Arts* (1994)

There remains a persistent class-based distinction between mass cultural participation and traditional or high culture in the distribution of attendance above. Working-class groupings consume predominantly mass media forms of film and popular music where audiences for classical music and the visual arts are drawn largely from the middle class. A striking feature is the high level of arts consumption for all middle-class respondents who have higher levels of consumption not just for the high arts but for all types of culture (see Di Maggio and Useem, 1978b). A greater proportion of middle-class respondents report attending popular music events and films than any other grouping. Film as a medium is popular with all social groups and similar proportions in each social class report attending traditional music and popular music. Classical music and visual arts exhibitions as already indicated remain substantially middle class and, interestingly, theatre alone of the high arts maintains a claim to being a more socially mixed art form. What this means is that cultural participation of any form is associated more with middle-class membership than with other socio-economic groups and that middle-class audiences enjoy what Gripsrud has called a privileged 'double access' to not only the historically bourgeois forms of art but also to mass forms of popular cultural expression (Gripsrud, 1989). At a more local level, there appears to be a growing impetus to consume and participate in the arts among the Irish middle class for whom culture has acquired a significance and a value that it did not possess previously. The process of modernisation begun in the 1960s, the change in Ireland's class structure from one based on family property to a meritocracy more typical of Western nations (Breen *et al.*, 1990: 53) and the general upward shift in mobility that was experienced in the decades following economic expansion can be said to have created fertile ground for the emergence of new forms of arts participation. What remains to be examined is the basis of such cultural confidence, the nature of audience's identification with the arts and the role, if any, that such cultural participation plays in middle-class identity.

## Cultural Hierarchy and Social Class

One of the most important contributions to discussion about the relationship between culture and class is that contained in the work of Pierre Bourdieu. In his sociology of culture Bourdieu outlines a hierarchy of aesthetic tastes which resembles a similar hierarchy of social classes in the economic field and reflects the stratified distribution of educational and cultural capital. While his aim is not to produce a classification of artistic tastes as such, the field of culture, according to Bourdieu, classifies its consumers better than almost any other object in the social world and revolves around that most prized possession of social positions: cultural legitimacy. The expression of aesthetic taste involves a process of competing for cultural stakes that in addition to informing one's sense of identity and belonging in the social world also mark by differentiation one's separateness from other positions and groups. In the analysis offered in *Distinction* (Bourdieu, 1984) the organisation of cultural taste is relational and rigidly hierarchical. The taste for legitimate, high brow culture, 'pure taste', dominates the field of culture and confers through its self-legitimating activity of aestheticisation a status of artistic and cultural dominance. Central to the operation of pure taste is the aesthetic attitude, the pure gaze of aesthetic distancing, characterised above all by a separation from practical function and a refusal to view objects in any other way than in purely aesthetic terms. The aesthetic disposition stands opposed to 'barbarous' vulgar taste, a zone of aesthetic taste associated most prominently with the practical, utilitarian attitudes of working-class respondents who consistently reaffirm a continuity between art and life and systematically resist the aestheticisation of objects as useless and pointless. Between pure and barbarous tastes lie the various dispositions and aesthetic strategies of the middlebrow field which reflect in various degrees an aspiration to cultural legitimacy while maintaining some of the experiential basis of popular aesthetic consumption. The discrete zones of taste form a hierarchy of aesthetic forms: legitimate art forms such as the symphony or appreciation of difficult, avant garde art dominate over types of lesser status such as popular folk music or such middlebrow forms as jazz and cinema. Between these zones of taste there exists a hierarchy of discriminatory competence shown in the increasing ability of arts consumers to produce meaningful distinctions based on knowledge and familiarity with the art forms concerned. With the differential and stratified distribution of resources, the cultural field comes to reflect the stratification of society as a whole. Ultimately, the game of culture is a competitive struggle expressed through stylistic distinction between occupational groupings and class fractions who seek to maximise the return from economic and cultural resources and whose trajectory in social space reveals a career of investment in social, economic and cultural capital.

The apparent reductionism between class and culture implicit in Bourdieu's model has been questioned by Di Maggio (1987). He observes that artistic tastes cluster far less in reality than we imagine them to do and that the social significance of taste lies in its role as a form of cultural currency in the complex world of social networks rather than as an expression of class interests. Consumption of the arts, Di Maggio suggests, has powerful symbolic functions which go some way towards explaining the emergence of distinct class-related aesthetic tastes but is not reducible to the class origins of the individual arts user (Di Maggio, 1987). The arts, for example, have an important screening role: possession of particular artistic interests and tastes is a convenient means of identifying membership of a social class and acts as a boundary marker to exclude outsiders (Di Maggio, 1982: 182). Cultural goods, style and competencies, what Bourdieu calls 'cultural capital' and which includes above all a familiarity with the high arts, function as effective means of class reproduction, ensuring the selection of members from the dominant, cultured status group and providing for the socialisation of new members into the class group. Furthermore, Di Maggio argues, arts consumption provides an important source of identity for the middle class, informing and building class solidarity through shared experiences, languages and aspirations (1978: 151). The collective participation in public forms of cultural entertainment acts as a social ritual which builds social solidarity through mutual identification and reinforces the social and ideological cohesion of the class or status group.

A common factor in the accounts of both Bourdieu and Di Maggio on the relationship between culture and class is that of education (Di Maggio and Useem, 1980; Bourdieu, 1993). Education, it is recognised, is one of the single most important variables in the distribution of arts consumption. Arts appreciation is a trained capacity; art exists as such only for those who have the appropriate knowledge to decipher it (see Bourdieu, 1993: 215) and access to the codes of literary and artistic analysis is predominantly achieved through the acquisition of recognised educational credentials. Strategically, acquisition of the appropriate forms of high culture can facilitate upward social mobility and as the preponderance of teachers among audiences for the arts reveals, the cultivation of highbrow artistic tastes in the absence of the appropriate economic capital enhances claims for at least marginal membership of the middle and upper middle class.

A sociology of arts consumption as indicated by this brief discussion illustrates some of the parallels that exist between an economy of practice in the cultural field and the social world of stratification. Whether in terms of how the arts contribute to class reproduction or act as source of classification between different social groups and class fractions, arts consumption is a phenomenon that is situated in the social and steadfastly rooted in the activity of social beings. To investigate the social character of the aesthetic in more direct fashion the following section presents data from a study of audiences for the radio arts magazine programme, *The Arts Show*, and examines some of the ways in which the arts have become important for sections of the Irish middle class.

## *The Arts Show*: The Middle Ground of Arts Support

*The Arts Show* is the flagship arts review programme of Ireland's national public radio service, RTÉ Radio 1. It was introduced in 1988 as part of a revamping of speech programming in order to meet competition from newly established local radio. The brief of the programme was to provide a compendium of current arts, popular and traditional, domestic and international, in an entertaining and accessible fashion. The programme was allocated relatively substantial resources with a team of three full time producers, a well known personality presenter and a strategically important time opening the evening schedule three times a week. The populist intentions of the programme were clear from the choice of Mike Murphy as presenter of the programme. Having had a successful career in light entertainment and variety in the previous twenty years, his pivotal role as presenter of a serious arts programme bemused many and caused consternation among more traditional-minded producers and audience members.[9]

The purpose of the present research was to investigate the middlebrow popularisation of legitimate, dominant culture that characterises *The Arts Show*'s approach and in particular to examine audience responses to the eclectic mix of art forms that it presents from across the cultural spectrum. A survey closely modelled on that for *The Public and the Arts* survey (Clancy *et al.*, 1994) was carried out and a self-selected sample of listeners recruited through the programme.[10] This is not a random sample of the audience but rather consists of a cohort of dedicated listeners to *The Arts Show*. The differences between this sample and that of the evening time radio audience are illustrated in Table 2. For comparative purposes, a demographic analysis of the general public derived from Clancy *et al.* (1994) is also presented.

Listeners to Radio 1 in the evening are traditionally thought to be older, often female, living alone and people who use the radio for company. Figures from the JNLR show that in the evening time female listeners slightly outnumber male listeners, are predominantly in the 35+ age group and disproportionately based in Dublin. It is also a largely middle-class audience with 58 per cent of listeners in the ABC1 category. By contrast, listeners to *The Arts Show* as shown in this survey are significantly younger and in comparison to the general population very highly educated. As such, they appear to constitute quite a

Table 2 *The Arts Show survey – sample structure (in per cent)*

| | Arts Show sample | Radio 1 evening (1) | National population (2) |
|---|---|---|---|
| **Age:** | | | |
| 15–24 | 6 | 8 | 23 |
| 25–34 | 28 | 10 | 19 |
| 35–44 | 34 | 16 | 18 |
| 45–54 | 23 | 21 | 14 |
| 55+ | 9 | 45 | 25 |
| **Gender:** | | | |
| Male | 45 | 54 | 50 |
| Female | 55 | 46 | 50 |
| **Region:** | | | |
| Dublin | 42 | 40 | 30 |
| Rest of Leinster | 13 | 24 | 26 |
| Munster | 30 | 22 | 26 |
| Connaught/Ulster | 13 | 14 | 18 |
| NI/UK | 2 | | |
| **Education:** | | | |
| Primary | 3 | | 17 |
| Secondary | 28 | | 64 |
| Third level | 69 | | 17 |

(1) Source: JNLR/MRBI 1993/94   (2) Source: The Public and the Arts
n = 106

distinctive group in contrast to the older profile of the Radio 1 listener in the evening set apart by their age, their cultural interests, their high levels of education and by middle-class membership.[11]

The main strategy of this research was to employ elements of discourse analysis in order to identify and analyse distinct audience discourses about the arts as well as some of the discrete interpretative positions adopted by listeners in their engagement with the programme. Drawing on the opposition within Bourdieu's sociology of culture between the legitimate taste of the pure gaze and the popular aesthetic (Bourdieu, 1984: 30), the research was premised on the availability of a range of discursive positions between the two extremes of elitism and populism in the arts. The discourse of elitism is characterised above all by the 'disinterestedness' of the aesthetic attitude, the belief that the appropriate relationship between the art object and spectator is a wholly aesthetic one, valued for its own sake alone (Stolnitz, 1961). The discourse of populism typically inverts elitist aestheticism and is perhaps best illustrated by the quintessentially populist observation by Marx in *The German Ideology* that:

'The exclusive concentration of artistic talent in particular individuals, and its suppression in the broad mass which is bound up with this, is a consequence of the division of labour' (Marx, 1846/1968: 416). As interpretative positions, elitism and populism constitute what Michael Billig would describe as the twin poles of an 'ideological dilemma' (Billig *et al.*, 1988) about art, the nature of artistic creativity, cultural participation and the source of aesthetic value. In this study, elitism and populism are viewed less as formal systems of discourse than as 'practical ideologies', rhetorically defined and argumentatively constructed positions produced by audience members in their responses to and evaluation of a radio programme.

Respondents to the survey were coded according to a series of Likert scaled items in the questionnaire which queried listeners' perceptions of a number of defining features of elitism and populism in the arts. An open-ended section on the questionnaire inviting listeners' comments on *The Arts Show* was also coded and a combination of these indicators was used to define membership of either category. Elitists therefore scored strongly on statements such as: 'Being able to appreciate things like classical music is a sign of being cultured' and tended to argue that *The Arts Show* was often very lightweight in its approach. Populists, on the other hand, scored more on statements such as 'I think popular arts like rock music and photography are as much an art form as the so-called high arts' and also tended to argue that the programme was not sufficiently populist in its approach. The spread of responses in this continuum produced outliers at both elitist and populist poles and a significant number of responses at both upper and lower quartiles. There was also, however, a substantial middle ground between the two extremes and the middle 50 per cent of the distribution was reworked as a middlebrow category defining the core listenership to the programme. An analysis of the three categories appears in Table 3 and gives an illustration of the variety of demographic backgrounds associated with these cultural positions.

Elitists are evenly mixed in age, gender and according to the geographical spread of listenership but are relative to other groups overwhelmingly in the highly educated bracket, with 50 per cent having postgraduate qualifications. Populists, by comparison, are younger and there is a greater proportion of female members. The middlebrow category is more mixed and is closer in gender and age to the evening time JNLR audience but again, like all of *The Arts Show* listeners, possesses a high level of education which goes hand in hand with an interest in arts and culture. Bearing out the observations of di Maggio and Bourdieu, possession and use of any aesthetic discourse is in this sense dependent on educational capital and further emphasises the exclusivity of this form of cultural consumption.

In an analysis of attendance at different types of art forms, elitists' preferences are, not uncharacteristically, consistently of a high cultural nature and

Table 3 *Demographic analysis of elitist, populist and middlebrow groups*
*(in per cent)*

|  | Elitist | Middlebrow | Populist | Total |
|---|---|---|---|---|
| **Age:** | | | | |
| 15–24 | 0 | 4 | 13 | 6 |
| 25–34 | 27 | 26 | 32 | 28 |
| 35–44 | 36 | 36 | 29 | 34 |
| 45–54 | 27 | 24 | 16 | 23 |
| 55+ | 9 | 9 | 10 | 9 |
| **Gender:** | | | | |
| Male | 50 | 51 | 32 | 45 |
| Female | 50 | 49 | 68 | 55 |
| **Region:** | | | | |
| Dublin | 41 | 38 | 48 | 42 |
| Rest of Leinster | 18 | 15 | 6 | 13 |
| Munster | 36 | 32 | 23 | 30 |
| Connaught/Ulster | 5 | 11 | 23 | 13 |
| NI/UK | 0 | 4 | 0 | 2 |
| **Education:** | | | | |
| Primary | 0 | 6 | 0 | 3 |
| Secondary | 27 | 30 | 26 | 28 |
| Third level | 73 | 64 | 74 | 69 |
| **Column Totals** | 100 | 100 | 100 | 100 |

count classical music, contemporary dance, art house film and visual arts exhibitions as events they visit more than six times per year. The populists' mix is more eclectic with mainstream film being the most commonly pursued event and including in addition to theatre, visual arts and classical music, the more typically populist forms of traditional/folk music and rock/pop. Middlebrow audiences have lower levels of frequent attendance and choose from a narrower range of events. Film, visual arts and theatre constitute the most popular choices and as such, as well as in the level of attendance, approximate the national average described in *The Public and the Arts* more so than either the elitist or populist segments.

Elitism and populism emerged most clearly as distinct discourses in the non-structured, qualitative data from the open-ended section of the questionnaire. As discourse, elitism and populism function as 'interpretative repertoires' (Gilbert and Mulkay, 1984; Potter and Wetherell, 1987) or registers of terms and categories used by listeners to describe and evaluate the programme. Elitists, for example, characteristically described *The Arts Show* as an 'important' programme which was 'intelligent', 'informative' and 'essential listening' for anyone with an interest in the arts. Some of the typical elitist appraisals of the programme included:

> *The Arts Show* fills a very important slot in radio listening, enjoyable and informative. Without it, keeping in touch would be very difficult.
>
> (Female, 35–44, Mature Art Student, Cork)

> It is intelligent. It is one of the only programmes on radio which presents intellectual discussion (which is non-political). I think there could be more of this.
>
> (Male, 25–34, Secondary Teacher, Dublin)

> I rate it a must when I'm home and think it should be extended to give an intelligent coverage for a mix of classical music – like Peer Gynt – Stravinsky, Moussorgsky – try and lead the Irish listener away from [what] Radio Éireann calls CHUNES. We hear far too much of rubbishy current noises without melody all day long.
>
> (Male, 55+, Hospital Pharmacist, Dublin)

Elitism as a distinctive discursive position is most marked in the view expressed by some listeners that the programme was too light and should, in effect, assume the higher cultural ground:

> Very predictable interviews with a soft approach to most issues – no real debate on any of the serious issues – just a token nod.
>
> (Female, 35–44, Teacher)

> My strongest criticism is that it's often too 'chatty', cosy; that it lacks sharpness, intellectual depth and adventurousness.
>
> (Male, 35–44, Financial Controller)

> On the whole I enjoy *The Arts Show* but sometimes I find it bland and uninspiring. Often I feel there is not enough meat in it because it tends to scan rather than delve into Arts issues.
>
> (Female, 35–44, Potter/Mature Student)

The elitist aesthetic espoused by some segments of the audience argued that the programme should incorporate more debate on intellectual and cultural affairs and include a greater number of specialised, in-depth features as opposed to the type of dabbling or delving into art which they associated with magazine programmes:

> Since my main area of interest is the visual arts – painting and sculpture – I would like a lot more informed coverage here.
>
> (Male, 45–54, Lecturer)

> I would like to see more thorough, in-depth reports on specific projects, artists, theatre etc. Also a critical review of institutions and their policies and impact they make on the arts in Ireland.
>
> (Male 25–34, Designer)

Populism as a discursive position stands opposed to this type of approach. Populists typically celebrated the wide-ranging, eclectic mix of arts on the programme and were happy to endorse its attempts to popularise high culture and make it more accessible to those with little background knowledge of the subject. The most important attribute in the populist repertoire was that of 'entertaining', 'enjoyable' listening, suggesting an entirely different set of aesthetic priorities:

> Excellent and entertaining and not elitist or high brow – but only with Mike Murphy!
>
> (Male, 45–54, Unemployed, Tipperary)

> I find it very entertaining and I enjoy listening to items about areas of the arts of which I know very little.
>
> (Male 25–34, Secondary Teacher, Cork)

Yet populists could also be critical of *The Arts Show*, perceiving it at times as not being quite populist enough:

> It's good but it comes across as elitist. Too nice, too cosy. Arts Awards show from Bank of Ireland had some years ago made me wonder if you wanted ordinary people ever to be involved. Art is for everybody not just the wealthy or formally educated. Cut out the 'arty' tartiness and put a little edge to what is happening.
>
> (Male, 45–54, Credit Union Manager )

> Show tends to be 'safe' sometimes – is it possible to question policy in arts, discuss new work without becoming totally high brow?
>
> (Female, 25–34, Primary Teacher)

One of the central criticisms in this respect is the identification of the programme with an exclusive arts clique consisting of people who all know one another and possess a language of their own:

> Some of the reviews are far too much like promoting the work of friends.
>
> (Female, 45–54, Arts Officer)

> The whole atmosphere of the show comes across as an exclusive or semi-exclusive club of Mike Murphy's friends having a chat and bit of banter about odds and sods in the arts world!
>
> (Female, 35–44, Management Consultant)

A priority of the populist position is that art should be available to all and in this context populists universally argued in favour of a greater involvement of ordinary people in the programme:

> Improvements: By engaging with 'ordinary people' and recording their responses to the contemporary arts.
>
> (Female, 35–44, Teacher)

> This programme initially launched itself as an arts show with a small 'a', sort of catering to the people, by the people for the people. Punters – those who support the arts should, I think, be given a voice I think sometimes. Having been a regular listener I'm getting a bit irritated by some of the permanent reviewers.
>
> (Female, Homemaker, 45–54)

Why not have 'punter reviewers' if they can articulate well what they review and do not usurp the 'professional reviewers' space/credit. The results might be surprising.

(Female, 55+, Manager Art Gallery)

Elitism and populism represent two extremes of the field of aesthetic discourse covered by *The Arts Show*. In fact, the programme might more properly be thought of as addressing the middle ground, middlebrow type of listener who is an arts enthusiast but without the professional knowledge of the expert and is not overly concerned with issues of cultural populism. In this survey there is a substantial middle ground among the audience for the programme who are both very satisfied and entertained by what they are listening to. Many of the comments returned in the survey were of this confirmatory and affirmative type:

It's informative and easy to listen to, the interviewing is relaxed and the information mainly forthcoming. It's topical and the coverage is wide and balanced in general.

(Female, 45–54, Retired)

Whenever I have listened I have found it interesting particularly in areas where I haven't been familiar with current events. Also I like to hear reviews of current shows.

(Female, 45–54, Secretary)

I am usually interested in what topics it is covering each night. Mostly by the end of the programme I find I have information, been stimulated and have enjoyed it.

(Female, 35–44, Counsellor)

Acclamation such as this would appear to endorse the very definite policy of the programme to be an accessible and listener-friendly vehicle for the arts. Producers of *The Arts Show* are conscious that any arts programme risks being elitist but are satisfied that their policy of a cultural bricolage presented in an entertaining populist fashion has met with the approval of the middle ground of arts interest in the country and it is a matter of some satisfaction to programme makers that *The Arts Show* has achieved credibility and a 'must hear' status among culturally-literate, arts-aware consumers:

I suppose I am pleased at the fact that we have gained a huge audience and I do really believe that and I do know that anybody who is – I was going to say kind of thinking and I suppose that is what I mean and I don't mean that to sound in any way elitist or exclusive or anything – it has become something that 'Oh yes did you hear that on *The Arts Show*!' or 'I was going into town and I heard it on *The Arts Show*!' or something and that the kind of snobbery that is associated with the arts could never really be associated with *The Arts Show* and I think that that's important. And that it is an accessible programme and that it is an interesting programme and in lots of ways it is a vitally important programme to listen to if you are involved in the arts.

(Producer – *The Arts Show*)

The middlebrow position defined by producers and articulated further by dedicated listeners to the programme constitutes an attempt to celebrate in populist fashion the practical, experiential enjoyment of the arts while retaining an appeal to the elitist sense of the arts as a cultural imperative, a sense of being 'important' and commanding respect for their intrinsic worth. The many uses of the arts for audience members consistently reproduce this conjunction of pleasurable enjoyment, an affirmation of the continuity of art and life, while appealing to art's quasi-magical powers to transform and enliven the mundane:

> I don't think I could live without having the visual arts around me, the written word around me, it's just, it would be unthinkable really, I just can't think of a duller life. It's just, it's always been a part of me and always will be a part of me.
>
> (Female, 55+, Manager art gallery, Cork)

> It's great enjoyment and it makes life not so dull.
>
> (Female, 35–44, Chiropodist, Dublin)

> It is basically entertainment. It is a way of spending leisure time. It's a way of getting my mind off the other stuff I'm thinking about all the day and maybe thinking about the big issues in life or the little issues in life or it'll make you laugh or cry or whatever in some way that will engage me.
>
> (Male, 25–34, Company Accountant, Dublin)

Listeners in this category very much support cultural eclecticism, the indiscriminate mix of high and popular culture that is seen as integral to the populist ethos of postmodern culture (Jameson, 1984):

> I am very pleased that so much of what was dismissed as popular art when I was young is now accepted as really important culture. For instance, popular music, The Beatles, my favourite Jimi Hendrix, for instance. But then also cinema. They were seen almost as escapism or bubblegum but now I really see no difference between good popular music and good classical music if you follow me so I'm happy that what was once derided as just popular or escapism is now accepted as good and valid.
>
> (Male, 35–44, Illustrator, Dublin)

For such listeners cultural legitimacy is no longer restricted to certain forms of art. They display a sense of cultural confidence that their cultural experience and background is just as valid and important as traditional high culture. Further, the culturally confident middlebrow expresses the belief that participation in the arts is available to all, even betraying a certain impatience with the suggestion that barriers to arts access exist:

> I think a lot of the barriers that people have in going to the arts is sometimes just the thought of walking into a particular institution that they have never walked into before. I think probably the thing of actually down to the Abbey box office and booking tickets and they go, well it's not for me. And that's in their own mind really.
>
> (Male, 25–34, Company Accountant, Dublin)

I can never understand people – I remember working with a colleague and he said they wouldn't let me into the Concert Hall. I mean all you do is go and pay your money. You know people have this most extraordinary idea – I don't know – do they want to put their hands under their feet to encourage them to go in.

(Female, 55+, Microbiologist, Dublin)

However, expressions of such confidence must be reviewed in the light of the fact that only 3 per cent of this sample of listeners had left school with only a primary education. While *The Arts Show* does seek to attract listeners with its light and easy mix of arts and entertainment, the audience remains an exclusive one of highly educated and largely middle-class arts enthusiasts who are predisposed to engaging in this form of cultural discourse. The programme has succeeded in raising awareness of the arts and popularising less accessible forms of art for its listeners but it is unlikely on the evidence of this research to have introduced listeners to an experience of the arts that was not prefigured in their background experience or education. What remains to be considered, then, in the final section is the function of such cultural confidence for this particular fraction of the middle class which *The Arts Show* has apparently been so successful in reaching.

## Conclusion: Middlebrow Cultural Confidence

Part of the success of *The Arts Show* has been in identifying and satisfying an audience of middlebrow arts enthusiasts which hitherto had gone unrecognised. In doing so, it also retains the support and admiration of elitist and populist arts listeners. Clearly, were *The Arts Show* to shift its emphasis radically and move significantly up to the higher cultural ground which the elitist group appear to call for or, alternatively, move in some of the directions indicated by populists, it would risk alienating some of its core middle ground support. Unifying the middle ground is a consensus which is broadly populist in tone expressed in the belief that the arts are for everyone, that they are primarily meant to be experienced and enjoyed and that most forms of cultural expression can legitimately claim to be art once they satisfy certain basic aesthetic criteria. The middle ground of *The Arts Show*'s audience responds positively to *The Arts Show*'s presentation of aesthetic experience as a source of both intellectual stimulation and personal enjoyment. It is an aesthetic experience characterised by immediacy: it requires no specialised knowledge; its mode of address is to the 'arts enthusiast', the amateur or ordinary listener who is literate, aware and possesses a love of art. This positive portrayal of middlebrowism, however, with its associated attitude of cultural confidence contrasts sharply with what is often perceived as the conservative and cautious nature of middlebrow culture (see Bourdieu, 1990b).

An important concept in Bourdieu's analysis of middlebrow taste in *Distinction* is the phenomenon he labelled 'cultural goodwill' (Bourdieu, 1984:

318) or the act of deference to dominant forms of culture. Cultural goodwill is, for example, expressed in the aspiration of the petite bourgeoisie to climb in social and cultural space but without either the cultural or economic means to do so. In consuming middlebrow versions of culture – accessible collections of art, listening to light classical music, reading popular but not avant-garde forms of literature – middlebrow arts enthusiasts perform an act of cultural goodwill, upholding the traditional sources of cultural legitimacy and sustaining the implicit hierarchy of the fine arts. Contemporary mass media like radio, television, magazines and newspaper supplements are among the most important of what Bourdieu calls 'cultural intermediaries', mediators and popularisers of dominant culture. Cultural intermediaries are, Bourdieu suggests, always cautious in their taste and 'resolutely avoid vulgarity' (1984: 326). They demand guarantees of the quality and authority of their aesthetic choices and avoid moving far from the legitimate centre even if they juxtapose new and traditional art forms in peculiar and sometimes contradictory ways.

The taste for a wide range of popular arts and popularised versions of high brow art among *The Arts Show* audience is certainly emblematic of middlebrow culture. The intention of the programme is to bring 'the wide world of the arts' to the non-specialist listener and for the committed group of listeners in this survey at least that appears to have been a successful venture. Following Bourdieu's account, one can argue that *The Arts Show* performs an act of cultural goodwill by affirming the value of the aesthetic as well as promoting the ability of its audience to participate in this heightened cultural practice. The evidence in this survey is that most committed listeners to *The Arts Show* do approve of what they hear and do participate in some active way. For Bourdieu, however, there is an element of self-deception about this. Middlebrow culture, for Bourdieu, is an imitative reflection of legitimate culture that disguises the social basis of its submission to dominant culture. Middlebrow arts consumers 'misrecognise' their place in social and cultural space and the hierarchical stratification of society that underlies a taste for the arts. They see in the arts a realm of legitimacy, refinement and status, and middlebrow culture appears to promise easy access to such cultural dominance. But just as the culturally dominant can, Midas-like, aestheticise whatever they touch, so, for the middlebrow, legitimacy remains an elusive goal: once popularised or incorporated into the middlebrow category, art is diminished and degraded in aesthetic status.

Bourdieu's account of the nature of middlebrow culture need not, however, be accepted in its entirety. The cultural confidence of the arts enthusiast appears to offer a strong countercurrent to the notion of 'cultural goodwill' and the conservatism traditionally associated with middlebrow culture. The self assurance of culturally confident middlebrows counterbalances the naive attitude of deference that Bourdieu supposes to be the basis of 'cultural goodwill'. It is perhaps a measure of the post-modernising of the contemporary cultural scene that the barriers between middle and high brow taste have been levelled to the extent that cultural supremacy has in fact passed to the zone occupied by middlebrow arts consumers who self-assuredly display their aesthetic prowess and independence from models of cultural hierarchy inherited from the past. There is no reason to think that the very rigid forms of cultural domination that Bourdieu described in 1960s France still apply in 1990s Ireland. But this is not to deny that hierarchies and stratification in the arts continue to exist and that social, cultural and geographical barriers to cultural democracy remain. There is ample evidence in these findings from *The Arts Show* survey that audiences for the arts remain strongly rooted in the educational and cultural experience of the middle class. What is suggested, however, subject to further research, is that the type of middle ground support that a programme like *The Arts Show* receives indicates just how significant the arts have become for the image and identity of an expanded and progressive new middle class and how class fractions such as this have become the repository of post-modern cultural values.

## Notes

[1] An earlier version of this chapter was awarded a postgraduate essay prize by Royal Irish Academy's Social Science Research Council. I am grateful to members of the Council for permission to reprint the work here. I would also like to acknowledge the helpful comments of Dr Brian Torode, Department of Sociology, Trinity College, Dublin.

[2] See the work of Michèle Lamont for a sympathetic application of Bourdieu's approach in an American context. Lamont's (1992) work is itself a comparison of the process of 'distinction' among the French and American upper middle class. (Lamont and Fournier, 1992) presents more wide-ranging studies of cultural consumption in the United States. Halle (1994) is another work inspired by Bourdieu offering a sociology of the uses of art in contemporary America. Bourdieu has also been particularly important in a revival of interest in the study of middlebrow culture and is evident in the work of Long (1986; 1987) and Radway (1989) on middle-class literary tastes.

[3] *Audiences, Acquisitions and Amateurs* (1983) was the first systematic survey of arts consumption in Ireland. *The Public and the Arts* (1994) sought to update this analysis and to compare the rate of change in arts consumption since that time. With the appointment of a new Arts Council in 1993, much greater attention has been given to arts research. See in particular *Views of Theatre in Ireland* (1995), the reports of the PIANO (1996) and FORTE (1996) working groups and *Poverty: Access and Participation in the Arts* (1997).

[4] These statistics are reported in *The Public and the Arts – A Survey of Behaviour and Attitudes in Ireland* (1994) Dublin: The Arts Council/UCD Graduate School of Business. The methodology and overall findings of this report are discussed in greater detail below.

[5] Further statistics on the size and employment potential of Ireland's cultural industries are reported in *The Employment and Economic Significance of The Cultural Industries in Ireland* (1995) Dublin: Coopers and Lybrand.

6   The full mission statement is as follows:

> As the statutory body entrusted with stimulating public interest in the arts and with promoting knowledge, appreciation and practice of the arts, An Comhairle Ealaíon/ The Arts Council believes that everyone in Ireland has an entitlement to meaningful access to and participation in the arts. The Council understands that it has a primary responsibility to encourage and maintain high standards in all art forms, especially in the living contemporary arts. It also understands that it has a clear responsibility to foster those structures which assist and develop dialogue between artists, the arts and the communities from which they emerge [reprinted in *Art Matters*, No. 16, Nov. 1993].

An equally strong endorsement in official arts policy of cultural populism is to be found in the discussion document of the Arts Council of Great Britain: *A Creative Future – the way forward for the arts, crafts and media in England*, London: Arts Council of Great Britain, 1993.

7   The first survey was commissioned and conducted in 1981 and provides the basis for comparison and analysis of growth trends in the 1994 survey – *Audiences, Acquisitions and Amateurs: Participation in the Arts*, Dublin: The Arts Council/An Chomhairle Ealaíon, 1983.

8   The aggregate attendance at arts events in RSGB Omnibus Arts Survey, 1991. Cited in *The Public and the Arts*, (1994: 81).

9   *The Arts Show* was introduced in the revamped Radio 1 schedule of 1988 when RTÉ faced competition from legal independent radio for the first time. The programme is hosted by the popular personality presenter Mike Murphy and maintained since its introduction in excess of a 1 per cent national audience share for its 7 p.m. evening slot which was considered to be good for the relatively 'dead time' of night time radio. Considered to be one of the successes of the evening schedule, the programme moved in September 1996 to an afternoon slot, 2.45 p.m. to 3.30 p.m., Monday to Wednesday, with an omnibus evening repeat where it has attracted up to four times its previous audience. An account of the production context of the programme is presented in O'Neill (1993).

10   The survey was conducted in May/June 1994 and advertised both through the programme and in the RTÉ Guide. 143 requests for questionnaires were received both by telephone and post and a total of 106 completed questionnaires were received.

11   BBC research has shown that the audience profile for Radio 4's *Kaleidoscope* also deviates from the norm and is in some senses a unique audience grouping. See *Radio 4 in the Late Evenings*. BBC Unpublished Report (BBC, 1989).

# References

Ang, Ien (1985) *Watching 'Dallas': Soap Opera and the Melodramatic Imagination*. London: Methuen.

The Arts Council (1983) *Audiences, Acquisitions and Amateurs*. Dublin: The Arts Council/An Chomhairle Ealaíon.

The Arts Council (1995) *The Arts Plan, 1995–1997*. Dublin: The Arts Council/An Chomhairle Ealaíon.

The Arts Council (1995) *Views of Theatre in Ireland: Report of the Arts Council's Theatre Review*. Dublin: The Arts Council/An Chomhairle Ealaíon.

The Arts Council (1997) *Poverty: Access and Participation in the Arts*. Dublin: The Arts Council/An Chomhairle Ealaíon/ Combat Poverty Agency.

Benson, Ciarán (1992) 'Towards a cultural democracy?' *Studies*, 81(1).

Billig, Michael *et al.* (1988) *Ideological Dilemmas – A social psychology of everyday thinking*. London: Sage.

Blundell, V., J. Shepherd, and I. Taylor (eds) (1993) *Relocating Cultural Studies: Developments in Theory and Research*. London: Routledge.

Bourdieu, Pierre (1968) 'Outline of a Sociological Theory of Art Perception', *International Social Science Journal*, Vol. 20.

Bourdieu, Pierre (1984) *Distinction: A Social Critique of the Judgement of Taste*. (translated by R. Nice). London: Routledge.

Bourdieu, Pierre (1990a) *Photography*. Cambridge: Polity Press.

Bourdieu, Pierre (1990b) *The Love of Art*. Cambridge: Polity Press.

Bourdieu, Pierre (1993) *The Field of Cultural Production*. Cambridge: Polity Press.

Breen, R., D. Hannan, D. Rottman and C.T. Whelan (1990) *Understanding Contemporary Ireland – State, Class and Development in the Republic of Ireland*. Dublin: Gill and Macmillan.

Clancy, P., M. Drury, A. Kelly, T. Brannick and S. Pratschke (1994) *The Public and the Arts: A Survey of Behaviour and Attitudes in Ireland*. Dublin: Graduate School of Business, UCD/The Arts Council.

Coopers and Lybrand (1994) *The Employment and Economic Significance of the Cultural Industries in Ireland*. Dublin: Coopers and Lybrand.

Davies, Ioan (1995) *Cultural Studies and Beyond – Fragments of Empire*. London: Routledge.

Di Maggio, Paul (1982) 'The arts in class reproduction' in M.W. Apple (ed.) *Cultural and Economic Reproduction in Education*. London: Routledge.

Di Maggio, Paul (1987) 'Classification in Art', *American Sociological Review*, 52, pp. 440–55.

Di Maggio, Paul and Michael Useem (1978a) 'Cultural democracy in a period of cultural expansion: the social composition of arts audiences in the United States', *Social Problems*, 26 (2).

Di Maggio, Paul and Michael Useem (1978b) 'Social class and arts consumption' *Theory and Society*, 5 (1/2).

Di Maggio, Paul and Michael Useem (1980) 'The Arts in Education and Cultural Participation: The Social Role of Aesthetic Education' *Journal of Aesthetic Education*, 14 (4).

Durkan, Joe (1994) *The Economics of the Arts in Ireland*. Dublin: The Arts Council.

Easthope, Anthony (1991) *Literary into Cultural Studies*. London: Routledge.

Fiske, John (1987) *Television Culture*. London: Methuen.

Fiske, John (1989a) *Understanding Popular Culture*. London: Unwin Hyman.

Fiske, John (1989b) *Reading Popular Culture*. London: Unwin Hyman.

Frow, John (1995) *Cultural Studies and Cultural Value*. Oxford: Oxford University Press.

Gans, Herbert J. (1972) 'The politics of culture in America: A Sociological Analysis' in D. McQuail (ed.) *Sociology of Mass Communications*. Harmondsworth: Penguin.

Garnham, Nicholas (1986) 'Extended Review: Bourdieu's Distinction', *The Sociological Review*, 34 (2).

Gilbert, G.N. and Mulkay, M. (1984) *Opening Pandora's Box: A Sociological Analysis of Scientists' Discourse*. Cambridge: Cambridge University Press.

Gripsrud, Jostein (1989) 'High Culture Revisited', *Cultural Studies*, 3 (2).

Halle, David (1994) *Inside Culture: Class Culture and Everyday Life in Modern America*. Chicago: Chicago University Press.

Inglis, Fred (1993) *Cultural Studies*. Oxford: Basil Blackwell.

Jameson, Frederic (1984) 'Postmodernism: or the Cultural Logic of Late Capitalism', *New Left Review*, No. 146.

Kelly, Anne (1989) *Cultural Policy in Ireland*. Dublin: Irish Museums Trust/UNESCO.

Kennedy, Brian P. (1990) *Dreams and Responsibilities: the State and the Arts in Independent Ireland*. Dublin: The Arts Council/An Chomhairle Ealaíon.

Lamont, Michèle (1992) *Money, Morals and Manners: The Culture of the French and the American Upper-Middle Class*. Chicago: University of Chicago Press.

Lamont, Michèle and M. Fournier (eds) (1992) *Cultivating Differences: Symbolic Boundaries and the Making of Inequality*. Chicago: University of Chicago Press.

Long, Elizabeth (1986) 'Women, reading and cultural authority: some implications of the audience perspective in Cultural Studies', *American Quarterly*, 38.

Long, Elizabeth (1987) 'Reading groups and the post-modern crisis of cultural authority', *Cultural Studies*, 1(3).

MRBI (1994) *Report of the Joint National Listenership Research*. Dublin.

Marx, Karl (1846) (1968 Edition) *The German Ideology*. Moscow: Progress.

McGuigan, Jim (1992) *Cultural Populism*. London: Routledge.

Moores, Shaun (1993) *Interpreting Audiences: The Ethnography of Media Consumption*. London: Sage.

Morley, David (1980) *The 'Nationwide' Audience*. London: BFI.

Potter, Jonathan and Margaret Wetherell (1987) *Discourse and Social Psychology*. London: Sage.

O'Neill, Brian (1993) 'Producing The Arts Show: An Ethnographic Study of Radio Producers at Work', *Irish Communications Review*, Vol. 3.

Radway, Janice (1988) 'The Book-of-the-month-club and the general reader: on the uses of serious fiction' *Critical Enquiry*, 14 (1).

Seaman, W. (1992) 'Active audience theory: pointless populism', *Media, Culture and Society*, 14 (2).

Stolnitz, Jerome (1961) 'On the origins of aesthetic disinterestedness', *Journal of Aesthetics and Art Criticism*, 20 (1).

Storey, John (1993) *An Introductory Guide to Cultural Theory and Popular Culture*. London: Harvester Wheatsleaf.

Strinati, Dominic (1995) *An Introduction to Theories of Popular Culture*. London: Routledge.

Turner, Graeme (1990) *British Cultural Studies: An Introduction*. London: Unwin Hyman.

Williams, Raymond (1958) 'Culture is Ordinary', reprinted in (1989a) *Resources of Hope*. London: Verso.

Williams, Raymond (1989b) *The Politics of Modernism*. Tony Pinkney (ed.) London: Verso.

Willis, Paul (1990) *Common Culture*. Milton Keynes: Open University Press.

Zolberg, Vera L. (1988) 'Tensions of mission in American art museums' in Paul Di Maggio (ed.) *Non-Profit Enterprise in the Arts: Studies in Mission and Constraint*. New York: Oxford University Press.

3

# Gender, Class and Television Viewing: Audience Responses to the *Ballroom of Romance*

*Barbara O'Connor*

The concepts of social class and gender have been systematically addressed within reception studies of television audiences since the early 1980s. Morley's (1980) benchmark study of the *Nationwide* audience marked the beginning of empirical research within this framework on the ways in which class based discourses influenced interpretations of television. Gender too (though more commonly the female) has been the focus of a substantial body of work on the uses, meanings and pleasures of television (for example see Hobson, 1980 and 1982; Ang, 1985; Brown, 1990; Seiter *et al.*, 1989; Press, 1991; Geraghty, 1991). Despite the substantial theoretical and empirical attention devoted to both topics, however, there has been remarkably little work on the ways in which social class and gender discourses articulate in television viewing contexts. This chapter focuses on such an articulation and is based on the findings of a qualitative audience study conducted in the mid-1980s on the uses and inter-pretation of television by women and men from different class backgrounds.

While the research was completed a decade ago, I feel that the findings are still relevant and instructive in a number of ways. Firstly, to my knowledge, it is an original piece of research which has not been replicated since that time and, on that basis, the findings themselves should be of intrinsic interest. Secondly, it provides a baseline study in terms of which subsequent and future work can be compared. In this context it raises questions about the extent to which class and gender-based taste cultures may have shifted since that time in the wake of social and technological changes affecting everyday life generally, and media consumption in particular.

## Methodology

The research was conducted in two stages, consisting of semi-structured interviews and group discussions. The interviews explored the socio-demographic characteristics of the selected group members, work and leisure activities, and media use and preferences. The group discussions were used to investigate responses to the television drama the *Ballroom of Romance*. In combining these two research phases it was hoped that the nature of the relationship between the groups' position in the social structure, their subcultural experiences, and their response to a particular programme could be mapped out.

Data from eight groups comprising a total of 71 respondents and data from 46 individual interviews with group members is included in the analysis. A socio-demographic profile of the eight groups included in the analysis is provided in Appendix A (p. xx). The research was conducted with extant groups of various types ranging from groups participating in educational courses to community groups. The discussions following each viewing also took place in diverse locations and contexts ranging from the formal setting (educational context) to the more informal (group member's homes). This chapter explores the responses to the *Ballroom of Romance* by analysing extracts from the group discussions and drawing on the interview data.

The film the *Ballroom of Romance* had been adapted from the short story of the same name by William Trevor (1972) and was a joint BBC/ RTÉ production. It was first broadcast on RTÉ1 on 31 October 1982. Its TAM rating for this first broadcast was 46, that is 46 per cent of homes owning a television set had it switched on. It won high critical acclaim including a BAFTA (British Academy of Film and Television) award.

The film is set in the west of Ireland in the 1950s in a remote rural ballroom to which the men and women flock every week until they marry or emigrate. The action of the film revolves round the main character, Bridie, a single woman living with and taking care of an ageing and semi-invalid father in addition to working their small farm. She cycles to the ballroom every Friday night, as she has done since she was a teenager, in the hope of meeting a suitable marriage partner. Her first love emigrated many years previously, married and settled in England. She would now settle for Dano Ryan, the drummer in the band who is characterised as a quiet, decent man who works on the roads. Her name has also been associated locally with Bowser Egan, one of the rowdy bachelor trio who spend the night in the local pub before putting in an appearance at the dance. One assumes that she has had some kind of relationship with Bowser in the past but the exact nature or quality of this relationship is never made explicit within the diegesis of the film. However, we are made aware that Bridie is not attracted to Bowser and that she regards him as lazy and feckless. On this particular night Bridie, in conversation with Dano, hints at the possibility of marriage but Dano makes it clear that he is not interested in moving onto a farm. With her hopes of marriage to the drummer dashed, she makes a decision never to return to the ballroom as she looks at herself and her ageing peers and realises the loss of dignity associated with her situation. Bowser Egan asks her to dance and during the dance tells her that his mother is ill, will die shortly and that he will then be free to marry. Bridie, disappointed and angered by Dano's rejection and presumably her sense of humiliation, tells Bowser how repugnant she finds him physically, how she has resolved never to return to the ballroom and leaves the hall alone to cycle home. However, Bowser overtakes her on the road, promises to change his ways and invites her 'into the field'. We see Bridie turning her bicycle. The next scene shows Bowser closing the field gate, taking the last slug from the whiskey bottle and throwing it away. Then there is a cut to a shot of Bridie cycling home alone against the dawn sky, a resolute but otherwise indecipherable expression on her face.

While the discussions themselves covered a number of topics and were substantially open-ended, the topics covered here include the general response to the film, the response to the representation of gender roles and response to the main character, Bridie. By general response is meant the extent to which the groups liked or disliked the film and the reasons why. The topic of the representation of women's roles was chosen for investigation because the researcher's 'preferred reading' at the time was that the oppression of women was foregrounded in the film by the privileging of the women's discourse (through the main character, Bridie) both visually and verbally. There was no assumption, though, that the researcher's 'preferred reading' would necessarily coincide with that of the group members. The object of the analysis was to investigate the extent to which, and the ways in which, the representation of gender roles was discussed by the various groups. Also, given the importance of characterisation in fictional film, it was decided to analyse the groups' response to the central character, Bridie, in order to examine the ways in which the various groups related to her.

## General Response

The three groups of working-class women expressed a dislike of the programme because it did not correspond to their idea of good television. One working-class group for example had this to say:

> . . . wasn't my type of programme.
> / A bit silly . . . a bit slow and a bit silly . . .
> / I watched it as well but I turned it off half way through.
> / There was no story in it . . . there was no dialogue to get interested in or anything

GF: So you'd like something with more dialogue . . . faster?
/ Yea . . . with more life in it.
/ I don't think the title of it suited it.
/ What was the title?
/ The *Ballroom of Romance*.
/ I mean there wasn't a bit of romance in it . . .

(Group A)

The above response can be partially understood in terms of this group's taste in television viewing. They rejected a genre which was perceived as too slow moving and lacking in a strong narrative element. Evidence from the interview data indicated that the women in group A were more involved with the action-packed, fast-moving police and adventure series, and with representations of the urban working class in naturalistic serials like *Coronation Street* and melodramatic serials such as *Dallas*. In fact the *Ballroom of Romance* was the antithesis of the series and serials which constituted their regular viewing, lacking in their view humour, suspense or excitement.

A second group consisting of young unemployed working-class women on a typing course were not very impressed by the film either. They felt that it was a film for older people because they might be better able to relate to that era. For themselves it was 'gloomy and 'boring':

. . . it's a film for older people who know what it was like in those days . . . not for the likes of us
GF: A lot of people said that it was boring [referring to the spontaneous remarks immediately after the viewing].
/ It was.
/ It would put you to sleep.
/ It was very gloomy . . .
(. . .)/ I think it was like that because they were only tryin' to show certain things that go on (. . .) I think it tried to just show . . . what sort of people there is in dances . . . not tryin' to show any more . . . just their personality . . . what they go through when they go to a dance . . . what is going through their mind . . .

(Group B)

The general response among the third group of young working-class women was one of complete boredom with the film, even more so than for the other two groups. The discussion was marked by what Morley (1980) has referred to as a 'critique of silence'. In other words they could not comment because they could not identify with the drama's representations which they perceived as being very remote from their own experiences and concerns. Despite repeated attempts on the part of the researcher to initiate conversation with all five in the group, only two made any sustained contribution to the discussion while two remained almost completely silent. A lot of probing was necessary and there were many long silences. In response to the question as to whether they had liked or disliked the film the response was:

. . . boring.
GF: Why was that?
/ It was the same thing all over again, every time there was a dance on
everybody was standin' around the room . . .
/ That never really happens.
(. . .)/ Stupid.
GF: Stupid? . . . why do you say that?
/ 'Cos it was.
GF . . . in what ways? . . . would you look at that if it was on tv?
/ No . . .
/ There was nothin' in it . . .

(Group C)

They expressed an awareness of the cultural distance between their own experiences and the referential world of the ballroom. Their comment on the type
of music and dancing represented in the film also revealed a distance from
their own musical taste:

GF: What did you think of the music?
/ (laughs) . . . it was too . . . the one music all the time . . .
/ All lovey-dovey . . . you know boy-girl kind of a jig yoke.
/ If you did that at a disco now you'd get thrown out . . .

(Group C)

Other references were made throughout the discussion to their distance from
the country and from rural experiences. One woman recounted her experience
of going dancing in the country in the following extract:

. . . sure we went to a disco in Wicklow on Saturday night . . . we went in . . .
you know . . . they were all kind of just jumping about ya know . . . they were all
very culchee . . . a crowd of us and they all started going mad . . . ya know . . .
like they were good dancers and they were jumpin' about . . . ya know . . . doin'
all the latest things . . . ya know . . . and this guy came over eventually and told
them they weren't supposed to be dancin' like that . . . that they weren't to
dance like that ya know . . . to dance the way everyone else was dancin' . . .
really stupid ya know . . . they were really amazed 'cos all the women came out
of the kitchen and stood there and looked . . . 'Janey! Dublin people . . . look at
the way they're dancin . . .'

(Group C)

In direct contrast to the working-class women, the middle-class women
responded very favourably to the film since it did correspond to their idea of
'good' television drama. There was some, though not extensive, comment on
the film as a constructed cultural commodity:

. . . it was awfully authentic . . . it was really very well done . . . they got all the
details which Teilifís Éireann miss . . . you know . . . the BBC in any play about
anything . . . they go for every tiny detail and by so doing you are completely
transported into the time . . . I was watching all the details . . . I mean the big
red faces and the hair brushed back . . . like out of the waxworks . . .

/ What I thought was very good . . . but it must be a theatrical device . . . is the way Mr. Dwyer was there at all the terribly important moments (. . .) he was a sort of link . . . I would say a theatrical device but I thought he . . . that was a very good thing . . . that couldn't have been in the book . . . well . . . if I were the director I would put it in there . . .
/ He was the father figure . . . he was kind of in charge of everything . . .

(Group D)

Their opinion that the film would have universal appeal was related to their knowledge of it as an acclaimed cultural product:

GF: Do you think it appeals only to people here or . . . ?
/ No . . . it has universal appeal . . . they might not understand the circumstance . . . the situation is the same anywhere . . . it has won awards hasn't it? . . .

(Group D)

The general response was one of total enthusiasm for the play by the group of rural middle-class women who had themselves experienced the ballroom of romance era. They had a very positive orientation to the representation of the ballroom and of rural life. This discussion was marked by a preponderance of personal reminiscences of their own dancing experiences in similar ballrooms in the 1950s. The film seemed to act almost exclusively as a trigger for the bitter-sweet nostalgic recollections of the ballroom days which added an air of exhuberance to the discussion. There was no critical comment on the film as a commodity or on the formal aspects of its construction:

GF: Did people like it or not ?
/ Great.
(. . .) GF: Well did people identify with it?
/ Oh yes! very much so [ (chorus of 'yes')].
GF: And had you seen it before . . . had anybody seen it before?
/ Yea . . . twice before.
(. . .)/ Yea . . . it brought back memories . . . sad . . . nostalgia.
GF why sad?
/ I don't know . . . the music was really beautiful . . . it just reminded me of the dances . . .

(Group E)

These women recalled the 1950s as being a happy and enjoyable time for them and the rural Ireland of their youth as classless. Much of the discussion was devoted to anecdotes of female cameradie and fun, of sexual innocence and naivety. Their reminiscences were tinged with nostalgia and they compared the ballroom days favourably with the dances and music of the present:

. . . you can't compare dances today with dances years ago . . . for instance a disco in no way compares to what we did (. . .) I think it would be great to see a return to the type of ballroom . . .
(. . .)/ It was smashing . . . the atmosphere was different . . .

(Group E)

A further striking feature of this group's discussion was the large number of references to sartorial elegence and fashion; what Dyer (1976) has referred to as 'sensuous materiality':

> . . . then when it came to the time of a dress dance . . . what we call 'the Dance' (. . .) and they'd all come in their long dresses . . . and I always remember . . . buttons and bows here (. . .) and a bustle under that and a big bow here at the back . . . and maybe a little flower here . . . and we used to meet them at the shop and we'd all know the dance and we'd all go up that night and they'd all come in in their different colours . . . satin . . . no . . . taffeta . . . it made a nice rustle and we'd watch them there and wonder who were they going with . . . it looked like something out of this world . . .
> / Fairyland.
> / Yea . . . fairyland . . .
>
> (Group E)

The response of the men's groups to the film was not as strictly demarcated by a social–class cleavage although there were class differences between groups and possibly within groups, although the latter is more difficult to substantiate given the limitations of the group discussion method. There was a mixed reaction to the film among group F (young urban working-class men), with the majority disliking it because they did not see it as realistic and a minority liking it because they did regard it to be so:

> GF: Did you like it or not or what?
> / Ok.
> / I thought it was great.
> GF: Why?
> / That's what goes on at a dance . . . at discoes . . . girls at one side and boys at the other side and they're scared to . . .
> GF: You're saying that happens now?
> / It fucking does . . . in the Tara Club . . . all the young ones . . .
>
> (Group F)

and again:

> . . . not really much of a story but it was good.
> GF: Yea . . . why do you think it was good?
> / Don't know . . . in the country . . . show what's goin' on down there maybe . . . it was good . . .
>
> (Group F)

The negative comments were expressed as follows:

> . . . just don't like it . . . it's very boring sort of . . .
> (. . .) GF: How was it different from what you would like on television?
> / I dunno.
> / If *Top of the Pops* was on one station I'd watch it . . . and if ( ) on the other station . . . just forget it you know . . . if there was cricket on one station and that on the other station . . . if you only had two[channels] I'd watch that . . . I wouldn't watch cricket anyway.
> (. . .)/ I dunno . . . it was too boring . . . not based on real life . . .
>
> (Group F)

The mixed-class group, though predominantly working class, and consisting of redundant workers, reacted favourably to the film. They claimed to like it because they saw it as a vignette of rural life in Ireland in the 1950s and there was an emphasis in the discussion on their interpretation of the social history of the period:

> . . . enjoyable
> GF: Yea . . . why did you enjoy it?
> / It told us what life was like a good few years ago down in . . . wherever it was . . . you know and it's all changed now . . . I think it has down around that area anyway because I go down there (. . .) dance halls and all . . . like Quinnsworth . . . modern . . . you know what I mean . . . there's a bar and all in there and they all do their own thing . . .
>
> (Group G)

The group of middle-class business men also liked the film very much:

> GF: Did you like it?
> / Do you mean technically or . . . ?
> GF: Did you like it?
> / I thought it was very good.
> / I thought that it did reflect something that did happen twenty or thirty years ago but I don't know whether it's so valid nowadays . . . not near as bad . . . even down around Ballycroy.
> / (. . .) I thought it was very realistic.
> / (. . .) I thought it was a very sad film even the first time I saw it . . . you know . . . the people there were really prisoners in that place . . . they couldn't even talk to each other . . . absolutely incredible . . . very very sad . . . brilliant technically . . . really brilliant.
> / I thought it was extremely authentic as well . . .
>
> (Group H)

We see how this group's initial reaction was to identify the film as a cultural commodity much like the urban middle-class women and to discuss it in terms of numerous production features such as technical aspects, performances, authenticity, and realism. There was also an awareness of the possibility of evaluating it at more than one level as the question 'do you mean technically or . . .?' indicates.

## Discussion of General Responses

Broadly speaking each group's response to the *Ballroom of Romance* could be usefully visualised on a continuum which places the working-class women's groups at the 'dislike' end, the middle-class groups of women and men at the 'like' end, and the working-class and mixed men's groups in the middle. However, it is necessary to go beyond this rather crude categorisation to begin to understand the meanings of the terms 'like' and 'dislike'. One of the most striking differences in response in terms of enjoyment emerged between the women's groups with the middle-class women expressing an enjoyment of the film and the working-class women stating a definite boredom with it. Enjoyment, or lack of, were expressed on two levels which are intertwined in practice but are separated out here for analytical purposes. The first was an identification with the form of the film as encapsulated in the remarks of the female and male middle-class groups. The second was an identification with aspects of the representation, for example, Bridie's pitiful situation (Group D) or with memories of the dance-hall era (Group E). Dislike of the film was also expressed in these two ways. The form was rejected in terms of it being slow, the music boring, the plot not sufficiently exciting and so on. The second way in which dislike of the film was expressed was in terms of an irrelevance to their own lives based on a perceived distance between their own lives and the lives of the characters portrayed in the film.

The form of the film had no attraction for the working-class women (groups A, B and C). They expressed a dislike of the film because they regarded it as slow and boring with no story line or action. Their lack of enjoyment can be linked to their genre preferences. The interview data indicated that the women in group A expressed a preference for fiction; naturalistic and melodramatic serials, police, detective and hospital series. Within these genres the elements which they appreciated were action, suspense, adventure and humour. The *Ballroom of Romance* could not be said to include any of these elements. On the contrary it was a once-off film, perceived to be slow-moving without a strong storyline and lacking in humour. It did not fit, therefore, into their criteria of good television and was rejected on this basis.

The second plane on which dislike was expressed was in terms of the distance between the representations in the film and the concerns of their own lives. Since the film was located in the past in rural Ireland they could not identify with the situations or characters represented. Group B for instance specifically rejected 'old-fashioned' plays and historical series. Generally, their television viewing was light, with music televison and melodramatic serials being their favourite programmes. Their own interest in music, fashion, pop stars and teenage magazines could be seen to be based on their involvement in a 'subculture of femininity' (see McRobbie, 1978) which was immediate, current and subject to constant change. Representations located in the past, therefore, were regarded as dated and *passé*.

The distance expressed by the working-class women's groups from the past and from rural life was not confined to media representations but could be seen to be a reflection of a more general rejection of a dominant strand of Irish culture which draws heavily on 'tradition' (associations with the past), and rural romanticism.[1] Their lack of involvement in a 'national' discourse and their orientation towards the popular culture of a more urbanised society was reflected in their preference for British television and print media. The involvement of teenagers in British and US media has also been documented by Dillon (1982:163) and Reynolds (1986:2). However, group A did engage with the public sphere through the viewing of RTÉ current affairs programmes on local issues particularly those which were seen to affect the family, such as programmes on crime and drugs. The working-class women's cultural reference points were, therefore, almost exclusively local or Anglo-American. Unlike the middle-class women who were involved in a 'national' discourse, they did not have the cultural experience which would help them to identify with the portrayal of rural life located in the past.

It is instructive to compare the groups of urban working-class women with the urban middle-class women with regard to media use and preferences. The latter group's reported television viewing included a mix of actuality programming and fictional genres. They regularly watched or listened to current affairs and documentaries thus involving themselves in a more 'public' and 'national' media agenda than their working-class counterparts. They also reported regular viewing of drama in the form of once-off plays, historical and costume drama, and films. They expressed a dislike of melodramatic serials and to some extent naturalistic serials (though response towards the latter was mixed) and violent programmes. It would appear that the elements which were rejected by this group – spontaneity, violence, participation – were precisely those which were germane to the working-class women's pleasure (see Bourdieu, 1980). It is not surprising then that the stylistic conventions of the genre and the modes of representation of the *Ballroom of Romance* were more likely to be more appreciated by middle-class than by working-class women.

While social class was shown to be a major factor in influencing the general response of the women's groups, gender was also important. This was evidenced in the differences in general response between the working-class women and men. The group of young urban working-class men (F) reacted to the film differently, with some members finding it enjoyable and others pronouncing a definite dislike. If we compare their response to that of their female counterparts (C), we see that more of the young men enjoyed it. It is noteworthy that the enjoyment of the film by the working-class men was based on their perception of it as a social commentary or documentary. The members of group F who liked it perceived it as realistic since it portrayed 'what's goin' on down there [in the country] maybe'. It was also clear from the remarks made by the mixed class-group (G) that they also treated the film as a vignette of social life in rural Ireland in the 1950s. As one of the men commented 'it seemed more of a documentary on the Mayo dance hall to me than anything else . . . it didn't develop any characters in the play . . . it told us what life was like a good few years ago down in . . .' A similar emphasis on the realism of the film was also apparent at the individual interviews during which remarks were made that it was very educational, a good view of the 1950s or 'more of a statement . . . it's just a social comment'.[2]

I would suggest that this factual orientation to the play on the part of group G can be usefully linked to the discourses which this group inhabited and which, in turn, influenced their media preferences for factual programmes such as news, documentaries and current affairs. These men were more involved in 'public' discourses than the working-class women who were confined to the domestic and private domains of life which influenced their radio and television genre preferences in the 'private' direction. In fact the working-class women had expressed a definite antipathy towards current affairs programming in terms such as 'I never understand them . . . all politics . . . I'm not interested'. Their viewing was very much in line with the 'public' and 'private' agenda documented by Hobson (1980). In her study of media use she found a polarity between the working-class women who worked full time in the home and their husbands who worked outside the home as regards television viewing. The women rejected programmes which were seen to belong to the 'man's world' including news, current affairs and, to a lesser extent, documentaries, and they actively chose viewing which was understood to constitute a 'woman's world'. These findings were also applicable to the women to whom I spoke. Alternatively, the men, given their involvement in more 'public' discourses both in terms of media use and greater access to other 'public' domains, had a greater claim to knowledge of rural life as expressed in references to emigration in the 1950s, the west of Ireland, community expectations of the characters and so on.

These observations on the differences in response on the part of working-class women and men would tend to suggest that both came to the viewing situation with different expectations and orientations and judged the film accordingly. It would appear that the women came to it with an emotional/romantic sensibility and were disappointed. As one of the working-class women commented when speaking of her reasons for disliking the film said, 'there was no romance in it'. It would appear that the men, on the other hand, came to the film with a factual orientation, were able to frame it in terms of social documentary, and could respond to it on that level.

The general response of all the middle-class groups was favourable though the sources of enjoyment varied between them. The rural women's group expressed their enjoyment in terms of the ways in which representations of the ballroom evoked nostalgic memories of their own dancing days in ballrooms similar to the one portrayed. For the urban middle-class women their enjoyment lay principally in their identification with Bridie's situation which reminded them of women they knew. The middle-class male group tended to emphasise the technical aspects of the film when asked for their response. They also found that the representations were sad in the sense that they perceived the characters as prisoners caught in a trap of social convention.

Regarding the form of the film, the female urban-middle class group regarded it as 'technically brilliant' and as having universal appeal, good acting and so on; comments which could be classified as metalinguistic or 'critical' (see Liebes and Katz, 1984). They were aware that it had won television awards which, for them, appeared to enhance its value as a cultural commodity. As in the case of the other groups, their response to the film can be linked to their preferences for once-off plays and 'serious' drama. The kind of critical comment made by this group would seem to indicate the operation of a certain level of 'disinterested and distanced contemplation' which Bourdieu (1980) has claimed to be germane to bourgeois aesthetic sensibilities.

However, while the response to this aspect of the film's form manifested a definite class cleavage, the group of rural middle-class women were the exception to the rule in that they did not make any 'critical' or 'metalinguistic' comment on the film. On the basis of their class position, one might have expected this group to be involved in a discourse which would elicit 'critical' comment on the programme. Its absence in the discussion can only be speculated on here. Their mean educational level was lower than their urban counterparts and it is likely that education is the primary factor in the acquisition of this form of cultural capital (see Bourdieu, 1980). In addition the strength of the rural group's identification with the ballroom era may also have militated against their commenting on the form of the programme.[3] The context of the discussion – one of female cameraderie and fun – also contributed, I would suggest, to the extra-textual thrust of the comments. It may well be that the demarcation of aesthetic codes by social class is stronger in cities since there are more opportunities for constructing cultural distinctions because of the greater availability of 'high' culture and the arts in the metropolis.

## Responses to the Representation of Women's Roles

Responses to the representation of women's roles in the film also varied substantially between the groups. The past/present opposition is useful in exploring the differences between them. As in the case of the general response the remarks of the working-class women on the representation of women's roles were substantially similar. They frequently activated the past/present axis in terms of the past being bad and the present good, or, at least, better. They claimed that life had changed dramatically for women since the era portrayed in the film – that women could now remain single if they wished because they had more education and better career prospects. The idea of freedom of choice for women generally was a motif in this discussion. With reference to the difference between women then and now, one group had this to say:

> . . . and they'd be more outspoken [referring to women in a contemporary context].
> / You don't go to a dance nowadays to discuss the farm . . . or the pigs or the sows or whatever else he had.

/ Women are more independent as well.
/ You wouldn't be depending on . . .
(. . .) GF: In what way are women less dependent?
/ In every way.
/ Women are better about themselves now . . . they are more educated . . .

(Group A)

Another group expressed the changes for women in terms of dancing etiquette:

. . . it would be insultin' if you weren't asked up to dance . . . you were like a wallflower
(. . .) I think the women were so desperate that they would take anyone . . . they would dance with anyone . . . it's rude to say no . . . so an awful lot of them are just gettin' up to dance because they feel they had to (. . .) the thing has changed a bit now . . . it was like that then . . . you know . . .

(Group B)

Yet another considered that women have more of a choice of career now than in the past:

. . . women have more of a choice these days . . . at that stage they hadn't got careers to look forward to or they had no variety of careers . . . it was either a secretary or a wife . . . or something like that you know . . . you hadn't a great choice but now they have a choice . . . you can choose what you want yourself . . . you are not forced into something . . .

(Group C)

By far the most feminist thrust came from the urban middle-class group (D) in response to the representation of women's roles. While they too operated with the concepts of past and present, they dissolved the dichotomous relationship between them maintaining that Bridie's situation continues today in a different guise:

. . . it doesn't have to be fellas like that . . . we all know fellas in clubs and in places who generally drink too much and [people say] 'he's a hard man' . . . he isn't a hard man . . . he should get a good kick . . . he is a bloody nuisance to everyone . . .

(Group D)

And:

. . . I mean if you take rural Ireland . . . it's all there you know . . . it might be dressed up a little bit . . . in a Ford Fiesta instead of a bicycle . . . but I don't think there is any difference . . . I really don't . . .

(Group D)

The treatment of women by the male dancers in the ballroom was also regarded as humiliating by this group:

. . . what I really thought was very sad about that thing was that when you went into the ballroom . . . the women on the one side and the men on the other . . . and the women could not make the first move.

/ They couldn't make any move.
/ The men . . . suddenly one will go and then the whole herd.
/ That's exactly what it is . . . a herd.
/ It's awful to be a woman in that situation to stand there and wait for these ignoramuses . . . when the herd has passed and you've been passed over . . .

(Group D)

There was little discussion of gender roles among the rural middle-class group (E). However, the comments they did make could be located at the other end of the spectrum from group D in terms of their perception of the oppression of women as an element in the film. The past/present dichotomy was, once again, activated by the rural group in respect of women's roles. In this case, though, they gave the past a positive value as they had direct experience of the era portrayed in the film and did not consider it to have been oppressive. They claimed, as we have already witnessed, that it was an era of sexual innocence and classlessness in which they had been poor but happy. They harked back after these 'good old days'. There was an awareness that things had changed for women – that women now have more freedom, but these changes were to some extent regarded as retrogressive and they felt that women were in a more vulnerable position currently than in the past:

. . . young girls now don't want to get married . . . it isn't their primary object in life.
/ No way . . . it's only secondary.
/ Do you think that marriage is going to die out?
/ I don't think they are any better . . . not very liberated living with those fellows because my reading of it . . . cases that I know . . . after a few years it's the fellas who want to bale out.
/ that's true . . .

(Group E)

There were also differences between the men's groups regarding the representation of women's roles in the film, ranging from the overt sexism of the young working-class group to the less overt form of the mixed-class and middle-class groups. The work roles of Bridie and her father were perceived by the former in the following way:

. . . I think it was the same . . . the woman workin' in the fields with her dad . . . [ his] leg amputated or something and she was doin' as much work as him and she brought him home in the cart and all this . . . and then yer one Bridie would be doin' things for her father like washing the eggs and keeping them out for Monday for him and doin' the rest of the things you know . . . I'd say it was the same.
GF: It was equal?
/ Yea . . . women did the same amount of work.
GF: Yea?
/ Well . . . that's what I saw in the film anyway . . .

(Group F)

The striking aspect of this recollection was that Bridie's workload was perceived as being equal to that of her father when, in fact, the film portrayed Bridie as doing most of the work. The fact that they perceived Bridie as 'helping' indicates the way in which preconceived ideas about gender work roles were brought to bear on their perception of the division of labour within the film.

Sexism also appeared to be a key element in their enjoyment of certain scenes. In response to the question:

GF: Were there any scenes in the film that struck you as being particularly funny?
/ That fat auld wan that was chasin' all the men.
GF: (. . .) Why do you say that?
/ The way she went on . . . she was dyin' to get a fella she was . . . I think (laughs).
GF: And did you think she was funny?
/ Yea . . . I thought she was funny . . . the way she was goin' on you know . . . tryin' to get off with someone . . . and she was goin' around tryin' everybody . . . she asked the man if he wanted a cigarette and she was waitin' and just puts his lighter back in his pocket . . . she was chasin' that new bloke . . . the fella that was fixing himself up in the room that time.
/ (. . .) he was dancin' and he wouldn't look at her . . .

Some of the conversation focused on relationships with the opposite sex. They saw women as waiting to trap men into marriage:

. . . women are too much into 'love' nowadays . . . talk about 'love' and all that and [they say] 'never leave me' . . . marriage and all this.
/ (. . .) I don't think blokes really want to be tied down.
/ The more they talk about lovin' ya and all the worse it is because they just . . . just puttin' ya under pressure all the time . . . you get a pain . . . that's what happened to me . . . I just got browned off . . .

There was a range of reactions to women's roles among the members of the mixed–class group. Some men were overtly sexist, others were not. However, much of the conversation was generalised rather than relating directly to the representation of women's roles within the film. While there was a consensus that women were now becoming more liberated, as in the case of the working-class women, the tone of the remarks suggested a a certain degree of resentment of the perceived changes:

. . . as regards women they are holding their own . . . it's not unreasonable to see a girl going over to a fella now an' sayin' 'are you gettin' up to dance?'and if he doesn't he'll get a slap in the jaw or whatever the case may be . . . it has gone to that stage.
/ (. . .) I don't think blokes really want to be tied down . . .
/ Yea . . . another thing there is drink . . . dutch courage . . . women are going into the pubs and going over with a half bottle of gin in them or whatever the hell is goin' . . .

The middle-class group, although less overtly sexist than the other two male groups, did not perceive that women, as represented in the film, were more oppressed than men. The main theme of the film was considered to be the trap of convention which was seen to be universal, current and equally applicable to men and women:

> . . . it wasn't sadness that struck me . . . it was sort of pathetic . . . they were caught . . . they were all caught and (. . .) I think the thing that struck me was that she [Bridie] accepted her reality and he [Bowser] wasn't her choice . . . and he accepted his reality (. . .) the reality was this structure and I thought . . . the fella and the girl . . . they were equally constrained . . .

It is also interesting to contrast their response to the group of urban middle-class women on the issue of men asking women to dance. The men perceived it, not as an exercise of male control, but as a source of vulnerability for themselves:

> . . . on paper it looks as if they have equal power . . . but when he goes up and gets a few refusals . . . it's more difficult for him to make . . . you know . . . to use that power I think because of the refusal and the hurt you feel in a refusal . . .

## Discussion of Responses to the Representation of Women's Roles

Because the working-class women felt that women's roles had changed dramatically since the era portrayed in the film, they thought that the relevance of the representation of the women in the film to the current social reality was severely limited. As we witnessed earlier, these groups displayed a distance from the past and from rural life both in terms of their media preferences and at a more general experiential level. Given the cultural distance, then, between the representations in the film and their own experiences, it would have been difficult for them to perceive a correspondence between women's roles in the film and women's roles in the current social reality outside the film.

The middle-class group, as already noted, was by far the most feminist in its thrust. The members of this group perceived the portrayal of women's roles in the film as having direct relevance to women's current situation. In contrast to the working-class women, this particular group discussion was marked by a claim to knowledge and understanding of rural life. Some of this knowledge was based on their personal experience and was encapsulated in comments such as 'people I had known'. It was also based on more general, public, socio-political knowledge as references to the EC grants, the breach-Gaeltacht, various geographical locations, Donagh O'Malley's free school scheme and the like, indicated. The differentiated knowledge of geographical areas of the country was in striking contrast to the undifferentiated perceptual map of the working-class women who generally distinguised only between Dublin and the rest of the country.

The middle-class group had access to discourses which were not at the disposal of the working-class women. Their cultural experience differed significantly in terms of class background and educational levels from the working-class women (see O'Connor, 1987). They were also more geographically mobile since some of the group had rural backgrounds but were educated 'out' of rural Ireland. Those with urban backgrounds also had a personal knowledge of the country. This group were actively involved in interests outside the home and were all members of an association aimed at the advancement of women in political life through their promotion within the mainstream political parties, signifying their involvement in a feminist discourse. The cultural experiences of this group, therefore, would have given them access to competences which would facilitate an understanding of the representations of women in the film and an ability to see connections between them and the extra-textual reality.

The uncritical orientation of the group of rural middle-class women to the representation of women's role in the film and their desire to uphold traditional gender values can again be accounted for by reference to the cultural discourses which this group inhabited. Because of their age and rural location, this group had direct personal youthful experience of the same type of ballroom as that portrayed in the film. As already noted, they recalled their experience of the era as being carefree and happy. They operated the past/present axis in favour of the past. They would have grown up in a climate of social conservatism in which both the ideology of the Roman Catholic church and of traditional rural society would have tended to emphasise the importance of the place of things in the natural order, and thus operated to maintain the social and political status quo.

The responses from the men's groups demonstrated that, while there were class inflections, they all displayed a distance from the portrayal of women in the film. As evidenced from the comments of the working-class group, they were the most overtly sexist in this respect. This is not an unexpected reaction given the cultural experience of being male, teenage and working class. The tendency of 'drop-out' working-class boys to be involved in their immediate environmental culture which emphasises 'macho' traits has been noted by Willis (1977) in Britain and by Dillon (1984) in her study of Irish youth subcultures.[4]

The emphasis in the mixed-class group's discussion was on the ways in which women's lives had improved since the 1950s and to this extent they were similar to the working-class women. However, one of the most obvious aspects of their comments on women's roles was that they contained a definite negative attitude to what they considered to be women's increasing liberation. The middle-class men's group focused on what they perceived to be the oppression of men within the film. They did this by reference to the trap of social convention which was perceived as operating equally on men and women, their own vulnerability in social dancing etiquette, and by focusing on areas in which they considered men to be oppressed by women, as in the case of the control which the Irish mother was perceived to exercise over her sons. The distance expressed by the men was not a distance from the past and rurality, as in the case of the working-class women, but rather a distinct lack of empathy with the experiences of women *qua* women and a refusal/ inability to acknowledge a wider asymmetry of power relations between the sexes in a patriarchal society.

## Responses to the Main Character

Responses to the main character, Bridie, were again characterised by variation between groups. The three working-class women's groups displayed a some-what ambiguous response to Bridie. Group A sympathised[5] with her because of her failure to get a man and because she was no longer considered to be attractive:

> GF: What did you think of Bridie?
> / I thought she was a right eejit.
> / She was very lonely.
> / I felt sorry for her as well and I thought . . . you know she wasn't all that great to look at . . . that she would suit anybody . . . you know.
> / I thought she was attractive enough in her own way.
> / I mean she was overweight and her age wasn't all that . . .
> / Compared to some of them that were there . . . she was a lot nicer than them . . .
> / Yea . . . but as I say what age would she have been . . . forty?
>
> (Group A)

Here we can see the importance which this group attached to the assets of youth and beauty in attracting a husband. Of interest in this context is the emphasis placed on physical beauty and sexual attractiveness for women as a resource in the sexual/marriage market place. While it must be acknowledged that these traits are valued for all women, they may have a more fundamental importance for working-class women as resources on the marriage market than for middle-class women who also usually have access to a career and/or money or property.

The expression of sympathy for Bridie on the basis of her inability to get a husband was also reiterated by the younger working-class women. Group C commented:

> . . . she seemed to be just . . . she was very unhappy . . . the first guy that she was going out with . . . he went off to England to work because there was no work where they were and she was just left there . . . and that seemed to be happening through her life
> / even the one she wanted she couldn't have . . . the ones she didn't want.
> GF: So do you feel sorrry for her in any way?
> / Yea . . . you'd feel sorry for her . . . it seemed as if she had terrible worries on her head you know . . . she's never goin' to get married . . . she wasn't goin' to the dance any more you know . . . somebody like that you'd feel sorry for them . . .
>
> (Group C)

It seemed to me that while the working-class women's groups did express a sympathy with Bridie because of her failure to get a husband, they did not have an immediate identification with her. There were few spontaneous expressions of sympathy, these coming only in response to specific questions, as can be seen in the comments from group C cited above, and even then the reply was in the conditional tense. One member of group A saw her as 'a right eejit' while others thought that she was somewhat stupid to tolerate her situation and that she should have done something about changing her life.

The urban middle-class women's group was the only one to strongly empathise with Bridie in a spontaneous and overtly emotional manner. Admiration for her character was encapsulated in remarks such as 'she was a very sensitive and intelligent person'. But most of their comments were directed at her sad and unenviable situation:

> . . . her face changed to people I knew . . . I was so interested . . . I have actually gone back in my mind . . . I can see the village I came from which is a very backward rural village and I know people like her and they are still there . . . their faces came on the screen and the things that happened to them . . . and I felt a lump here [pointing to her throat] . . .
>
> (Group D)

This group also referred to Bridie's humiliation and powerlessness at the dance:

> . . . when she was dancing with that young lad he had been talking about . . . for example the Bowser . . . he just brushed him aside . . . she couldn't do anything . . . my reaction would be if I could I would knock him down . . .
>
> (Group D)

The empathy for Bridie was also expressed in relation to Bridie's efforts to woo the drummer:

> . . . you know the saddest thing for me . . . where poor Bridie was talking to the drummer and trying to get him over to her side . . . gosh . . . you know . . . the goose pimples were bursting out on me . . . I think it was beneath her to grovel like that . . .
>
> (Group D)

We have already seen how the rural middle-class women did not consider Bridie's situation to be pitiable in any way and consequently did not express either sympathy or empathy with her. In fact, they did not identify at all with Bridie's pressing need to find a husband. As one woman commented 'well . . . we were never in that position . . . so we don't know'. For the most part their references to Bridie were really only incidental to their own reminiscences. This lack of identification with Bridie is most likely attributable to the fact that their primary point of engagement with the film was in terms of the identification with the feeling of romance which the music and dance evoked, rather than with the personality or situation of particular characters. Given the nature of the engagement with the film by this group, it is not implausible to suggest that they projected *themselves* as characters in the film.

The men's group did not make extensive spontaneous reference to Bridie either. Group F, for example, in response to a direct question had this to say:

> GF: What do you think of Bridie?
> / The wan that was tryin' to get fixed up with the drummer? (general laughter)
> GF: Yea.
> / She was alright most of the time . . .
>
> (Group F)

While both the middle-class urban group and the mixed-class group did actually state that they felt sorry for her (see general response), a more fundamental indication of their attitude towards her, I would suggest, is encapsulated in their use of language which was to a large extent distancing and at times disapproving and/or patronising. A particularly striking feature of their linguistic pattern was the use of game and sporting analogies when discussing her (and, indeed, when discussing the other women characters).

Group G expressed a sympathy for Bridie but in the tongue-in-cheek manner communicated in comments such as:

> . . . poor ould Bridie felt very sorry for herself . . . didn't she? . . . 'cos she was gettin' left on the shelf . . . wasn't she?
> / (. . .) She didn't want to . . . you know what I mean . . . be like everybody else . . . didn't want to accept Bowser at the start . . . she wanted to be a bit better up the ladder if you like . . . (. . .) a gentleman she was lookin' for . . . but she had to bow down to what everybody else was.
> / She was a bit of a liberator . . .
>
> (Group G)

The members of the middle-class group were also unsympathetic to Bridie. They suggested ways in which she could have handled her situation better and they also hinted at what they regarded as characteristic female duplicity in her dealings with Bowser:

> . . . I don't think she really means that she's not going back to the dance (. . .) I think it's only a facade in front of the other people that she . . . you know . . . buzzed off on him [Bowser] . . . your man was cycling up behind her and she was cyclin' way ahead . . . he didn't leave for maybe five or ten minutes afterwards . . . but she seemed to be waiting close to the field.
> GF: you think she planned it?
> / Oh yea . . .
>
> (Group H)

Later in the conversation Bridie is criticised for breaking the rules of the game:

> . . . she turned around and went into the field with him.
> / She suffered from sexual frustration or something.
> / She's meant to say 'no'.
> / Well . . . you see she's broken the rules of the game here . . .
>
> (Group H)

## Discussion of Responses to the Main Character

The alignment of responses to Bridie was substantially similar to how groups responded to the representation of women's roles in the film, with the middle-class women's group displaying the most empathy with Bridie's situation. Both the working-class women and and working-class and middle-class men expressed what I have termed a conditional sympathy with Bridie but their sympathy was based on different 'situated logics'. For the working-class women, their sympathy was based on a 'feeling for' her situation as a woman and expressed in terms of her inability to get a husband, her ageing and loss of looks. The sympathy expressed by the men's groups for Bridie was in terms of the general constraints on people's lives, both men and women, in the era and location portrayed in the film. What is interesting in the latter case is that while her 'femaleness' was brought into play, it was in a critical rather than a sympathetic way. The fact that she was accused of being a 'bit of a liberator', duplicitious in her dealing with Bowser, incompetent and/or wilful in 'breaking the rules of the game', all indicate an emotional distance from her as a character.

## Conclusion

In this chapter I have examined the ways in which eight selected groups of working-class and middle-class women and men responded to the television film the *Ballroom of Romance*. Through discussion of three aspects of the film, the general response in terms of like or dislike, responses to the representation of women's roles and, finally, responses to the main protagonist, Bridie, the groups arrived at distinctive orientations to, and interpretations of, the film which were largely determined by social-class and gender-based discourses. The full significance of the film for each group included not only their interpretation of specific scenes and sequences but also their response to the film in terms of the pleasure which it afforded and the perceived relevance to their own lives. Because they inhabited different kinds of discourses and had access to different cultural competences, the viewing situation was framed in ways which differentially influenced the pleasures and meanings of the text. Or to put it another way, the groups had different ways of seeing the film based on different kinds of enjoyment, different levels of emotional involvement, and different points of engagement with the text.

By including a range of groups in the discussions, the analysis was able to go beyond some of the more generalised gender and class-based theories regarding the meanings and pleasures of television and could indicate the specific ways in which gender is differentiated by social class and social class, in turn, is differentiated by gender.

If the findings are considered in terms of the broader debate about power in this volume, more specifically the balance of freedom and constraint in the activity of television viewing, it is clear that audiences are not free to construct meaning in an infinite number of ways around the text. In this case there was a limit to 'semiotic democracy' (see Fiske, 1987), a limit imposed by the disourses of social class, gender, age, and to some extent, urban/rural locale. However, in arguing for the effectivity of structural constraints on the viewing activity, I do not want to subscribe to a reductionist analysis. It is patently clear from the findings that there were differences within groups which cannot be fully accounted for in social class or gender terms. For instance it is still unclear why some members of the urban working-class group of young men liked the film and others disliked it. A more truly ethnographic methodology would be essential in providing a fuller understanding of the situation.

In the introduction I raised the issue of the possible changes in media consumption since the time of this study. It is not possible to make any definitive statements in the absence of sufficient research evidence, but the available research indicates (see for example O'Connor, 1990, and Kelly in this volume) that gender differences continue to be an important dimension of response to at least some media genres. However, given the rapid social and economic changes in Ireland since the mid-1980s, it would be reasonable to assume that there already are gradual and parallel changes in patterns of media use and taste which will soon become apparent. To get a clearer picture of the nature and extent of both stability and change around media use, though, one would need to consider, not only the reception of particular programmes, but also the broader relationships between social class, gender and television consumption. In this regard some of the research questions which one might pose are the extent to which women's and men's changing position in Irish society has altered their media consumption. For example if more women are now working in paid employment outside the home are they listening to less radio and with what consequences, or, alternatively, if there has been an increase in certain kinds of male unemployment which confines them more to the home, has this led to a greater viewing of daytime television including daytime soaps, traditionally perceived as a 'woman's genre'? Another relevant issue might be the extent to which the 'national' discourse which some of the groups inhabited and which were constructed by the national broadcasting service in the past will be altered by the increasing pressures on public service broadcasting and the availability of alternative 'imagined communities' through the newer media technologies. One might also query if 'ironic viewing' as part of a contemporary or postmodern sensibility has become a more widespread form of engagement with television generally. The answer to these questions and others awaits further empirical investigation and analysis of media consumption in Ireland.

# Appendix

## Discussion Group Profiles

| NAME | SIZE | GENDER | SOCIAL CLASS | MEAN AGE |
|------|------|--------|--------------|----------|
| A | 13 | female | working | 25yrs. |
| B | 08 | female | working | 17yrs. |
| C | 05 | female | working | 17yrs. |
| D | 08 | female | middle | 42yrs. |
| E | 12 | female | middle | 55yrs. |
| F | 07 | male | working | 17yrs. |
| G | 10 | male | mixed | 30yrs. |
| H | 08 | male | middle | 35yrs. |

## Notes

1   For a fuller discussion of the dominance of a conservative rurally-based culture in urban Ireland see McLoone (1984).
2   While the film's status as a social document was also commented on by other groups, it was not nearly as extensive as in group G.
3   I would also suggest that the evocative nature of the music exercised a powerful identificatory pull on this group especially since it was associated with the pleasures of youthful dancing. For a fuller discussion of the correspondence between musical and emotional rhythms see Langer (1955).
4   The sexism of group F is also likely to be partially context-related in that the members of the group were more willing to criticise women when talking amongst their peers. It is suggested that in the latter context they acquire a bravado which would probably be less pronounced in a one-to-one discussion with the group facilitator.
5   A distinction is drawn between the related terms 'empathy' and 'sympathy'. The former is defined for the purposes in hand as an 'appreciative understanding' or 'feeling with' a person or situation. 'Sympathy' is taken to refer to a compassion which is not based on a full appreciation or understanding – a 'feeling for' a person or situation. I am grateful to Dr Helen Burke, formerly of the Department of Social Administration, University College Dublin, for initially clarifying this distinction for me.

## References

Ang, Ien (1985) *Watching 'Dallas': Soap Opera and the Melodramatic Imagination*, London: Methuen.
Bourdieu, Pierre (1980) 'The Aristocracy of Culture', *Media, Culture and Society*, 2(3): 225–54.
Brown, Mary Ellen (ed.) (1990) *Television and Women's Culture: The Politics of the Popular*. London: Sage.
Dillon, Michelle (1984) 'Youth Culture in Ireland', *The Economic and Social Review*, 15(3):153–72.
Dyer, Richard (1976) 'Entertainment and Utopia', *Movie*, 22:2–13.
Fiske, John (1987) *Television Culture*. London: Methuen.
Geraghty, Christine (1991) *Women and Soap Opera: A Study of Prime Time Soaps*. Cambridge: Polity.
Hobson, Dorothy (1980) 'Housewives and the Mass Media', pp. 105–14 in S. Hall, D. Hobson, A. Lowe, P. Willis (eds), *Culture, Media, Language: Working Papers in Cultural Studies, 1972–1979.* London: Hutchinson/Centre for Contemporary Cultural Studies.
Hobson, Dorothy (1982) *Crossroads: The Drama of a Soap Opera*. London: Methuen.
Langer, Suzanne K. (1955) *Feeling and Form*. London: Routledge.
Liebes, Lamar and Elihu Katz (1984) 'Once Upon a Time in *Dallas*', *Intermedia*, 12(3): 28–32.
McLoone, Martin (1984) 'Strumpet City – the Urban Working Class on Television', pp. 53–8 in M. McLoone and J. MacMahon (eds), *Television and Irish Society: 21 years of Irish Television*. Dublin: RTÉ/Irish Film Institute.
McRobbie, Angela (1978) 'Working Class Girls and the Culture of Femininity', pp. 96–108 in Centre for Contemporary Cultural Studies Women's Studies Group, *Women Take Issue*. London: Centre for Contemporary Cultural Studies/Hutchinson.
Morley, David (1980) *The 'Nationwide' Audience*. London: British Film Institute.

O'Connor, Barbara (1987) 'Women and Media: Social and Cultural Influences on Women's Use of and Response to Television'. PhD dissertation. Dublin: University College Dublin.

O'Connor, Barbara (1990) *Soap and Sensibility: Audience Responses to 'Dallas' and 'Glenroe'*, Dublin: RTÉ.

Press, Andrea (1991) *Women Watching Television: Class and Generation in the American Television Experience*. Philadelphia: University of Pennsylvania Press.

Reynolds, Marian (1986) 'Young People and the Media', paper presented to the Annual Conference of the Sociological Association of Ireland, Trinity College, Dublin.

Seiter, Ellen, Hans Borchers, Gabriele Kreutzner and Eva-Maria Warth (eds) (1989) *Remote Control: Television, Audiences and Cultural Power*. London: Routledge.

Trevor, William (1972) 'The Ballroom of Romance', pp. 50–72 in *The Ballroom of Romance and Other Stories*. London: Bodley Head, 3rd. impression, 1979.

Willis, Paul (1977) *Learning to Labour: How Working Class Kids get Working Class Jobs*. Hampshire: Saxon House.

# 4

# 'Going to the Pictures': The Female Audience and the Pleasures of Cinema

## Helen Byrne

A tearful woman gazing in rapt attention at a flickering screen has become one of the most enduring images of women's relationship with the cinema. We have read it in Kracauer's account of the 'little shopgirls' (Kracauer, 1947), we've seen it in *Sleepless in Seattle* and more recently in a television advertisement for soup![1] Probably this stereotype is in need of revision but the persistence of the image suggests a cultural awareness that women have, or have had, particularly intense responses to the screen. Women's particular passion for cinema has been linked to the cultural, social and economic position of women at a particular time (see Petro, 1989). This linking of female passion for cinema with specific social, cultural and historical circumstances and the fact that little work has been done on Irishwomen and cinema prompted me to undertake a study of the female cinema audience in 1940s/ 1950s Waterford. This chapter is based on the findings of my research and focuses primarily on the relationship between women's experience of cinematic pleasure and their social, cultural and economic position in Waterford of the time.

The material[2] on which the chapter is based was collected through group and individual interviews with 22 people (17 women and five men) between the ages of 55 and 77, in June, 1994. Apart from one woman who described her family as wealthy, all the participants were from urban backgrounds and were in working-class or middle-class occupations during the 1940s and 1950s, such as factory workers, hairdressers, shop assistants, usherettes, housewives, clerical workers/typists and were generally single for most of the period under research. Individual profiles of the women in the study can be found in the Appendix, p. 104.

One of the first discourses to emerge from the interviews and discussions was of cinema as a social outlet, one of the few available to women, particularly working-class women, at the time. As the discussions progressed, however, it became obvious that cinema fulfilled more than just a need for cheap entertainment. Using the interview material as a focus, I will argue that cinema played a dual role in women's lives in the 1940s and 1950s. Firstly it created for them a 'utopian space', or in Richard Dyer's (1985) terms a 'utopian sensibility' where they could experience pleasure, excitement, and a sense of liberation which contrasted with the sense of frugality, repression and control emanating from the social forces of family, church and work. Secondly, the experience of cinema opened up a window onto modernity by presenting alternative worlds and role models for women and, in some cases, acted as a source of aspiration to what was seen to be a more modern, less restrictive, lifestyle. The dual role of cinema as a utopian space and as a socialising agent into 'modernity' is the theme of this chapter.

## Utopian Sensibility

'The cinema was magic. It was kind of magic' (Bee Foley, 66).

Life for women in 1940s and 1950s Waterford, as perceived by the women in the study, was relatively monotonous, rigid and controlled. Material scarcity meant 'plain living' and few luxuries. Commentators suggest that Ireland at the time was an authoritarian society in which parents, church and employer decided much of what one should think and how one should behave (for example see Lee, 1979; Inglis, 1987; Kelly, 1995). Life was, as described by the women, 'regulated. We walked a narrow path'. In the midst of this were the cinemas, or as the women called them, the picture houses, whose very names, Coliseum, Theatre Royal, Savoy, Regal, Regina, suggested another space, a different sensibility. In this space women could transcend their daily existence and escape into the world of cinema. As Pauline O'Neill commented, 'You'd come back floating on air. You'd live the picture, you know. You'd really live it and you'd be so happy that you'd be part of it.'

'Magic', 'dream', 'fantasy', 'enrapture' and 'escape' were other key terms used to describe this transcendence. Richard Dyer's concept of 'utopian sensibility' is useful for exploring the relationship between entertainment and 'escape'. He argues that entertainment offers us an image of something better to escape into, something not provided for in our day to day lives (Dyer, 1985:222). It does this at the level of sensibility, of feelings, presenting us with what Utopia would *feel* like, rather than how it would be organised. Dyer lists five categories of utopian sensibility to specify the emotional appeal of entertainment. These are: 'abundance', the 'enjoyment of sensuous material reality', which compensates for poverty or material scarcity; 'transparency', a quality of open relationships which compensates for manipulation; 'intensity', the experiencing of emotion directly without holding back, and which compensates for dreariness, monotony and predictability in one's life; 'energy', potential, the capacity to act upon, which compensates for exhaustion, the daily grind of work and urban living and, finally, 'community'[3], a sense of belonging, a network of phatic relationships which compensates for fragmentation, arising *inter alia* from job mobility and legislation against collective action. (Dyer, 1985:228). Dyer therefore links the pleasure of entertainment directly to the inadequacies experienced in society. Three of the above categories – 'abundance', 'transparency', and 'intensity' – are particularly relevant to this study.

## Abundance / Material Scarcity

One of the most directly satisfying cinematic pleasures for women at this time was the feeling of abundance and 'enjoyment of sensuous material reality' (Dyer, 1985:228) provided by the glamour, style and fashion on the screen. The post-war years saw chronic unemployment, large-scale emigration, and the visible presence of underemployment in Waterford (see Hearne, 1991:29). In 1947, for example, 1,400 people lived more than four to a room; of 5,684 dwellings, 1,236 had no private water supply. Lack of financial resources meant material scarcity and few luxuries. However, once one could scrape together the cost of a cinema ticket, one could bask in the sensuous luxury of the cinema image and, at least temporarily, forget the harsh realities of one's real life. The popularity of the biblical epics, *Ten Commandments*, *Ben Hur*, *Salome*, and the musicals, *Ziegfeld Follies*, *Merry Widow*, *Singing in the Rain* at the time could be explained by the need for sensuous spectacle and extravagance. The women themselves often chose musicals as their favourite films for the luxurious costumes and scenes:

> Oh! I loved those old films . . . they'd come out in those big dresses and be bouncing around. It used be lovely to watch 'em . . . what's this the other one was when they wore the dresses? The *Merry Widow*, Lana Turner was in that. They played the *Merry Widow* Waltz. You'd want to see her and she all in black. Ah, you want to see the black dress she had on her. 'Twas beautiful, magnificent. All them films that they had, big gowns on them. I used love 'em and one gown nicer than the other.
>
> (Elizabeth McGrath, 56)

The sensuousness and glamour seemed to have seeped into the cinema building itself. In fact, as early as 1927 an article in *Theatre Management* argued that 'the film and theatre itself must be geared to pleasing women's sensibilities' (quoted in Stacey, 1994: 85–6). In Waterford, the women's appreciation of the decor of the picture house is captured in comments like:

Then all the music would start and this big silk screen would go back wouldn't it? (. . .) There'd be this lovely big coloured screen and it'd all just go back slowly. In the Col. [colloquial for Coliseum] I think they used have a red velvet one with a motif at the end.

(Norah Power, 65)

Sometimes even the people working in the cinema were described in the sensuous terms usually reserved for film stars as the following comment on the 'Queen Donoghue', the lady who worked in the Savoy box office, suggests: 'She used be laid out [Waterford term for beautifully dressed] (. . .) She always had style. She was glamorous and blondy. She used to have the diamante ear-rings' (Kitty Casey, 63). The pleasure taken in observing the clothes, jewellery and hair is obvious. Considering that femininity has been culturally constructed as 'image' and that women were the usual creators of the domestic environment (Stacey, 1994:101), women had a particular need to experience this sensuous material reality as it was intimately bound up with their feminine identity and role. The cinema, therefore, became a utopian space for women because it temporarily allowed them to satisfy the need for abundance at a time of material scarcity.[4]

## Transparency / Social and Cultural Manipulation

Apart from financial constraints, there were social and cultural constraints on women which forced them into specific roles. At this time the attitude to women and expectations of them were largely defined by the prevailing Catholic and nationalist ideology which was evident in many of the state laws and institutions, for example censorship (see Kelly, 1995: 190). Women were ideologically assigned the role of 'devoted mother' or 'innocent virgin', and this is reflected in the women's accounts of their experience at the time. Many women, for example, refer to the fact that one had to give up work on marriage or that it was totally unacceptable for a woman, particularly a young woman, to go to the pub. Studies of the social climate of the time support the women's sense of inhibition and regulation which operated through the social forces of family (particularly the mother), church and work (see Lee, 1979; Inglis, 1987).

While permeating many aspects of life, inhibition was quite obvious in relation to sexuality. The social legacies of post-famine Ireland and the influence of Victorian England had ensured that sexuality became equated with shame, and so was rarely discussed with one's family or, indeed, in any public forum, except perhaps the church (see Inglis, 1987). Through sermons, missions, pamphlets and, indeed, the schools, the church made public the topic of sexuality in Irish society but generally through the discourses of shame, guilt, sin and self-control – discourses, of which women seemed particularly aware. In the utopian space of the cinema, however, a different discourse operated.

While sometimes romance and sexuality were seen as dangerous infringements of patriarchal taboos, they were also shown in terms of pleasure, eroticism, and overwhelming love.

Cinema was one of the few public expressions of these feelings, principally through romantic fantasy and the male star. Not only did women enjoy the male star's screen presence but also discussions about him in the workplace where 'everyone had a little place on the wall' for their favourite:

> If there was a nice photograph of the fellow you liked then you'd cut that out. No one would have women now. That'd be extraordinary now. I remember Mary O'Connor – Gregory Peck . . . she loved his films [she used to say] 'Now I don't care what the film is, I don't care what it's like. If Gregory Peck is in it, I'm there tonight'.
>
> (Kitty Casey, 63)

Robert Taylor was loved for his good looks, 'Jet black hair and military style mac', Robert Mitchum and Paul Newman for their 'cool' approach, Orson Welles for his 'mystery', and Charles Boyer, 'just for the sound of his name' (French pronunciation, of course!). Dark hair, voices (Ray Milland, Richard Burton, James Mason) and eyes (Omar Sharif) were the most frequently mentioned attractive features of the male star. Face and voice are said to be the centres of eroticism for the female gender, since female desire is allegedly based on identification with others through knowledge of the personal (Laplace, 1987: 160). The close-up of the star's features on the cinema screen was perfect for creating the illusion of personal knowledge. This description of Richard Greene's face and smile indicates the pleasure women experienced from these scenes:

> Oh, he was magnificent in it, Richard Greene. That thing [song] played all the way through– 'Capri when we fell in love one day. Capri when we met and our hearts were gay', 'twas beautiful (. . .) he was gorgeous. He used to smile then he'd have this big dimple in his chin. When he'd smile we'd be linking one another and digging one another. You'd be really wrapped up in the whole thing.
>
> (Kitty Casey, 63)

Considering Laplace's (1987:160) comment on female desire and Bazin's (1971) concept of the heightened erotic power of the cinematic image in times of censorship, I would suggest that the women's responses to the male star included an erotic element. This intensified the women's pleasure in the male star and the associated romantic fantasy as illustrated by the quotations above and below:

> Do you remember when the male star would kiss the girl? You'd actually get a thrill (laughter). Really because it was so lovely (. . .) And you know when the fellow ran his fingers through the girl's hair, you know, romantic. Nothing sordid.
>
> (Mary Kiely, 66)

We should note here a possible discrepancy between a romantic discourse and an explicitly sexual one. Mrs Kiely emphasises that it was the 'lovely' romantic discourse she enjoyed as opposed to an explicitly sexual discourse which could be considered 'sordid'. This emphasis not only indicates an awareness of the more 'sordid' explicitly sexual discourses operating in cinema since the 1960s, but also an awareness of the differences between the cinematic and other discourses surrounding sexuality in Ireland in the 1940s and 1950s.

The pleasure women experienced through the male star and romantic fantasy has further significance if we consider Modleski's (1984) and Radway's (1987) work which links women's responses to the heroes of romantic fiction with a need for nurture. Robert Taylor, being the epitome of glamour seemed to be the most popular choice of screen hero. If one wanted to describe 'a really handsome man, you'd say, "he's a real Robert Taylor"' (Mary Kiely, 66). The gentle, considerate, more romantic heroes like Charles Boyer, Franchot Tone and Rock Hudson were generally preferred to the tough ones:

> I loved him [Franchot Tone]. He was always nice in it and kind of gentle in it.
>
> (Mary Smith, 60)

> I always preferred a more moderate type of character, more gentle, considerate, not that tough image that might shove you around.
>
> (Maire Redmond, 69)

> Now he was a lovely actor [Gary Cooper]. He mostly did cowboys. He was a gentle kind of man. You never saw anything violent in him.
>
> (Pauline O'Neill, 72)

Some women admired a hero who might not have been the 'Tyrone Power type' but portrayed more strength and power:

> He was smouldering and dark and big and strong (. . .) Yes, he wasn't an evil man in the type of film. He was a leader that's how you saw him, Zorba the Greek . . . Anthony Quinn.
>
> (Bee Foley, 66)

Yet one woman admired the hero who was quite hostile in his treatment of the female character:

> Anytime we saw him [Rock Hudson] in them films he was rich or something like that, you know. He never dirtied his hands kind of thing. We used to endure him all the same. The films were lovely but we'd be thinking of someone else taking his part in the film. Now like *Gone with the Wind*. Clark Gable, he was fabulous in that, really fabulous
>
> (Elizabeth McGrath, 56)

> GF What did you like about him in that?

> He didn't take much nonsense from her [Scarlett O'Hara]. She was spoilt now, she was a spoilt brat to me. But he wasn't having any of it. He didn't take much notice of her and then it was lovely the way he walked out at the end and told her he didn't give a damn. Someone like that you want in those films.
>
> (Elizabeth McGrath, 56)

John Wayne in *The Quiet Man* was also considered to be a 'real he-man'.

(Kitty Byrne, 69)

Now when he tore her over the moors coming off the train. He wasn't taking any of her nonsense then and he fired her back to her brother.

(Elizabeth McGrath, 56)

The gentle hero is said to represent a closing of the gap between the sexes and is admired for the nurture he symbolises (Modleski, 1984: 17) whereas the hostile hero, as in the cases quoted above, is said to be driven to hostility by the force of his love (Radway, 1987: 215). Either way, the women's responses to these heroes suggest a need for nurture, for the reassurance of romantic love which was not being met in their real lives. This implies Dyer's category of 'transparency', the feeling of an open, direct relationship like 'true love' which compensates for being manipulated or confined to a particular role in real life. Norah Power, for example, contrasted Paul Henreid lighting the two cigarettes in *Now Voyager* with the reality of the man posing the indifferent question, 'Do you want a fag?'

The women wanted to experience some of the screen romance: 'You would be wishing that they [boyfriends] could look like them [film stars] and would *act like them* (. . .) You knew it was [fantasy] when you were logical but you kept wishing and hoping' (Norah Power, 65). However one soon left behind screen romance and entered the reality of marriage and 'Then you'd forget them then in the long run. It was all a fantasy. You got married then (Mary Smith, 60).

The patriarchal positioning of women as wives and mothers and the lack of nurture for them in these roles is also indicated. Kitty Casey reported one woman as saying 'Supposing 'twas only Mickey Mouse was on, I'd go just to get J—— [her husband] to mind the children'. Kitty continued on to remark that 'she had a hard life with him'. For a couple of hours in the utopian space of the cinema, through romantic fantasies about the male stars, the female audience could vicariously satisfy an emotional need for nurture and escape the frustrations experienced as women in their daily lives.

## Intensity/Monotony

The women in this study spoke about escaping from the monotony, predictability and rigidity of Irish society at the time. The lack of variety in social outlets for women seems to have been one reason for this monotony. The women suggested that while men were more likely to have been involved in sports clubs, women, particularly working-class women, had few options[5], apart from films, which allowed them to escape the ordinary and humdrum (see O'Connor, 1989:258):

They [films] were a great outlet physically and mentally. You could switch off from the humdrum.

(Teresa Daly, 62)

So you left the ordinary, everyday things behind when you went to the cinema.

(Bee Foley, 66)

And if you were browned off. Remember if you were browned off [you'd say] 'I think we'll go to the pictures'. It'd take us out of ourselves.

(Mary Kiely, 66)

Dyer suggests (1985:225) that entertainment compensates for the monotony and dreariness of life by creating 'intensity' in the spectator by which he means the experiencing of emotion directly, fully, unambiguously, authentically without holding back. The intensity of these emotions was often indicated by frequent references to crying at a film. In fact, crying was one test of a good film:

It was a great picture. You'd be crying your heart out.

(Pauline O'Neill, 72)

'Twas a great picture, you'd be crying your eyes out. 'Twas so sad. 'Twas lovely.

(Mary Kiely, 66)

I'd cry at it but I'd love that feeling.

(Elizabeth McGrath, 56)

Why did women love 'that feeling'? Why was it so satisfying? Modleski (1984:328) feels that perhaps women are attracted to melodrama because 'it provides an outlet for the repressed feminine voice'. Certainly, the stories most described as 'lovely' or as generating intense emotion involved issues concerning the female sphere which Irish society had not acknowledged in any meaningful way such as family disagreements and upset in *Ice Palace*, *Imitation of Life*; problem pregnancies in films like *How Green was my Valley*, *Secret Interlude*, *Blossoms in the Dust*; social and moral obstacles to relationships in *Waterloo Bridge*, *Intermezzo*, *Madame X*, and *All that Heaven Allows*. Consequently at a time of social constraint and authoritarianism, what seemed to engage the women's emotions most were narratives where personal emotions and desires were in some way bound by social convention and duty. One woman recalled being particularly sad at *How Green was my Valley* because the boy's whole career was jeopardised since he had to marry the girl who was going to have his baby. 'He was forced into it' (Mary Kiely, 66). Kitty Casey made a similar comment on *Secret Interlude*: 'She became pregnant. Of course they couldn't tell the family. He would be disgraced. He said he'd leave and give up everything for her (. . .) He forsook the family for her'.

These themes, while underlining patriarchal taboos, also allow women to experience vicariously intense emotions related to breaking the taboo without the real life risks and complications. This 'playing with reality' in Ang's terms (1982: 134) is a liberating experience. Similarly the 'tragic structure of feeling' –

the acknowledgement that life is a series of ups and downs – usually associated with television soap opera (Ang, 1982), also seemed to operate in film melodrama. When asked why they went to these sad films Kitty Byrne replied: 'There was a story to them, to see what was happening to other poor people'. From the context of this comment, I would suggest that 'poor' refers to emotional hurt rather than material poverty and therefore suggests an identification with, and a recognition of, a pattern of feeling which they themselves had experienced. In fact some women suggested that their favourite female stars were often those whose screen personae had similar problems to the women themselves: 'They always had those kind of roles where they had a bit of bother and trouble and they overcame it all. Naturally it had a happy ending. They were always working hard for a living like ourselves' (Norah Power, 65).

The aesthetic devices of melodrama particularly 'pathos' and 'melos' (see Elsaesser, 1985) were successful in arousing pleasure and intense emotion in the women in this study. 'Pathos' is aroused by the audience's awareness of the social determinants of a character's dilemma. A number of the scenes which the women chose for their intense emotionality seemed to have been effective because of this awareness. For instance, this emotion was evoked in response to a scene from a film in which Orson Welles had been so badly disfigured that he pretended he was dead and did not return to his wife, Claudette Colbert. Having become reacquainted with her years later, he finally decides to leave without revealing his identity:

> The minute she saw the medal [he had given to her child] she knew it was him. She ran out. He was going off in the taxi and she was screaming after him. He completely went out of her life because she was so happy he couldn't break up her marriage. It was a lovely story.
>
> (Kitty Casey, 63)

The death scene in the prison cell in *Madame X* was also remembered for intense emotion. It was interesting that three women in separate interviews mentioned the scene from *King's Row*, where Ronald Reagan had his legs amputated, as particularly memorable. One gave the following description:

> Anyway what did he do and he really did it for spite, he cut off his two legs. One of his legs was injured and he said he had to amputate his legs and you'd see him. I can see him to this day, sitting up in the bed and 'ah, ah, ah' screaming and looking for his legs. It ended up lovely. He got the girl afterwards but I can remember that scene, doctor's bag and he coming up the stairs and looking at the leg and he deciding what to do and you could see him because he was really bitter, the old doctor, but he actually amputated his legs.
>
> (Mary Kiely, 66)

We can imagine the intensity of emotion experienced by this woman in watching the scene and the 'pathos' of knowing that patriarchal spite had caused the pain and suffering to which a scream is an inadequate response. 'Melos' –

comprising lighting, montage, visual rhythm, decor, style of acting, and music (Elsaesser, 1985: 176) – also contributed to this effect as the frequent references to the bag and actors' movements and facial expression confirm. 'Melos' was significant in other scenes also:

> *Imitation of Life*. The clothes she wore in that. It was only magnificent. The scene in that where the mother was dead and the funeral was going through the streets and the young one was running after her and telling her 'I'm sorry mother' and we were roaring crying standing at the back so we could get out fast. Oh, the auld bitch to do that to her mother.
>
> (Elizabeth McGrath, 56)

> When he recovered and saw all this [in the paper] he couldn't go back to his wife. He was after getting old. He was shuffling along and the snow was falling and this Christmas he came back to the town and he saw his wife and children around the Christmas tree and the tears just flowed down.
>
> (Minnie McGrath, 77)

The scene from *All that Heaven Allows* where Jane Wyman gazes out a huge window on to an idyllic snow-covered landscape also caused intense emotion and was probably effective because of the 'melos'. Yet, while enjoying the spectacle, women were sufficiently attuned to the 'melos' to sense the contradiction in the text, as this account shows:

> *All that Heaven Allows*. That scene where she is up in the snow with him, that big, big window and she looking. Ah Jesus, that was beautiful. I'd be saying to myself 'Are there places like that in it, you know, or is it really only in our mind or is it all only make believe?' To see the scenery, the window, there, you know she just standing at the big window. Ah, 'twas magnificent.
>
> (Elizabeth McGrath, 56)

This liberating experience of intense emotion and the vicarious experience of playing with reality in the cinema compensated for the monotony and predictability of life for these women.

## Into Modernity

Cinema was an intense and utopian experience for women, but did it move them towards a more modern, less restrictive lifestyle? It is notoriously difficult to assess the effect of these cinematic experiences. Yet being lived experiences, 'just as lived as kicking a ball around a football pitch or going to a dance' (McRobbie, 1984: 142), they can flood into the more social sphere and become a source of shared or common knowledge. By exposing them to other ways of living in a context of pleasure and excitement, cinema gave women a positive sensibility to a less traditional, more modern way of life and so primed them for change. The interview material suggests that this occurred through three channels. Firstly, cinema provided role models for new images of femininity.

Secondly, it circulated consumer discourses which increased material expectations and, finally, it generated discussion, however limited, on issues which were generally taboo in Irish society at the time.

## New Images of Femininity

Since the cultural construction of femininity is as 'object of the look', women were particularly conscious of style and fashion. In the 1940s and 1950s when these women had limited access to material goods, they looked to the female film stars as role models so that they could satisfy their need to construct their own femininity in a particular way. So from the screen came the Lady Hamilton and Mrs Miniver hats and Audrey Hepburn's version of the 'new look'. Significantly it was the 1950s when Hollywood was reflecting the affluence and consumer boom of post-war America that produced the stars most remembered for style and fashion – Doris Day, Lana Turner, Audrey Hepburn, Elizabeth Taylor. Doris Day became the new image of the attractive woman, stylishly dressed yet displaying a girl-next-door or even tomboyish innocence. Through the cinema this more modern image of femininity became part of cultural consciousness:

> Remember when the beautiful fitted dresses came in. Remember we used to say 'Give us a look, you're the image of Doris Day'. It was so important to us.
>
> (Mary Kiely, 66)

Occasionally this modern image clashed with the more traditional view of Irish womanhood. One woman recalled her sister appearing 'with big, dangling earrings (. . .) My father really thought she was a fast woman' (Margaret Halpin, 62).

While all the women were aware that they could not achieve the beauty and glamour of the female star, many did suggest that the stars gave them a sense of their own potential. Two women were particularly struck by Scarlett O'Hara's resourcefulness and daring when she used the green velvet curtains to make a dress in *Gone with the Wind*:

> I often think about it. It was a clever thing to do, you know.
>
> (Mary Walsh, 68)

> She just took the curtains down, lovely green velvet. I could even see 'em now and she had this dress and this hat and she walked into the hall, all the looks. She stood out to the whole lot of them.
>
> (Dolly Casey, 74)

Some women responded most positively to the film *Now Voyager* particularly to the iconic image of the transformed Bette Davis on the gangplank of the ship. When asked specifically why she liked this scene, Kitty Byrne replied 'because it showed what could be done'. There is also a sense of removing constraints and finding one's own potential in the following:

She was like an old maid, wasn't it?

(Kitty Casey, 63)

The mother had her like that.

(Kitty Byrne, 69)

And she left the house, walked through the town, then on the ship, looking for clothes, hairdos. She let her hair down.

(Kitty Casey, 63)

Paradoxically, the film, *Now Voyager*, though perpetuating the construction of women as image, also suggests some sense of 'empowerment' for women (Laplace, 1987: 145). This sense of empowerment, which women vicariously experienced in the cinema, was positive and self-enhancing. Similarly Doris Day was chosen as a favourite star not because the woman wanted to look like her but because she felt she could *be* like her:

> Doris Day to me she was the real girl-next-door type (. . .) I felt I could do the things she was doing and I was kind of like her. I don't mean like her in looks but the same type.

(Kathleen Malone, 59)

The choice of these two stars is interesting, in the light of Molly Haskell's (1987: 215–21) remarks about Bette Davis, whom she perceives as a woman who pursued her own vision both in her screen persona and her own career. Doris Day, for all her girl-next-door image, 'escapes the chains of motherhood' (Haskell, 1987: 268) and 'tries with plenty of odds against her to find where she belongs and what she can do' (Haskell, 1987: 267). It is not that women began to act or behave in a similar way but that this experience of potential in the cinema made them more receptive to the idea of their own possibilities.

## New Material Expectations and Lifestyle

During the 1950s there was a consumer discourse operating where the cinema screen became a shop window for the myriad consumer goods being produced in post-war America and so had an effect on audience expectations (see Brown, 1985: 225). In this context there is a notable difference between the experience of older and younger women in the study. Those women who were in their teens and twenties in the 1940s admired the star's style but, being unable to afford the products, concentrated instead on less expensive techniques – a change of hairstyle or a way of wearing a scarf – to come closer to the screen image.

> Long 'go in the films, like the neckscarves we'd be wearing now, while they'd be smaller they'd [film stars] wear them around their hair and have it flipped down. We'd be buying bits of ribbon and tying it down like this. You'd compare yourself all the time to the stars and to the styles.

(Kitty Casey, 63)

Hairstyles were very frequently mentioned as were requests to the hairdresser to copy styles from the films:

> It was when she was a . . . princess. Audrey Hepburn. She used have hair all out in . . . kind of little bits of curl coming out and then we all started wearing our hair like that.
>
> (Norah Power, 65)

> O'Grady's [hairdressers] on the Mall used to have a sign 'Models Wanted'. Crowds would go down. You'd say 'Do it the way Betty Grable had it in such a film'.
>
> (Teresa Daly, 62)

Those who were in their teens and twenties in the 1950s, however, seemed more able to afford consumer goods.[6] This was particularly true of the younger women in this study, who were skilled bookkeepers or typists and had acquired jobs in offices, or those who became shop assistants. The increased ability to purchase consumer goods is reflected by Kathleen Malone (59) who remembers buying an outfit in Dublin because it was similar to one worn by Doris Day in a film. She also recalled seeing a film called *A Paris Affair* and remarking to her boyfriend that she would love to see Paris. He replied 'Well, we'll go there on our honeymoon'. They did! So for some women, particularly the younger and more affluent ones, the aspirations generated by the cinema screen could at times be attained.

Other small changes in lifestyle which suggest a move towards modernity were often associated with the cinema. As with consumerism, there were, also, some small differences between the older and younger women as they described social life. The older women described the camaraderie of the queue, the heckling of the audience, buying sweets before going to the cinema, occasionally buying chips on the way home. Younger, perhaps more affluent, women referred to cinema more as a night out, dressing up, going for coffee afterwards. There were also one or two references to smoking:

> I'd say some people would [imitate gestures of the stars]. In those days it was very fashionable to smoke and they had these big cigarettes. I never smoked. I tried it and had burned eyebrows (. . .) They had these gestures. You could see it from the films.
>
> (Maire Redmond, 69)

One of the initial visible signs of movement towards a more modern lifestyle was the practice of going for a coffee:

> I remember going in for an occasional cup of coffee. By the way coffee wasn't drunk as much then, maybe we didn't like it but it was the done thing to have a cup of coffee and a chocolate biscuit. We probably would have gone instead of going to the pictures. The money wouldn't have stretched both ways.
>
> (Bee Foley, 66)

In Dublin it would have been a more social experience. You would have more than one person with you, possibly up to four people and you would go in for coffee afterwards and you'd talk about it [the film], moon over some fellow, you know, say 'He is absolutely gorgeous'.

(Margaret Halpin, 62)

Then there was the cafe upstairs and all of us when we'd go [to the cinema] we always went for a cup of coffee . . . that was the first place I ever drank coffee . . . you'd sit there feeling really cosmopolitan. Oh, it was lovely.

(Mary Kiely, 66)

The last quotation, perhaps, points to an interesting change in social life for at least some women during the 1950s. The 'coffee bar' ambience and its association with cosmopolitanism as opposed to the more homely 'cafe' or, perhaps eating/drinking in public at all, indicate the more modern aspirations and expectations of young middle-class women at the time.

## Discussion Topics

Finally, cinema played some role in the socialisation of women into modernity by bringing into the public sphere issues which were generally repressed in Irish society. An essential aspect of cinema at the time was its role in social intercourse, especially for women, and part of the pleasure of cinema was talking about it with friends and workmates:

They'd go into work the next morning and the whole picture would be discussed and everything, especially if a lot of them had been there on a Monday night.

(Maureen Cotter, 72)

What he said and what she said and what he done and what she done. That was all part of it. You just didn't go and look at it and come out and shut off. I didn't anyway.

(Norah Power, 65)

Certainly stars, fashion and stories were discussed, but often through these discussions other topics revolving around relationships, sex, pregnancy and their social implications emerged. Some examples were recalled. The 'long kiss', a screen kiss reputedly lasting three and a half minutes was 'the topic whispered about, as anything sexual was taboo' (Maire Redmond, 69). *How Green was my Valley* and *Secret Interlude*, already referred to, raised questions about problem pregnancies. *Blossoms in the Dust* raised discussion about illegitimacy as Greer Garson was campaigning to have the word 'illegitimate' removed from birth certificates:

There's no such thing as a bad girl or an illegitimate child only illegitimate parents [recalling the sentiments of the film].

(Kitty Byrne, 69)

GF: Would you discuss that sort of thing?

You would, in jobs (. . .) It would work in to a row then because some would be in favour and others against.

(Kitty Casey, 63)

In this way, cinema in the 1940s and 1950s may have played a similar role, though on a much smaller scale, to that of television in the 1960s and perhaps the radio phone-in in the 1990s (see Chapter 8). It made repressed and hidden issues public by generating discussion even on a limited scale and made these women more aware of a wider range of views on such issues.

## Conclusion

This study of women who went to the cinema in Waterford in the 1940s and 1950s has shown that one important role of cinema was to provide a utopian space in which these women could experience pleasurable emotions and which temporarily satisfied needs which were frustrated or denied in Irish society at the time. The research clearly indicated that women's pleasure in the cinema revolved around three aspects: glamour, stars and stories. Each of these had a role to play in creating this utopian space. The experience of glamour, fashion, decor and spectacle in the cinema allowed women to experience feelings of abundance and enjoyment of sensuous material reality at a time of material scarcity, thus vicariously satisfying a need which has its origin in the cultural construction of femininity and the female role. The male star and romantic fantasy allowed women to experience 'transparency' – the feeling of sincere and open relationships rather than the sense of shame and guilt which surrounded sexuality in Irish society. Women's choice of screen hero would also suggest that they felt a need for romance and explicit nurture which were again frustrated in everyday life. The cinema played a role somewhat similar to television soap opera today by providing some public expression of female concerns, and through melodramatic elements of 'pathos' and 'melos' and 'the tragic structure of feeling', allowing women to experience emotion intensely. In this way it helped to compensate for the monotony and predictability of daily life. These elements constituted the 'magic' of cinema for these women in the 1940s and 1950s and as I have shown were related to the specific social and cultural circumstances of the time.

Cinema played a second role in the lives of the women with whom I spoke. It became a socialising agent into modernity providing women with the possibility of considering alternative roles to those prescribed by the dominant institutions of the time and generated a desire for a less traditional way of life. The female stars provided new models of femininity, primarily in relation to appearance and fashion, but also suggested new potential and possibilities for women. The cinema screen, particularly in the 1950s, became a huge shop window for consumer goods and thus raised women's material expectations and prompted certain changes in lifestyle. Finally, the cinema gave public expression to topics such as sexuality and reproduction which were taboo subjects in Irish society and so allowed the women in the study to consider a wider range of viewpoints. In the words of Teresa Daly (62) 'They [films] were windows on the world, they broadened our horizons'.

# Appendix

## Profiles of the Women in the Study

**Byrne, Kitty:** B.1924. Primary Certificate. Housekeeper, factory worker. Married in 1951.

**Casey, Dolly:** B. 1920. Left school at 14. Single.

**Casey, Kitty:** B. 1931. Left school at 16. Worked in printing works. Single.

**Cotter, Maureen:** B. 1922. Left school at 15. Shop assistant. Married in 1943.

**Coughlan, Eileen:** B. 1918. Left school at 18. Family wealthy, trained horses and ran a car. Married in 1948.

**Daly, Teresa:** B. 1932. Completed some years at secondary school and a commercial course. Clerk/Typist, usherette, assistant manager in cinema. Married in 1959.

**Foley, Bee:** B. 1928. Left school at 15. Clerk. Married in 1956.

**Halpin, Margaret:** B. 1932. Leaving Certificate. Clerical worker with local authority. Married in 1955.

**Kiely, Mary:** B. 1928. Intermediate Certificate. Shop assistant in large drapery store. Married in 1959.

**Malone, Kathleen:** B. 1935. Intermediate Certificate. Clerk in office of large provisions store. Married in 1957.

**McGrath, Elizabeth:** B. 1938. Left school at 15. Cloakroom attendant, factory worker. Married in 1960.

**McGrath Minnie:** B. 1917. Intermediate Certificate. Married in 1941.

**O'Neill, Pauline:** B. 1922. Primary Certificate. Usherette. Married in 1945.

**Power, Norah:** B. 1929. Primary Certificate, Technical school to study bookkeeping. Factory worker. Married in 1954.

**Redmond, Maire:** B. 1925. Intermediate Certificate and commercial course. Bookkeeper/Typist. Married in 1952.

**Smith, Mary:** B. 1934. Completed Primary school. Hairdresser. Married in 1957.

**Walsh, Mary:** B. 1926. Left school at 18 and qualified as a shorthand typist. Shop assistant and shorthand typist. Married in 1951. Widowed in 1964.

# Notes

I would like to thank the following whose help made the project possible. They shared their memories, their time and their personal stories with me: Martin Breen, Kitty Byrne, Dolly Casey, Kitty Casey, Teresa Daly, Margaret Halpin, Patrick Kenny (for his time and resources), Kathleen Malone, Elizabeth McGrath, Norah Power, Mary Smith, The Waterford Active Retired Association and their members who participated: Maureen Cotter, Eileen Coughlan, Bee Foley, Jack Keane, Mary Kiely, Minnie McGrath, Thomas Mulhall, Pauline O'Neill, Maire Redmond, Mary Walsh and Tony Wentworth. Four of the above names are pseudonyms to comply with requests for anonymity. I would also like to thank Ciara O'Reilly.

1 This advertisement for Hotcup Quick Soup was transmitted by RTÉ television during 1994–95. It shows a young woman curled up in a soft armchair, watching a black and white movie flickering on the television screen. Tears are streaming down her face, yet she seems to be enjoying the experience and is somewhat comforted by the mug of soup she cradles in her hands. It is interesting that this stereotypical image of intense female response to the screen, though perhaps dated, is still being exploited, even if humorously, by advertisers in the mid-1990s.

2 The oral history approach adopted in this study raises some consideration about popular memory, unconscious processes, and treating the material only as text. Yet, allowing for these difficulties, I feel it is worthwhile to consider the interview material in conjunction with theoretical studies of women and cinema to illuminate women's experience of cinema in the 1940s and 1950s.

3 The camaradie and fun of being in the cinema audience, and indeed in the cinema queue, was referred to frequently and suggests a shared experience which may relate to Dyer's 'community' category. It certainly added to the women's delight in cinema going as a social activity.

4 It is interesting that the 'wealthy' woman in the study felt that cinema was not so important for her as she had other outlets; horse-riding, hockey club, season of hunt and Beagle Balls, etc.

5 The dance (though more expensive than cinema) was an occasional option. Evening strolls and radio were also mentioned and the books, *Miracle* and *Oracle*. These 'were classed as bad books' because they had 'a bit o' love in them' (Kitty Casey, 63).

6 From some of the comments made it is possible to speculate why this was so. Waterford was somewhat cushioned from the national recession (Hearne, 1991: ii), factories with largely female workforces had opened and emigrants were sending money home. Female office workers had higher wages than factory workers and shop assistants sometimes had arrangements with their own and other stores for accounts and discounts, etc.

# References

Ang, Ien (1982) *Watching 'Dallas'*. London: Methuen.

Bazin, Andre (1971) *What is Cinema? Vol. 2.* Berkeley & Los Angeles: University of California Press.

Brown, Terence (1985) *Ireland: A Social and Cultural History 1922–1985.* London: Fontana.

Dyer, Richard (1985) 'Entertainmant and Utopia' in Bill Nichols (ed.) *Movies and Methods, Vol. 2.* Berkeley and Los Angeles: University of California Press.

Elsaesser, Thomas (1985) 'Tales of Sound and Fury, Observations of the Family Melodrama' in Bill Nichols (ed.) *Movies and Methods, Vol. 2.* Berkeley and Los Angeles: University of California Press.

Haskell, Molly (1987) *From Reverence to Rape: The Treatment of Women in the Movies.* Chicago and London: University of Chicago Press (first published 1974).

Hearne, John (1991) 'The Waterford Economy 1945–1962: The Interaction of Government Politics and Local Initiative'. MA thesis, University College Cork.

Inglis, Tom (1987) *Moral Monopoly: The Catholic Church in Modern Irish Society.* Dublin: Gill & Macmillan.

Kelly, Mary (1995) 'Censorship and the Media', pp. 185–211 in Alpha Connelly (ed.) *Gender and the Law in Ireland.* Dublin: Oak Tree Press.

Kracauer, Siegfried (1947) *From Caligari to Hitler.* Princeton: Princeton University Press.

Laplace, Maria (1987) 'Producing and Consuming the Woman's Film: Discursive Struggle in *Now Voyager*, pp. 138–66 in Christine Gledhill (ed.) *Home is where the Heart is.* London: British Film Institute.

Lee, J. J. (1979) *Ireland 1945–1970.* Dublin: Gill & Macmillan.

McRobbie, Angela (1984) 'Dance and Social Fantasy', pp. 130–61 in A. McRobbie and M. Nava (eds) *Gender and Generation.* London: Macmillan.

Modleski, Tania (1984) *Loving with a Vengeance: Mass-Produced Fantasies for Women.* New York: Methuen.

Mulvey, Laura (1985) 'Visual Pleasure and Narrative Cinema' in Bill Nichols (ed.) *Movies and Methods Vol. 2.* Berkeley and Los Angeles: University of Californa Press.

O'Connor, Emmet (1989) *A Labour History of Waterford.* Waterford: Waterford Trades Council.

Petro, Patrice (1989) *Joyless Street: Women and Melodramatic Representation in Weimar Germany.* Princeton: Princeton University Press.

Radway, Janice (1987) *Reading the Romance.* London: Verso.

Stacey, Jackie (1994) *Star Gazing: Hollywood Cinema and Female Spectatorship.* London: Routledge.

# SECTION THREE
# NORTHERN IRELAND, ETHNICITY AND THE DOMINANT IDEOLOGY

## 5

# Screening the Message: A Study of Community Relations Broadcasting in Northern Ireland

## Paul Nolan

The idea that negative media messages have a harmful effect on public consciousness has an obvious corollary, which is that positive media messages can create socially useful effects. The former proposition is the one which stirs public controversy, but it is the latter proposition which continues to be most influential, underpinning most public service broadcasting. Media studies has tended to be drawn by the gravitational pull of the public debate and to concentrate on the real or imagined effects of sexually explicit or violent programmes; by contrast very little attention has been paid to what has become known as 'prosocial' media. The purpose of the study which is the subject of this chapter was to test the assumption that television can act as a force for enlightenment; more specifically to look at how far it can promote tolerance and understanding within the divided communities of Northern Ireland.

The research focuses on one particular programme, a thirty-minute documentary called *Orange, Green and Yellow*, which was broadcast by the BBC in Northern Ireland in Spring 1991 as part of the series entitled *A Sense of Place*. What distinguished this series was that it was made with the overt intention of improving relations between the two religio-political communities and received financial support from the government-sponsored Cultural Traditions Group. The research was framed around a simple, or seemingly simple, question: did the programme succeed in its aim of improving community relations? It would be disingenuous to pretend that this line of enquiry could proceed along established methodological paths; before any answers could be glimpsed a forest of theoretical and methodological questions had first to be cleared.

## Theoretical and Methodological Questions

Yeats's famous question:

*Did that play of mine send out*
*Certain men the British shot?*

was of course rhetorical; or at least at a literal level unanswerable. We cannot know the precise effects of a Yeats play or a Heaney poem or a television documentary for that matter. In certain exceptional cases we are aware of direct causal connections: Michael Buerk's famous 1984 documentary on the famine in Ethiopia did in observable ways create a tide of sympathy for the famine victims and subsequent media events like *Bank Aid* or *Comic Relief* have produced effects measurable in the amounts of cash aid sent in by viewers. These are, however, exceptional cases. Communication research has, over the decades, consistently failed to deliver what government and sponsors require of it: clear evidence of the effects of the media on society, particularly on forms of anti-social behaviour. In a survey of the research on media effects commissioned by the Broadcasting Standards Council the authors Cumberbatch and Howitt (1989: 25) are forced to the conclusion:

> The history of mass communication research is conspicuously lacking in any clear evidence of the precise effects of the mass media. Theories abound, examples multiply but convincing facts that specific media content is reliably associated with particular effects has proved quite elusive . . . there is a certain consistency in the research over this.

The lack of certainty in the discipline forced its early practitioners to retreat into a search for a more rigorous, more scientifically based research methodology, which in practice tended to privilege quantitative survey methods. The hoped for clarity of this empirical method failed to arrive and, although the history of mass communication research is too complex to summarise here, the term 'mining in the sand' used by Cumberbatch and Howitt well encapsulates the efforts made by American media researchers in the 1960s and 1970s to respond to government imperatives. The new consensus which emerged in the 1980s accepted that human communication eludes scientific methology (Lull, 1990). The natural-science pretence was let slip and recognition made of the difficulty of separating out media messages from the mass of influences in people's lives (Willis, 1981). The question of media effects then had to be re-framed to allow for a heuristic enquiry into how people interact with television; how they bring their existing beliefs, values, experiences and knowledge with them to the viewing experience. In effect this has meant a shift towards the active viewer as the proper subject for research, a shift which has drawn media studies into the territory of ethnographers. It is a shift which has brought forth new methodological imperatives: to understand the viewer's response inside the familial, societal and ideological contexts in which the readings take place opens up many new lines of enquiry, and also the danger that reception studies could go spiralling into the orbits of ethnographic theory. The focus on audience response in some writings displaces any analysis of the actual content of the media text or the intentions of the writers, producers and broadcasters. There are obvious problems, however, in accepting 'meanings' for television programmes that float free of any reference to the actual text. As David Miller argues (Miller, 1994 : 267), anyone who watches an image of urban violence and reads it as a scene of beautiful countryside must be said to be performing a misreading, and not just an interpretation. Texts cannot be infinitely open. The insights from reception analysis must be balanced with the knowledge gained of the broadcasting institutions, the intentions of the producers and analysis of the context. In other words researchers must attempt an analysis which integrates both the encoding and decoding stages in the construction of meaning.

In the final chapter of their important work on international audience responses to televised news accounts of political conflict the authors Cohen, Adoni and Baritz (1990 : 195) admit that insufficient emphasis was given to the intentions of producers and journalists. They call for future research to take a 'start-to-finish' approach, that is 'research that begins with the producers and journalists of the news, continues with the product they manufacture, and terminates with the audience'.

Insofar as my research project followed a particular model it was the start-to-finish approach recommended in this passage, the added complication arising from the fact that the study concerned itself with prosocial broadcasting. Stuart Hall's encoding/decoding paradigm (Hall, 1977) was a useful frame of reference, and one easily mapped on to the model advocated by Cohen, Adoni and Baritz.

In practical terms this meant interviewing those in the Community Relations Council and Cultural Traditions Group who first conceived the programme; then the BBC personnel with editorial responsibility for buying in and broadcasting the programme; following through with interviews with the actual programme-makers, and finally, interviews with selected groups of viewers to discover how successfully the original message had conveyed itself to different audiences. I will now follow the same sequence to describe my findings.

## The Cultural Traditions Group

In January 1990 the Community Relations Council was formally launched at Stormont Castle, Belfast, by the then Education minister, Dr Brian Mawhinney. Built into the structure of the new body was the Cultural Traditions Group which had enjoyed an antecedent existence since 1988. It had first been brought together at the urging of civil servants from the Northern Ireland Office, keen to draw on the insights of academics and the wider intellectual community in order to assist in the formulation of government policy on a range of social and cultural issues. The Anglo-Irish Agreement of 1985 had marked a paradigm shift in the way in which the British and Irish governments defined the nature of the political problem in Northern Ireland. While the main thrust of the Agreement was the harmonisation of formal struc- tures, the more significant concord was on the need to recognise that both nationalist and unionist aspirations would have to be accommodated in any future political developments. Implicit in that recognition was an imperative for government to take further steps to address the internal conflict in Northern Ireland in the terms in which it was now being described: in terms of culture, of identity, and of the dysfunctional relationship between the two communities. From this point on, government abandoned the drive to persuade the people of Northern Ireland to accept a single, integrative identity which would render difference unimportant; instead the thrust was not only to recognise difference, but to legitimate and even to celebrate the two identities as two competing, but nevertheless compatible, forces. For the civil servants, whose task it was to reinterpret the mission of government in policy terms, this new direction immediately signalled some problems. It was time to call upon the strength of Northern Ireland's intellectual community.

There had never been, as Professor John Whyte observed in his inaugural lecture at Queen's University in 1993, any form of rapprochement between the policy makers in the Northern Ireland Office and the policy analysts in the universities. Professor Whyte's subsequent publication, however, *Interpreting Northern Ireland*, (1990: 258) was an important landmark in the coming together of the two because it was Whyte's formulation which crystallised a new consensus:

> Both the traditional nationalist and traditional unionist interpretations have lost their popularity . . . [in favour of] . . . the internal-conflict interpretation. According to this interpretation, the crucial conflict is between the communities in Northern Ireland. Though this conflict is influenced by the relations which Northern Ireland has with Britain on the one hand and the Republic on the other, those relations are not at the heart of it.

From 1985 onwards there followed a series of unorchestrated but nonetheless harmonious developments. The Institute of Irish Studies at Queen's University, Belfast was one centre for the ethnographic exploration of culture or, more cor- rectly, for the exploration of the many different cultures operating within and beyond the sectarian divisions. Equally uneasy with the dichotomised world of orange and green was the constellation of writers and critics involved in the Ulster literary scene. Poets like Seamus Heaney, Michael Longley and Derek Mahon had, throughout the troubles, resisted the appeals for them to take a committed stance, and their troubled rejection of easy allegiances had itself become a theme of Northern poetry in this period. It was a theme that broadcasters could relate to as the identities of their various audiences swam in and out of focus and while there was nothing that could be described as a 'movement', there was an eagerness to share experiences and to define a common project. It was in this climate that Dr James Hawthorne, a former controller of the BBC in Northern Ireland, was invited to the Northern Ireland Office, where it was suggested to him that he might convene a meeting of those with the appropriate experience to help advise government in the formulation of policy in the area of cultural identity. Thus was born the Cultural Traditions Group, described by its first paid coordinator, Maurna Crozier, in a conference paper (1992) in these terms:

> Its members were mainly academics, with backgrounds in history, conflict studies, the Irish language, geography and music, but included those who had left the lecture theatre for publishing, broadcasting and poetry. The Group was charged with the task of bringing the notions of pluralism and diversity, so familiar to the academics, into the public arena for debate, to people for whom diversity seemed mostly to have murderously green or orange colours.

The early meetings of the Group took the form of an intellectual salon – deliberately informal, with a strong emphasis on social interaction, the non-institutional settings helping to mark the distance from daily work practices. With the incorporation into the newly-formed Community Relations Council in 1990 (resented by some members as a shotgun marriage) the Cultural Traditions Group found itself with a budget to spend, and the need therefore to identify a clear programme. Certain things immediately suggested themselves: financial support for the publishers of works on local culture or identity, for festivals, conferences, for literary events or anything that could be thought to encourage the acceptance of cultural difference.

It is hardly surprising that the Cultural Traditions Group thought to add television to their repertoire. Although they were quite unaware of it, the burgeoning conflict resolution industry internationally, guided by the same instincts, had come to the same conclusions. As the Australian magazine *Conflict Resolution News* (Antennae, 1993: 9) put it:

> The time has come to use one of our most valuable assets for Conflict Resolution (CR): the mass media. There is little doubt of the need. The rapidity of global and profound change leaves dysfunctional societies with massive unresolved conflicts.

The Cultural Traditions Group was fortunate in having as its first Chairperson Dr James Hawthorne, whose experience as Controller of the BBC told him that any naive attempt to intrude a political agenda into public service broadcasting would backfire. Speaking at a Cultural Traditions conference in March 1989 he said '. . . any attempt to present information in an anti-sectarian mode runs the risk of misinterpretation. If the media are seen to have an agenda then they will lose their audience'.

Nonetheless the Media Sub-Committee of the Cultural Traditions Group was excited by the idea of having its ideas explored through the powerful medium of television. The BBC at the time had a programme idea waiting for production funds, the idea being for a series which would explore local cultural traditions. 'There was', said Dr Hawthorne 'a true co-incidence of purpose and ideas'. One remaining difficulty was the propriety of the BBC accepting money from an external agency to fund programmes with a particular political agenda but, quoting Dr Hawthorne again, 'an elegant solution was found'. The programme makers, not the BBC, could receive grants to help them develop programme ideas to a brief offered by the Corporation. The brief was to produce programmes which would help the divided communities of Northern Ireland better understand the forces shaping communal identities.

## The Programme Makers

The BBC Controller Pat Loughrey was, like his predecessor Dr Hawthorne, a member of the Cultural Traditions Group. Another thing they held in common was that, prior to taking up the Controller's post, both men had established their reputations in the BBC's Education Department, and both felt secure with the original, Reithean definition of the Corporation's purpose with its emphasis on the edification of the viewing public. A different ethic, however, has come to dominate British broadcasting, through a process well described by Tom Burns (Burns, 1977: 25) as:

> . . . the transition of broadcasting from an occupation dominated by the ethos of public service, in which the central concern is with quality in terms of the public good and of public betterment, to one dominated by the ethos of professionalism, in which the central concern is with quality . . . [marks] . . . a shift from treating broadcasting as a means to treating broadcasting as an end.

The two production companies which won the contract to produce the programmes for the series, Bridge Television and Flying Fox, both subscribed fully to the professional ethic described above. Barry Cowan from Bridge Television and David Hammond from Flying Fox are amongst the most distinguished broadcasters in Ireland: they have both, at one time or another, been employed by the BBC and they have both gone on to carve their professional reputations in the world of documentary film-making. Their personal reputations, and the reputations of the production companies they founded, were sufficient to ensure that the series could be seen to be in safe hands. The integrity of each of these two film makers, however, militated against them working to any imperative other than their own professional standards. The agenda of the Cultural Traditions Group, they stressed in individual interviews, was foreign to them. In emphasising the distance between their own standpoint and that of the Cultural Traditions Group, they were anxious to establish that

they would have accepted no outside interference with their editorial independence (nor, insist both producers, was any attempt made to interfere), and
anxious also to express reservations about government attempts, or attempts by
government-funded bodies, to use cultural politics as a way to shape attitudes
and behaviours. David Hammond commented: 'I've never understood this
Catholic and Protestant thing, I've never pretended to understand it, and I've
certainly never tried to preach on the subject through my programmes'.

Barry Cowan expressed himself with equal finality, voicing also his particular concern at the community relations project:

> I believe what they would have liked from those . . . programmes was to help
> feed the communal sense of guilt, because that's the line they're pushing at the
> moment . . . I didn't see that as my function at all. I see my function as a
> researcher, as an historian, and as a programme-maker to say that these are the
> roots of sectarianism in Belfast. And if you don't like it – tough.

## The Programme

The series, *A Sense Of Place* was broadcast by BBC (Northern Ireland) in the
months of March and April, 1991. There were six programmes in all. The first
three, made by Flying Fox, were quiet, affirmative studies of local landscape
and culture, and tended to emphasise those things held in common by the two
traditions. The next two programmes, made by Bridge Television, took an opposite approach: in providing a history of sectarianism in Belfast they focused on
the urban rather than the rural, and on areas of antagonism rather than on the
things which unite. The final programme was a studio discussion on sectarianism.

The heterogeneity of the individual programmes presented me with a
methodological problem as no single documentary could be taken, synecdocally,
to represent the series as a whole; on the other hand asking groups to view all
six would have presented even greater methodological problems. In the end
I selected a programme made by Bridge Television called *Orange, Green And
Yellow*. My selection was determined by the fact that the subject of the commentary – sectarianism – was the one most likely to stimulate measurable
responses; and, secondly, because its approach seemed most typical of television
documentary approaches to the issue.

The format of the programme is a familiar one: the early part follows the
convention of a chronological narrative illustrated by contemporary visual references with appropriate sound effects (e.g. rioting mobs) on the soundtrack. As
events move closer to the present tense a series of witnesses are interviewed by
the presenter who threads a theme through their individual testimonies. The
presenter is Barry Cowan himself and the programme opens with him speaking
directly to camera. Against a sombre black background he explains the purpose

of the programme which is to explore the causes of sectarianism in Belfast. His presence at the start of the programme was at the suggestion of the BBC and serves two main functions. Firstly, the considerable personal weight of the man who is, arguably, Northern Ireland's most respected broadcaster is placed up front to add gravitas to the programme which follows; secondly, the introduction serves to establish where authorial responsibility lies – not with the BBC but with Barry Cowan. His personal signature there helps to validate the programme for the BBC while at the same time indemnifying the corporation by accepting individual responsibility for the message.

This devolution of responsibility down from the institution to the professional presenter is by no means particular to this programme; it is, as Kumar (1977: 248) observes, part of the corporate strategy of the BBC to base its claims to neutrality in the presentational style of its presenters. The tone that is favoured, 'quizzical, amused, slightly sceptical', was first described in the BBC handbook of 1973 and it remains the hallmark of today's presenters. It is a professional style which Barry Cowan has mastered and which is put to work in this programme to assure us, the viewers, that we are in the hands of a detached media professional. This integrative function, as Cohen *et al.*, (1990) describe it, is of crucial importance because of the way it seeks to recruit the audience to what is presented as a common sense view of the world.

Cowan draws from his first witness, Dr Gerard Cleary, an academic historian, a brief synopsis of Belfast history with the emphasis on economic development as the dynamo driving the changing social relations. After this there are six interviews with contemporary witnesses. In each one the interviewer is shot in a head and shoulders frame in front of a collage of images of the city's history. The first two to be interviewed are public servants who speak from their experience of administering policy in a divided society: Charles Brett, former Chief of the Housing Executive speaks on housing, and Bob Cooper, Director of the Fair Employment Commission speaks on employment. The rueful tone in which these two men reflect on the tragedy of sectarianism is continued through the next two interviews which are with politicians, the Official Unionist Cecil Walker and the SDLP's Brian Feeney. Like the civil servants before them the politicians speak of sectarianism as a force outside and beyond their control. The responsibility of the political parties in reinforcing historical divisions is not probed by Cowan, whose interviewing style at this point is gentle, concerned and sympathetic, encouraging us to see these individual political figures as moderate influences. The programme then cuts to its final two interviewees: the writer Sam McAughtry and trade unionist Paddy Devlin. Both are seasoned media performers and both have maintained a pride in their working-class origins while distancing themselves from any form of extremist politics. McAughtry the Protestant and Devlin the Catholic occupy the same approximate political space, and it is from there they contribute their

sometimes humorous, sometimes sad recollections of the excesses of their communities of origin. Cowan's final question is to McAughtry: 'Are you proud of
Belfast?' and McAughtry's warm affirmative answer is followed by the closing
music, the Maurice Craig ballad *May The Lord in His Mercy be kind to Belfast*.
As it plays the programme finishes with a long tracking shot of Belfast by night.

In assembling its political message the programme is careful to conform to
BBC conventions of balance. The nationalist and unionist perspectives are maintained in symmetry throughout the programme, but in conformity with BBC
tradition the editorial balance does not have to weigh all political views, only
those within a certain consensus. In the words of a former controller, Sir Charles
Curran, 'One of the senior editors said recently in a phrase which I treasure:
"Yes we are biased – biased in favour of parliamentary democracy"'. *Orange,
Green and Yellow* operates its own exclusions: Paisleyism, at one point identified with atavistic sectarianism and republicanism, by implication is also
consigned to politic's irrational fringe. There are other, more subtle exclusions:
having posited in his opening remarks, that religious affiliations are less important then economic forces, no church figures are invited to speak, nor does
anyone else contribute any views on the religious dimension of the conflict. No
women are interviewed in the programme. The speakers are all male, and
while it might be inexact to level the familiar accusation that they, like most
authority figures, are 'male, middle aged and middle class', it would be true to
say that the programme does not attempt to express the specific experiences of
the young, or of women, or of working-class communities of Belfast today.

The experiences of the interviewees are assembled into a shared consensual
perspective which rejects sectarianism and political extremism. To be outside
that consensus is, by implication, to be against common sense. The other political message of the programme – that changes in the economic infrastructure
have been responsible for changes at the social, cultural and political level –
might provoke an interesting debate in those circles were structuralist Marxists
squared up against the Gramscian revisionists. Alternatively, the evidence of an
economic determinist argument might fit well with those right-wing conspiracy
theorists who scrutinise all BBC programmes for evidence of a Marxist bias. In
truth, however, the concerns of the left or right were unlikely ever to surface in
the solipsistic universe of Northern Ireland politics. None of our respondents
sought or found evidence of any political leaning other than those that could be
painted in the colours of green and orange. But, as we shall see, even with that
limited palette, they still managed a considerable degree of inventiveness.

## Responses to the Programme

The audience research was conducted with nine differentially situated focus
groups, and which, taken together, could be seen to be broadly representative

across the categories of gender, class and religion. Contact was initially made by letter with 43 different groups, and follow-up phone calls allowed me to negotiate a sample of twelve which, in addition to their willingness to participate, provided the socio-demographic spread I wanted. I had originally intended to include rural groups in my sample, but given the limited scope of the research, and given also the specific content of the programme (a history of sectarianism in Belfast), it seemed prudent to trim the ambitions of the study and restrict it to the Belfast area. In the event practical difficulties forced two of the twelve groups to drop out of the schedule, and one other group which did participate in the study had to be excluded from the sample because the preponderance of 'outsiders', who had turned up to take part in the discussion, put a question mark beside the representatives of the participants on the day. The nine groups in the sample were:

*The Conway Mill Writers' Group:* A group of mainly unemployed people from the Falls Road who meet regularly as a writers' workshop.

*Women's Institute, South Belfast:* Generally perceived as a middle-class organisation, the Women's Institute brings women together for cultural, social and charitable purposes.

*East Belfast Protestant Community Workers' Group:* A sense that Protestants were being marginalised in the area of community development prompted the formation of this informal grouping in the mid-1980s.

*Orange Order, North Belfast:* Through contact with the Grand Orange Order it was agreed that the Clover Hill Temperance Lodge would participate in this survey.

*Falls Community Council (Women) and Falls Community Council (Men):* The Falls Community Council is the longest established and largest community organisation on the Falls Road, and takes as its bailiwick the whole of nationalist West Belfast. For the purpose of this focus group study, its management committee convened two groups, a group of men and a group of women to view the programme.

*Protestant and Catholic Encounter:* This ecumenical grouping has headquarters in the university area. It was formed in the early years of the Troubles to promote mutual understanding.

*Olympia Women's Group:* This group is drawn from a working-class Protestant community known as the Village. Its members meet regularly for social and educational purposes.

*The Cornerstone Community:* Situated right on the 'frontline', on the interface between Protestant and Catholic West Belfast the Cornerstone Community aims to give practical expression to its christian vision.

Focus group interviews are increasingly significant in media research and their role and function are described by Arthur Asa Berger (1991: 91) as follows:

> Focus groups are group interviews that are held to find out how people feel about some product, service or issue . . . They are a kind of collective depth interview, and it is hoped that the discussion will lead to important insights that will help manufacturers or sellers of services function more effectively.

Methodological problems, however, remained. The first consideration was the need to fix opinions on this particular thirty-minute documentary against the backdrop of general attitudes to the media. To calibrate the degree of perceived bias required some scale on which it could be measured, so I thought it necessary to ask all participants to complete a short written questionnaire at the beginning of the ˙session, detailing their general perception of television's portrayal of local events. A second consideration, which required the use of a short questionnaire, was the problem of ascertaining the views of less confident group members. The danger in open discussion (see Lewis, 1991) is that one or two dominant members can set the frame for discussion and create the appearance of consensus, when in fact other views exist but remain unspoken. The second questionnaire, then, was introduced to establish the immediate responses of individual informants to the programme before discussion inside the group led by its more dominant members could gravitate towards a collective view that would suppress the variety of individual responses.

The engagement with the group had to be probing enough to get in under the radar that the informants put up around themselves. Following Morley (1986) I returned to tackle the same questions from different angles, to ensure that anyone adopting a persona could be challenged, and that, under this complex form of interrogation, artificial poses would give way to real attitudes. Finally, there was one further problem, in many ways a problem without a solution. My name would immediately betray my origins in the Catholic community and there was therefore always the possibility that groups, consciously or unconsciously, would allow that to affect their perception of me in the interlocutor role. It has been suggested elsewhere (Lewis, 1991) that in situations of ethnic difference it is preferable that the researcher share the identity of the informants. I would not wish to disagree with this suggestion but, given the limited resources of this particular study, it was not feasible to employ interviewers from the two traditions.

## Group Responses: Some Common Themes

*Orange, Green and Yellow* was broadcast on 29 April, 1991. Following its transmission there were no complaint calls to the BBC, nor did anyone contact the BBC to praise the programme. No reviews of it appeared in newspapers or magazines. No public statements were issued about it. Two nights later the BBC broadcast the sixth and final programme in the *A Sense of Place* series, a studio discussion in which various panellists were invited to contribute their views on the issues the programme had raised. This device is often used when the BBC fears controversy after a broadcast, as the studio discussion helps to defuse public anger by creating a forum for criticisms to be ventilated. In the event, however, there was no controversy to defuse. On the panel were: Peter Taylor, the BBC journalist, Dr Mari Fitzduff, Director of the Community Relations Council, Lord Fitt of Bell's Hill, Gusty Spence, the ex-UVF commander, and Ivor Oswald, Chairman of the Belfast 1991 committee. (Barry Cowan was also invited to participate, but declined the invitation because, he said, he felt the discussion would be freer without him present.) The panellists all paid brief respects to *Orange, Green and Yellow* before going on to discuss sectarianism as a social and political phenomenon without further reference to the style or content of the programme. No other public comment ever followed.

It is useful to remember this when we move from the particular group responses towards generalisations of any kind. The sometimes quite extreme reactions of group members ('I found it excruciating. I couldn't bear it'. PACE member) cannot be assumed to correspond to how the same people, or others like them, would react to this programme outside of the control situation.

One other interesting measure of this can be seen in the responses to a question I asked all the groups after we had concluded our formal interview: could anyone remember seeing it when it was first broadcast? Given that the BBC's viewing figures show that it enjoyed 22 per cent of the audience share when it was first broadcast (some eighteen months before the interviews), it might have been expected that approximately twenty or more individuals would have remembered the programme. In actual fact, only three people could remember it at all although, to pitch the claim at its lowest, a percentage of the others are likely to have been in the vicinity of a television at the time of the programme's transmission and to have been part, therefore, of its notional audience.

The exaggerations, then, we can take to be a feature of the control situation which invited people to participate in a group viewing with much higher degrees of concentration than they would normally bring to their television viewing. We must also allow for the fact, demonstrated by the questionnaires, that many people brought to the interview strong feelings about the media generally and used the opportunity of a discussion with an outside interlocutor to vent these feelings. And in many ways that is what they were encouraged to do: the questionnaires and the interviews were structured in such a way as to allow for this possibility and to ensure that the responses to the programme, and the responses to the media generally, could be separated out.

None of the qualifications that have just been made take away from the fact that groups of people took similar attitudes, and that the patterns of response tell us something significant about 'the cultural glue that binds so many of us together in clusters of common interpretation' (Lewis, 1991: 57). That cultural glue was of course most evident inside each group's own discussion, but there are in addition certain common features threaded through the group interviews which show a deeper patterning of response.

The most striking common feature is the resistance shown to the integrative embrace of the programme. With the exception of the Olympia Women's Group, and certain sections of the PACE and Cornerstone groups, most respondents performed a resistant reading of the programme. For a documentary which was so studiously 'middle-of-the-road', it is remarkable how far it failed to recruit sympathy from the groups. Previous studies have shown how television tends to cultivate attitudes sympathetic to a centrist, or what appears to be a centrist view point, through a process described as 'mainstreaming'. As Morgan (Gerbner, Gross, Morgan and Signorielli, 1982: 246) puts it:

> Some people are to the left of the television mainstream, and others are to the right; in order to maximise its audience, television appears to steer a middle course – and in the process absorbs and homogenises people with otherwise divergent orientations. This process of convergence is called mainstreaming.

The ability of the interviewees to maintain a resistant reading obviously derives from their strength of feeling about television bias generally but, as the interviews demonstrate, they were able to apply their general critique to the detail of this programme in highly specific ways.

The selectivity employed by the interviewees in picking through the evidence of the programme in order to construct their case is itself quite striking. It is not surprising, perhaps, that Catholics detected a unionist bias, while Protestants found evidence of the opposite: in this way the programme functioned rather like the Rorschach ink blot test. Just as the interpretations of the ink blot help the psychologist to understand how people create meanings, so too these interviews show how the selectivity of perception is framed by the ideological and cultural backgrounds of those viewing the programme. As Morley (1986) has observed, the viewer creates the meaning of the programme from the restricted range of cultural resources which his or her structural position has allowed them access to. The two dominant ideologies at work here are, clearly, nationalist and unionist, but before turning to look at how they frame their own specific meanings it is important to look at the influence of gender and class.

Women, generally speaking, were more open to accepting, or at least to negotiating with, the intended message of the programme. This is in keeping with previous research (e.g. see Loomis, 1990), which shows that while men were more likely to adopt a tone of superior knowledge, women are more likely to confess to deficits in their own knowledge. In accordance with this the Protestant working-class women of the Olympia Women's Group offered no resistance to the presentation of history provided by the programme. As one woman said 'It taught me things I didn't know'.

This open acceptance of the educational purpose of the programme was accompanied by a regretful admission from most of the women that they didn't know enough about their own history – 'All that history . . . we didn't go into that at school'.

This same sense of ignorance would, it seemed, on other occasions give rise to feelings of impotence and anger, particularly in the face of unfavourable media presentations of the Protestant community. Before viewing the programme all those present had used the questionnaire sheets to indicate their belief that both the BBC and Ulster Television are biased in favour of a nationalist outlook, and this belief was given forceful expression in the discussion as indicated by remarks such as, 'Many's the time I felt like lifting the poker and putting it through the TV' and ' It makes us feel like we're wrong and we don't know why'.

Without wishing to surrender their belief that all television is somehow biased against them, the women could find little fault with *Orange, Green and Yellow*. The discussion concluded with a remark which was almost, but not quite, an endorsement: 'There hasn't been the programme yet that's unbiased. This is the first one to come near'.

The Catholic women from the Falls Community Council were also, in their individual questionnaires, able to accept that the programme had fulfilled its educational purpose: five out of the group of eight indicated that they had learned something. The discussion however opened up several lines of critical enquiry which quickly began to undermine confidence in the neutrality of the programme. An early challenge was made to one of the more fundamental parts of the programme's construction, the cartographer's map of the city from which the programme takes its title: 'If you take the map, orange, green, and yellow. The shipyard was in yellow. And like, immediately I thought, well, that should be in orange'.

This observation brought immediate murmurs of assent, and the point was then elaborated by another group member: 'The industrial and commercial parts were shown as yellow when they definitely are not'.

This was taken by the group to be a telling fault, and further evidence of the same bias. One woman provided an articulate overview of what she saw as the main fault of the programme:

> It didn't show a causal effect between things happening and other things happening . . . it was as if sectarianism had happened by accident. Take the man from the Housing Executive, he said we were set up at the time of general unrest. He didn't explain the reason why they were set up was because Catholics couldn't get houses . . .

A strikingly similar deconstruction was performed by the group of men from the Falls Community Council who, in a separate discussion, attacked the programme's presentation of sectarianism as a force operating outside any human agency:

The British government never gets mentioned. To my knowledge of Irish history there was always some exploitation, but here sectarianism is talked about without any mention whatsoever of the British government.

Another speaker added:

You have to remember that all those people who had power were involved in the Orange Order. The Orange Order is one of the most sectarian forces going, but it doesn't even get mentioned in it. I think the BBC and Ulster Television are afraid. They daren't do an in-depth investigation of the Orange Order because it would ruffle too many feathers . . . I think the BBC is afraid of the Orange Order.

The view that the BBC is influenced by the Orange Order was not shared by the members of the Orange Order themselves, or at least by the members of the Clover Hill Temperance Lodge who viewed the programme in the Orange Order offices in Clifton Street. On the contrary, they watched the programme alert for signs of a quite different bias, a bias against the Orange Order and the Protestant people of Ulster. They were not to be disappointed. A significant fault occurred at the very start of the programme. The opening shots of *Orange, Green and Yellow* are old magazine illustrations of the Home Rule riots. Images of mob violence, accompanied by the sound of hubbub on the soundtrack, provide a striking illustration of how sectarianism has long been a feature of Belfast life. One alert member of the group, however, himself a writer and researcher, was able to point out that only two of the four illustrations, taken, he said, from the *London Illustrated News* of the time, were actually of the Belfast riots; the other two images were published in the same issue of the *London Illustrated News* but were actually illustrations of riots which had taken place in France fifty years previously. [In interview with me Barry Cowan conceded that some licence may have been taken with these graphics in order to convey a strong visual sense of a riot.] This sleight-of-hand was not regarded as exceptional, but rather was seen by the group to be typical of the dissembling nature of the BBC:

I lost my faith with the BBC, and even with their news programmes when they showed a scene of burning refuse at the start of the Belfast Corporation worker's strike, and that was given out as a scene of a riot in the early 1970s. And I contacted the BBC, and I couldn't get a response.

These instances were not taken by the group as simply the tricks-of-the-trade of programme production; instead they were seen as evidence of a deeper malaise inside the media. Before viewing the programme the group had given a 100 per cent 'yes' to the question 'Do you believe that the BBC is biased?', and had responded in the same way and with the same unanimity to the question of bias in Ulster Television. Their deep conviction that the media are biased against Unionism, and against the Protestant people, was confirmed by this programme, which was described by one member as a 'classic':

GF:   In what way a classic?

I said it was a classic because it was the stereotype view we've had to endure from the days of the Civil Rights movement, of Protestant guilt and Catholic grievance, that's the underlying theme which comes through.

When asked to give detailed references to show how that bias manifested itself in the programme, the group was able to see evidence at every point:

The programme began with an historical account but as it went on it said that gerrymandering occurred because the Protestant community so established it. That's where I started saying to myself now this is propaganda and the whole thing has taken a nasty turn . . .

By contrast with the strongly oppositional readings performed by the Orange Order and the members of the Falls Community Council, albeit from diametrically opposed political perspectives, the more middle-class members of the PACE and Cornerstone communities were able to accept the programme's presentation as conforming in general terms to their own view of Belfast's history. Class is obviously a factor here, but the pattern is by no means a clear one. If women and middle-class groups both tend to be more accepting of the programme, then one might expect the greatest degree of acceptance to come from the Women's Institute. The reality is that the Women's Institute group evinced a strong distaste for the programme. Their resistance, it should be said, was not based on an oppositional reading of the facts presented, but rather on the belief that television should find other ways to assist mutual understanding. Members of the group could see no social or political benefits deriving from this form of historical enquiry:

Why must we always be asked to look backwards? There was a programme on last night – did anyone see it? It was about the massacre of Protestants in Drogheda, and it was simply dreadful. And it horrifies me, absolutely horrifies me, to think that this could be going out to schools.

These things may be real but, you know, they hold the mirror up too much.

When challenged by the view that the media must report reality, the group did not feel any need to withdraw:

GF: Well what about the reporting of Bosnia? We don't expect the news bulletins to tell us all about the good things that happened in Bosnia today, do we? We expect to hear about conflict, about violence.

Why not hear the good news about Bosnia? Why not? I'm sure there are plenty of things we'd all be interested in hearing about. I would be very interested for example, to hear about handicrafts in Bosnia. But of course we only hear about shootings and about the terrible things that are going on at the moment.

The idea that television should do more to try to tell the 'good news' found strong echoes in the PACE and Cornerstone communities. Working-class groups had a diametrically opposite view. For the East Belfast community workers, or the men and women of the Falls Community Council, programmes like *Orange, Green and Yellow* fail because they do not face up to the harsher realities of life in Northern Ireland. However hard-hitting the programme may have seemed to those who produced it, or those who broadcast it, the documentary still seemed, to those who live in the deprived areas of Belfast, to be soft around the edges. Studies done by Cohen, Adoni and Baritz (1990: 190) show that this is the pattern in other international conflict situations:

> . . . viewers [in conflict societies] perceive 'real' social conflicts as more severe than their portrayal in the news . . . They accept the notion that there is a picture of severe social conflicts on television, but at the same time they believe that in the real world the degree of severity is even greater.

This is not the only area of congruence between the Catholic and Protestant groups. While, in an obvious sense, the readings made from a nationalist and a unionist perspective oppose each other, the alienation described by both communities seems to stem from a common source, or at least to converge to a common point. This might best be described as a vexation with the tendency of television to exclude the more authentic voices of Belfast's communities in order to promote a safe and reassuring view of the city's sectarian divisions. The widespread irritation with Sam McAughtry, for example, would not seem to be based on any strong dislike of McAughtry as an individual, or on any offence caused by his contribution to the programme, but seems directed rather at the editorial decision to select him to speak on the Protestant experience. In the eyes of both Protestants and Catholics he is too moderate, too liberal and too practised a media performer to have any credibility in this role. Even politicians like Brian Feeney and Cecil Walker, despite their electoral mandate, fail to convince as representatives of working-class experience. For Protestant groups there is, as the discussion with the Orange Order and the East Belfast Community Workers revealed, a poignant concern with the inarticulacy of their own community running underneath a range of their criticisms, but a programme like *Orange, Green and Yellow* only serves to confirm their belief that the media are not interested in hearing their viewpoint in any case: 'I find that media people are very cynical and don't have immediate rapport with the Protestants because of their own cultural and philosophical background' (Man in Orange Order group).

For groups like the Falls Community Council, the Broadcasting Ban (still in existence at the time of the survey) is the clear proof that spokespersons from their community will not be given access to the airwaves, but the blame for excluding other, non-Sinn Féin spokespersons is placed firmly at the feet of the broadcasters, not the government:'You don't have to get politicians. You can get people who are involved in their community and who are fighting for their community' (Woman from the Falls Community Council).

The absences are read as exclusions. The broadcasters are seen to be instrumental in promoting an establishment view – dissembling, complacent, and unwilling to make space for dissident voices. For the Catholics and Protestants from the troubled parts of the city interviewed in this study the mirror that is held up by television succeeds in rendering them invisible. It is ironic that a programme which set out to explore the reality of a divided city only served to unite them in that belief.

## Conclusions

On the evidence of this research it could be concluded that the hopes of the Cultural Traditions Group failed to be realised in the consumption of this programme, and for reasons which should prove significant for other ventures of this kind. Before detailing these reasons it should be emphasised that this venture was only a first tentative exploration of the use of the mass media by the Cultural Traditions Group, and that many other imaginative ventures have followed. The lessons from *Orange, Green and Yellow*, however, remain of interest to others beyond the world of community relations, though they are lessons that have to be drawn carefully.

The first of these is that no matter how carefully the message is encoded by the programme-makers, or written into the DNA of the programme, it is still capable of a wide range of oppositional interpretations by those who view it. The simple idea of an undifferentiated audience passively absorbing the content of a television documentary and, consciously or unconsciously, being shaped by the experience must be discarded, and replaced by an awareness of many different audiences, all of them performing their own reading of the text and capable of using those readings to confirm their existing beliefs.

A second important message concerns the role of the programme makers, in a structure like the BBC which guarantees a degree of editorial freedom. As can be seen from the approaches taken by Flying Fox and Bridge Television, the professional ethos of programme makers militates against any attempt to recruit them to work to the agenda of any external agency. While this degree of professional integrity provides a reassuring guarantee that the medium cannot be abused for any suspect purpose, it provides an equal bulwark against it being employed to transmit other messages, however laudable in intent. An additional feature of the independence of the media professionals is the creation of a self-referencing value system which amounts, in practice, to a solipsistic indifference to the views of the audience. This is particularly regrettable in the Northern Ireland situation where the alienation from television's messages is both deep and widespread.

For many of those interviewed in this study, television fails to provide a credible account of experience, and is therefore mistrusted in its representation of other communities and other viewpoints. Common to groups on both sides of the sectarian divide is the belief that television selects opinions from a narrow range of the social spectrum, and deliberately excludes the voices of working-class communities in order to preserve a self-serving set of middle-class values.

# References

Antennae (1993) 'Hope And History: Using Broadcasting For Community Relations Purposes in Northern Ireland'. A consultancy report for the Community Relations Council.

Berger, Arthur Asa (1991) *Media Research Techniques*. London: Sage.

Burns, Tom (1977) *The BBC: Public Institution and Private World*. London: Macmillan.

Cohen, A., H. Adoni and C. R. Baritz, (1990) *Social Conflict and Television News*. London: Sage.

Crozier, Maurna (1992) 'Cultural Traditions: Long Term Politics', paper delivered to the American Committee for Irish Studies, Galway.

Cumberbatch, Guy and Denis Howitt, (1989) *A Measure Of Uncertainty*. London: John Libbey.

Gerber, George, Larry Gross, Michael Morgan and Nancy Signorielli (1982) 'Charting the Mainstream: Television's Contributions to Political Orientations', *Journal of Communication'*, 32(2): 101–27.

Hall, Stuart (1977) 'Culture, The Media, and the Ideological Effect' in James Curran, Michael Gurevitch and Janet Woollacott (eds) *Mass Communication and Society*. London: Edward Arnold.

Kumar, K. (1977) 'Holding The Middle Ground: The BBC and The Public Broadcaster' in James Curran, Michael Gurevitch and Janet Woollacott (eds) *Mass Communication And Society*. London: Edward Arnold.

Lewis, Justin (1991) *The Ideological Octopus*. London: Routledge.

Loomis, A. (1990) 'Semiotics And Ideology: A Textual And Audience Study Of A Documentary Video Text', Master's Thesis, University of Massachusetts.

Lull, James (1990) *Inside Family Viewing: Ethnographic Research on Television's Audiences*. London: Routledge.

Miller, David (1994) *Don't Mention The War*. London: Pluto.

Morley, David (1980) *The Nationwide Audience*. London: British Film Institute.

Morley, David (1986) *Family Television*. London: Comedia.

Morley, David (1992) *Television, Audiences and Cultural Studies*. London: Routledge.

Whyte, John (1990) *Interpreting Northern Ireland*. London: Clarendon.

Willis, P. (1980) 'Notes On Method' in S. Hall, D. Hobson, A. Lowe and P. Willis (eds) *Culture, Media, Language*. London: Hutchinson.

# 6

# Dominant Ideologies and Media Power: The Case of Northern Ireland

*David Miller*

The representation of political controversy is itself regularly a matter of political controversy. This suggests that the parameters of public debate are often informed by assumptions about the power of the media to shape public opinion and political decision making. Yet the investigation and specification of media power has slipped almost entirely off the research agenda of sociology and especially of media and cultural studies. This chapter examines the highly influential critique in sociology of the 'Dominant Ideology Thesis' (Abercrombie *et al.*, 1980; 1986; 1990). This was an attack on those theories which emphasised the role of ideology in the reproduction of class inequality and in particular in winning consent for the dominant order (Hall *et al.*, 1978; Hall, 1977). Although this chapter accepts many of the criticisms of the dominant ideology thesis, it will also be argued that the critique and its theorising of the relationship between the material and the ideological is seriously adrift from contemporary empirical evidence.

The argument will be illustrated by reference to empirical research on responses to media coverage of the Northern Ireland conflict. There is a strong case for examining these arguments in relation to the Northern Ireland conflict, because here there have been long running and consistent attempts to win popular consent and to police the media by the state. The extent to which such attempts are successful ought to illuminate debates about the importance of ideology in the reproduction of contemporary power relations.

Briefly, the critique of the dominant ideology thesis challenged the

> Marxist argument that the stability of capitalism could be explained by reference to the existence of a dominant ideology which had the consequence of incorporating the working class into the capitalist system, whether by leading them to

accept false beliefs, by obscuring the real character of economic exploitation in capitalism, or by blocking the development of oppositional ideas (Hill, 1990:2).

The authors contested this on both empirical and theoretical grounds arguing that

> ideology does have significant effects but these are primarily on the dominant rather than subordinate class. What has been important for the stability of capitalism is the coherence of the dominant class itself, and ideology has played a major role in securing this. The Marxist position was criticised for its failure to analyse the apparatus or mechanisms by which dominant beliefs were transmitted and how such beliefs were received by subordinates; and for its assumption that the human subject was an ideological dupe, incapable of independent thought and rational action (Hill, 1990:2)

The critique of the dominant ideology thesis applies especially to structuralist Marxism (and to structural functionalism) and apparently less so to the more sophisticated Gramscian influenced theorising in media and cultural studies. Nevertheless, as Abercrombie has argued, there is no fundamental break between some Gramscian writing on hegemony (e.g. Bennett, Mercer and Woollacott, 1986) and the cruder versions of the thesis. In both

> it is not clear what mechanisms will normally produce a hegemonic outcome out of the mélange of social forces; to have a principle that guaranteed such an outcome would reproduce the crudest features of a dominant ideology thesis (Abercrombie, 1990: 202; see also McGuigan, 1992).

The conclusion of the critique was that there is no necessary relationship between culture and economics: 'In late capitalism . . . the cultural becomes increasingly independent from the requirements of capitalism as an economic system' (Turner, 1990: 252) and that the stability of capitalism was best explained by reference to what Marx called the 'dull compulsion of the economic'. The position advanced in this chapter is that the dominant ideology thesis does indeed overplay the integrative function of ideology, but equally, it is seriously underplayed by Abercrombie, Hill and Turner. Whether it is a necessary requirement for the reproduction of capitalism or not, powerful organisations and institutions do in fact engage in information management (secrecy, censorship and propaganda) in order to pursue their interests and legitimate their actions. Furthermore the pursuit of such strategies do make identifiable differences to the distribution of power and resources in society.

Abercrombie *et al.* rightly criticise theorists of dominant ideology and in particular Hall (1988) for concentrating on 'content analysis of the ideological message without any informed investigation of how this message is received, and thus fall into the trap of uncritically attributing effects to ideologies' (Hill, 1990: 21). Elsewhere Abercrombie (1990[1]; 1996) emphasises that a proper examination of the media needs to examine the 'three moments', by which he means media content and reception, but also the process of media production.

(Such a position was of course, as Abercrombie states, advocated by Hall, in the early 1970s). However, this neglects two further 'moments' which need to be examined. These are first the moment of 'promotion' and second that of 'outcomes'. That is, there is a need to examine first promotional strategies of government departments, business interests and pressures and interest groups and their interaction with media institutions, and second, the extent to which media coverage or public opinion are translated in to public action and the extent to which opinion or action impact on decision making and outcomes in society.

Extending the number of moments to include promotion and outcomes and acknowledging that there is no necessary determinate relationship between each, clearly makes the demonstration of ideological effects even harder than is suggested by Abercrombie. However, it also has the effect of enabling us to see the mechanisms by which media content is (or is not) related to the promotional strategies of dominant (and subordinate) groups. The key mechanism missing from the dominant ideology thesis is of course human agency which operates within the context of already existing structures and remakes them. This opens up the question of outcomes. That is, what are the consequences for human action and decision making of particular beliefs and ideologies and how does this affect the distribution of power in society? Both of these moments have been given less than full attention in recent media and cultural studies.

Even if greater attention is given to the genesis of propaganda and public relations messages on the one hand and to the impacts of public belief and ideology on the other, we are still left with empirical questions about the precise links between each of the five moments – promotion, production, definition, reception and outcomes – on specific occasions over different issues. The next sections deal in turn with each of these as they apply to Northern Ireland, with a much heavier emphasis on the moment of reception since it has been the area where there has been the most doubt and uncertainty over the last decade and a half.

## Moments in Media Production and Reception

### The Moment of Promotion

Since Abercrombie and colleagues do not examine the link between social institutions and cultural production, a very important part of the process is missing from the critique of the dominant ideology thesis. Even if some sociologists think that there is no link between state power and matters ideological, it is clear that governments are not so sanguine; hence the large sums which are spent each year on managing the media and public opinion (Cockerell *et al.*, 1984; Franklin, 1994; Miller, 1994b). In the case of Northern Ireland, official bodies have in recent years markedly increased their promotional expenditure. By 1992–93 official figures show a spend of more than £22m per annum by the NIO, Industrial Development Board and Tourist Board alone (not including the Army and RUC) (Miller, 1994b: 292).

However, the ability of the British state to construct and impose primary definitions of the conflict in Northern Ireland is subject to a number of limitations, such as internal rivalries and divisions as well as contradictions in PR strategies. On the one hand, terrorism is portrayed as a major threat to democracy which must be countered by extraordinary means, and on the other, Northern Ireland is marketed as a peaceful and attractive inward investment and tourist destination. The Northern Ireland 'you'll never know, unless you go' as the Tourist Board advertising campaign has it (see Miller 1993a).

Furthermore, official definitions necessarily compete (or are engaged in struggle) with alternative and oppositional definitions for media space and are not always successful. Finally the official approach is also likely to run into problems if it changes dramatically as it appeared to do in the peace process with changed official orientations towards Sinn Féin (see Miller and McLaughlin, 1996).

## The Moment of Production

Even without such problems, official sources are not able always to set media agendas in all the ways they would like (Miller, 1993a; 1993b; 1994b). This relates in part to the fact that media and state agendas do not always converge. News values do not easily accommodate the 'good news' image of Northern Ireland. However, official sources have tended to dominate the good news which does appear.

It is also true that a significant public service ethos remains in broadcasting and the ideology of the 'fourth estate' remains in parts of the press although there are clear limits to the practice of a watchdog role (Murdock, 1991; Murphy, 1991). Most importantly, however, the reporting of 'security' matters and the frameworks of understanding utilised by the mainstream British media have tended to take their cue from official sources (Miller, 1994b).

## The Moment of Definition

For Abercrombie 'It is difficult to see textual ideology in television as a whole let alone popular culture as a whole. The modern cultural experience is of a pluralization of texts' (1990: 212).[2] However, this is not the case in relation to coverage of Northern Ireland. Official definitions do tend to dominate media accounts of the Northern Ireland conflict. The language of 'terrorism' and 'security forces' is almost universal and the British state is very rarely seen as anything other than a neutral arbiter in the conflict on British television. However, the extent to which official accounts dominate depends also on matters of genre and format as well as on where and when the material is published (Miller, 1994b; Schlesinger *et al.*, 1983).

So far I have argued that the first three moments do on occasion show a strong causal relationship each tending to reinforce the other in favour of official definitions, especially in security matters. I have also argued that there is no necessary link between each of the moments. Each requires active ideological labour on the part of a myriad of politicians, decision makers, promotional and media professionals.

However, the next moment, that of audience reception, is the one where there has been the greatest doubt and uncertainty in media and cultural studies and to a lesser extent in sociology. Below I review the empirical evidence from my own audience research and from the other available evidence. First of all it is worth reviewing the arguments put forward by Abercrombie in his critique of the dominant ideology thesis.

## The Moment of Reception

The 'most important' problem of the dominant ideology thesis is that the 'audience is presented as relatively uncreative in its responses to an ideological text' (Abercombie,1990: 201) and that audiences absorb 'the ideological content of television, film, or popular music without reflection' (1990: 216). However, as Abercrombie notes 'in most of the literature audience passivity has been discarded in favour of audience activity' (1990: 216). He goes on to highlight three aspects of activity: choice, differentiation and creativity.

By choice he means that viewers do not usually watch all episodes of a particular series, may be inattentive during programmes and that many people end up not watching the programmes they prefer 'largely because of compromises within the family' (1990: 217). Viewing habits are seen as somewhat chaotic and if they have effects these must be varied and contradictory. According to Abercrombie this 'must suggest an incoherent ideological effect' (1990: 217). However, this is only the case if it is accepted that there are a diverse range of meanings equally available across television on Northern Ireland. Furthermore this ignores the fact that the television programmes which gain the largest audiences also tend to be the most closed around official perspectives.

By differentiation, Abercrombie means that people watch and respond to television in different ways and by creativity that audiences give their own meanings to what they watch. Both of these points are the familiar territory of the theorists of the 'active audience' and I will consider them together. A key problem for theories of the active audience is the way in which the concept of 'meaning' is used. This confusion can be traced back at least as far as the 'encoding/decoding' model advanced by Stuart Hall (Hall, 1980) amongst others (see Harris, 1992). Reception is conceived to be a process where audiences make 'readings' of programmes. Crudely, audiences are thought to 'read' messages either in accordance with the dominant code, to negotiate their meaning or to decode them oppositionally. The problem is that this blurs together understanding and response (e.g. agreement/ disagreement, interest/ disinterest etc.). The concept makes it difficult to account for a person who might understand the information or ideology in a programmes, but disbelieve or disagree with it. The vast majority of people in my own research read or decoded media coverage of violence in Northern Ireland in a similar way. The real question is, did they agree or disagree with the media definition of the violence and thus to what extent were they influenced by the media.

Much current work on the audience starts with assumptions about media power which actively prevent the investigation of influence. Indeed, even the theorisation of influence has become 'awkward' and it has slipped almost entirely off the research agenda (Corner, 1995). If we restore questions about beliefs, sources of belief and media influence, then audience research would look somewhat different. In what follows, I want to take the examples of two separate pieces of research conducted by myself on media coverage of Northern Ireland. The first, which takes the SAS killings in Gibraltar in March 1988 as its focus, examines the impact of misinformation on British public belief. The second looks more broadly at perceptions of violence in Northern Ireland. In both it will be argued that the media can be shown to influence beliefs and ideas about the conflict. Of course, such influence is not direct nor is it guaranteed by media content. People do actively evaluate, interpret and respond to media coverage. The recognition that such processes intervene between media texts and 'effects' does not mean however, as some have concluded, that the media have no influence or power.

## Audience Reception: Method and Sample

The research reported here examined the processes by which people come to 'make up their minds' about the conflict in Ireland. It seeks to establish what people 'know' and then to trace the sources of this knowledge and belief. I asked groups of people to write their own news bulletins using photographic stills taken from previous television news programmes covering the Northern Ireland conflict. This was to investigate whether they could recall and reproduce news programmes. The bulletins were then compared with what the groups actually believed to be true and the reasons for their acceptance or rejection of the television message. These questions were examined by the administration of a small number of questions which each of the participants answered in writing and then a period of group discussion.

The research was carried out between November 1988 and February 1990. At first it concentrated simply on perceptions of the Northern Ireland conflict in general and a total of nineteen groups including 144 people took part. Two types of group were selected. Firstly, groups of people who might be expected to have some special knowledge about the conflict in Northern Ireland. These included four nationalist and two unionist groups living in the North as well as one group of serving British soldiers. The other groups were selected because they were not necessarily expected to have any special knowledge of the conflict and included four Scottish groups and three English groups. All the discussions were conducted with pre-existing groups of people who work, live or socialise together, chosen to reflect different sociodemographic factors such as age, region, nationality, class and gender (see list of groups in the appendix, p. xx). However, it also appeared from comments in some of these groups that it was important to try to investigate beliefs about specific incidents in more depth. An obvious candidate for investigation, due to the intensity of controversy surrounding the event itself and its coverage, was the Gibraltar shootings which had occurred on 6 March 1988. Not only was there an offical version of the event available, but an alternative version of the killings was, perhaps, more widely distributed than in the case of any other special forces killings in Northern Ireland itself. As a consequence, the Gibraltar killings ought to have the potential to show wide public disbelief in the official version. Eleven further groups, seven Scottish groups, one group of British soldiers, two Northern Ireland groups and two groups of American students, altogether including 143 people, took part in this second phase of the study (see list of groups in the appendix, pp. 143–4).

Each group was divided into up to six news teams and given identical sets of photographic stills. In the first phase of the research on perceptions of the Northern conflict, the pictures were taken from actual news bulletins and represented different aspects of routine coverage of Northern Ireland. The groups which took part in the research on the Gibraltar killings were given eight pictures specifically about the Gibraltar killings in addition to some of the photographs used in the first phase of research. A series of questions were asked immediately following the 'presentation' of the news bulletin. All questions were open ended and explored perceptions of the news, perceptions of Northern Ireland and sources of information, belief and memory.[3]

## The Gibraltar Study

All publicly available information about what happened in Gibraltar had come via the mass media. Even in Northern Ireland the only publicly available sources of information in addition to the mainstream media are the alternative and radical papers of each community. The only people who knew what had happened in Gibraltar first hand were those that were killed (Mairead Farrell, Dan McCann and Sean Savage), their killers, the eyewitnesses and (possibly) the other member(s) of the IRA unit. There was a range of information available, with a quite clear division in the press between the majority of papers which supported and actively propagandised on behalf of the official view promoted by the state (*Sunday Times, Sun, Sunday Telegraph, Daily Express, Daily Mail, Daily Star* and *Daily Mirror*) and those papers and television current affairs journalists (*Observer, Independent, Guardian, This Week,* BBC Northern Ireland's *Spotlight, Private Eye*) which attempted to investigate the discrepancies in the official line and come to a judgement about what had happened in Gibraltar. In television news some questions were asked, but the emphasis was on the official state version (see Miller, 1991). The question is which version did viewers and readers believe?

Respondents varied in their beliefs about many of the 'facts' of the case and there were sometimes disagreements about what had happened. But a substantial proportion of respondents did believe various of the details of the official version which turned out to be false, such as reports that the IRA members had planted a bomb or that they were armed. Some also believed subsequently emphasised details of the official case, such as the alleged challenges made by the SAS or the alleged 'movements' in response by the IRA members.

The motivations of the SAS in shooting Farrell, McCann and Savage were hardly questioned by the groups. Even amongst those who did not believe the IRA members were armed, there was wide agreement that the SAS men had *believed* that Farrell, McCann and Savage had planted a bomb and were able to set it off. For one group 'the fact that the terrorists proved to be unarmed created an international incident. But the shooting had taken place in the belief that these people had been armed.' Another group wrote that the fact that there was no bomb had only been discovered after the shooting: 'Three members of the IRA were shot dead in Gibraltar, suspected of placing a bomb in a car. When the bomb disposal unit set off a controlled explosion there was no bomb' (Retired women, Paisley). Even groups which were otherwise very critical of the shootings appeared to believe that the lack of a bomb was only discovered after the shooting: 'After the bomb disposal team were called in to search the car in which the three had parked, it was discovered that there were no explosives in the car' (Nationalist group, West Belfast).

Although it was more common for respondents to believe key elements of the official case than details associated with alternative explanations, some respondents did reject official 'facts' and believed instead in alternative versions. In general these 'alternative facts' had also been gleaned either from the press or by culling details and fragments from television news. This can be seen most clearly in relation to what was believed about Carmen Proetta, whose photograph was among the photographic stills given to each of the Gibraltar groups.

Perhaps the most bitter of the definitional struggles over the Gibraltar killings was that for the reputation and credibility of key eye witness Carmen Proetta. Following Proetta's appearance on *Death on the Rock*, Thames Television's investigative programme, official sources in Gibraltar and one government minister provided journalists with information which resulted in a series of defamatory stories about Proetta, which alleged among other things that she used to be a prostitute. The allegations were untrue and seven national newspapers were forced to apologise and pay substantial damages. All the apologies were of much less prominence than the original stories, appearing on inside pages and taking up no more than a few sentences in a single column.

In my study, 30 per cent of the general Gibraltar sample did feel able to say they believed Proetta to be a prostitute or similar and a further 15 per cent that she was possibly a prostitute. This is in itself a remarkable finding, given that the stories discrediting Proetta appeared almost exclusively in the press, mainly in the English tabloids, and were wholly false. There were similar stories discrediting Proetta in the *Sunday Times, Daily Telegraph* and *Sunday Telegraph*, but by and large television news stayed clear of recycling false information about Proetta.

Unsurprisingly the nationalist group in West Belfast were uniformly critical of British TV news regarding it as 'pro-British' or 'anti-Irish'. Although the majority of the group (six out of eight) listed nationalist papers such as the *Irish News, Andersonstown News* and Sinn Féin's *An Phoblacht/ Republican News* among their reading matter, five also listed English tabloids, predominantly the *Sun*. Five members of the group were aware of the allegations against Proetta, but rejected them in comments such as 'we were told by the British news and papers that she was a prostitute, which I do not believe'.

The rejection by the bulk of this group of the Proetta 'story' is testament to the power of political identity in withstanding propaganda assaults. However, one of the group who listed the papers he read as the *Sun*, the *Star* and the *Irish News*, did believe that Proetta was a prostitute, even though he also stated that 'we want the British soldiers off our streets and we want our nationality back'. This is evidence that even when an oppositional political identity is a strong part of everyday life it is possible for elements of official propaganda messages to be accepted.

The media assault on the credibility of Proetta had continued throughout the summer of 1988, but reached its apotheosis during the inquest in September. Official sources had suggested that she would change her testimony and when she gave evidence the bulk of the press, and significantly, television news, misleadingly reported that she had (see Miller, 1994b: 233–6).

Although perceiving Proetta as a prostitute did not necessarily lead to scepticism about her evidence or truthfulness, such perceptions did have their role to play. Many of those who thought that Proetta was a prostitute also believed that she had withdrawn her account or given a different version at the inquest. For example, one participant held up the picture of Proetta and asked the rest of the team 'Is she the witness?'. Another participant replied to general assent 'Yes, she retracted her evidence'. Some of the Scottish ex-prisoners group were also convinced that Proetta had retracted:

> An eye witness saw the whole view of what happened and said the SAS just pulled guns out and shot them without warning. But later on when she was being interviewed by police she denied all knowledge (Group from Scottish Association for the Care and Resettlement of Offenders – SACRO, Glasgow).

The other SACRO group echoed this: 'She said the SAS shot them down in cold blood, but later on in the inquiry she said that she made it up'. These groups had mostly believed that Proetta was a prostitute and that she had changed her evidence, but were nonetheless very critical of the actions of the SAS in the killings.

In the above examples the people who believed Proetta had retracted also believed that she was a prostitute. But there were also some groups who believed she had retracted even though they did not believe that she was a prostitute. Here again we can see the influence of media misinformation. The retired women in the Paisley group were critical of the shootings and did not believe that Proetta was a prostitute. They were, however, confused about what had happened in Gibraltar primarily because they had become doubtful about Proetta's testimony. As one of the woman in the group put it 'can we believe in the integrity of the eye-witnesses? Through the newspapers we were led to believe that at least one was of doubtful character and not always truthful.' Perhaps more surprisingly, some of the participants in the nationalist group in West Belfast accepted that Proetta had changed her evidence. They had explicitly rejected the story about prostitution, but they believed as one put it that 'She said one story, then she said another'.

Many groups were thus influenced by the smear campaign against the credibility of key witness Carmen Proetta – thinking that she was a prostitute and/or that she had retracted her evidence. Nonetheless considerable ambivalence remained regarding the Gibraltar affair, especially among groups critical of the government on other political grounds. They were particularly unsure of the legitimacy of the SAS action and what had happened in Gibraltar. One team of Scottish pensioners, who thought television news to be unbiased, who read the *Daily Record* or the *Daily Express*, and most of whom thought Carmen Proetta was a prostitute, sounded a note of caution at the end of their news bulletin:

> Was the army right to shoot? We must leave that for future generations to decide. Nobody has sympathy for the IRA but in the shooting at Gibraltar had we taken a leaf from their book?

# Perceptions of Violence in Northern Ireland

The second study examined perceptions of violence in Northern Ireland. As noted above a similar method of investigation was used here – groups writing their own news stories using photographic stills taken from actual television news programmes covering the Northern Ireland conflict, followed by questions and group discussion. Respondents from both studies were almost universally agreed that television showed life in Northern Ireland as mostly violent (more than 95 per cent), but more than half of the respondents rejected this as a factual picture of life in Northern Ireland.[4] Nonetheless a large proportion of the English and Scottish respondents (42 per cent) were unwilling to visit Northern Ireland, almost all because they were scared of the threat of violence. As evidence for this most cited the media, some commenting 'Because of what I hear on TV I believe it to be very violent', while others regarded media coverage as a transparent reflection of life in Northern Ireland, as in 'TV news seems to be merely reporting the facts'.

It was evident that many people not living in Northern Ireland had heard accounts which suggested that life in Northern Ireland was not all violent, but that some had difficulty in accepting this even at an intellectual level. They continued to believe what they saw as the news account or remained unsure or confused. One respondent whose only sources were listed as TV and newspapers wrote 'It's seen as mostly violent but it's probably not like that everywhere', while another who had listed 'friends' as one of her sources put 'I don't know, I've never been there, but I've *heard* it's mostly peaceful' (her emphasis). Others commented 'I don't know. My son said it was nice'; 'would probably think it was more violent than it is in reality', and 'I couldn't say for sure as you see violence on the TV, but friends who live there say it's fairly peaceful and condemn any violence'. In other cases people were simply confused about the amount of violence in Northern Ireland. The clearest reason for this was media coverage of the conflict.

However, the more common response for those who had heard indirect evidence that life in Northern Ireland was not all violent, was a rejection (at least at the intellectual level) of what was seen as the TV news account. Sources for these rejections were many and varied. The main sources of indirect experience were respondents speaking with people who had been to Ireland on business, holiday or in the army, or to people who had lived in Ireland or their relatives. Such accounts can be used to strengthen a critique gained from alternative sources of media information. One retired woman who quoted the *Guardian* and TV documentaries as a reason for rejecting the TV news account also mentioned an ex-colleague as a source, 'I worked beside a man from the suburbs eight miles from Belfast. He had never seen any violence except results of bombing in the city.'

The credibility of personal contacts with people who had been to Northern Ireland or whose close friends or family had been there tended to be higher than the credibility of television news. But the highest credibility source seemed to be the experience of actually visiting Northern Ireland. One retired person from Shepherd's Bush said simply that 'When I was there it seemed to be quiet'. One woman from Paisley had been to Belfast City for 12 July, a time of heightened tension for Catholics. She wrote 'I've been during the 12th July celebrations. I didn't see any "activity" but heard "opinions"'. This visit informed her analysis of what Northern Ireland was like, 'TV news emphasises the violent aspects of life, but most people are too busy getting on with their lives'.

A small number of people gave alternative media information or said that they had compared different accounts as reasons for rejecting the TV news account that Northern Ireland was mostly violent. Respondents cited plays, documentaries or other media. For example one wrote 'Documentaries which actually talk to the people in Ireland who live there day to day', another put 'Information comes from interviews in specific documentaries with Irish people themselves who say that things aren't all violence all of the time'. Alternatively 'Plays on NI sometimes present a peaceful picture'. Two retired people said that they had gained other perspectives from religious broadcasts. Religious material had also provided one young woman ex-offender with information which she had used to evaluate television news, 'The portrayal of NI is an image of constant conflict. There is peace in some areas but the news is always about violence in the community'. This perception and partial critique of television reporting had come in part from the religious magazine, *The Tablet*. 'It's helpful to have written reports' she pointed out.

Other respondents said they had evaluated other TV news stories against different sources of information, and thus learned to critique news construction of events. One woman had evaluated news coverage of student demonstrations against her understanding of what students were like and had used this critique of the news to inform her views of the coverage of Northern Ireland:

> the newspapers created the impression all the students were hoodlums and all the rest of it, but they wouldn't have been students if they hadn't have got through their exams. It's always the ones who step out of line a wee bit or take a different opinion from the media that are highlighted as trouble makers. That seems to be the way that reporters work.

One pensioner had evaluated coverage by comparing TV news with the fact that there didn't seem to be any great rush by people to leave Northern Ireland. He wrote: 'People live there and are not doing an East German scramble to S[outh] Ireland or GB'. A number of respondents were able to distance themselves from media accounts of Northern Ireland by reference to a critique of television news and news values in particular. Several referred to 'common-sense' interpretations of the media. As one explained there is 'no story in rural peace, therefore pictures show violence in a minority of areas . . . TV only pictures confrontations'.

The answers given by the Northern Ireland groups and the British soldiers reflected their own personal experiences of life in Northern Ireland. The Northern Ireland groups were all from Belfast and in the main came from working-class areas closely associated with the conflict. Such areas are in fact the focal point of much political violence, army and police patrolling and sectarian tension. Similarly the British soldiers who had been to Northern Ireland had been as part of a tour of duty. As such they were at the sharp end of patrolling and coming into contact with the (nationalist) population in particular parts of the North. In both sets of groups the propensity of people to see or experience the conflict is clearly much higher than in some other parts of Northern Ireland.[5] Even then, a large majority rejected what they saw as the television account of the North. For one woman in the Shankill area television 'mostly tells about violence. When something does happen it's blown out of all proportion and the good things are hardly ever shown or talked about'. Such coverage was uniformly thought to damage British perceptions of Northern Ireland as in this comment from a nationalist woman in the Lower Ormeau area: 'I think British people would be very afraid. They are under the impression that people are shooting each other at every street corner'.

Such criticisms of television and accounts of their own experience of violence were also occasionally developed into an analysis of the perception of the relative danger of various areas of Belfast. Here there is an extent to which the media may play a part in informing Belfast residents about the areas which are particularly dangerous or violent. In the following example two women from the Lower Ormeau discuss perceptions of their area. The nationalist Lower Ormeau Road borders the mixed university area and the loyalist Donegall Pass area. Further up the road, over the Ormeau bridge is the loyalist Annadale area. It is an interface which has seen many sectarian killings in the period of the troubles and is sometimes referred to as 'murder mile' because of this. These two women had lived in the nationalist Lower Ormeau area for most of the period after 1969 and gave their view of the level of violence:

1 I have yet to see anything – I honestly mean that
2 I've seen one gun the whole troubles
1 Yet when you say where you live, people say 'What? Murder mile?'

For the British soldiers, perceptions of violence seemed to be linked to whether they had been to Northern Ireland on a tour of duty as well as where they had been posted and their experiences while in Northern Ireland. The small number who had not been on a tour (seven) universally said that life in Northern Ireland was mostly peaceful. They had gained this impression from other soldiers who had been (six), from 'non-news television programmes'/ 'media' (three) and in one case (a member of the Royal Irish Rangers) from living in Ireland. Of those who had been on a tour of duty the predominant view was that Northern Ireland was mostly peaceful and that television distorted events there. One corporal wrote: 'TV does no good for the peacefulness of the province. It makes it out to be like Lebanon.'

Both the soldiers and the Northern Ireland groups were in general very sceptical about British network news coverage of the conflict in ways which the general British groups simply were not. The Northern Ireland groups in particular showed a great complexity of views on television coverage of the conflict. Their critique of British news was clearly rooted in their own experiences and culture.

In summary the clearest reason for rejecting the message of television was the actual experience of living in or visiting Northern Ireland. The Northern Ireland groups and the British soldiers were the most emphatic in rejecting the message. However, some of the English and Scottish respondents had evaluated television news portrayals against other media images, or by reading alternative accounts in the press or magazines. Still others had rejected the television news picture by drawing on critiques of news values or by using personal experience from other topics or simply by processes of logic. It was also the case however that a significant minority were prepared to say that life in Northern Ireland was mostly violent and that nearly half of the British sample stated that they were afraid of visiting Northern Ireland.[6]

## Some Questions Regarding Outcomes

In the research reported above media information clearly affected public views on the prevalence of violence in Northern Ireland and on the killings in Gibraltar. But how many people would have to believe official propaganda (and for how long) for it to matter? In both the dominant ideology thesis and its critique there is a lack of specificity on what would count as a dominant ideology. How dominant would it have to be? Hall (1977: 332–3) argues that the '"definitions of reality", favourable to the dominant class fractions, and institutionalised in the spheres of civil life and the state come to constitute the primary "lived reality" as such for the subordinate classes'. However, 'even under hegemonic conditions, there can be no total incorporation or absorption of the subordinate classes' (1977:333). By contrast Abercrombie, Hill and Turner (1980; 1990) cite extensive opinion poll evidence to show that large sections of the population apparently do not believe key elements of the 'dominant ideology'. Yet even using the data they quote, it is also clear that substantial numbers of people do believe the propositions in question. Either way, demonstrating that particular beliefs or ideologies are held by significant numbers of the populace does not resolve the argument for there are a further set of relationships to be investigated: those between public opinion and actual outcomes in society.

This brings us to the fifth 'moment' which is the question of 'action' or 'outcomes'. This can be seen as a very complex series of 'moments' which are collapsed here. For example, there is the question of the relationship between public belief and political conclusions and between conclusions and action. A key conclusion of my research was that significant numbers of people in Britain do believe key elements of the official definition of the conflict in Northern Ireland as a result of media portrayals of the conflict. This manifestly makes it less likely that some people will oppose government policy in this area. Indeed only a very small number of people in Britain (three per cent in 1977 and 1983) are prepared to say that they regard the IRA as 'freedom fighters' (De Boer 1979; Hewitt 1992). But the bulk of the population do not necessarily come to the same political conclusions as that of the government's public position: a majority of British public opinion has been in favour of British withdrawal from Ireland for most of the period between 1972 and 1994 (see Miller, 1994b, Ch. 6 for a discussion). Furthermore, political conclusions do not necessarily lead to political action, as can be seen by the lack of support in Britain for organisations openly campaigning for British withdrawal.

Then there is the relationship between action and influence, such as whether public opinion or popular protest influences government or other decision making. The influence of opinion and action on state decision making is itself an extremely complex process. On occasion decision makers may be forced to react to changes in public opinion, political protest or even media coverage. The fact that official sources perceive managing the media to be necessary is itself strong evidence that media coverage and 'public opinion' can be important in constraining state actions. In the case of Gibraltar, as with other state killings in Northern Ireland, managing the media is an important means of averting public criticism and adverse judgements in the international arena (such as at the European Court of Human Rights). It also helps to protect 'security force' personnel from the full rigours of the legal process.

Alternatively decision makers may feel able to simply ignore public opinion or political protest. For example the majority of British opinion in favour of British withdrawal from Ireland seems to have made little impact on the policies of the main political parties. Conversely, coalitions of interest may at times be strong enough to change government policy even though the policy attracts a high level of public support. It can certainly be argued that the Ulster Unionists were able to influence British government policy on the peace process because of the Conservative government's slim majority. In such cases any version of the dominant ideology thesis would be inadequate for explaining political change since public opinion assumes a much less important role in state decision making.

Thus there exists a whole range of factors, ideological, political and organisational that need exploration if 'outcomes' or the consequences of ideology or public opinion for maintaining or changing the staus quo are to be fully under-stood. Furthermore, the exploration of the processes, which may contribute to maintaining or changing public opinion needs much further analysis. The impact of the media and public opinion on decision making and outcomes contributes to the reproduction and transformation of power relations and to the circumstances in which new promotional strategies are planned and executed and news decisions made. The interaction of the five moments (promotion, production, definition, reception and outcomes) outlined above, in the context of already existing conditions, constitutes and reconstitutes contemporary power relations. This does not mean that the 'stability of capitalism' is perpetually and functionally assured, as in the dominant ideology thesis. But it does mean that the relationship between ideology and the distri-bution of power and resources needs to be examined. The approach advocated here redirects attention from assumptions about the economic, military or strategic 'interests' of the British state in Northern Ireland (which tend to be associated with arguments about dominant ideologies). Instead, investigation of the actual promotional strategies of the state is required.

## An Agenda for Media Research

The critique of the dominant ideology thesis does not match the empirical evi-dence offered in this chapter in relation to audience response to media coverage of Northern Ireland. The critique overemphasises the heterogeneity of media processes and the 'activity' of audiences. Furthermore the authors do not deal with questions of propaganda, public relations and lobbying (the moment of promotion) at one end of the cycle nor with impacts of the media or public opinion on policy, decision making or on the social distribution of harms and benefits (the moment of outcomes). To be fair, such problems also afflict a wide variety of contemporary writings on the role of the media generally.

In the 1970s and early 1980s the relationship between the media, other social institutions and the stratification of class, gender, ethnic and sexual hier-archies were central to media studies (Hall, 1977; Curran, Gurevitch and Woollacott, 1982). Many of the approaches available at the time for extending media analysis ended up by focusing too narrowly on one of the 'moments', whether it be on the 'text', or on the 'active audience' or alternatively found themselves up the postmodern cul de sac. One result has been that questions of ideology and power have left centre stage to be replaced by the ideology that ideology is not important. It has been my argument that there is a complex, variable and interactive relationship between the five moments outlined here, and that the methods and conceptual apparatus for investigating them, are available. The suggestion is that these questions urgently need to be put back at the centre of an expanded agenda for media research.

# Appendix

## Groups Taking Part in the General Study

|  | No. of groups | No. of participants |
|---|---|---|
| **General Scottish groups** | | |
| SACRO | 1 | 8 |
| Society of Telecom Executives | 1 | 4 |
| Glasgow School of Art, 2nd Year Students | 1 | 5 |
| Bruntsfield Hospital staff | 1 | 14 |
| Total | 4 | 31 |
| **General English groups** | | |
| Harrow Victims Support Group | 1 | 10 |
| Chislehurst Neighbourhood Watch | 1 | 7 |
| Pensioners Keep Fit, Shepherds Bush | 1 | 12 |
| Total | 3 | 29 |
| **Soldiers** | | |
| Redford Barracks | 1 | 19 |
| Total | 1 | 19 |
| **Nationalist groups in Northern Ireland** | | |
| Cromac Street | 1 | 2 |
| Lower Ormeau Road Women | 1 | 2 |
| Turf Lodge, West Belfast | 1 | 5 |
| Suffolk Community Services Group | 1 | 4 |
| Total | 4 | 13 |
| **Unionist groups in Northern Ireland** | | |
| Shankill Womens Group | 1 | 8 |
| Dee Street retired women | 1 | 6 |
| Total | 2 | 14 |
| **Mixed group** | | |
| Farset | 1 | 8 |
| Total | 1 | 8 |
| **American Students** | 1 | 26 |
| **Totals** | 20 | 140 |

# Groups Taking Part in the Gibraltar Study

|  | No. of Groups | No. of Participants |
|---|---|---|
| **General Scottish groups** | | |
| Saltcoats Workers Educational Association | 1 | 7 |
| SACRO | 1 | 15 |
| Glasgow College of Technology | | |
| 2nd Year Communication Studies students | 1 | 9 |
| Ardrossan Senior Citizens | 1 | 32 |
| Paisley Retired women | 1 | 6 |
| Glasgow School of Art Second year students | 1 | 14 |
| Total | 6 | 83 |
| **Soldiers** | | |
| Redford Barracks, Edinburgh | 1 | 20 |
| Total | 1 | 20 |
| **Northern Ireland groups** | | |
| West Belfast Parent Youth Support Project | 1 | 8 |
| Suffolk Community Service Group | 1 | 4 |
| Total | 2 | 12 |
| **American Students** | | |
| US Students at Manchester University | 1 | 24 |
| US Students at Glasgow University | 1 | 4 |
| Total | 2 | 28 |
| Totals | 11 | 143 |

## Notes

1   Abercrombie is dealing specifically with 'popular culture' by which he appears to mean fictional media. However, the critique of the dominant ideology thesis could be made in relation to factual programming too. If it were not, then this would be a serious weakness of the argument in itself. Here it is assumed that both factual and fictional media are potentially important and require to be investigated.

2   This view is partially contradicted by one of Abercrombie's collaborators. Stephen Hill writes of the large section of the media industry which has extolled Thatcherism (1990:32), which does somewhat undermine the view that there is little coherence in textual ideology.

3   More details of method and sample and a discussion of some of the other findings can be found in Miller, 1994b, Chapter 5. The contrast between US and British audience responses is discussed in Miller, 1994a.

4   53.8% believed life in Northern Ireland was mostly peaceful; 15.4% thought it was mostly violent and a further 11.9% thought it 'probably' mostly peaceful.

5   It should be pointed out, however, that since the early 1980s, ordinary squaddies have rarely become involved in actual military engagements with the IRA. Such confrontations became mainly the preserve of undercover operatives (Urban, 1992: 69 and 217).

6   An anonymous reader of an earlier draft of this chapter suggested that a problem with this analysis is that it assumes that people who come to share the official view based on their own reading of the evidence are uncritical viewers. There is not space to adequately deal with this point here. Suffice to say that the position adopted here is that those viewers who came to believe that there was a bomb in the car in Gibraltar can be considered 'active' in that they interpreted the information available in the media, as do we all. The key point however, is that what they came to believe supported an official propaganda offensive and was false. This remains true however critical of other official views they might be or however self interested they might be in believing the official account.

## References

Abercrombie, Nicholas (1990) 'Popular Culture and Ideological Effects', in N. Abercrombie, S. Hill and B. Turner (eds) *Dominant Ideologies*. London: Unwin Hyman.

Abercrombie, Nicholas (1996) *Television and Society*. Cambridge: Polity Press.

Abercrombie, N., S. Hill and B. Turner (1980) *The Dominant Ideology Thesis*. London: Allen & Unwin.

Abercrombie, N., S. Hill and B. Turner (1986) *Sovereign Individuals of Capitalism*. London: Allen & Unwin.

Abercrombie, N., S. Hill and B. Turner (1990) *Dominant Ideologies*. London: Unwin Hyman.

Bennett, T., C. Mercer and J. Woollacott (eds) (1986) *Popular Culture and Social Relations*. Milton Keynes: Open University Press

Cockerell, Michael, Peter Hennessy and David Walker (1984) *Sources Close to the Prime Minister*. London: Macmillan.

Corner, John (1995) *Television Form and Public Address*. London: Edward Arnold.

Curran, J., M. Gurevitch and J. Woollacott (1982) 'The Study of the Media: Theoretical Approaches', in M. Gurevitch, T. Bennett, J. Curran and J.Woollacott (eds) *Culture, Society and the Media*. London: Methuen.

De Boer, Connie (1979) 'The Polls: Terrorism and Hijacking', *Public Opinion Quarterly*, 43: 410–18.

Franklin, Bob (1994) *Packaging Politics*. London: Edward Arnold.

Hall, S. (1977) 'Culture, the Media and the "Ideological Effect"', in J. Curran, M. Gurevitch and J. Woollacott (eds) *Mass Communication and Society*. London: Edward Arnold.

Hall, S. (1980) 'Encoding/Decoding', in S. Hall, D. Hobson, A. Lowe and P. Willis (eds) *Culture, Media, Language*. London: Hutchinson.

Hall, S. (1988) *The Hard Road to Renewal: Thatcherism and the Crisis of the Left*. London: Verso.

Hall, Stuart, Chas Critcher, Tony Jefferson, John Clarke and Brian Roberts (1978) *Policing the Crisis: Mugging, the State and Law and Order*. London: Macmillan.

Harris, David (1992) *From Class Struggle to the Politics of Pleasure: The Effects of Gramscianism on Cultural Studies*. London: Routledge.

Hewitt, Christopher (1992) 'Public's Perspectives', in David L. Paletz and Alex P. Schmid (eds) *Terrorism and the Media: How Researchers, Terrorists, Government, Press, Public, Victims View and Use the Media*. London: Sage.

Hill, Stephen (1990) 'Britain: The Dominant Ideology Thesis', in N. Abercrombie, S. Hill and B. Turner (eds) *Dominant Ideologies*. London: Unwin Hyman.

McGuigan, Jim (1992) *Cultural Populism*. London: Routledge.

Miller, David (1991) 'The Media on the Rock: The Media and the Gibraltar Killings', in B. Rolston (ed.) *The Media and Northern Ireland: Covering the Troubles*. Basingstoke: Macmillan.

Miller, David (1993a) 'The Northern Ireland Information Service and the Media: Aims, Strategy, Tactics' in Glasgow University Media Group, *Getting the Message*. London: Routledge.

Miller, David (1993b) 'Official Sources and Primary Definition: The Case of Northern Ireland', *Media, Culture and Society*, 15 (3): 385–406.

Miller, David (1994a) 'Understanding "Terrorism": US and British audience interpretations of the televised conflict in Ireland', in Meryl Aldridge and Nicholas Hewitt (eds) *Controlling Broadcasting: Access, Policy and Practice in North America and Europe*. Manchester: Manchester University Press.

Miller, David (1994b) *Don't Mention the War: Northern Ireland, Propaganda and the Media*. London: Pluto.

Miller, David and Greg McLaughlin (1996) 'Reporting the Peace in Ireland', in Bill Rolston and David Miller (eds) *War and Words: The Northern Ireland Media Reader*, Belfast: Beyond the Pale.

Morley, David (1992) *Television, Audiences and Cultural Studies*. London: Routledge.

Murdock, Graham (1991) 'Patrolling the Border: British Broadcasting and the Irish Question in the 1980s', *Journal of Communication*, 41: 104–15.

Murphy, David (1991) *The Stalker Affair and the Press*. London: Unwin Hyman.

Scammell, Margaret (1994) *Designer Politics: How Elections are Won*. Basingstoke: Macmillan.

Schlesinger, Philip, Graham Murdock and Philip Elliot (1983) *Televising 'Terrorism': Political Violence in Popular Culture*. London: Comedia.

Turner, B.S. (1990) 'Conclusion: peroration on ideology', in Abercrombie et al. *Dominant Ideologies*. London: Unwin Hyman.

Urban, Mark (1992) *Big Boys' Rules: The SAS and the Secret Struggle Against the IRA*. London: Faber.

# 7

# Northern Ireland Audiences and Television News

## Raymond Watson

Ang (1990) comments on the highly controversial reception of Rushdie's novel, *The Satanic Verses* to illustrate how a clash of cultural understanding can express itself with world-wide consequences. One of the main issues raised by the Rushdie controversy, how people in multi-ethnic societies understand media texts, has been addressed, though perhaps less dramatically, by researchers of media audiences. David Morley (1980:6) in a somewhat different context quoted Counihan (1972) to argue that media research was being transformed because the research focus had:

> . . . shifted from what the media do to people; to what people do to the media . . . (audiences) receive messages in a selective way, to tend to ignore or subtly interpret those messages hostile to their viewpoint.

Morley further argued that the capacity of an audience to subject a media text to different readings needed to be investigated in a way that accounted for the cultural context of that audience's reception of media output. Indeed, other researchers such as Findahl and Hoijer (1991) also viewed audience interpretation of the media as occurring within the framework of the existing cultural knowledge of audiences.

Similarly, Lindlof (1987) arguing for the 'interpretative' approach, and researchers who wished to identify the cultural competence of their sample audience groups (Morley, 1980), recognised that cultural and political attitudes could be identified by research that focused on the participants' discussions of their everyday lives. Reports of such discussions, it is argued, illustrate cultural competences and the interpretative strategies that group members use to makes sense of their world. The research reported on below set out to identify aspects of the cultural competence of groups in Northern Ireland and how these influenced readings of a television news text.

How might a selected group of people from Northern Ireland read a television news text? To what extent might the readings of that audience be influenced by their cultural and political circumstances? The research conducted in 1991–92 (Watson, 1993), explored aspects of the cultural and political experience of a number of people in Northern Ireland and subsequently analysed how they responded to a television news broadcast. The research sought to establish the level of influence that cultural experience exerted on television news' comprehension. The Northern Ireland audience provided a good case study scenario because it consists of a group of people who share the same geographical locality but who possess opposing historical/political aspirations and experience.

The research (for a complete account of methods and findings see Watson, 1993) was based on two phases of in-depth interviews which were tape recorded. The first phase of interviews was complemented by written diary records kept for one week by the participants and other observational data noted by the researchers. The method of gathering the relevant data had to be specifically designed to account for the potent sectarian situation that exists in Northern Ireland. For example, this involved the use of a second field work researcher whose religious and cultural beliefs were seen as being compatible with the expressed religious and national identity of some of the participants. This was seen as necessary for two reasons: for the personal security of the researcher, and because it was felt that participants might respond in a guarded manner if they believed that the researcher was from, what they viewed as, 'the other community'.

The first phase of in-depth discussions provided the respondents with the opportunity to relay, in their own words, what they believed to be their ethno-political identity and to describe their cultural and political experience.

The research material generated was analysed by organising the evidence thematically around the topics of attitudes towards history, religion, politics, paramilitaries, the police, the British Army and the media. The second phase of the discussions/interviews was conducted after the audience had viewed a simulated news bulletin. This was to establish if the audience members had understood the news text in different ways, and if so, the ways in which these interpretations connected to their cultural and political viewpoints.

Six families were interviewed. Three families declared themselves to be aligned to the unionist community and lived in a medium-sized town close to Belfast, while the other three families declared themselves to be aligned to the nationalist community and lived in a medium-sized town close to the border. A profile of the participants by name, age, occupation, marital status and residential status is provided below.

*Nationalist Families*

1  Larry (38) Self-employed tradesman
   Mary (38) Housewife
   Patrick (17) one of their three
      children
   Council house

2  Dermot (37) Teacher
   Brenda (37) Civil servant
   Two children aged 10 and 12 years
   Private house

3  Benny (36) Labourer
   Siobhán (37) Housewife
   Two children aged 8 and 10 years
   Council house

*Unionist Families*

4  Tony (55) Self employed pig
      farmer
   Susan (57) Housewife
   No children left at home
   Private house

5  Isaac (28) Shop floor worker
   Rachel (25) Store worker
   No children
   Council house

6  Cedric (50) Store worker
   Janice (52) Housewife
   Gilly (25) Store worker and
      youngest of their three children
   Council house

## Discussions on Identity

Those designated as the nationalist sample audience were all Roman Catholics and most declared that Sinn Féin would be the political party that they would vote for. There were two exceptions: Patrick said that he would vote for the SDLP (Social and Democratic Labour Party) and Mary said that although she had once considered herself a republican she had now become politically apathetic.

Dermot, who aligned himself with Sinn Féin, clearly stated his reasons for supporting that party: 'They're a republican party and I believe in republicanism'. Larry explained his reasons for voting for Sinn Féin by referring to the pre-1972 Northern Ireland regime: '. . . we would probably still be running with the old Stormont . . . biased voting . . . religious discrimination in employment'. Mary accounted for her political apathy by stating: 'Because I honestly don't think it makes a difference who gets in'.

All these nationalist participants had attended Roman Catholic schools and the males felt that school friends had been influential in the formation of their political outlooks. The political viewpoints of all the nationalists towards the British Government and the security forces (British Army and RUC) tended to be negative. For example, Dermot told how he believed that there was a lack of consensus government in Northern Ireland: 'It depends if you think the State is legitimate'. Larry similarly said: 'If the law isn't just it's what is in your own head that is right. A British soldier can do whatever he wants and get away with it'. Siobhán expressed her alienation in terms of a class-based ideology:

'Thatcherism, there's Benny [her husband] out working, look at the money he's getting, it's a pittance . . . I'm totally against the Government'.

The nationalists tended to view the Protestant religion as being linked to the unionist political ethos to which they objected. Elements of the discussion revealed important 'us' and 'them' attitudes. Larry said: 'The Prods. [Protestants] think that they are a better class of people than we are'. Siobhán and Benny were of the view that Protestants were of a different cognation, saying literally that they were a different 'breed of people'. They also spoke negatively about Orange parades [the traditional celebrations of the Orange Order, a Protestant organisation] 'in their town'. They explained how they believed that the marchers were 'outsiders' from the 'other' community. Benny's own words demonstrate the depth of his antagonism towards the Orange marchers; 'Most of the time it makes me sick'. With the exception of Patrick, the nationalist sample said that they had attended republican parades and gatherings.

The nationalist sample also declared a preferential interest in Gaelic sports and spoke negatively of rugby and hockey although most identified a common link with soccer. Dermot gave this opinion: 'I think that everybody is aware, no matter what . . . the gaelic games are associated with nationalism . . .'. He continued by saying that other games were associated with unionism and quoted specific examples of overt unionist political influence in non-gaelic games. Benny told how he was a member of the local Celtic Social Club, a club that displayed nationalist tendencies through its activities. Patrick, who was the youngest respondent, related that he was only interested in playing in a pop group with his mates and that he viewed the sectarian divisions within Northern Irish sport as being unacceptable.

The three families designated as the unionist sample stated their voting preferences as follows: Cedric, Janice and Gilly stated that the DUP (Democratic Unionist Party) represented their political outlooks. Isaac and Rachel said they voted for 'a unionist party' and did not state which party. Tony and Susan said they voted for the Alliance Party, a small party with non-sectarian policies. While voting for the Alliance Party is not an indication of affiliation with the unionist community, Tony and Susan were Protestant, who like their co-religionists described their nationality as 'British'. Cedric articulated his reasons for voting for the DUP in both class-based and sectarian terms: 'Well, we thought we would have a better standard of living with the DUP'. He added that the DUP was an effective counter balance to the nationalist/Catholic SDLP. Janice, his wife, agreeing with Cedric, said: 'It's really the only party you have, Protestant party, not being bitter . . .'. Rachel and her husband Isaac related why they voted for a unionist party. Rachel said, 'Yea, one of ours [meaning a unionist part]'. Tony and his wife Susan said they were Alliance Party voters and spoke negatively of the DUP whom they viewed as sectarian.

The unionist sample generally agreed that civil disobedience was a matter for an individual's conscience. This attitude was displayed by most of these participants when they spoke in nostalgic terms of the 1974 Ulster Workers' Strike that brought down the power-sharing Northern Ireland Executive Government. For example Gilly recalled: 'I remember everybody marching up the Doagh Road, and you [her father, Cedric] cooking out the back on a camp fire'.

The unionist sample generally expressed the belief that the current Northern Ireland judicial system was fair. Tony said that he believed many of the negative accusations levelled against the justice system were motivated by nationalist 'propagandists'. This type of belief in the judicial system and the security forces was construed as an expression of support by this group toward the state.

Most of the unionist sample believed that the civil rights demonstrations of 1968 were responsible for the return of political violence to Northern Ireland. In Cedric's words, 'Where the Troubles started from was "One man one vote", the march to Derry . . . Bernadette Devlin. They just actually spread to Belfast around republican areas . . .'. Alternatively Tony and Susan, who repeatedly appeared politically moderate, believed that the issue of civil rights should have been addressed and that, consequently, the current Troubles might have been avoided. Gilly was dismissive about the issue of civil rights and believed that discrimination existed against Protestants rather than Catholics: 'I feel that they [Catholics] get the better jobs'.

In relation to paramilitary organisations the unionist sample were highly critical of the IRA. Gilly said: 'I have a lot of bitterness towards them'. There was a general feeling that IRA violence had hardened attitudes and increased sectarianism.

Like the nationalist group, many of the unionists displayed 'us and them' attitudes. This was articulated by Cedric when he recalled the historical separation of the communities and how people felt safer '. . . within their own community'. Cedric told how he felt, 'You can only trust your own and that's it'. Isaac expressed his attitude toward what he viewed as the '"other community" . . .'cause they [Catholics] are a different species, so they are, than we are'. Tony and Susan expressed a more positive attitude towards the Catholic community. Susan told how she belonged to an Irish cultural group, Comhaltas Ceolteoirí Éireann (an organisation that promotes Irish language, music and dance), although she confided that she felt compelled to conceal this from her Protestant friends. This type of attitude would suggest that although Susan stated her nationality as British, she has a positive attitude towards what is identified as Irish culture. She explained this by saying that she believed that these cultural pursuits belong to everyone, meaning both communities, and '. . . not to one side only'.

In relation to symbolic representations of culture such as parades and sport, the unionist sample viewed Orange demonstrations favourably. For example, Cedric viewed Orange parades and the Twelfth of July (annual Orangeman's day) as festive occasions that did not give offence. In relation to sport, the unionist sample were negative towards gaelic games, saying that they were Catholic sports, whereas they viewed rugby, soccer and hockey as being '. . . enjoyed by the whole community'. Isaac objected to gaelic games because he saw the activities as the slippery slope to demands for further cultural expression by nationalists: 'Once you let the gaelic football in, they [Catholics] will be wanting to talk it [Irish language] to you like'.

## Media

Members of the two sample groups stated that they preferred to read newspapers which they believed presented political and cultural values closely aligned to their own outlooks. Most of the unionists said that they only read what they perceived as unionist newspapers such as the *News Letter*, and that they would not read what they identified as Catholic/nationalist daily papers. Indeed, two of the unionist sample described the *Irish News* as merely a 'republican scandal rag'. Similarly, members of the nationalist group said that they would never buy the *News Letter* because they perceived it as being a unionist paper. Dermot's stated attitude is a good example of how certain members of both groups viewed the press; he said that sometimes he might purchase some of the 'British papers just to see what they were saying'.

In relation to broadcasting, interviewees from both groups expressed their belief that television output had at times been at odds with their political interests. The nationalist interviewees tended to see television bias as the result of both the organisation of broadcast institutions and of journalistic practices. For example, Dermot spoke of how he believed that television news selectively portrayed stories from his home town that were unfavourable to Sinn Féin, and added: 'Sinn Féin are denied access to it [broadcasting], you know'. He referred to the broadcast ban that effectively censored Sinn Féin from the airwaves at the time of the research (1992). Dermot's perception is comparable to that of a unionist interviewee. Cedric told how he believed that news reporters had paid children to, 'sing rebel songs . . . to act like rebel songs'. Thus, in his view, journalists had initiated the children's activities to create a good news story.

Despite the participants' display of caution towards television news, all the interviewees agreed that television constituted a primary source of factual information and, importantly, they believed that they were able to distinguish between fact and fiction. All the interviewees' examples of how the media might be biased involved the selection of texts which were perceived as being critical of their communal group interests or political outlooks. They did not provide examples of bias that might have been regarded as adversely effecting the interests of the 'other side'. It appears, therefore, that for these participants television news is selectively viewed and that the regional press is selectively purchased and read.

## Television News

Following the collation of contextual information it was decided to explore how a television news text might be interpreted by the selected audience members. A news programme compiled by the researcher was shown to the sample audiences. This compiled news programme simulated the format of the UTV evening news (local Northern Ireland news that is transmitted daily at 6 p.m.). At the time of research, sport ran as the lead item. The news stories used for the compilation were selected from a two-week period of news broadcasts in 1992. The simulated news programme provided the opportunity to show a variety of culturally charged news topics alongside other news topics which possessed no overt cultural or political significance.

The news programmes were screened in the interviewees' homes. Immediately after the screening they were given the opportunity to discuss the programme in an effort to identify how they read or interpreted the viewed programme. These discussions were wide ranging and audience led, and addressed topics such as perceived thematic content of the news programme, personal opinion of the issues presented, and confidence in the performance and ability of television news to present the issues fairly.

The textual content of the simulated news programme included the following items:

1 *Sport*
   (*a*) Gaelic football. A report on a Down v Meath football match.
   (*b*) Soccer football. A report on a Linfield v Ards football match.
   (*c*) Greyhound racing. The Big Race from Dunmore Stadium.

2 *Sion Mills bombing*
   This story reported an IRA bomb attack on a small rural RUC station in Sion Mills in the north west of Northern Ireland. Many houses in the village were destroyed and it was reported that the attack was devised to lure the security forces into 'the line of fire' of a second bomb left close by. This item also included an interview with the DUP's William McCrea, MP, and the NI Security Minister, John Cope.

3 *Grenade attack*
   A report of a grenade attack on a Belfast RUC station during which two suspected IRA men were apprehended as they made their escape.

4 *Peace people*
A report on grant aid of £61,000, awarded to the Northern Ireland Peace People. This report briefly explored the history of the Peace Organisation. This group are what remains of the Peace People, consisting predominantly of women who were inspired in 1976 by the violent death of a mother and her three children to hold mass demonstrations against violence in Northern Ireland.

5 *Orange parade*
A report of the annual Orange parade held in Co. Donegal. Orange parades are viewed as being a core element of the unionist and Protestant identity in Northern Ireland. It is important that the portrayed Orange parade occurred in the Republic of Ireland, a state that Northern Protestants politically oppose.

6 *Shankill girl*
A report of an appeal for a missing 13-year-old Shankill Road girl including an interview with her mother who pleaded for her to return home.

7 *Romanian orphans*
A report on the welfare of Romanian orphans, and how a group of Northern Ireland volunteers were assisting the orphans in Romania.

## Discussion of the News Programme

The discussions of the viewed programme were analysed with reference to the cultural views and opinions portrayed by the audience members in the earlier phase of the research in an effort to understand how the cultural interpretative strategies of audience members influenced their understanding of the programme.

The first question put to all the participants after viewing the news programme was: 'What for you was the most important item on the news?' Then they were asked to discuss the news item that they had recalled. Key selections of how the interviewees responded are presented below.

### News Story 2 – Sion Mills Bombing

Most of the designated unionist audience members recalled the Sion Mills bombing as the most important item. The narrative accounts used to describe this item varied a great deal. This group recalled the incident in strong terms that generally indicated perceptions of disgust, anger and bitterness toward the IRA for carrying out the attack:

Tony: The most devastating part was the Sion Mills business, you know.
Cedric: It really annoys you to see that, really annoys you.
Gilly: So much disregard for human life . . . the devastation to those people's homes, you know, for what?

Various members of this audience used loaded terms to describe the IRA who had carried out the attack. For example, Cedric – 'Faggots', Isaac – 'Fuckin' Bastards!', Gilly – 'Cold blooded murderers'.

Members of this group referred to particular visual images of the footage that were used to portray the devastation. Tony said: 'Imagine your house . . . It's just a bundle of rubbish . . . the slates and everything . . . think of what it's done to your things inside?' Susan's response was, 'Someone was to get married and all'. Isaac referring to the devastation said of those who carried out the bombing that they had 'No regard for anything!'

The news item aroused feelings of communal sympathy with those affected by the bombing. Tony said: 'I suppose they [IRA] feel that anything goes for the Prods [Protestants]'. Cedric related the attack to himself and his family and neighbours: 'Like us sitting here tonight . . . and some one driving a van down the street . . . and where do you go from there?' Gilly, indicating that she viewed the incident as an attack on the local Protestant community said: 'There was no police in the station so it obviously wasn't the police they were going for!'

These sentiments contrast sharply with the initial response of the nationalist sample. More than half of this group recalled the 'Romanian Orphans' item as being the most important news story. When asked specifically about the Sion Mills bombing the tone of the responses was quite different from those quoted above. The nationalists seemed to be less enraged by the news report and seemed to generally share the view that it was 'Just another attack'. The nationalist responses appeared to lack any obvious evidence of condemnation and they also tended to play down the seriousness of the attack.

Members of the nationalist group discussed this attack in terms of a failed attack on the RUC. For example Siobhán said: 'Why do that [bomb the RUC station] whenever there was nobody inside?' And went on to say: 'Difference, you see, if it was full of police'. This critical view was partly shared by other nationalists. For example Benny, her husband, said that 'a ten lbs bomb' could have been used and related how the smaller bomb would have lured the RUC into the second explosion without causing so much damage to local residents. Larry, sharing a similar opinion, said: 'What do I think of it, it was a pity there was nobody inside it [meaning the RUC Station], ha!' To which his wife Mary retorted: 'That's a very staunch Republican attitude Larry!' Paddy, Larry and Mary's son, seemed resigned to such attacks: 'Just another bombing in the history of Northern Ireland'. But he went on to say that although he did not agree with such activities, he believed the IRA were, 'politically motivated'.

Mary was the only one of the nationalist group who referred negatively to the Sion Mills news item. She criticized the bomb attack saying it was close to civilian houses and that, 'It was obvious that they [IRA] weren't just going to hit the police station. The IRA know that when they plant a bomb . . . there is going to be damage other than the original target'. Mary seemed to be objecting to the fact that a large number of civilian homes were destroyed and damaged. She concluded that this type of action made her 'angry . . . What is going to happen to change it all? It's just a vicious circle, that's all it is!'

Dermot mentioned the damage but did not appear to condemn it. 'So it wasn't new or anything, just it looked a fairly destructive bomb in terms of doing damage to buildings and that'. Brenda, his wife, said that she knew Sion Mills to be, '. . . a nice wee Tudor type place'. Asked if the portrayed destruction annoyed her she replied; 'No, not really, it's just a way of life here'.

Visual elements of the news item which the nationalist group recalled went unmentioned by the unionist group. A significant portion of the text involved an interview/confrontation between DUP MP, Rev. William McCrea, and the Northern Ireland Office Minister, John Cope. This interview drew substantial comment from the nationalist sample. Benny's opening remarks on the news item were; 'Sion Mills, with your man McCrea giving off about the local people'. He was cynical about the interview saying; 'McCrea done all the talking'. Similarly Dermot said; 'The wee confrontation with Willy McCrea and the State Minister, it was a bit staged'. Brenda agreed with this: 'I remember more about Willy McCrea than the actual bomb . . . it was a bit contrived. But he [McCrea] rants and raves a bit like that'. The terminology used to describe the interview is generally negative and serves to deride the unionist MP and his speech.

This could be seen as another way in which the nationalist group selectively make use of a section of the text that does not challenge their declared subjective political outlooks. The unionist sample, alternatively, made no mention of the McCrea interview and perhaps felt secure discussing the bomb devastation as proof of their established attitudes towards the IRA.

Larry attempted to articulate his view that the Sion Mills reportage was an example of the way in which Northern Ireland broadcasting told the news in a biased fashion. He said: 'It tries to lean you towards a certain way. It's [the text] presented in such a way that it leans you toward a certain way [of thinking]'. He believed that the coverage was not '. . . middle of the road . . . it's not straight down the line. Like you are hearing the story that the ministers are putting across, the security ministers, the police. You are never hearing the other side of the story'. Explaining that the 'other side' means, 'Sinn Féin and the IRA . . . who are not allowed to talk'. Paddy tended to agree with this critical view saying that he believed that the textual information that the RUC Station was 'unmanned' was 'a lie!'

## News Story 3 – Grenade Attack

The interviewees continued by discussing other news stories generally in the order of presentation. The grenade attack aroused relatively little discussion from the unionist group. Those who did refer to this news text did so in vague terms apparently unsure of what they had seen. For example, Susan referred to the, 'Belfast bombs . . . Well, there was, aye, was it fire bombs thrown in? Aimed at the police station near Royal Avenue?' To which Tony responded: 'Where was this, on this programme'?

Isaac mistakenly said; 'The shooting at the police station'. Rachel interrupted, although equally unsure, saying: 'It wasn't a shooting. Get your facts right, somebody had thrown a bomb or something, or a hand grenade or whatever, as two off-duty police officers went in'. Tony later referred to the incident as, 'the terrible devastation of bombs'.

The apparent lack of discussion data on this news story is noticeable and the researcher can only speculate about the reasons for this. One possible explanation is that this news item was overshadowed by the longer and more graphic Sion Mills story. Remarks expressed by Rachel would tend to confirm this view, for example: 'Sion Mills was an extreme . . . it's not every day there is a massive bomb like that'. No attempt was made by the researcher to reconstruct the textual content of 'news item 3' in order to elicit an interpretation. It was felt that if the participants failed to interpret the details under these research conditions then it would be most unlikely that the audience members would recall this text under everyday viewing conditions.

The nationalist sample appeared slightly more attentive to the grenade attack story. Most were unsure of the actual content of the item. For example Benny referred to 'Where the two policemen were shot and eleven civilians or whatever it was?' Dermot failed to recall the news item and when prompted stated frankly: 'If you hadn't asked us we just would not have remembered it'. The reason given for this lack of recall was that it was just an average story. This view was also presented by Larry: '. . . it was just one of those things that people are tired listening to'. Other interviewees responded in a similar fashion: '. . . so small an incident'. And, 'just another attack'.

Mary gave her reasons more specifically: 'Because they weren't killed they were just wounded! You know that's how little of an impact it makes on us, human life . . . You know what I mean? They were just another casualty'. In the above quote Mary articulates her view that people have become apathetic in Northern Ireland and are only concerned about more extreme or spectacular news stories.

Larry spoke of this news story in greater detail, seeing it as a means of casting doubt on the reliability of the media. He said that despite what the text said, he believed the two suspects were arrested by, 'Plain clothes policemen [as opposed to civilian by-standers as stated in the text]', and who, he believed, must have been '. . . walking close by'. Patrick similarly expressed scepticism about the credibility of the story, saying: 'Two fellas ran off, if you can believe what you hear on the news'.

A further interpretation of this incident, specific to the nationalist audience, was an expression of sympathy with the 'plight' of the apprehended bombers. For example Brenda said: '. . . those two wee lads are in for a time of it [rough treatment at the hands of the RUC] . . . I remember the fact that them two wee lads got caught, you know'.

## News Story 4 – Peace People

Within the unionist audience, gender appears to have emerged as an important element in the discussions of the Peace People news story. All the women from this group responded enthusiastically to this story, while the male members of this group were critical. Janice, referred the Peace People story as the most important one on the programme and was not critical of the portrayed theme of a revitalised peace movement. In the following statement she speaks enthusiastically of the Peace People and their goal of bringing violence to an end: 'Bringing back what the Peace People were years ago . . . to try to get it [the peace movement] going again to see if they can get peace back to this country'. Susan stated clearly how she felt about the Peace People: 'Well I think they [peace movement/Peace People] were marvellous'. Rachel also spoke positively of this story; 'I think their ideals are good and what they are aiming for is . . . what most people would want'. Gilly said that she would actively support today's peace movement: 'Well I would go along with the young ones now. You are [her generation] trying to correct what your parents' generation created, really'. The women appear to have identified with the peace movement whose founders and mass membership were overwhelmingly female. It could also be argued that support for this movement would not compromise the political outlooks held by the women in this sample.

In contrast, the reactions that this item provoked from the male members of the unionist group were much more critical. Isaac expressed some cynicism about the women out marching for peace saying: 'But it's okay all these women out marching but if their men's out shooting?' He continued saying how, in his view, the founders of the movement who were awarded the Nobel Peace Prize, '. . . took the money and pissed off to the States'. Cedric discussed this item in similar terms: 'They never done anything for us . . . They got a lot of money out of it, where did they go after that?' Tony said, 'The boyos [paramilitaries] weren't ready to listen to them'. The above critical discussions appeared to centre around the interpretation of the Peace People as a women's organisation that was either corrupt or powerless in the face of male action.

Most of the nationalist sample group had to be prompted to recall details of the Peace People news story and there appeared to be no evidence of gender-orientated interpretations. With the exception of Mary, the male and female members of this group tended to react to the contents of this story in a similar way. Siobhán referred to the Peace People story in the terms; 'No, that peace thing. I wouldn't even be interested'. Her husband Benny referred to the Peace organisation negatively, saying, 'They [Peace People] are not there for peace. They are there for their own pockets'. This criticism of the grant aid was shared by Patrick who said that it was noticeable that the grant money came from 'the British Government'. He was suspicious saying that it was an attempt by the Government to 'buy out' the 'organisation'. Larry agreed with this view and added; 'Where does it [the money] all come from? What is it spent on?'

Dermot and Brenda spoke of this story in nostalgic terms, saying that it brought back memories, especially the footage of the large crowds that attended the peace rallies. Dermot added that he was suspicious of government motivation for supporting the peace movement, and contrasted this instance of support with the financial support shown to other groups: 'I mean it compares quite vividly with what the Irish language movement gets!' Brenda agreed with this argument, saying that there were other more deserving causes such as 'community groups'.

Mary was the only member of the nationalist sample who discussed this news story in a similar way to the unionist women; 'I thought it was good to see [the grant aid]'. Mary continued to speak positively of the Peace People saying that they were active, 'for a couple of years . . . then they faded away'.

The nationalists tended, with varying degrees, to be of the opinion that this story might have implications that could undermine republican interests. Their perception that the 'grant aid' originated from the British Government appeared to have been motivated not only by the text – the announcement was made by the NI Minister, Dr Brian Mawhinney – but also through arousal of their existing political ideologies. The text stated twice that the grant aid was provided by 'The European Commission's Programme for Community Relations', a segment of textual information that appears to have been ignored by all audience members.

## News Story 5 – Orange Parade

The unionist sample audience had to be prompted to recall the story of Orange parades in County Donegal. They then tended to recall this item in a particular way, with Susan being the only exception. Cedric's initial comments were: 'There again, County Donegal was always known for having Orange parades over the years . . . as far as I can remember'. He continued to compare this to similar nationalist parades: 'It's like St Patrick's Day, it's the same, you have the Ancient Order of Hibernians [a Catholic organisation] . . . They [Catholics/nationalists] have their day and we [Protestants/unionists] have ours'. Isaac said bluntly that the Orangemen were, '. . . just right to be doing it [marching in Donegal]'. A view with which Rachel quickly agreed: 'Yea, everybody has their own belief, or whatever, you know'. Tony similarly discussed the news item but added that Donegal should have been 'brought in' to the United Kingdom during partition. He spoke of those who participated in the portrayed parade as a community who were, in his own words, 'making their last stand nearly, you know'.

In contrast, Susan responded with a view that appeared to be at odds with others from the unionist group. She stated: 'I think it was provocative. I mean to have it [the parade] in Donegal wasn't it? Why should they have it in Donegal?' She went on to argue that she believed that there should be no parades at all. Susan appeared to view parades from either community as being provocative expressions of sectarianism.

The discussion data on this news item referred to some visual details of the text. Tony spoke of the 'security presence' that was mentioned by the narrator and presented visually in the text through a hovering Irish Army helicopter. Cedric referred to a one-to-one interview between the news presenter and an Orangeman. Isaac recalled that 'the parade appeared peaceful', and also recalled sections of the dialogue. Rachel agreed, saying: 'It's nice to see that it [the parade] could pass off peacefully in the South'. She was referring to the fact that the Republic is perceived by many Northern Ireland Protestants as being a state dominated by Catholicism, and a state that lays sovereign claim to the territory of Northern Ireland.

Generally the unionist sample audience discussed this news story in terms that supported and justified the right of the Orangemen to parade in Donegal. Again, these responses to the text would appear to be motivated by their own particular political interests.

The nationalist sample responded rather more negatively to the Orange parade story. As with the unionist sample, their discussions of the story centred on the Orangemen's right to march in the Republic. Larry believed that republican parades were not given the same rights to march in Northern Ireland, saying, 'Yea, how easy it was for the Orangies [Orangemen] to march down South [the Republic] when republicans can't march up here . . . the same liberties aren't granted to the other side up here'. Mary and Patrick agreed, but Patrick again used this text as an opportunity to question the credibility of television news. He told how he believed that television gave more favourable coverage to Orange parades than it did to nationalist parades. Dermot spoke of how he believed the Orange Lodges complained that their rights would be infringed in the Republic. Dermot pointed out that the parade story illustrated that Orangemen had complete freedom; '. . . and yet there they are, thousands of them, marching down in Donegal'.

Siobhán and Benny had both previously expressed their dislike of Orange marches and these sentiments were evident again in their discussions of this story. Siobhán dealt with the topic by bluntly dismissing the news item, saying, 'They are a breed of their own . . . nothing sinks in when I'm watching something like that'. Siobhán's response to this story is probably generated by her attitude towards what she perceives as symbolic representations of the 'other community' and provides yet another illustration of how textual information can be framed by, and understood within, an existing cultural attitude.

Despite the fact that the news story stated that, instead of the 'oath of loyalty to the Queen', the Order in Donegal pledged an 'oath of loyalty to the organisation's forefathers', Benny objected to the Orange march saying: 'I don't think they should be allowed to march there and say their allegiance is to the Queen'. Again, this was an indicator that textual information was ignored and that his established attitude to the topic was activated by the story.

Dermot referred to a section of footage that served to illustrate his negative view of this story. He spoke of parading Orangemen saying: 'I remember that, funny enough, when it was on . . . there was a couple of big fat men in it [the parade]'. This type of negative response by Dermot is consistent with his earlier response to the Sion Mills story. In the Sion Mills story he selected small sections of the text and referred to the portrayed characters by negative stereotyping in a way that served to reinforce his political viewpoint.

The discussions on this news story, like the previous stories, illustrate just how selective the interpretative activity of audiences can be. It also shows how audience beliefs can be aroused by textual content and how these beliefs can be more influential in formulating responses to the content than the actual textual information shown. For example, the issue of the legitimacy of Orange parades occurring in the Irish Republic was not mentioned by the text, yet both groups felt compelled to discuss it.

## News Story 6 – Missing Girl

The responses of the unionist sample to this story indicate that it was barely remembered. For example, when prompted to recall the story, Rachel replied: 'Oh aye, the wee girl going missing'. Similarly, Susan replied: 'Yes, that's right. There was the wee girl that was lost'. Tony added: 'You get a big appeal put out for one person that is missing, because of the concern that is in people'. Rachel and Isaac's comments were slightly different but they probably articulated how this story was received by most of the unionist sample. They said: '. . . it's not the most memorable part of the news'. And then went on to say that if the story had some relevance to them then they might have remembered it in more detail. There appeared to have been little interpretation of this human interest story and little of the textual information was recalled. It is interesting, though, to contrast and compare the differences between the nationalist responses to the story.

The nationalist sample discussed textual elements of this story. Most importantly, they all mentioned the one-to-one interview with the missing girl's mother and the news reporter. With the exception of Larry, this sample audience all used expressions that appeared to be critical of the mother of the missing girl. Referring to the interview Siobhán said: 'Well, like, the mother hesitated when she was asked, "Did she [the missing girl] ever do this before?" . . . Why? I think there is something going on in the house . . . She's covering her tracks'. In relation to the same piece of text Benny suspected that the mother had a 'drink problem or something'. He went on to say that the mother looked, 'very tired and hang-overish looking'. Dermot and Brenda engaged the text by addressing the same theme: 'I was just thinking, I wonder did she [the girl] ever get beat?' Mary was also critical of the mother and said that she thought the mother appeared to be 'a bit of a hypocrite'.

Benny referred to the same piece of text but the theme of his criticism differed slightly. He said: 'There is no sign of the father, like . . . it's usually mother and father would sit in front of the camera and say "please come home"'. Like the unionist group, some members of the nationalist group also said this story was not particularly significant. Larry said: 'It didn't register at all, except when it was on'. As with so much of the news text, only small fragments of the story were actually recalled. But it is noticeable that the nationalist sample were much more critical of this story and recalled much more textual detail. One reason for this could be that the nationalist group all have young children and consequently the story may have been one to which they could more easily relate. The fact that some of their criticisms revolved around family relations would indicate this as a possibility. For example, they wondered if the girl had been physically beaten, noticed the absence of a father, and that the mother appeared hung-over. The story also indicated that the girl's mother lives in the Shankill Road area [perceived by all sections of the community in Northern Ireland as a staunch unionist area] so it is also possible that the nationalist responses indicated a level of negative stereotyping towards the 'other community'.

## News Story 7 – Romanian Orphans

The discussions of this story were uncomplicated and shared many common features. Members of both the nationalist and unionist audiences spoke of the good will shown by the young Northern Ireland volunteers who travelled to Romania to help the orphans. The common audience reading addressed the theme of how both sections of the community appeared to be represented amongst the volunteers in Romania.

Cedric's comments were fairly representative of how all the unionist sample referred to the story: 'It was great to see that, you know. So it just goes to prove, all sides [meaning both communities] can do things together . . . they were from all sides like, you know what I mean?'

Gilly added that it was 'strange' that people from the North [meaning representatives from both communities] could work together while abroad but seemed unable to function in the same way at home. She said: 'It's strange how . . . here [in Northern Ireland] it's different – you know what I mean?'

Isaac and Rachel responded to this story by using· it as an opportunity to display hostility towards the IRA and providing yet more evidence of the use of highly selective interpretative strategies. Rachel said: 'It wasn't IRA men went out to help in Romania'. And she went on to explain herself saying that '. . . they [the IRA] were too busy bombing the like of Sion Mills'.

Significantly, many of the nationalist group stated their opinion that the Romanian story was the most memorable item in the programme. When asked the initial question of what they remembered about the news programme, over half the nationalist group recalled the Romanian story first. For example, Dermot said that of all the stories the Romanian item 'would stick out more'. Larry and Paddy both replied when asked which story was most important, 'Romania and Sion Mills'.

The nationalist sample tended to interpret the thematic content of the Romanian story in the same way as the unionist sample. They spoke of the good will of the volunteers from both communities who were trying to help those less fortunate. For example, Mary spoke of the fact that the same cross-community spirit would not exist in Northern Ireland, '. . . because of the continuing situation here'.

The largely common response to this story, that the volunteers should be admired, may well be due to the fact that it was perceived as not overtly threatening or representing either group's interests in a partisan way. The cross-community effort referred to by the audience members was not directly mentioned in the text. The story appears to have been read in this way by most of the sample audience members because the volunteers were identified by name and urban area in the story. These details, to people from Northern Ireland, are normally a clear indication of which community that person might belong to. For example, volunteers were named and identified as being from the Shankill and others as being from north Belfast, consequently the audience members appear to have conferred nationalist or unionist identities on them.

## News Story 1 – Sport

Although the sports coverage was the first news item on the programme, all the participants discussed the other news items first. This was probably because the serious and graphic nature of the subsequent 'hard news' stories such as Sion Mills overshadowed the sports coverage.

Most of the unionist audience utilised particular discourses when speaking about the sports coverage. Cedric and Janice initially stated that they believed sport to be divorced from politics. The labile nature of conversation was revealed when this discussion developed. Cedric eventually became more specific, referring to details of the sports text. He said that gaelic football was 'a Catholic game', and added:

> It's ah . . . well, let us put it this way, they say it's an RC [Roman Catholic] game, you know what I mean, cause it's GAA . . . it's what, Gaelic what . . . Amateur Association or something like that. It's like, Protestant children brought up to go to church and Catholic children brought up to go to chapel. Well, their game goes along with their religion.

Cedric related how he believed that soccer was also caught in the sectarian divide, saying: 'It's like the Blues [Linfield] would never sign a Roman Catholic, You know what I mean?'

Cedric, Rachel and Isaac said that they viewed sport as being divorced from politics. Rachel said that, 'It's all right as a sport, you know'. But when asked if she would ever watch Gaelic, she quickly replied in mock horror: 'No. Ha, ha!' Isaac added: 'No, I never watch Gaelic. Sometimes I watch football [meaning soccer]'. When first asked about the sports coverage, Isaac immediately replied, 'Linfield beat Ards 5:2', thus indicating which sports item was most important to him.

Tony and Susan's responses to the sports story were thematically different from other members of the unionist audience. Susan said that her only interest in sport was when the coverage was actually about something that had local relevance to either herself or Tony. Tony, like Cedric, struggled to correctly interpret gaelic football's title of 'All Ireland', but also added; 'Yes, well I do, I love a bit of Gaelic, although I'm a rugby follower'. Referring to the text he said: 'It was Down playing Meath. Last year Down won the . . . [he could not recall the title of All Ireland] it was the first time Down had won . . . That was a big accomplishment for Down'. Tony continued by criticising some of the unionist politicians who refused to congratulate the Down gaelic team on their 'athletic accomplishment' [winning the All Ireland Championship]. Tony also talked about how sport in Northern Ireland is affected by sectarian attitudes. Speaking of gaelic and rugby he was of the opinion that they are 'two sets of sports. They are completely separated. You never get gaelic people playing in it [rugby]'.

Those members of the nationalist sample audience who discussed the sports story displayed favourable attitudes toward Gaelic and less favourable attitudes toward soccer. Mary, Larry and Patrick joked when asked about the sport, saying that they had no interest in sport. Referring to the television footage of the match Dermot said: 'Aye, I enjoyed the . . . with Down winning the All Ireland, it was good to see them back on again playing Meath. I think that it's a good idea. Especially with the BBC, they seem to be giving Gaelic a bit more coverage'. In this discussion Dermot was speaking of his enthusiasm for television coverage of gaelic football which he believed was underrepresented until recently. Benny responded similarly and added, 'It was a draw [Meath v Down]. There wasn't great support there. There wasn't a big crowd there even after them winning the All Ireland'.

Brenda and Siobhán had little to say in relation to the gaelic coverage, but their attitude towards soccer was unfavourable. In reply to a reminder question from the researcher: 'There was the Linfield match and the dog racing?' Siobhán said, dismissively: 'Just as I said, I'd love to go to the dogs'. The researcher judged Siobhán's failure to respond to the reminder question about the Linfield match and use of the term 'I'd love to go to the dogs' as a means of reply that was derogatory, showing her dislike for Linfield.

Benny discussed the Linfield match in terms of his recent experience of Linfield supporters: 'I went down to watch a football match when Linfield were playing here. They [the Linfield supporters] weren't there to watch a match at all, they are just bigots. They wrecked the club and everything after the match'.

## Discussion

The presentation of sections of the narrative accounts of the news programme illustrates a variety of audience reactions. Foremost, was the mobilising of pre-existing belief structures by the audience members. A good example of this is the Sion Mills story, which produced the most divergent interpretations and which appear to be determined by pre-existing attitudes towards the IRA. This reaction is also evident in relation to other news stories, for example, responses to the Orange parade story. In this case the audience referred to the legitimacy or illegitimacy of Orange parades occurring in the Irish Republic, while this issue went unmentioned in the text. The arguments about the legitimacy of Orange parades in what is perceived as a nationalist area must have been known by the audience before they encountered the news text.

Many responses also seemed to be motivated by, and functioned to reaffirm, particular social group interest. When Cedric spoke of the Orange parades, he couched his discussion in the terms that Catholics have 'their day and we have ours'. This implies that if the same marching tradition exists within both communities then Orangemen are justified in parading. Rachel uniquely managed to use the Romanian orphans' story to reinforce her opinion of the IRA. When praising the work of the volunteers, whom she identified as being from both communities, she added her opinion that IRA members would not volunteer for such work.

There was evidence of audience recall of fragments of textual information which again occurred within communally patterned ways. For example, Dermot frequently recalled specific textual content to allow him to talk about news stories in a way that was not threatening to his political attitude. For instance, in relation to the Sion Mills story he recalled the interview between the

Government Minister, John Cope, and the DUP MP, William McCrea, saying that it was staged, and ignored the rest of the text. In response to the Orange parade story he recalled that there were a number of big fat men marching in the parade.

Similarly Cedric recalled details of the Sion Mills bombing story that portrayed the destructive nature of the attack. These details served to validate his negative attitude towards the IRA. The respondents' selection of specific fragments of the text and failure to recall significant amounts of detail or information illustrates how they actually attended to only small and selected parts of the total news stories.

The stories about the Peace People and Romanian orphans elicited the least divisive interpretations. In relation to the Peace People story, there was some evidence of diverse interpretations particularly aligned to gender. The male members of both cultural groups were critical of the Peace People; all responded with their opinion that the founder members of the organisation had misappropriated funds. Some of the male members also viewed the Peace People as being a women's organisation. All of the female participants from the designated unionist group responded in positive terms to the Peace People story. They nostalgically recalled the early days of the movement and appeared to favour the objectives of the current movement. Mary was the only member of the nationalist group who responded in a positive way to this story when she welcomed the announcement of the grant aid awarded to the Peace People.

So despite the importance of ethno-political discourses in mediating audience responses, we can see from the above that other discourses such as gender were also brought to bear on the negotiation of meanings. And there are indications that other responses may have been generated by the family circumstances of the selected groups. The designated nationalist group all had young children, whereas the unionist group were either older with adult children, or in the case of Rachel and Isaac had no children. In reply to the missing girl story, all of the nationalist group criticised elements of the textual content. Benny asked why the mother was alone in the televised appeal for the girl's safe return and he wondered about the absence of the girl's father. Dermot wondered if the missing girl had been beaten and Mary wondered if she had run away from home before. The unionist group who had no young children significantly made little or no response to this story. This serves to demonstrate the possibility that people selectively choose to ignore a piece of text because it is perceived as serving no purpose in their lives.

Finally, the audience groups through their cultural and social differences were able to generate radically different responses to a single television news programme. This activity occurred especially in response to media information about which the audience already possessed fixed ideas. The audience responses were most diverse when they viewed news stories that they perceived as having direct relevance to their everyday lives.

# References

Ang, Ien (1990) 'Culture and Communication: Towards an Ethnographic Critique of Media Consumption in the Transnational Media System', *European Journal of Communication*, 5 (June): 239–60.

Ang, Ien (1991) *Desperately Seeking the Audience*. London–New York: Routledge.

Buckland, Patrick (1981) *A History of Northern Ireland*. Dublin: Gill and Macmillan.

Cathcart, Rex (1984) *The Most Contrary Region: The BBC In Northern Ireland 1924–84*. Belfast: Blackstaff Press.

Curran, James (1990) 'The new revisionism in mass communication research: a reappraisal', *European Journal of Communication*, 5 (2–3).

Habermas, Jürgen (1969) 'Reason and the Rationalization of Society', *The Theory of Communicative Action*. Vol. 1, London: Heinemann.

Habermas, Jürgen (1987) 'Lifeworld and System: A Critique of Functionalist Reason', trans. Thomas McCarthy, *The Theory of Communicative Action*. Vol. 2. Cambridge: Polity.

Laganbank Alliance (1996) 'Laganbank Focus, news sheet', Belfast: Laganbank Alliance.

Lindlof, Thomas (ed.) (1987) *Natural Audiences: Qualitative Research of Media Uses and Effects*. New Jersey: Albex Publications.

Lindlof, Thomas (1988) 'Media Audiences as Interpretive Communities', in J. Anderson (ed.), *Communication Yearbook* II, pp. 81–107.

Lull, James (1990) *Inside Family Viewing: Ethnographic Research on Television Audiences*. London–New York: Routledge.

Melody, William (1988) 'Pan-European Television: Commercial and Cultural Implications of European Satellites', in P. Drummond and R. Patterson (eds) *Television and Its Audience: International Research Perspectives*. London: BFI Publishing.

Morley, David (1974) 'Reconceptualising the Media Audience: Towards an Ethnography of Audiences', Stencilled Occasional Paper, C.C.C.S., University of Birmingham.

Morley, David (1980) *The 'Nationwide' Audience*. London: BFI.

Morley, David (1981) 'The *Nationwide* Audience: a critical postscript', *Screen Education*, 39.

Morley, David (1986) *Family Television*. London: Comedia.

Watson, Raymond (1993) 'How Do People Interpret Television News?: Northern Ireland – An Ethnographic Case Study'. Master of Philosophy thesis, University of Ulster, Coleraine.

# SECTION FOUR
# POWER AND THE PUBLIC SPHERE

8

# 'The Ryanline Is Now Open . . .' Talk Radio and the Public Sphere

## Sara O'Sullivan

'It used to be the parish pump. But in the Ireland of the 1990s, national radio seems to have taken over as the place where the nation meets' (Frank McNally, *The Irish Times*, 29 November 1995).

'. . . if radio is genuinely the sound of the nation talking to itself . . . we are for the most part a stinking, non-thinking talking-ship of fools' (Jonathan Philbin Bowman, *Sunday Independent*, 5 November 1995).

Talk radio provides a rare opportunity for Irish audiences to participate in mass mediated debate and discussion. Despite the popularity of the genre, it has been given limited attention by Irish sociologists.[1] In this chapter I wish to analyse the forum offered by one Irish talk radio show, *The Gerry Ryan Show*, and to consider the significance of this active audience participation. This discussion is based on a qualitative study of telephone callers to *The Gerry Ryan Show*, involving an analysis of the calls made to the show during the week 9–13 May 1994, and, subsequently, the undertaking of 27 in-depth interviews with these callers.

*The Gerry Ryan Show* is broadcast on 2FM each week-day from 9.00–12.00 and has been on the air since 14 March 1988 (Russell, 1991: 27). It is the most popular show on 2FM, with a reach of 382,876, and an average quarter-hour audience of 228,085 (MRBI, 1995: 81).[2] My interest is in those audience members who call *The Gerry Ryan Show* and participate in this live, on-air discussion. What makes this show particularly interesting is that it offers access to listeners, and in this way allows the audience to participate in meaning making. We have here a clear example of public debate occurring within a media context. This chapter is broadly located within what Corner (1991) terms the 'public knowledge project' and will focus on analysing the kind of participation offered by *The Gerry Ryan Show*. I have used Habermas's concept of the public sphere to help frame this discussion.[3] My interest is in whether *The Gerry Ryan Show* can be seen as part of the public sphere, or whether the show is 'just' entertainment, masquerading as debate. I am also interested in the space provided by the show for private sphere issues to be raised in a very public forum. I will argue that this study does not offer any evidence to support the suggestion that *The Gerry Ryan Show* is part of the public sphere, as defined by Habermas. However it would be wrong to see the show simply as entertainment. Callers to *The Gerry Ryan Show* may not be engaging in rational-critical debate, but their participation must be systematically analysed, rather than being dismissed.

Most of the American research on talk radio has taken a functionalist approach to the genre, and the focus has been on audience uses and gratifications.[4] This work can be divided into two main areas. Talk radio is often thought of in relation to its democratic functions; researchers have focused on the role talk radio plays in keeping listeners up-to-date with political issues, and how talk radio shows provide a forum where these issues can be discussed by ordinary citizens (see Levin, 1987; Hofstetter *et al.*, 1994). In a survey of local households and local leaders in Terre Haute Indiana, Crittenden (1971: 210) found that *Speak Out*, a local talk radio show, 'certainly seems to stimulate political communication and to formulate political issues to some degree'. Listeners found the programme educational, and frequent listeners were more likely to be involved in local political and civil issues. Crittenden (1971: 209) concludes that this programme 'makes an important democratic contribution' in the Terre Haute area. Verwey (1990: 39) argues that radio call-ins provide public service information for listeners, allow social criticism, and work as an instant 'complaint channel'. An important unintended consequence of Canadian call-in shows 'was their capacity to get regional public works done and public complaints attended to more quickly than . . . any other way' (Verwey, 1990: 233).

In a different approach Turrow (1974) introduces the idea that talk radio can be analysed as a form of interpersonal communication. His hypothesis was that calling a talk radio show is a substitute for the interpersonal contact that is missing in people's lives, due primarily to the problems associated with urban living. Thus 'callers will not mention influencing the audience when asked why they like speaking on radio' (1974: 174). Bierig and Dimmick (1979) also argue that callers to talk radio shows are seeking human contact rather than trying to mobilise others into action. They do, however, suggest that the difference between their findings and Crittenden's may be linked to the different functions provided by talk radio shows in different areas. In their study of a late night talk show it was found that 'callers were more likely to be single, alone and not a member of any organisation' (Bierig and Dimmick, 1979: 92). In a smaller community such as Terre Haute it is possible that a lack of interpersonal communication is relatively rare.

Tramer and Jeffres (1983) argue that people use talk radio both as a forum and as a companion. A survey of 181 callers to three different talk shows found that 24 per cent called to use the programme as a forum, while 27 per cent called to chat. The authors (1983: 300) point out the similarities with the uses made by women of soap operas, which functioned both as an escape outlet, and as a source of information about the problems of everyday life: 'Just as Herzog found radio soap operas functional outlets for escape some forty years ago, today's talk radio formats are providing a similar outlet for today's isolated listeners'.

These studies can all be located within a uses and gratifications perspective. Talk show audiences are presented as having found a genre that meets some of their informational or interpersonal 'needs'. Morley (1992: 118) has pointed to the limits of the uses and gratifications perspective, and I would agree that people's responses to the media cannot be understood 'in terms simply of individual psychologies . . . [but] are founded on cultural differences embedded within the structure of society – cultural clusters which guide and limit individual's interpretation of messages'. The uses and gratifications theoretical framework was not found to be particularly useful in relation to callers to *The Gerry Ryan Show*.[5] This study aims to go beyond this type of approach in order to uncover the meaning and significance of participation in *The Gerry Ryan Show*, both for the individual callers and for the wider audience.

## 'Types' of Calls

Calls to *The Gerry Ryan Show* are not homogeneous, and include the bizarre and the entertaining, as well as the serious. A complex framework is required to include these very different call 'types'. From my analysis of the 83 calls over one week to *The Gerry Ryan Show* I have identitifed four 'types' of calls (see Table 1 below), each of which I will discuss in turn.[6] It must be noted that 65 per cent of these callers are women; this can be compared to the average audience, which is 57 per cent female and 43 per cent male (MRBI, 1995: 90).

### The Expressive Call

The expressive call allows the caller to express his or her views on a subject. The call may be emotive, 'concerned to reveal one's own personality and interests' in relation to the subject under discussion, or it may be connotive, 'a means of influencing others' (Crisell, 1986: 183). In the expressive call the mode of discussion is debate, and many of these calls are focused on public sphere issues. The great majority of the 34 expressive calls over this week can be classified as emotive and both men and women are represented in this group. Only two callers can be classified as connotive, that is as trying to influence listeners in some way.

Table 1 *Types of Calls*

| Call Type | | Callers to The Gerry Ryan Show 9–13 May | | | No. of Research interviews with each type of call | | |
|---|---|---|---|---|---|---|---|
| | | Men | Women | Total | Men | Women | Total |
| **A** | **Expressive** | | | | | | |
| (i) | Emotive | 11 | 21 | 32 | 5 | 7 | 12 |
| (ii) | Connotive | 2 | 0 | 2 | 1 | 0 | 1 |
| **B** | **Exhibitionist** | 8 | 5 | 13 | 3 | 1 | 4 |
| **C** | **Service Encounter** | | | | | | |
| (i) | Advice Seekers | 0 | 2 | 2 | 0 | 1 | 1 |
| (i) | Advice Givers | 0 | 3 | 3 | 0 | 2 | 2 |
| (iii) | Asking a question | 4 | 14 | 18 | 1 | 1 | 2 |
| (iv) | Answering a question | 4 | 5 | 9 | 0 | 2 | 2 |
| **D** | **Troubles-Telling** | 0 | 4 | 4 | 0 | 3 | 3 |
| | | N=29 | N=54 | N = 83 | N=10 | N=17 | N = 27 |

## The Exhibitionist Call

In contrast, with an exhibitionist call 'the caller's aim is not so much to vent his opinions on a particular topic as to project his personality, to become a performer' (Crisell, 1986: 185). The context of these calls must not be forgotten; callers are ringing a popular radio show and for some callers getting on-air is the purpose for their call. Thirteen calls from this week can be categorised as exhibitionist calls; this is the only grouping where males outnumbered females. These calls usually take the form of either telling an amusing story, or reciting a poem the caller has written. These calls revolve around entertainment not debate. One respondent explains this difference:

> . . . I think it depends on you know the reason why you'd be phoning up [(yeah)] I mean *if it was just something like that, just an amusing story I think half the time it's just to be there to tell it*, do you know what I mean [(yeah)] and if it's a much more serious topic and you, you know, you're probably more inclined not to be concerned with being on the radio as opposed to, you know you want to put your point across.
>
> (Caller 21: Englishman, living in rural Ireland, works from home)

## The Service Encounter

Parallels can be drawn between some calls and what conversation analysts term the service encounter.[7] The service encounter can be seen as an instrumental encounter, where talking is a means to a non-verbal end; 'the Service Encounter's business may be characterised as Solving a Problem . . . the focal object is the "problem and its properties"' (Jefferson and Lee, 1981: 411). The service encounter can deal with advice; here the problem is a personal one, involving self-disclosure, and the five calls in this sub-group (two advice seekers and three advice givers) were all made by women. Another form of service encounter is the question/answer format. *The Gerry Ryan Show* often features in-studio 'experts' who are there to answer listeners' questions. In the week 9–13 May two such 'experts' appeared on *The Gerry Ryan Show*. The show also features callers who ring in with practical questions for listeners; as one caller put it, '. . . you tend to go to The Ryan Show because he has a large listenership [(uhum)] (. . .) I thought there's bound to be somebody out there with an answer' (Caller 15: unemployed man, living in rural town, but brought up in Dublin).

## Troubles-Telling[8]

Troubles-telling is an expressive encounter where the talk is an end in itself, and 'the focal object is the "teller and his experiences"' (Jefferson and Lee, 1981: 411). While troubles-telling and service encounter can be seen as quite similar, insofar as both deal with troubles, an important difference between the two is that advice will usually be rejected in a troubles-telling, particularly if it comes early on in the discussion. It is inappropriate to respond to a troubles-telling with advice; the speaker is aligned as a troubles-teller, not an advice-recipient, and must be allowed to tell the full trouble (Jefferson and Lee, 1980: 410). In the week in question there are four instances where callers have rung the show to recount a trouble. Again these calls frequently involve self-disclosure and this group is also exclusively female. I would argue that this 'type' of call shares characteristics with troubles talk in 'ordinary' conversation, in particular the caller is looking for emotional reciprocity rather than advice. This reciprocity is provided by subsequent callers, who call to recount similar experiences. Gerry Ryan also provides these callers with sympathy and support.

My interest is in the space provided to callers by *The Gerry Ryan Show* to express a 'private' opinion on public matters, and to discuss the 'private' in a very public fashion. This is part of a general trend in Western society identified by Meyrowitz; 'private and public behavior are no longer separated. People's personal feelings are shown – visually on television, audibly on the radio' (Reiner, 1995: 67). Therefore I wish to focus on expressive calls, and those calls involving self-disclosure, namely troubles-telling and advice seeking advice-giving. Here I shall be drawing extensively on my interviews with those who called *The Gerry Ryan Show* during this week. I am interested in two related issues, whether talk radio can be seen as a public sphere, and what the significance of this public discussion of private matters might be. To help frame this discussion I will briefly introduce Jurgen Habermas's work on the public sphere. I will then move on to a presentation of each of these two caller group-ings, followed by a discussion of the participation offered to these very different kinds of callers by *The Gerry Ryan Show*.

## The Public Sphere

In *The Structural Transformation of the Public Sphere* (1989), Habermas analyses the rise and the fall of the eighteenth century public sphere. He begins his discussion by locating the bourgeois public sphere within a general model of state and society. Habermas argues that in the eighteenth century there was a clear division between what he terms the 'private realm', and what he terms the 'sphere of public authority' (see Table 2 below). Within the private realm Habermas differentiates between the private sphere, consisting of the family and the economy, and the bourgeois public sphere, 'a public sphere constituted by private people' (1989: 30). In this bourgeois public sphere 'private citizens debate issues of public concern . . . in an environment free of power relations', where the force of the better argument wins (McLaughlin, 1993: 601). Discussion cen-tered on issues of the common good, and involved 'the problematization of areas that until then had . . . remained a preserve in which church and state authorities had the monopoly of interpretation' (Habermas, 1989: 36). Habermas locates the public sphere in the world of letters, in the coffee houses and salons of eighteenth-century Europe. He argues that debate here was shaped by the reading material read by individuals, and that novels and newspapers served as 'organs of public information and debate' (McCarthy, 1989: xii).

Table 2 *Social Realms in the Eighteenth Century*
*(adapted from Habermas, 1989: 30)*

| Private Realm | | Sphere of Public Authority |
|---|---|---|
| Civil society (realm of commodity exchange and social labor) | Public sphere in the political realm | State (realm of the 'police') |
| | Public sphere in the world of letters (clubs, press) | |
| Conjugal family's internal space | 'Town' (market of culture products) | Court (courtly-noble society) |

Habermas argues that both the private and the public spheres were trans-formed with the development of the welfare state. He focuses on two main developments here, both involving a breakdown of the separation between state and society that can be seen in Table 2. Firstly the state penetrated the private sphere; here he simply means that the development of the welfare state involved state intervention in both the family and the realm of commodity exchange and social labour. The second development he notes involves 'organized private interests' invading the public sphere (1989: 179). These organised private interests would include public relations companies, special interest groups, political parties and so on, that is groups that are 'not representative of the interests of private people as the public' (Habermas, 1989: 189). This development is significant as it changes the nature of the public sphere. The public sphere becomes a forum for competition between these private interests; this precludes any orientation to the common good, a key requirement for the public sphere. The net result is that the public sphere 'becomes the court before whose public prestige can be displayed – rather than in which public critical debate is carried out' (Habermas, 1989: 201). The public sphere becomes 'a public sphere in appearance only' (Habermas, 1989: 171). He also identifies a move from a culture-debating to a culture-consuming public (Habermas, 1989: 159–62).

There are numerous problems with Habermas's account of the degradation of the public sphere and it is certainly doubtful whether his account is historically accurate (see for example Ryan, 1993; Eley, 1993).[9] Feminist scholars point to the patriarchal character of the bourgeois public sphere and argue that a central feature of this model is women's exclusion from this rational-critical debate, and their relegation to the private sphere.[10] The link Habermas identifies between mass mediated communication and democratic politics is, however, of interest in relation to talk radio. The mass media are central to any discussion of the contemporary public sphere. Kress (1986) argues that the potential for dialogue exists in relation to talk radio, although the caller always remains in a position of disadvantage, as control ultimately rests with the host (see also Moss and Higgins, 1986; Avery and McCain, 1986; Karpf, 1980).[11] The first question I wish to address is whether *The Gerry Ryan Show* can be seen as part of the public sphere.[12] Here I will draw on my interviews with expressive callers.

The second question that will be considered is whether self-disclosure in the public sphere can be seen as emancipatory, or as part of what Habermas (1987) terms the colonisation of the lifeworld by the system.[13] Some writers dispute Habermas's insistence that discussion in the public sphere should be confined to issues of general concern, as this works to situate the private sphere 'outside the realm of justice' (Benhabib, 1993: 92). Fraser argues that both public and private 'are cultural classifications and rhetorical labels. In political discourse they are powerful terms frequently deployed to delegitimate some interests, views and topics and to valorize others' (1993: 131). Labelling something as private excludes it from debate.[14] As a result, the 'private domain, women's traditional "sphere", is very often the realm of the oblique and unspoken' (Meaney, 1993: 241). A belief that private sphere issues should not be automatically excluded from the public sphere is central to feminist thinking, as is suggested by the slogan 'the personal is the political'. The feminist emancipatory project involves the renegotiation of public and private boundaries, in order to make 'what were hitherto considered private matters of the good life into public issues of justice' (Benhabib, 1993: 92). Fraser sees the opening up of the private sphere as an emancipatory process. As private needs come into public view they 'lose their illusory aura of naturalness as their interpretations become subject to critique and contestation' (Fraser, 1989: 160). Habermas (1989: 158–9), on the other hand, is pessimistic about this 'floodlit privacy', which he views as a symptom of 'the destruction of the relationship between public and private spheres'. We have here two very different ways of viewing this 'opening-up' of the private sphere.

## Expressive Calls

Callers in this group had rung the show to disagree with points others had made (seven callers), to express agreement (two callers), or to add a new point to the discussion (three callers). The mode of discussion here is debate, and callers offer different forms of evidence to support their contributions. Some callers offer no 'proof' to support their opinion, but instead draw on traditional norms or values. This caller is clearly appealing to traditional norms about femininity:

> Em just I suppose, just on impulse when I heard the people saying, some people saying it [body hair on women] was attractive and saying would they not think it was attractive, just you know I didn't think it was attractive so I just thought I'd say it.
>
> (Caller 19: Dublin woman, working in the home)

Similarly, although this male caller claims his contribution is factual and objective, it is clear that it is not a 'fact' but a belief or an opinion that he is expressing:

> Just about *the fact* that eh you know there could be an attempt made on him [Nelson Mandela] or whatever, you know. Em on his life, you know (. . .) em, well it's not so much that I feel strongly on the issue of South Africa. I feel strongly that too many people are being naive about the whole thing (. . .) *People have got to be objective* about the whole thing and see it from both sides of the coin rather than sort of saying oh its terrific for the black community, you know that em there is going to be trouble.
>
> (Caller 2: Rural man, self-employed)

In contrast other callers draw on their own experiences or observations to support their point. For these callers, the show allows them to challenge statements which contradict their own lived experience; these calls have a powerful authenticity. One woman called to disagree with two previous callers who were arguing that women were useless drivers; to support her argument she explained

'. . . I drive for a living, I'm a taxi driver . . .' (Caller 18: rural woman). Gerry Ryan offered support to a caller making similar claims: '. . . you should know, you do 1,000 miles a week . . .'. Another caller draws on her childhood experiences to back up her point:

> Em well there was a lot of violence in *The Family*, you know and somebody rang up Gerry and said Charlo is not a real person, and things like that don't happen. *And they do, I was reared in that, I seen it* you know. And there's a lot of children out there still being physically abused and mentally tortured, you know [(uhum)] . . .[15]
>
> (Caller 25: Dublin woman, self-employed)

## The 'Set-Up'

The topic that attracted the most callers during the week was the discussion about women drivers, introduced by caller 5. This call provoked quite a response both from women and other men and the topic ran for the rest of the week. However all was not as it seemed; although several times during the week Gerry Ryan commented that he was surprised that this one was still running, this call was apparently set up by the show:[16]

> . . . But in reality when I rang *The Gerry Ryan Show* I rang to say could you find out where they get those statistics from, that women are proven to be better drivers than men (. . .) so the next morning a guy rang me back and said, *The Gerry Ryan Show*, blah, blah, blah, you were on yesterday about women drivers and I said yeah and he said well, could you go on the air today and really stir it up [(laughs)] you know he kind of said well we want you to go on and gizz people up, you know, not just get on with a straight face and say, where did those statistics come from, but we want you to get on – I knew what he was saying, you know. He wanted me to go on and condemn women drivers into the ground and in other words aggravate the women driving population of Ireland. [(uhum)] Just to stir things up, which is really what his show is all about, you know. So eh I did and then it took off from there . . .
>
> (Caller 5: Dublin man, sells telecommunications equipment)

So, although this caller had rung in with a quite serious question, someone working on the show saw the call had the potential to 'gizz people up' and he was only too happy to oblige. It is interesting that the call backfired on him and had real world consequences that he had not anticipated:

> But eh I was surprised that a few friends of mine (. . .) suddenly jumping down my throat [(uhum, uhum)] (. . .) Normally these are people who would be very calm and collected and weigh up all possibilities and let you be entitled to your opinion without getting uptight about it. [(uhum)] But in this case I was entitled to nothing ((laughs)) [(uhum)] I was just slaughtered, you know.
>
> (Caller 5)

He invokes the democratic ideal of freedom of speech here, but does not see the irony in discussing his experience as if the call was not a set-up.

This caller has a very negative view of the participation offered by the show. This is not surprising given his experience of calling the show. For him stirring things up 'is really what his show is all about'. However he moves beyond his own experience of calling and suggests that the show is about manipulation not participation. The show works because Gerry Ryan turns all callers into good radio material, no matter what their original purpose for ringing was, 'he has a wonderful ability for someone just to ring up off the street and suddenly make an engrossing story out of them, just on the spot, instantaneously [(uhum)]' (Caller 5). All credit goes to Gerry Ryan; he has the talent to make mundane calls engrossing. After all the purpose of the show is entertainment. It can be argued that this challenges the idea that *The Gerry Ryan Show* can be seen as a valuable forum.[17]

## The *Gerry Ryan Show* as Public Sphere?

*The Gerry Ryan Show* can be said to provide a space for these expressive callers to air what they think. Furthermore it is ordinary people's views and not those of 'experts' that are broadcast. One respondent makes this distinction clearly:

> I think its important, you know, so many people, so many people, you know, you get a good understanding of other people's points of view and general public's point of view on a certain topic [(uhum)] (. . .) I think that's important, because you know usually when you're listening to em, em, television programmes and radio programmes all you are hearing is *reported views* of people in the business [(uhum)] And its, you know, I think public opinion is very important and I think its good that you can, you know get a chance to hear it and air your own points of view.
>
> (Caller 21: Englishman, living in rural Ireland, works from home)

This can be seen as important given the widespread fear that the lifeworld is being colonised by 'experts' (see Livingstone and Lunt, 1994). However on this evidence I find it difficult to be optimistic about the participation taken up by these expressive callers. The show may allow for the expression of different opinions, but, from the evidence of this week, this is at the expense of any critical discussion of social and political issues.[18] Furthermore, as Calhoun (1993: 29) argues, communication in a public sphere is 'not merely sharing what people already think or know but a process of potential transformation in which reason is advanced by debate itself'. The rules of debate in the public sphere demand that 'arguments are analysed rather than simply aired' (Livingstone and Lunt, 1992: 14). These findings lend support to Tuchman's argument that 'modern media may encourage citizens to know more, even to be more opinionated, but to do less about public affairs' (cited in Livingstone and Lunt, 1994: 15). As one respondent puts it:

> It wasn't really a very serious conversation that people were going to come to blows over, you know. It was really *just opinions* [(yeah)] (. . .) Two different points of view and that was that . . .
>
> (Caller 12: Rural man, self-employed and works from home)

Crucially it can be argued that this expression of public opinion is not translated into social or political action. Only two callers in this grouping were
looking for any action consequences from their call to the show.[19] One of these
explains the response she was hoping for when she made the call:

> But em the morning that I rang Gerry Ryan I was hoping that a nun or a priest
> would ring up and say right we can look into this, look into areas and we'll
> actually do something for children. They didn't. But I was glad that I did put that
> little thought out there and hoping that somebody would ring up and argue with
> me, you know. [(uhum)] Gerry might even ask me back and I'd argue with them.
> I'd tell them to do this and that that does goes on and that they don't bother
> looking into it.
>
> I: Uhum, uhum. So were you disappointed that it didn't go on any further?
> / A little bit, yeah. I was. Like that's not Gerry's fault. He was there open and
> ready to take it, but it just proves my point.
> (Caller 25: Dublin woman, self-employed)

This caller hoped she would provoke those in authority to respond. No one
picked up on this and there were no more calls on *The Family* that day (11
May). It is interesting that the caller blames those whom she felt should have
responded and this disappointment does not affect her attitude towards Gerry
Ryan.

The show does offer access to its listeners and as such positions the
audience as citizens, not simply consumers. All listeners are included in Gerry
Ryan's invitation to phone the show, from anywhere in Ireland for the price of
a local call: 'The Ryanline is now open on 1–850– . . . You tell us and we'll tell
them'. Talk radio therefore allows minority groups the possibility of speaking
'rather than only being spoken about' (Kress, 1986: 417). However, in practice
access to the show is controlled by those working on the show and callers must
make it past the show's broadcasting assistants.[20] This control on participation
makes it difficult to see how the show might have a contribution to make to the
public sphere, where, in theory at least, access should be open to all (Habermas,
1989: 37). Furthermore the discovery of a 'set-up' raises some serious questions
about how this on-air debate is managed, or perhaps even manipulated. It must
also be acknowledged that although RTÉ is a public service broadcaster, a significant proportion (51 per cent) of its revenue comes from advertising (RTÉ,
1995: 22). The main purpose of *The Gerry Ryan Show* is to attract as many
listeners as possible, rather than to provide a forum for debate. To keep its
listenership high the show must be entertaining. The production team are
proud of the 'zany' reputation that the show enjoys, and are wary of 'boring'
material (see Russell, 1991). The main news stories of the day are seen as RTÉ
Radio 1's 'turf'.[21] The show attracts an audience on the basis that it is different
to *The Gay Byrne Show*, *Liveline* or *The Pat Kenny Show*. Entertainment then
can be seen as the key production value, and the team would seem to take the

position that while rational–critical debate does not always make 'good' radio, 'crack' does.[22]

Finally, on a more positive note, *The Gerry Ryan Show* can be seen to offer more to the daytime listener than its 'pop and prattle' predecessors.[23] Radio stations have tended to view daytime listeners as housewives and consumers, with limited interests. As Barnard (1989: 143) has noted,

> We [Essex Radio, UK] call our average listener Doreen . . . Doreen isn't stupid but she's only listening with half an ear, and doesn't necessarily understand long words. That doesn't mean that we treat her like a fool but that we make sure she understands first time.

*The Gerry Ryan Show* does not assume either that its listeners are all women, which of course they are not, or that those women who are listening have limited interests and are uninterested in public sphere issues.[24] Instead the show keeps listeners up-to-date with important social, political and moral issues. Over recent years the show has dealt at length with range of weighty topics, covering international, national and local issues. These have included, for example, child sexual abuse, the role of the Catholic Church in Irish society, rape, domestic violence, the war in the former Yugoslavia, French nuclear testing in the Pacific, conditions in Romanian and Chinese orphanages, the Beef Tribunal, Travellers' rights, environmental issues, and so on. These topics have not been dealt with in a trivial manner, and so it would be wrong to see the show simply as providing entertainment.

## Self-Disclosure: Troubles-Telling and the Service Encounter

For other callers *The Gerry Ryan Show* offers a space in the public sphere where matters of public concern may be discussed with others in similar situations. Here experience is privileged and it is people's own direct experience of the topic that motivates and legitimates their call to the show. It is the callers who are setting the agenda with these calls and it is primarily other listeners they are addressing rather than Gerry Ryan; callers are looking for a response from others who have experienced what they are currently going through (advice-seekers/givers), or are sharing their own experience with a previous caller (troubles-telling). The key mechanism here is identification rather than debate and there is a consensus among these callers that the show can help people overcome everyday troubles.

For those calling with a problem the call can be seen as an active strategy to gain information, advice or support. The show is one of a number of possible sources of help. For one of these callers *The Gerry Ryan Show* was a last hope:

> It's just I was fed up going to doctors (. . .) and getting no answer. So I heard Gerry a couple of times helping people on the radio with different, you know,

subjects and things, about children and that, so I said well, blast it, I might as well try him. He was only the last resort . . .

> (Caller 4: Rural woman, working in the home)

This caller found others' experiences reassuring:

> . . . when you go into a doctor and you say to him about vertigo, he'll say you've an infection in your inner ear and you've to put up with it and that was that. (. . .) But when I phoned Gerry as I said to you he said 'Well maybe there's someone else suffering with it', and then there was someone else and then there was another lady, she came on. There were I think four or five that morning. It was great to listen to them all having the same problem. I knew I wasn't an outcast.
>
> (Caller 4)

So the other callers helped alleviate the isolation that this woman was feeling, and also gave her some idea of what she could expect from her illness.

Those who responded to these calls explained that it was their own experience of the subject that prompted them to ring. Following from Weiss (1976: 11) these callers can be termed 'fellow participants', who 'can offer the immediate understanding that comes only from being in the same boat':

> She [caller 4] just seemed to have, you know she was puzzled, will this go on kind of thing, she was nervous and being through it I just rang up to tell her that once they got her on the right medication (. . .) she'd be ok. I wanted to put her out of that situation, you know that kind of a way?
>
> (Caller 3: Dublin woman, semi-invalid)

This woman identified with caller 4's situation, she too suffers from vertigo and was eager to do what she could to help her. Another advice-giver offered a different motive for ringing. She had heard a previous call and felt that it would have frightened her when she was first diagnosed:

> . . . the second caller, she would have frightened the wits out of me. She seemed despondent and made it seem so bad (. . .) I felt I'd have to, I had to ring, to let the first caller [caller 4] know that you can adjust your life to it and you do learn to live with it and that was my reason for calling. So, eh, I hoped at the time it was of some consolation to the first caller [caller 4] [(uhum)] (. . .) she was a middle-aged person like myself and I didn't want her to think that well, because she got it and there was no cure for it she might as well be dead . . .
>
> (Caller 6: Dublin woman, working in the home)

This caller doubly identifies with the woman who is seeking advice; both suffer from vertigo and both are middle-aged. Thus she sees her experience as more relevant than the caller she refers to here, who was in her twenties. It is interesting that she does not hint at this disagreement while on-air and this only comes through during the interview. The caller is not trying to prove that she is correct and that the previous caller was wrong. Instead her focus is on her own experience of the condition and she hopes that this will console caller 4.

The ethos here is comparable to that of a self-help group. Experts are excluded; help comes from those 'fellow participants' who have previously experienced same problem, and so are the best qualified people to help:

> . . . It's all very well talking to professionals (. . .) [but] its like an Al Anon meeting or an AA, if you can eh identify with someone well then you'd say 'Well, that was me', and you'd kind of say 'Well, what did she do?'. Well then you can go from there. But when you have the, the professionals in they're telling you how to do it. It's just going over the surface I think. Whereas if you get in deep, in and somebody identifies, you can go from there.
>
> (Caller 24: Dublin woman, self-employed)

Calling is a practical way to help others:

> . . . I feel that by my phoning up and being able to tell people, this is what you can do, it helps other people to get around it . . . [talking about the difficulties she encountered when she discovered her husband was a transvestite]
>
> (Caller 22: Dublin woman, works in horse stables)

Another important feature of these calls is that they can allow for horizontal communication between listeners. Gerry Ryan sometimes puts callers directly in contact with one another on-air. There is also evidence that callers and listeners get in touch outside of the confines of the show. Another vertigo sufferer got in touch with caller 3 after she had been on-air:

> . . . A gentleman rang me after that. He got in touch with Gerry Ryan and they rang me after that to see if I would talk to him, because seemingly what I said he was going through (. . .) he thought he had it and he just wanted to talk. [(uhum)] And we talked and he said it was great to talk to someone. So, that time is ( ), I helped someone like that, yes I did.
>
> (Caller 3: Dublin woman: semi-invalid)

Another respondent tells how as a result of an earlier call she made to the show, about her husband who is a transvestite, one couple in a similar situation contacted her and this led to them meeting:

> In fact there was one couple actually contacted me [(uhum)] through your show em and they ended up coming to Dublin to come to the transvestite club with me [(uhum)]. So I mean I feel I've helped that one person if nothing else. And how many people got helped that didn't even contact you or me? . . .
>
> (Caller 22: Dublin woman, works in horse stables)

Thus participation can have real world consequences.

Respondents also give us a glimpse into the benefits these calls may have for those who listen but do not call. Firstly the show is informative:

> You just pick up titbits as well [(yeah)]. Even if it's nothing to do with you, somebody might say something to you about so and so and you'd say 'Ah yeah, listen, I heard so and so that you could do such and such about that problem' [(uhum)] (. . .) He's very informative apart from being entertaining.
>
> (Caller 22: Dublin woman, works in horse stables)

It also gives listeners an insight into the problems and suffering of others:

> Ah yeah. You could wake up and often in the mornings I wouldn't feel too good in myself and I mean I'd listen to Gerry and I'd hear other people's complaints and I'd say, 'Ah God, you know to meself, you know what you have, you know what you take to cure it', so, you know.
>
> (Caller 3: Dublin woman: semi-invalid)

> . . . I'm here, I won't say in the lap of luxury, if you seen it! But my family reared and him and I and we've everything we've kind of wanted, built it up over the years and I'm cribbing that I'd love to change this, I'd – there's some poor auld bitch on the radio and she's broken hearted over something really important and it makes me feel low because I'm looking for a new this or a new that and I don't really need it [(uhum)]. The programme makes me stop and listen and say, 'Well thank God for what I have. That poor bitch has nothing'. [(uhum)]. You know, maybe her house has been taken off her or the fellow has ran off and left her in the lurch or with babies. And, you know they're, they're great problems now [(uhum)]. They're the big problems and it's lovely that he listens to them (. . .) It makes the likes of me stop and say, 'Well feck it, I'm happy with what I have, get in and clean it'.
>
> (Caller 20: Dublin woman, working in the home)

The feeling with which this is said is remarkable. Others' 'big' problems give her a sense of perspective and allow her count her blessings. This respondent has identified something 'really important' herself; it would appear that she is correct and it is usually 'some auld bitch' calling with a personal problem. All the troubles-tellers and advice-seekers from this week are women (see Table 1). Several callers show they are aware that calling is gendered in this way:

> . . . I've heard people, especially women for some strange reason, it's probably because they're more emotional than men, and maybe, probably because they ring in the first place, will ring and say they have a problem about something . . .
>
> (Caller 5: Dublin man, sells telecommunications equipment)

Furthermore from the evidence of this week it is also women who respond to these calls.

In contrast several male respondents mention that calling the show with a problem is a low status activity.[25] One argues that calling the show looking for help would be a sign that you have no-one else to talk to (Caller 5). Another terms calling with a problem 'silly'. Even the word silly has feminine connotations; women and children are called silly, not men:

> . . . I don't think if it was anything in my personal life or problem I'd ring a radio station about it. I think that'd be a bit silly now.
>
> I: Why silly?
>
> / Silly? [(yeah)] Why? Eh I think you should be able to sort out your own problems without expecting the nation to ring in [(uhum)] and tell you what to do, like. [(uhum)] I think you should be mature enough to sort out your own problems without going onto the radio and talking about it.
>
> (Caller 12: Rural man, self-employed and works from home)

Central here is the belief that people should be self sufficient, not dependent on others for help.

Male callers would also seem to have a different sense of what it is appropriate to introduce to the public sphere and what should remain 'private'.[26] This is illustrated quite nicely by one respondent: 'Ah give us a break. I don't want to discuss my personal problems with half a million people in Ireland. I suffer from impotency, please help, me name is —— . . . ' (Caller 7: Dublin man, office worker).

It is not surprising to find that advice-giving is primarily associated with women callers. Advice-giving draws on traditional female competences associated with women's role in the private sphere, where women are used to taking responsibility for others' health and well-being. As Rapping (1991: 36) argues, 'In the sexual division of labour, these matters of emotional and relational care-taking and socialization have always been seen as "women's domain"'. Of course this is not to suggest that these matters are somehow 'female', but simply to point out the resonance here. This also helps explain the scorn used by the male respondents in relation to this type of call; like most other unpaid work, this 'caregiving' has always been undervalued, particularly by men (Lynch and McLaughlin, 1995).

## The *Gerry Ryan Show* – Private Talk in Public

The respondents in the troubles telling and service encounter groupings are very positive about the role the show can play, particularly in relation to its problem-solving, educational and support functions.[27] I am also interested in the significance of this public form of self-disclosure, this 'outpouring of personal information usually only revealed to one's close friends, family, minister, therapist' (Priest and Dominick, 1994: 75).[28] In Ireland over the last thirteen years, major political issues have centered on the private sphere, particularly 'on questions of socio-sexual control' of women's bodies so central to the abortion referenda in 1983 and 1992, and the divorce referenda in 1986 and 1995 (Smyth, 1995: 34). The current affairs debates around both abortion and divorce were essentially dominated by 'experts', politicians, and members of the clergy, while women with first hand experience of these issues were excluded. In relation to abortion, for example, the focus of current affairs programming was on 'how the legal and social institutions should address the question of reproductive rights, while the emotional and personal experience of abortion is deemed relevant only to the private realm' (Fletcher, 1995: 63).

In contrast talk radio provided a space where these, and other, socio-sexual issues could be discussed by those with direct experience of them. This is seen as a positive and empowering development by some commentators. Gibbons has argued, 'The only place that ordinary people could discuss these matters was the despised format of talk radio, which can hold its head high in this regard' (cited in McNally, 1995; see also Fletcher, 1995). Talk radio has also provided a space where ordinary people can use their own experiences to bring the powerful to task directly, rather than by proxy. Lavina Kerwick's harrowing phone call to *The Gerry Ryan Show*, is probably the most famous example of this.[29] Both these developments would seem like positive developments if viewed from a feminist standpoint (but see Fennell, 1993 for a different view of the Lavinia Kerwick case).[30] Talk radio can be seen as having a role to play in forcing women's private experiences into a very public arena; once these experiences have been articulated, they become much more difficult to ignore. Parallels can be made between this process and the process of 'conscientization':

> When people get together and reflect upon their lives . . . they become aware that they are victims in common together . . . when people are thus fully aware, they can act together to change those patterns that oppress them (Dodson Gray, 1989: 86).

Furthermore the power of callers to help one another, without the help of experts, can be seen as particularly important given the established power of the medical profession, a power which some writers have suggested is exercised primarily over women (see for example Davis, 1988). Karpf (1980: 51) suggests that phone-ins typecast women 'in the role of people-with-problems'. While this might be true in relation to the question/answer format involving an expert of some sort, as we have already seen *The Gerry Ryan Show* also offers us the reverse, women who have overcome their problems and are now competent and confident in the role of advice-giver (caller 3; caller 6; caller 22). The emphasis placed on callers' experience of events, rather than on expert advice, can perhaps be seen as involving a reversal of the colonization of the lifeworld. However, following from Foucault (1977), it might be suggested that these calls simply open up the life-world to another form of surveillance, a form which may be just as oppressive as that exercised by the Catholic Church or medical profession in the past.

However a note of caution must be raised in relation to these calls. Hobson (1980: 113) suggests that such calls could limit action by fooling callers into thinking they have done something simply by voicing the problem, 'the very fact of recognition and seeming discussion or consideration by some "outside" or "independent" authority gives an impression that the problems have been aired'. This could prevent the caller from taking any further action that might improve her situation. Rapping (1991: 38) raises similar issues in a discussion of American television talk shows:

> . . . what's most infuriating about them is not that they are sleazy or in bad taste. It is that they work to co-opt and contain real political change . . . They are all talk and no action . . . This makes perfect sense. It is the nature of the mass media in a contradictory social environment to take progressive ideas, once they

gain strength, and contain them in the large, immobilizing structure of the political status quo.[31]

One of the respondents in this study has also pointed out a possible negative effect on the listener of the 'poor auld bitch on the radio' (Caller 16: Dublin woman, working in the home); others' troubles invite the listener to make comparisons with her own life, which could lead her to count her blessings and so ignore her own problems.

The focus on the individual, and the individual's problems may also work to hide the social, political and cultural forces which have caused these problems, or which exasperate them. However, following Fraser (1989), I would argue that these problems, once made public, are increasingly open for critique and contestation. I would agree with O'Connor (1995: 151) that talk radio has had an important role to play in 'exposing' private issues to Irish listeners, and that women such as Lavinia Kerwick 'have inadvertently shattered the collusion of silence surrounding various aspects of patriarchal control in the legal, sexual, familial and ideological spheres'.

## Conclusion

*The Gerry Ryan Show* allows callers to express an opinion on public matters; it also allows the private to be articulated in a very public forum. This study does not suggest that the show can be seen as part of the public sphere as defined by Habermas, that is as a forum for rational-critical debate. However it does offer a forum where listeners can 'meet' and discuss important issues, although as entertainment is the producers' top priority, the value of this forum is somewhat limited. Whilst recognising these limitations, I would argue that the evidence presented here would not support the view that the listeners and callers to *The Gerry Ryan* Show can be seen as 'fools'.

It is also significant that both men and women participate in this public discussion. Previous research has found that women reject what they see as masculine genres, for example news, current affairs and political programmes, seeing them as both boring and depressing (see for example Hobson, 1980; O'Connor, 1987; Morley, 1992). Perhaps this female participation can be linked to the format; many of the discussions on *The Gerry Ryan Show* are grounded in experience, and, from the evidence of this week, it can be argued that more abstract discussion is rare. This can be seen as an important change in the rules of the political 'game', given that the differences in men and women's styles of talk, and 'the language people use as they reason usually favors one way of seeing things [i.e. male] and discourages others [i.e. female]' (Fraser, 1993: 119). Women listeners can relate to these topics by taking 'the perspective of the concrete other', by identifying with other callers' stories. This makes these issues relevant, by providing 'elements within the situation to which she can relate' (Hobson, 1980: 112). This could be of particular importance given that it has been argued that Irish women are 'more weakly oriented to the political system' than men, with only 50 per cent discussing politics at least occasionally, compared to 68 per cent of men (Hardiman and Whelan, 1994: 109).

The Gerry Ryan Show can also be seen as challenging the public/private divide; topics belonging to both spheres are considered legitimate topics for discussion and are discussed with the same seriousness. From the evidence presented here it would appear that it is overwhelmingly women callers who are involved in this public discussion of private sphere issues. This can be seen as potentially empowering, for both callers and for listeners. As O'Connor (1995: 151) has suggested, talk radio provides 'the opportunity for listeners to compare feelings and attitudes about activities, relationships and institutions which, until very recently, were protected by the boundaries of marital loyalty and/or the confessional seal'. It is not clear however what the consequences of these on-air discussions might be, and whether they will lead to any action, either by callers or by listeners.[32] As Hobson (1980) and Rapping (1991) have suggested, perhaps shows such as The Gerry Ryan Show work to contain frustration and anger that might otherwise lead to political action.

In conclusion it can be argued that this study of callers to The Gerry Ryan Show would suggest that calling the show is an important social activity, and that this form of participation might have consequences for Irish society, as well as for individual callers; 'public debate is social action, however indirect, having consequences for the Zeitgeist of public opinion and social pressure' (Livingstone and Lunt, 1992: 13).

## Notes

I would like to thank Willie O'Reilly, Executive Producer of the show, for all his help with this study. He arranged that a member of the production team would contact callers; the study was explained and callers were asked to give permission for their phone numbers to be passed on to me. The phone numbers of those who gave their consent were then given to me. Respondents were contacted between four and six weeks after their calls to the show and asked if they could suggest a time when they would be free to talk about their call. The majority of interviews were completed then and there, and only two respondents asked me to ring them back at a later stage. The time lapse between the original call and the interview was largely due to the time it took for the production team to contact the 83 callers in question, and was therefore unavoidable. The interviews were all taped, with the respondents' permission and were transcribed at a later stage. I am indebted to all these respondents for being so generous with their time.

I would also like to gratefully acknowledge a postgraduate essay prize awarded by the Social Science Research Council for an earlier version of this chapter.

[1]   But see Fletcher, 1995 and O'Connor, 1995 for some discussion of the genre.

[2]   2FM is RTÉ's second radio station, and combines Top 40 hits, 'oldies', and Irish pop and rock music. Apart from The Gerry Ryan Show, the focus is on music rather than talk. 2FM is aimed at a younger audience than Radio 1.

3   Livingstone and Lunt (1994: 32–3) use a similar framework in their discussion of television talk shows, and argue that this format shares some characteristics with the public sphere.

4   There has also been work done using a discourse analysis approach to calls to talk radio shows (see for example Moss and Higgins, 1982; Moss and Higgins, 1986; Hutchby, 1991). See also Scannell (1991), for an analysis of on-air talk.

5   For example it could not be argued that callers to *The Gerry Ryan Show* were calling to fulfil interpersonal needs. Athough two callers mentioned that ringing helped combat their loneliness, five callers in the sample had rung from work, while six of those who had called from home mentioned that there had been somebody else there with them when they made their call.

6   All 'ideal types', following Weber (1949).

7   Several writers suggest parallels can be made between radio talk and ordinary conversation (see Scannell, 1991; Hutchby, 1991; Kress, 1986). It would therefore seem legitimate to draw on the work of Jefferson and Lee (1981), in relation to ordinary conversation, to discuss calls to the show.

8   Again I have 'borrowed' this term from conversational analysis.

9   I will only deal with those problems that I feel are directly relevant to this discussion.

10   Habermas has accepted this criticism in recent years (see Habermas, 1993).

11   This can be viewed as a serious obstacle to seeing talk radio as part of the public sphere; in Habermas's model participants bracket their status differences and participate in the debate as equals.

12   I am using Habermas's concept of the public sphere as a normative ideal against which callers' participation can be compared.

13   Following from Habermas, the life-world can be defined as that taken for granted milieu of cultural traditions, social solidarities and bodily centered experiences, in which we are always already situated. It is in the lifeworld that mutual understanding and communication are possible. The lifeworld is seen as under threat from system imperatives, for example bureaucratisation [political system] and monetarisation [economic system]. The threat of encroachment into the lifeworld by these sub-systems is what Habermas terms the colonisation of the lifeworld.

14   'To assign an event to the sphere of the private is at once to declare it void of power, and to assign responsibilities to individuals . . . to classify an event as . . . private is to say that individuals have responsibility while offering no social theory that can provide an account beyond that. To classify an event as belonging to the public domain is to assert that it is beyond individual responsibility and within the domain of social control' (Kress, 1986: 400).

15   *The Family* was a four-part drama series written by Irish Booker Prize winning author Roddy Doyle and broadcast on RTÉ 1 during May 1994. At the time there were some objections both to the language and the brief nude scene in the first episode. This was a topic of discussion on *The Gerry Ryan Show* the previous week. This call is in relation to the second episode.

16   I have no evidence to support this caller's claims as I have no observational data from this period to draw on. This incident introduces many questions about the production of the show which are of obvious relevance to my interest in the public sphere, and I accept that this lack of corroborating evidence is problematic. It also must be acknowledged that Gerry Ryan may not have been aware of the 'set-up'.

17   Another serious challenge to the participation offered by the show comes from a caller who argues that Gerry Ryan does not tolerate callers who do not agree with him, and that he dictates what is said on the air: 'All the people who rang in were basically

saying how wonderful this show was [*The Family*]. And I really think it was . . . because Gerry Ryan thought it was a good show' (Caller 23: rural woman,works in the home).

18 The five topics with the most calls over this week were women drivers (19 calls), the World Cup (10 calls), women and body hair (10 calls), questions to an in-studio vet (9 calls) and *The Family* (8 calls). No other topic involved more than four on-air calls and there were 20 topics in total.

19 The other caller wanted to challenge a point made by a spokesman for the insurance companies, but he was dissatisfied with his call to the show, and felt that he didn't get the point he wanted to make across: 'it just didn't come to me you know ( ) with the pressure on the radio' (Caller 17: Truck driver from Derry).

20 They make judgements about potential legal problems – slander, libel, contempt of court, whether topics are interesting or uninteresting, whether the caller is articulate or not etc. Balance is another key production value.

21 I am drawing on conversations with the production team here.

22 The concept of 'good' radio refers to a set of general assumptions oriented to by media professionals 'when making decisions about . . . a radio programme' (O'Neill, 1993: 70).

23 Karpf (1987: 170) argues that radio offers us private women and public men, and that daytime radio 'has a domestic ideology . . . threaded into its very fabric'. Hobson (1980: 108) suggests that the background chatter of radio DJs works to reinforce 'the dominant ideology of domesticity'.

24 Although, as mentioned already, the average quarter-hour audience for *The Gerry Ryan Show* is 57 per cent female and 43 per cent male, it must be pointed out that housewives are seen by Irish radio stations as their target audience: 'Station after station wanted it known how well they were doing among this audience, listening to music and advertisements, and making decisions as to how the family will spend its disposable income' (Foley, 1994). It might be expected that priority is given to attracting this powerful consumer group.

25 See Weatherill, who also raises the question of stigma: 'There's an insistence on transparency in all things which I think is destructive from a psychotherapeutic point of view. It might be alright for Princess Diana to tell everybody she suffered from bulimia, but for someone less famous than she is that still carries a stigma' (cited in McNally, 1995: 13).

26 Of course not all female callers would ring the show with a problem, though six female respondents said that they would. However those that would not call were not so outraged by the question. For example two respondents simply mentioned that they would be embarrassed to ring the show with a problem, while three other respondents said that they would be afraid someone might recognise them on-air.

27 Parallels can be drawn with Levin's (1987: 26) findings here: 'Talk radio in this posture is enormously reaffirming. The number of people who wish to help is large and their reservoir of good will seems unbounded. It is here that one senses the essence of a true community'.

28 As this quote might suggest, in an Irish context it was the Catholic Church which traditionally exercised control over women's bodies, and regulated sexual activity. In recent years this 'moral monopoly' has been challenged, particularly by the mass media: 'The media have lifted the veil of silence which previously shrouded moral issues. Discussions on sexuality and sexual morality . . . have been removed from the dark confines of the confessional and brought to the forefront of public debate' (Inglis, 1987: 90).

29 On July 15 1992 Lavinia Kerwick rang the show in despair the day after the man who had pleaded guilty to her rape walked free from the Central Criminal Court, with only a suspended sentence. She spoke on-air about the rape and subsequently appeared on the Nine O' Clock News, where she appealed to the Minister of Justice for a retrial. Following a public outcry Padraig Flynn, the then Minister for Justice, met with her on several occasions. This case is thus considered to have had considerable influence on the Criminal Justice Act drafted by Padraig Flynn in 1993.

30 Of course it must be acknowledged that the opening up of the private sphere was not the invention of the feminist movement, but, following Habermas, can be linked to the development of the welfare state, where 'the private becomes social' (Carpignano *et al.*, 1990: 52).

31 This echoes Radway's findings in relation to romance reading, an activity she describes as both combative and compensatory. While the readers enjoy reading these novels, and relish this time away from their husbands and children, it must also be noted that 'romance reading . . . supplies vicariously those very needs and requirements that might otherwise be formulated as demands in the real world' (1987: 23).

32 This is a question that I hope to address with further research on callers to the show.

# References

Avery, R.K. and T.A. McCain (1986) 'Interpersonal and Mediated Encounters: A Reorientation to the Mass Communication Process', pp. 121–31 in Gary Gumpert and Robert Cathcart (eds), *InterMedia: Interpersonal Communication in a Media World* (third edition). New York and Oxford: Oxford University Press.

Barnard, Stephen (1989) 'Mother's Little Helper: Programmes, Personalities and the Working Day', pp. 135–55 in Stephen Barnard *On the Radio: Music Radio in Britain*. Milton Keynes: Open University Press.

Benhabib, Seyla (1993) 'Models of Public Space: Hannah Arendt, the Liberal Tradition, and Jürgen Habermas', pp. 73–98 in Craig Calhoun (ed.), *Habermas and the Public Sphere*. Cambridge MA: MIT Press.

Bierig, Jeffrey and John Dimmick (1979) 'The Late Night Radio Talk Show As Interpersonal Communication', *Journalism Quarterly*, 56: 92–6.

Calhoun, Craig (1993) *Habermas and the Public Sphere*. Cambridge MA: MIT Press.

Carpignano, Paolo, Robin Andersen, Stanley Aronowitz and William Difazio (1990) 'Chatter in the Age of Electronic Reproduction: Talk Television and the "Public Mind"', *Social Text*, 25: 33–55.

Corner, J. (1991) 'Meaning, Genre and Context: The Problematics of Public Knowledge in the New Audience Studies', in J. Curran and M. Gurevitch (eds) *Mass Media and Society*. London: Methuen.

Crisell, Andrew (1986) 'Phone-Ins', pp. 181–90 in Andrew Crisell, *Understanding Radio*. London: Methuen.

Crittenden, J. (1971) 'Democratic Functions of the Open Mike Radio Forum', *Public Opinion Quarterly*, 35(2): 200–10.

Davis, K. (1988) *Power Under the Microscope*. Dordrecht, Holland: Ferris Publications.

Dodson Gray, Elizabeth (1989) 'The Daytime Talk Show as a Women's Network', pp. 83–91 in Ramona R. Rush and Donna Allen (eds), *Communications at the Crossroads: The Gender Gap Connection*. Norwood, NJ: Ablex.

Eley, Geoff (1993) 'Nations, Publics, and Political Cultures: Placing Habermas in the Nineteenth Century', pp. 289–339 in Craig Calhoun (ed.), *Habermas and the Public Sphere*. Cambridge MA: MIT Press.

Fennell, Caroline (1993) *Crime and Crisis in Ireland: Justice by Illusion.* Cork: Cork University Press.

Fletcher, Ruth (1995) 'Silences: Irish Women and Abortion', *Feminist Review*, 50: 44–66.

Foley, Michael (1994) 'Radio Stations See Housewives As Prime Audience', *The Irish Times*, 25 August 1994.

Foucault, Michel (1977) *Discipline and Punish: The Birth of the Clinic.* London, Penguin.

Fraser, Nancy (1989) *Unruly Practices: Power, Discourse and Gender in Contemporary Social Theory.* Minneapolis: University of Minnesota Press.

Fraser, Nancy (1993) 'Rethinking the Public Sphere: A Contribution to the Critique of Actually Existing Democracy', pp. 109–42 in Craig Calhoun (ed.), *Habermas and the Public Sphere.* Cambridge MA: MIT Press.

Habermas, Jurgen (1987) *The Theory of Communicative Action, volume 2, Lifeworld and System: A Critique of Functionalist Reason.* T. McCarthy (trans.), Boston: Beacon Press.

Habermas, Jurgen (1989) *The Structural Transformation of the Public Sphere: An Inquiry into a Category of Bourgeois Society.* Thomas Burger (trans.), Cambridge: Polity Press.

Habermas, Jurgen (1993) 'Further Reflections on the Public Sphere', pp. 421–61 in Craig Calhoun (ed.), *Habermas and the Public Sphere.* Cambridge MA: MIT Press.

Hardiman, Niamh and Christopher T. Whelan (1994) 'Politics and Democratic Values', in Christopher T. Whelan (ed.), *Values and Social Change in Ireland.* Dublin: Gill & Macmillan.

Hobson, Dorothy (1980) 'Housewives and the Mass Media', pp. 105–14 in S. Hall *et al.* (eds), *Culture, Media, Language.* London: Hutchinson.

Hofstetter, C.R., M.C. Donovan, M.R. Klauber, A. Cole, C.J. Huie and T. Yuasa (1994) 'Political Talk Radio: A Stereotype Reconsidered', *Political Research Quarterly*, 47(2): 467–79.

Hutchby, Ian (1991) 'The Organisation of Talk on Talk Radio', in P. Scannell (ed.), *Broadcast Talk.* London: Sage.

Inglis, Tom (1987) *Moral Monopoly: The Catholic Church in Modern Irish Society*, Dublin: Gill & Macmillan.

Jefferson and Lee (1981) 'The Rejection of Advice: Managing the Problematic Convergence of a "Troubles-Telling" and a "Service Encounter"', *Journal of Pragmatics*, 5: 399–422.

Karpf, Anne (1980) 'Women and Radio', *Women's Studies International Quarterly*, 3: 41–54.

Karpf, Anne (1987) 'Radio Times – Private Women and Public Men', pp. 169–175 in Kath Davies, Julienne Dickey and Teresa Straffort (eds), *Out of Focus: Writings on Women and the Media.* London: The Women's Press.

Kress, Gunther (1986) 'Language in the Media: The Construction of the Domains of Public and Private', *Media, Culture and Society*, 8: 395–419.

Levin, Murray B. (1987) *Talk Radio and the American Dream.* Toronto: D.C. Heath.

Livingstone, Sonia and Peter Lunt (1992) 'Expert and Lay Participation in Television Debates. An Analysis of Audience Discussion Programmes', *European Journal of Communication*, 7: 9–35.

Livingstone, Sonia and Peter Lunt (1994) *Talk on Television: Audience Participation and Public Debate.* London and New York: Routledge.

Lynch, Kathleen and Eithne McLaughlin (1989) 'Caring Labour and Love Labour', in Patrick Clancy, Sheelagh Drudy, Kathleen Lynch and Liam O'Dowd (eds*)* *Irish Society: Sociological Perspectives*, Dublin: Institiute of Public Administration.

McCarthy, Thomas (1989) 'Introduction', in Jurgen Habermas, *The Structural Transformation of the Public Sphere: An Inquiry into a Category of Bourgeois Society.* Thomas Burger (trans.), Cambridge: Polity Press.

McLaughlin, Lisa (1993) 'Feminism, the Public Sphere, Media and Democracy', *Media, Culture and Society*, 15: 599–620.

McNally, Frank (1995) 'Confessional on the Airwaves', *The Irish Times*, 25 November 1995.

Meaney, Gerardine (1993) 'Sex and Nation: Women in Irish Culture and Politics', pp. 282–99 in Ailbhe Smyth (ed.), *Irish Women's Studies Reader*. Dublin: Attic Press.

Morley, David (1992) *Television Audiences and Cultural Studies*. London and New York: Routledge.

Moss, Peter and Christine Higgins (1982) *Sounds Real: Radio in Everyday Life*. St Lucia: University of Queensland Press.

Moss, Peter and Christine Higgins (1986) 'Radio Voices', in Gary Gumpert and Robert Cathcart (eds) *InterMedia: Interpersonal Communication in a Media World*, (third edition). New York and Oxford: Oxford University Press.

MRBI (1995) *Joint National Listenership Research 1993/4*, Dublin: MRBI/JNLR.

O'Connor, Barbara (1987) 'Women and Media: Social and Cultural Influences on Women's Use of and Response to Television', unpublished PhD thesis, Department of Sociology, University College Dublin.

O'Connor, Pat (1995) 'Understanding Continuities and Changes in Irish Marriage: Putting Women Centre Stage', *Irish Journal of Sociology*, 5: 135–63.

O'Neill, Brian (1993) 'Producing the Arts Show: An Ethnographic Study of Radio Producers at Work', *Irish Communications Review*, 3: 65–72.

Priest, P.J. and J.R. Dominick (1994) 'Pulp Pulpits: Self-Disclosure on "Donahue"', *Journal of Communication*, 44(4): 74–97.

Radio Telifis Éireann (1995) *Annual Report 1994*, Dublin: RTÉ.

Radway, J. (1987) *Reading the Romance: Women, Patriarchy and Popular Literature*. London: Verso.

Rapping, Elaine (1991) 'Daytime Inquiries', *The Progressive*, October: 36–8.

Reiner, Bo (1995) 'The Media in Public and Private Spheres', pp. 58–71 in Johan Fornas and Goran Bolin (eds), *Youth Culture and Late Modernity*. London: Sage.

Russell, Paul (1991) *Ryan on the Radio*. Dublin: Gill & Macmillan and RTÉ.

Ryan, Mary P. (1993) 'Gender and Public Access: Women's Politics in Nineteenth-Century America', pp. 259–88 in Craig Calhoun (ed.) *Habermas and the Public Sphere*. Cambridge MA: MIT Press.

Scannell, Paddy (1991) 'Introduction: The Relevance of Talk', in P. Scannell (ed.) *Broadcast Talk*. London: Sage.

Smyth, Ailbhe (1995) 'States of Change: Reflections on Ireland in Several Uncertain Parts', *Feminist Review*, 50: 24–43.

Tramer, Harriet and Leo W. Jeffres (1983) 'Talk Radio – Forum and Companion', *Journal of Broadcasting*, 27(3): 297–300.

Turrow, Joseph (1974) 'Talk Radio as Interpersonal Communication', *Journal of Communication*, 18: 171–9.

Verwey, Norma Ellen (1990) *Radio Call-Ins and Covert Politics*. Averbury: Aldershot.

Weber, Max (1949) *The Methodology of the Social Sciences*. Edward A. Shils and Henry A. Finch (trans. and eds), New York: Free Press.

Weiss, Robert S. (1976) 'The Contribution of an Organisation of Single Parents to the Well-Being of its Members', in Gerard Caplan and Marie Killilea (eds), *Support Systems and Mutual Help: Multidisciplinary Explorations*. New York: Grune & Stratton.

# 9

# Divorce Referendum Coverage, Programme Formats and Television Audiences[1]

*Stephen Ryan*

This chapter sets out to examine the television coverage of the divorce referendum in the Republic of Ireland held in November 1995. The focus is on the different types of programme format used by RTÉ in their coverage of the campaign, and on how a variety of audience groups interpreted and responded to these programme formats.

These findings will be related to the issues of concision and 'soundbites', and to expert and lay roles in television discourse. To contextualise this material, I will firstly look at the referendum campaign itself, and how RTÉ approached the problems of covering it. I will then examine the themes focused on during the campaign, and how the electorate voted, before briefly outlining some of the theoretical and methodological aspects of qualitative audience research. Following this, the chapter will then discuss the audience responses to the referendum coverage.

## Political Context and RTÉ's Coverage

Following the defeat of the 1986 divorce referendum, the various coalition Governments in office in the lead up to the 1995 referendum acted to implement legislation in the areas of judicial separation, welfare rights and inheritance in order to guard against the re-use of anti-divorce arguments in these areas that were so successful in 1986 (for accounts of the 1986 campaign see Dillon, 1993; Girvin, 1987; Inglis, 1987; O'Brien, 1995; O'Reilly, 1992; and Prendiville, 1988). In the five years before the 1995 referendum the five main political parties were all involved in coalition Governments (Fianna Fáil/ Progressive Democrats, Fianna Fáil/Labour, and Fine Gael/Labour/Democratic

Left), all of which were formally committed to the holding and supporting of a new divorce referendum (for full detail on the range of approaches considered, see Stationery Office, 1992).

The 1995 campaign was contested on the Yes (pro–divorce) side by the Government and main Opposition parties, and the Right to Remarry Campaign (RTRC). The No side was represented by the Anti-Divorce Campaign (ADC), and the No Divorce Campaign (NDC), with the Catholic Church playing a less central role compared to 1986, but nonetheless making a number of important interventions during the course of the campaign.

The campaign was essentially played out in the mass media, with the more traditional methods of canvassing and leafleting taking a back seat. The fact that for much of the campaign the Yes position had a comfortable lead in the opinion polls, led to a situation where complacency began to effect the pro–divorce campaign. Marketing companies advised the Government 'to run a low-key campaign, avoiding major publicity which might alarm people, and get the amendment through quietly' (Coulter, 1995b: 11). This approach was informed by the view (stated by Garret FitzGerald, who was Taoiseach during the 1986 campaign) that it 'is just much easier to argue passionately *against* divorce than *for* it; easier to frighten people about the uncertain consequences of a radical social change than to worry about an unsatisfactory status quo' (1995: 11). In other words, the Government felt that it would risk losing support if it got into a protracted and detailed discussion of the possible consequences of the introduction of divorce. Because of this, there was a certain amount of tension between the Government part of the pro-divorce campaign, and the non party-political part represented by the RTRC.

The RTRC was an umbrella group comprised of the Divorce Action Group (DAG), the Irish Council for Civil Liberties, and other groups and individuals. Representatives from the Dáil parties sat on a committee of the RTRC. The various constituent groups would also campaign separately from the RTRC, and differences in approach emerged. Mags O'Brien, Chairperson of the DAG, argued that 'the Government and the Right to Remarry wanted to be nice people and unfortunately if someone else is playing a different set of rules, there's no point in you playing the nice guy rules' (interview with the author).

The Government decided at an early stage that they would spend £500,000 of taxpayers' money on a mixture of information and advocacy advertising. It would inform the electorate of the legislative changes made since the previous referendum in 1986, and it would advocate a Yes vote. This was a very contro–versial measure that was opposed not only by anti-divorce campaigners, but also by a number of pro-divorce politicians who saw it as being counter-productive. A legal challenge by Green Party MEP Patricia McKenna (who supported a Yes vote) was eventually successful, and the Government was forced to cut short its advertising campaign. There were two main effects of this short-lived advertising strategy. The first was that the anti-divorce camp was widely seen as having to struggle against a far better financed campaign, that was also undemocratically funded by taxpayers' money. A second effect was that many pro-divorce individuals felt that there was no need to make donations to groups such as the RTRC. This could be summed up as a situation whereby 'one poorly funded campaign [on the Yes side] faced two well-funded voluntary campaigns on the other side, with little active support from the Government parties' (Coulter, 1995b: 11).

The anti-divorce side was represented mostly by the Anti-Divorce Campaign (ADC), and the No Divorce Campaign (NDC). The ADC was a relaunch of the same-named body that so successfully campaigned against divorce in 1986, and had the same leading figures. The NDC was a newer organisation which took a more radical approach to the campaign. The differences between the two groups have been characterised as being between 'those whose pitch is deliberately secular and sociological [the ADC] and those lay Catholic organisations which use these arguments, but whose agenda is essentially religious [the NDC]' (Coulter, 1995a: 7). The differences could further be attributed to a fundamental divide between those (in the ADC) who are dedicated to working within existing political institutions (in this case Fianna Fáil), and those (in the NDC) who feel that their agenda would be better promoted through new political parties such as the Christian Solidarity Party and Muintir na hÉireann.

RTÉ's coverage of the referendum came under the remit of a steering group that comes into effect during all referenda and elections. The group was chaired by the Director of Radio Programmes, and included several representatives from RTÉ radio and television news and current affairs departments and also the Assistant Director General of RTÉ. The premise of the group was, according to Tony Fahy, the secretary of the group during the campaign, that 'the issue which faces the people is a simple one of Yes and No, we are not concerned about (. . .) how the parliament decides to stack up, on one side of any issue' (interview with the author).

In other words, the steering group intended originally to allocate a Referendum Broadcast to each of the five main Dáil parties, irrespective of the fact that all five were advocating a Yes vote. After some further consideration, they decided to give two extra Broadcasts each to the non party-political pro and anti campaigning groups. However, this still left a ratio of seven to two in favour of the pro-divorce side. In contrast to this, the steering group stipulated that any programme (including news and current affairs, and talk shows) featuring the divorce issue must divide time absolutely equally between the two sides. For instance, a live radio phone-in programme would have to time each caller, and attempt to ensure that each side in the debate would enjoy an equal share of the time available within that programme.

Monitoring this allocation of time, and the general approach of programme makers to the divorce issue was the primary role of the steering group during the campaign, but it was also responsible for dealing with any legal challenge to RTÉ's coverage that might arise. In this campaign, two High Court challenges were instigated. The first was from the ADC, and was concerned with the allocation of Referendum Broadcasts mentioned above. The second was from Muintir na hÉireann, and was about the amount of news coverage that the party was receiving over the course of the campaign. Both challenges were defeated, with the High Court stating that RTÉ had been conforming fully to its statutory obligations.

## Campaign Themes and Voting Patterns

Probably the single most noticeable difference between the 1995 and 1986 divorce referenda was the climate of scandal that surrounded the Roman Catholic Church in 1995. A series of major scandals erupted in the two years preceding the referendum, concerning paedophilia, a Bishop and a number of priests fathering children, and also a number of financial scandals. These were traumatic facts for Irish Catholics, and the Church appeared to lose moral authority because of them. An opinion poll conducted for an RTÉ religious affairs programme transmitted in March 1995, showed that '59 per cent either tended to agree or strongly agreed that people will have less respect for the Catholic Church's position on divorce' (Pollak, 1995: 6). Similarly, the research also indicated that '49 per cent of Catholics did not feel dependent on the Church for moral guidance'.

Hornsby-Smith and Whelan (1994: 44) argue that what Ireland has been experiencing in recent years is 'not so much secularisation as the emergence of the "new Catholic"'. Part of this 'new Catholicism' is particularly relevant here, as it involves 'an outlook that questions the church's right to speak with *absolute* [my emphasis] authority on matters of personal morality or to speak out on Government policy'. However, it could be argued that even though people were less likely to support uncritically the Church's position on an issue such as divorce, many may still have seen the Church, for all its troubles and faults, as being a source of certainty and reassurance. In an analysis of the campaign, Fintan O'Toole argued that 'precisely because Ireland has been changing so rapidly, the church represented for many people the last bastion of stability and security' (1995: 6). He went on to assert that the very undermining of the Church's position of moral authority had in fact acted to lessen the scope for social change: 'fear and insecurity seldom have the effect of encouraging people to embrace change'.

In examining the television coverage, leaflets, and advertising used by both sides in the campaign, a number of central themes emerge. On the Yes side the main arguments came under the following headings:

1. People have a civil right to remarry if their marriage has irretrievably broken down

2. The whole issue of marital breakdown should be properly addressed

3. Ireland should embrace more pluralistic values, and respect the position of minority churches

4. Children are affected by remaining in unhappy home situations more so than they are by divorce

5. Those who are in subsequent relationships should be allowed to formalise their position, or else the institution of marriage will be undermined

6. There is no need for Catholic Church law to be reinforced by State law

7. The peace process in Northern Ireland would be adversely effected by a No vote.

An Irish Times/MRBI opinion poll published in early November (see Jones, 1995: 7), indicated which of the pro and anti arguments were striking a chord with the electorate at the time. According to the poll, 56 per cent of those intending to vote Yes were doing so because people 'should have the choice to remarry/should have right to choose', while 24 per cent said that people 'should be given [an] opportunity for a fresh start, and [be allowed to] get on with their lives' (the polling company used an open-ended question for this issue, i.e., they did not give a list of options to the respondents).

On the other hand, the main areas covered by No campaigners were:

1. The effect of divorce on children is extremely negative and long-lasting

2. Once divorce is introduced, a 'divorce culture' develops whereby people begin to take the institution of marriage less seriously

3. The financial and taxation effects would be considerable

4. The constitutional position of the 'first family' would be seriously undermined

5. The nature of marriage would be changed from being permanent to being essentially temporary

6. An individual may be divorced against their will

7. Society is threatened by the spread of radical individualism.

The above mentioned poll showed that 28 per cent of those who said they would vote No would do so because divorce 'would destroy family life'; 16 per cent because divorce was an 'easy option/would be abused', and 15 per cent because they believed that 'marriage is for life'.

These two sets of arguments clearly show that the divorce referendum campaign was a struggle between two widely divergent world-views. Where the pro-divorce position was based on notions of individual rights and respect for minority views, the anti-divorce position was instead based on ideas about the 'greater good' of the society, and on the legitimacy of Catholic social teaching being enshrined in the Constitution. Where the anti-divorce camp argued that divorce would irrevocably harm family life in the Republic, the pro-divorce camp countered that the far greater danger lay in unhappy marriages that could not be legally ended (for further detail on these arguments see Ad hoc Commission on Referendum Information, 1995; Government Information, 1995; Hamilton, 1994; Irish Council for Civil Liberties, 1995; Little, 1995; O'Brien, 1995; Office of the Minister for Equality and Law Reform, 1995a and 1995b; and Ward, 1993).

A further poll, conducted on referendum polling day, proved afterwards to be accurate on the overall outcome, and provides an insight into how voter groups divided on the issue. According to this *Irish Times*/MRBI poll (see Coghlan, 1996: 2), women were split evenly on the issue, while 54 per cent of men indicated support for divorce. Two-thirds of 18–34 year olds said they had voted Yes, while three-quarters of over 65s said they voted No. Fifty-nine per cent of urban dwellers said they had voted for the introduction of divorce, while large farmers were the group most opposed, 76 per cent indicating that they had voted No. Seventy-seven per cent of separated people supported the divorce proposal.

There had been a dramatic decline in the number of people declaring support for the divorce proposal over the preceding weeks of the campaign. Earlier polls had shown a lead of up to 42 percentage points for the pro-divorce position (this example being from May 1995; see Coghlan, 1995: 7), by the final week of the campaign, this had closed to just three points. When the actual votes were counted, the gap had closed even further. The referendum had the closest result in the history of the State: 50.28 per cent voted Yes for the introduction of divorce, while 49.72 per cent voted No.

## Audience Research: Some Theoretical and Methodological Issues

This research was influenced by the 'reception analysis' tradition of qualitative audience research, in both its aims and methods. The word 'reception' has been used as a 'common term signifying viewers' interpretations, decodings, readings, meaning productions, perceptions or comprehension of programmes' (Höijer, 1990: 15). Similarly, Klaus Bruhn Jensen (1987: 23) sees mass communication as being essentially the production of meaning in society. 'The media produce and circulate signs and symbols in society, and it is in this capacity that they make a difference to individuals as well as to social institutions' (see also Jensen, 1988; Jensen, 1991; and Jensen and Rosengren, 1990).

Reception analysis is characterised by an emphasis on the polysemic nature of media texts, and on the possibility of audiences moving beyond the preferred reading of a text, to construct their own particular meaning. Because of this, the production of meaning from a media text is identified as a 'site of struggle'. Jensen (1986: 78) argues that 'meaning production is circumscribed by a social totality and is *likely* [my emphasis] to reproduce the limits of hegemony' (that is, the combination of coercion and consent that characterises the exercise of power by one social group over another – see Simon, 1982 and Jensen, 1990).

Of course, no audience research perspective is capable of producing a complete explanation of the relationship between a media text and its audiences. Schrøder (1994: 341) argues that despite this, we should:

> get on with it and produce *in*completely articulated accounts of audience readings and practices which may, in spite of their (no doubt) multiple shortcomings, provide illuminating insights into the polysemic and polymorphic relationship between media and people in the world we live in.

The choice of methodology for this research was informed by the emphasis of reception analysis on both the 'momentary experience' of viewing, and the 'result of a reflection on the momentary experience' (Gripsrud, 1995: 108), that make up the process of meaning production. In this light, it was decided to use focus groups, because of their suitability for generating discussion about the viewers' thoughts and reactions to the media text in question. Also important was 'their ability to explore topics and generate hypotheses' (Morgan, 1988: 21). In addition, focus groups are particularly adept at highlighting 'diversity and difference, either within or between groups' (Lunt and Livingstone, 1996: 96; see also Carey, 1994; Lewis, 1991; and Sarantakos, 1993).

On a more practical level, it was obviously important to talk to as many different people as possible within the period of the referendum campaign itself, something individual interviews could not have offered. The focus groups in this research were shown three video clips of RTÉ referendum coverage. The clips were chosen to cover both a range of campaign themes and of programme formats. The themes covered were:

1. The role of the Catholic Church, and its relationship with the State

2. The effect of marital breakdown on children

3. The 'floodgates' argument that rates of marital breakdown will increase once divorce is introduced into a jurisdiction.

These themes were covered by the following programme formats respectively:

1. A short news report (*Six-One News*: duration three minutes approx.; broadcast Friday 27 October 1995)

2. A current affairs recorded report (*Prime Time*: duration eight minutes approx.; broadcast Thursday 27 July 1995)

3. A studio audience discussion programme (*Davis*: duration 12 minutes approx.; broadcast Wednesday 6 September 1995).

The three clips were shown separately, with specific discussion of each clip being followed at the end of the session with a more general evaluation of the media coverage of the campaign, and a comparison of the worth and interest value of the three different types of programme. The groups were held between 8 and 21 November 1995, the referendum itself being held on 24 November. The four groups featured in this chapter cover a range of ages, socio-economic backgrounds, rural/urban backgrounds, and of course, both men and women. The focus groups can be categorised as follows:

Table 1 *Research Groups*

|         | No. in Group | Male | Female | Age   | Class | Area     |
|---------|--------------|------|--------|-------|-------|----------|
| Group A | 12           | 8    | 4      | 15–24 | WC    | N.Dublin |
| Group B | 10           | 7    | 3      | 18–54 | WC/MC | S.Dublin |
| Group C | 6            | –    | 6      | 25–34 | MC    | S.Dublin |
| Group D | 6            | 4    | 2      | 25–64 | MC    | Co.Clare |
| Total   | 34           | 19   | 15     |       |       |          |

The next section will look at the video clips shown to the groups in more detail, and will outline the reactions of the focus groups to those clips.

## News Report and Audience Responses

The first clip shown was from the *Six-One News*, and featured the response of the Taoiseach, John Bruton to the press conference of the Catholic Hierarchy which had been held the previous day. Bruton described the Church's stance as being counter-productive, and he warned that if divorce was rejected, 'fewer and fewer people might choose to go into civil marriage', according to the newsreader. The Bishops had described the Government's proposal as 'bad law', and they argued that divorce would 'make it harder for married couples to remain true to their marriage promise'. The item stressed Bruton's argument that the State must 'make regulations for society as it is, and not as one might wish it to be'. Visually, the item used images from the Hierarchy's press conference, shots of Bruton in his office, exteriors of Government Buildings, and a series of captions stating the main points of the Taoiseach's argument, before file footage of polling stations from the 1986 referendum ended the report.

The responses to this item by all the groups were much briefer than their responses to the two other clips shown to them. The group participants made quite general comments about the balanced nature of the item, and about the difficulty in taking in a lot of information in a relatively short period of time. A number of comments were made about the use of statistics, and some of the language used by politicians: 'I think that both sides are giving figures and statistics that they can't back up. I mean Bruton said there that you have a lot more people cohabiting' (Man, 55–64, No Voter, Group D). However, a member of the same group favourably compared Bruton's use of language in the clip to that of the Minister for Social Welfare, Proinsias de Rossa (who did not actually appear in the item):

> You can say the same thing using different language which wouldn't offend people. and I mean everyone's entitled to disagree, but I think the ferocity of the language he [de Rossa] used wasn't a good idea. Bruton would probably be much more softly, softly in terms of responding to the Church
> (Woman, 25–34, No Voter, Group D).

Another woman in the group commented on the superficiality of the item, and news coverage in general:

> I think most of the coverage that has been on television anywhere has lacked a depth . . . they're not giving enough depth of reason for voting on either side – I feel that very strongly. I think it's patronising to people; it's just the Government in particular, you know; 'vote Yes or we'll have loads of people living together'
> (Woman, 25–34, No Voter, Group D).

These responses indicate a frustration with the level of political discourse as conveyed by the mass media, and with the manner in which this material is often presented: 'You're so cluttered nearly, with information being fired at you, and you just get annoyed and say 'OK forget it, I'm going to make up my mind' (Woman, 25–34, Yes Voter, Group C). A number of young participants felt that the entire item was completely irrelevant to them, because of their age, and the fact that they themselves were not married.

Looking at the responses, there are indications of distaste for the way in which the divorce debate was proceeding, and a feeling of dissatisfaction with the constraints of the medium itself: constraints that were seen as being responsible for a lack of depth, and an overload of information for the viewer. Also, the news bulletin format appears to be so deeply ingrained and familiar to us that we find it hard to conceive of any different way of doing it. Unlike the discussions surrounding the two other video clips, participants at this stage of the focus groups, did not make any suggestions for alternative ways of structuring and presenting programmes such as the *Six-One News*.

## Current Affairs Report and Audience Responses

The recorded report from the *Prime Time* current affairs programme focused on foreign research reports on the impact of divorce on children, and used this information as a starting point to examine two Irish 'case histories'. Two separated parents and their respective daughter and son discussed their feelings about how the breakdown of the marriage affected them. The discussion was preceded by contributions from Don Lydon, the Head of the Department of Psychology in St John of God Hospital, and Maura Wall-Murphy, Co-ordinator of the Family Mediation Service. Lydon is shown arguing that the 'further you go away from something that's seemingly natural, the more trouble you run into', while Wall-Murphy asserted that 'marriage is a reflection of what's going on in our society and vice versa'.

John Power and his daughter Lisa were then interviewed about their experiences of marital breakdown, with the father talking about his fears that 'she [Lisa] might sort of wander off'. Lisa herself then stated that she 'was very mixed up', when her parent's marriage broke down, and that, at the time, she 'didn't know what was going to happen in the future'.

Agnes Edwards was then introduced as a member of the Separated Parents Association, the same as John Power. She talked about how she had returned to her marriage time and again after walking out, and how she was a 'staunch Catholic', who believed in 'sticking to my vows'. However, she explained that as her children grew up, her 'miserable marriage, where there was an awful lot of conflict', was having an adverse effect on them. Her son, Richard Barcoe, explained then how he and his brothers had reacted to the marriage breakdown:

> We all just broke free; it was like sort of being in prison and you get out. The first thing you do is get outside, go down to the pub and get pissed, but when you're a kid you can't get pissed, so you do all the things that you couldn't do, and that's what we did: we just went wild.

Following this, Don Lydon stated that 'all the studies show that children prefer to stay even in a violent marital relationship, or family relationship rather than see the parents separate'. This was then countered by Edwards and Wall-Murphy. File footage of the 1986 campaign was then shown, accompanying information about the growth in the numbers of separated people in Ireland. The piece continued with comments about whether or not divorce would actually make any difference in terms of trauma or distress for people already involved in marital breakdown. Richard Barcoe commented that divorce would allow him to 'understand that my mother and my father can both love someone else'. Lisa Power ended the report with her view on how she would approach marriage: 'just make sure that like, I'm going to stay with the person'.

The responses to this clip were more detailed than those for the *Six-One* item. The *Prime Time* clip was longer, and also would have been viewed by the groups mid-way through the discussion, after they had settled in, and before they may have become tired or bored with the material and the discussion itself. A member of Group B felt it was the best clip of the three shown:

> It's more real life – you're hearing what the adults have to say, and you're hearing what the professionals have to say . . . and the children, that was the only one there that the children came in.
>
> (Man, 35–44, Yes Voter, Group B)

Another man in that group stated that:

> The language is 'ground language', like the guy [Richard Barcoe] said; 'we broke loose', 'we went wild', you know, and that's, there's no baloney with that, while the other language in the last thing [the studio audience discussion programme] was very political language, statistics, and so on.
>
> (Man, 35–44, Yes Voter, Group B)

The fact that the two families in the *Prime Time* clip were both from a working class Dublin background clearly influenced the way in which they were perceived by the group participants. A member of Group A, himself a working class Dubliner, indicated his preferred clip of the three shown, when he talked about 'the one with the *actual people* [my emphasis] in it, [that] was the best' (Man, 15–24, Yes Voter, Group A). However, it was not a case of all the groups identifying with the families featured. A member of the rural group; Group D, even joked that he had problems understanding the accent of one of the interviewees: 'I didn't know what he [John Power] was saying; I couldn't understand him!' (Man, 55–64, No Voter, Group D).

A middle-class woman from Group C stated that 'I would like to know how they picked those two particular couples' (Woman, 25–34, Yes Voter, Group C). It is interesting to note here that those people who saw the featured families as being 'actual people', never questioned the rationale for including them in the programme, or the manner in which they were chosen. However, those who did not identify with them tended to raise a question mark over their participation in the programme, reflecting the unusualness of hearing working class voices in the mass media.

Closely related to this is the way in which one person's authenticity can be another person's inarticulacy. By this I mean that the definition of articulacy that is dominant in the mass media in Ireland, as elsewhere, is essentially an urban middle class one. Group C, the most middle-class and urban of the groups discussed here, produced a number of comments about the two families, such as: 'they weren't very literate' [sic], and 'they should have [been] better educated'. A pair of comments by two women in the group further illustrate this point:

> / They would have been more credible if they had been, mm, if they had been more middle class – that sounds terrible, but . . .

/ It does, yeah, but they weren't literate [sic] – they didn't come across, they didn't give you their story.

(Women, 25–34, Yes Voters, Group C)

Another group member said: 'no fault of the people that they actually interviewed, but I didn't think they were actually articulate enough to make their point' (Woman, 25–34, Yes Voter, Group C).

The idea that there should have been a greater range of backgrounds covered by the item, was also raised by members of this group:

/ . . . those two people would appear to me, came from the same social background, but that's not a variety of opinions . . .
/ And they were both from Dublin as well . . .
/ Like it's a whole country that's at issue here, not just two families from Dublin . . . they seemed to be more or less identical families, but where's the balance, there's no balance.

It seems very likely that it is the fact that these audience members did not identify with the two featured families, that led them to raise the issue of their representativeness. Those who did identify with the families never questioned their representativeness.

Another aspect of balance in the programme was raised by a member of Group D, who mentioned the way in which the recorded item was introduced in the studio by the *Prime Time* presenter:

Miriam O'Callaghan's introduction was very biased in that she said it [the research reports on the impact of divorce on children] would be 'manna from heaven' that would be *exploited* you know, which is very biased language to use.
(Woman, 25–34, No Voter, Group D)

It is interesting, if not very surprising, that allegations of bias tend to be made against people who are perceived as disagreeing with you, and rarely against someone seen as being on your side. This No voter clearly felt that O'Callaghan's use of language identified her as a supporter of divorce, but no Yes voters made the same observation. It would seem that we tend to be blinded to bias as long as it is bias in favour of our own preferred position.

The central issue in the discussions about the *Prime Time* clip was the way in which the item focused on 'real people', instead of experts or professionals. This area has been discussed by Livingstone and Lunt (1992 and 1994) in relation to how experientially-based knowledge is becoming more valued by some, over conventional academic and professional knowledge, in television debates and discussions. Traditionally, 'lay' contributors (such as Agnes Edwards and her son, or John Power and his daughter), were seen as being 'subjective', 'emotional', and as basing their comments on 'supposition', and were thus not as highly valued as 'expert' contributors. Increasingly though, lay contributors are being seen, by some, as 'authentic', 'relevant', and their comments as being 'grounded in experience'. This is problematic, however, because while the tendency towards giving air time to those who traditionally might not have received it is welcome, it is not the answer to all the problems of communicating complex and emotive issues such as divorce in Ireland. Mags O'Brien, the Chairperson of the DAG, took issue with the increasing drive towards the use of 'real people', or 'case histories':

> Journalists do it all the time, this idea, they think that if they show case histories, that really gets things across to people (. . .) I think they had this idea that people wanted to see fresh faces, but that was all very well, but when the issues are complex you can't put out people who only know their own little bit (interview with the author).

However, the use of case histories is, for some, a popular alternative to the traditional authority of psychologists, economists, sociologists, and so on. What is not so clear, is whether or not the case histories approach is more effective in communicating the issues of the day. It is apparent, though, that a lack of identification with the people featured in the case histories, on the part of an audience member, tends to lead to a concentration on the way in which the message is communicated, rather than the substance of the message itself. In other words, the novelty of hearing working-class accents in a serious socio-political discussion seems to prove, for middle-class audiences, to be at best distracting, and at worst irritating. On the other hand, those who identify with the accents in question, find their presence in such discussions to be a welcome change from the usual diet of middle class voices.

## Studio Audience Discussion Programme and Audience Responses

The final clip shown was from *Davis*, a programme that features a range of participants in a studio discussing a particular topic. In this case there were 30 to 40 members of the studio audience, with a mix of well known television performers – lawyers, campaigners, etc., and lesser known faces (the better-known participants were the first to be brought into the discussion, and were the only ones to be given captions when they spoke initially, stating their name and occupation or position). The excerpt chosen started with Mags O'Brien of the DAG being asked by the programme's facilitator/presenter, Derek Davis, about the idea of marital breakdown only affecting a small minority of the Irish population. Joe McCarroll of the ADC replied to O'Brien, setting the style of the programme, with Derek Davis alternating between pro and anti speakers throughout. The other speakers included in the clip were Tom Cooney of the Irish Council for Civil Liberties; Dr Seamus Grimes of the Department of Geography, University College, Galway; Maura O'Toole, a barrister with the Lawyers Divorce Campaign; Nora Bennis, Leader of Solidarity; Adrian

Hardiman, a Senior Counsel; and David Quinn, a columnist with the *Sunday Business Post*.

The argument covered the issue of whose rights should take precedence – those of the parents, or those of the children; the already existing provisions for separated people; and the situation where people may be divorced against their will. The discussion moved on to a research report by an American academic, Judith Wallerstein, with Joe McCarroll and Tom Cooney arguing about whether or not the research's findings about the effect of divorce on children were reliable or not. The segment ended with the 'floodgates' argument, about the possible increase in marital breakdown, once divorce is introduced to a society. Derek Davis then brought the discussion to a close by announcing the advertisement break, and trailing the topics that were to be covered in the second half of the programme.

Programmes such as *Davis* follow a clearly set pattern established by American programmes such as *The Oprah Winfrey Show* and *Geraldo* (both available to Irish audiences on British channels), and by programmes that reinterpreted the genre for British audiences, such as *Kilroy*. The similarity of *Davis* to these kind of programmes stretches beyond the use of a personal name for a title. There is a strong emphasis on the views of 'ordinary' people, a confrontational style, and fast pacing. At a recording session for a different edition of *Davis* that I attended, Derek Davis spoke to the studio audience before the programme started. He asked us not to be long-winded in our contributions. He said that anyone beginning their statement with 'I've got twelve points to make, the first one is . . .', would inevitably be cut off before they could finish.

Another aspect of programmes like *Davis*, is the way in which the focus of attention tends to be on the presenter, more so than on the studio audience members. Dr Gerard Casey, the Vice-Chairman of the NDC, and leader of the Christian Solidarity Party, was in the studio audience of the programme edition in question. He described the programme as:

> A waste of time. It's a waste of time because it's a solo run for Derek [Davis], I mean Derek is the one who talks all the time, I mean Derek talks one to one with everyone, which means if you have twenty six people, Derek talks twenty six times (interview with the author).

While this gives all, or at least most, of the studio audience the opportunity to contribute, it also means that, according to Casey, 'it's only soundbite, so you're sat with all these people, and they basically have one little thing, and it looks marvellous, but it's a one-man show'.

The idea that a programme is based on soundbites, would indicate that it was very quick-moving, and effective in holding the attention of the audience. However, definitions of what is fast-moving and interesting vary from person to person. The young working-class people in Group A were not impressed with *Davis*. They felt that it was 'totally boring', and one group member said that, 'If I saw that I'd turn it off'. Various members of the group made comparisons between *Davis* and the American programmes *Geraldo*, and *The Oprah Winfrey Show*:

> I love the American ones. . .
> / . . .The Americans are more emotional. . .
> / The Irish is always a lot more level-headed, isn't it, like?
> / The Americans is all a big gag, like.
> / They must sit down for hours to think up ideas for shows, like.
> / If I've nothing better to do, I'd watch them, like. . .
> / If divorce was on it, I wouldn't watch it – it's too boring, you know, in the Irish.
> / If the Americans were doing divorce, I'd watch it, 'cause they'd go hyper about it an' all.
>
> (Men and Women, 15–24, Yes and No Voters, Group A)

It would seem from this, that while a programme such as *Davis* may be considered to be a pale imitation of the 'soundbite' style of some American programmes, for others, it is far too close to them for comfort:

> Something that's just relying on soundbites and not allowing people to get a real in-depth discussion, isn't very helpful – Davis is limited in that sense, because people have got thirty seconds to say what they want to say and you can't say it in thirty seconds, so it's limited – they're always cut off before they've finished making their point.
>
> (Woman, 25–34, No Voter, Group D)

Similarly to the case histories issue discussed above, there seems to be a strong relationship between social class and perceptions of modes of television presentation. Broadly speaking, the more working-class group members tended to prefer the soundbite approach, while more middle-class members tended to distance themselves from it.

## Discussion: Soundbites and the Status Quo

This issue of the use of soundbites is important in our political and media lives, because research indicates that not only is the average length of a soundbite reducing, but there is evidence that this reduction affects comprehension by the viewer. Hallin (1992: 5) states that the average length of soundbites in USA Presidential elections fell from over 40 seconds in 1968, to under ten seconds in 1988. Robinson and Levy (1986: 193) demonstrated a link between news story length and their comprehension by audiences. Their evidence indicated that longer news stories were less likely to be poorly comprehended (this supports the views expressed by group members about the difficulty of taking in all of the information presented in the *Six-One* clip, for example).

Changes in broadcasting technology, increased competition between television stations, and between different programmes on the same station, have contributed to a situation where contemporary television news is fast-paced, with tight edits, and thereby more tightly packed with information than before. This can be seen as a simple professional consideration, concerned with concise and interesting presentation of information, or it can be viewed as a structural constraint with important ideological implications. In other words, the constraint of concision that was seen by the research groups as being a feature of the *Six-One* and *Davis* clips makes the task of communication more difficult, but this difficulty effects some more than others.

As Noam Chomsky put it: 'the beauty of concision, you know, saying a couple of sentences between two commercials – the beauty of that is you can only repeat conventional thoughts' (Achbar, 1994: 147). To argue for a complex and difficult social or political proposal for change simply takes more time than to defend the status quo. The range of reasons, arguments, and evidence that should be produced to construct a convincing case for a radical social change (such as that which was needed for the pro-divorce camp), are ill-suited to the structural constraint of concision, whereas the defence of a familiar situation (such as the Constitutional ban on divorce) can rely more on conventional wisdoms and common sense. Chomsky's argument (featured in the *Manufacturing Consent* documentary film: see Wintonick and Achbar, 1992) is that if 'you say something that's the least bit unexpected or controversial', then you need to be able to defend your statement:

> You better have a reason, you know, better have some evidence (. . .) because that's a pretty startling comment – you can't give evidence if you're stuck with concision. That's the genius of this structural constraint.

It is relevant here to recall the statement by Garret FitzGerald (1995: 11) that 'it is just much easier to frighten people about the uncertain consequences of a radical social change than to worry about an unsatisfactory status quo'.

This was a point that was addressed in very different ways by two leading campaigners from the opposing sides of the argument. Dr Gerard Casey of the NDC, in outlining his group's media strategy, stated that:

> Long complicated arguments and long bouts of statistics (. . .) are things that leave most people cold, so we had to find ways of putting a message across, which, if were *not exactly clinchers*, were at *least penetrating* (interview with the author; my emphases).

What this means is that the value was placed less on arguments that might be fully sound, and more on ones that could be expected to have an impact on the audience. While these categories are not necessarily mutually incompatible, it would seem from this statement that they were perceived as being in conflict in this instance. The benefit of this strategy from the point of view of those espousing it, was that a more elaborative and qualified approach would have come up against the 'genius' of the structural constraint of concision, and would arguably have been less effective.

This was certainly how this type of campaign was perceived by one of their opponents. Mags O'Brien of the DAG, argued that:

> The anti-divorce people were always saying we'll end up like America [in terms of a 'divorce culture'] and yet what they did was use totally American type of advertising, and that kind of soundbite stuff.     (interview with the author)

The implication of this is that the kind of arguments and slogans that were employed by many in the anti-divorce camp ('Hello Divorce, Bye Bye Daddy', or 'You Will Pay!' [more tax]), were ideally suited to the demands of a media soundbite culture. Conversely, the kind of arguments that were used by the pro-divorce camp, (such as 'Divorce is a Civil Right', or that Ireland should adopt a more pluralistic outlook), were less suited to those same demands, because of the need to rely on supporting arguments and evidence that were difficult to supply under the kind of time constraints discussed by the research participants above.

This contention is supported by a study by Liebes and Ribak (1991: 203), which found that Israeli television news 'inadvertently privileges a non-compromising attitude towards the Arab-Israeli conflict', because political 'hawks' could decode the news at 'face value in order to reinforce their position', without having to draw (as the political 'doves' would have to) on what they referred to as 'a sophisticated understanding of (. . .) the relationship between news and social reality, in order to do so'. In other words, a discourse that could rely on conventional wisdoms without needing to have recourse to a lengthy set of supporting arguments and evidence, was more readily decoded by the audience, because of the way in which television works.

Another issue that arose in relation to this programme was the element of confrontation that appears to be central to studio audience discussion programmes. There were mixed comments from group members about this aspect of the *Davis* clip: 'They're not going to listen to each other – when I see two groups of people trying to argue a point, but no-one's listening to anyone' (Man, 25–34, Yes Voter, Group B). This sense of distance from this approach was not shared by all the group members: 'I think it needs to be a bit controversial as well, to make people think. Like *The Late Late Show*, to really see passions going, and that gets you thinking' (Woman, 25–34, Yes Voter, Group C) (*The Late Late Show* edition referred to was broadcast in late October 1995, and featured a very heated and rancorous debate on the divorce referendum).

The use of statistics, and the programme's perceived over-reliance on political campaigners, were areas that were also criticised. One member of Group B, referring to the use of statistics, said:

> They're things that they've worked out on a piece of paper. They're not the real facts. They're just picking out a couple of people in one area and saying . . . right, multiply that by the population, and they're just getting a number.
> (Man, 25–34, Yes Voter, Group B)

This growing cynicism regarding politics and political communication, and its perceived manupulative intent, is again evident in the questioning of the use of campaigners instead of 'ordinary people'.

> Because you're not learning anything, you know. They [the campaigners] are not going to be asking relevant questions, they're going to be asking questions that they know their person up front has the answer for.
>
> (Man, 25–34, Yes Voter, Group B)

## Conclusion

The main issues raised in response to the *Six-One* clip were: firstly, the problem of taking in a large amount of information over a relatively short period of time, and secondly, the dissatisfaction with politicians' use of language and statistics. The *Prime Time* excerpt produced a number of responses about the appropriateness of using lay contributors in current affairs television, and about the ability or inability of audience members to identify with those lay contributors. The *Davis* clip provoked many comments about the use of soundbites, with responses to this kind of approach dividing broadly along social class lines. Working-class group members tended to welcome the energy and dynamism of this style, compared to more traditional Irish current affairs programming, while middle-class group members tended to distance themselves from it, seeing it as being superficial and inimical to proper debate.

This issue of soundbites in the context of the 1995 divorce referendum is an important one, because of the particular intensity and complexity associated with the debate. The referendum provided a good example of a situation where two very different political discourses came up against the structural constraint of concision, with very different results for the two sides. The need for pro-divorce campaigners to provide supporting evidence and arguments was more pressing than for anti-divorce protagonists, because they (the anti-divorce camp) were more readily able to rely on the kind of 'conventional thoughts' that were referred to by Chomsky earlier. This led to a situation whereby the proponents of 'a radical social change' were at a disadvantage when communicating their ideas through television, compared to the defenders of the 'status quo'. How much this factor may explain the drop in support for divorce over the course of the campaign, is, however, a matter for further research.

Another important issue raised by the group members in this research was that of 'expert' and 'lay' roles in news and current affairs television. While *Prime Time* focused on lay contributors, *Davis* relied more on expert ones. In this instance, the reactions to expert and lay voices depended very much on whether or not the audience member could identify with them. The working-class (and lay) voices of the *Prime Time* clip were highly valued by working-class group members, on the basis of their perceived authenticity, grounded in real life experiences, not in academic literature. The predominantly middle-class (and expert) voices of the *Davis* clip, were seen by the middle-class group members as articulate, educated, and more convincing than what they saw as the over-personalisation employed by the *Prime Time* clip.

Which approach is better suited to the discourse of a process such as the 1995 divorce referendum? Is it better to highlight lay voices that have long been unfairly marginalised in the mass media (along with their experience-based knowledge), or should we rely on the academic/intellectual knowledge of the more familiar experts of Irish society? Both paths are problematic. Whatever way a news or current affairs programme chooses to structure their coverage, there will be difficulties for the communication of meaning. The three programme excerpts chosen for this study all drew both praise and criticism from different research group members. How we conduct our political television obviously has major ramifications for how we conduct our politics. Tendencies towards greater concision, and reliance on soundbites, on the one hand, and case histories and personalisation, on the other, have important implications for how we discuss and make decisions about our futures. If a programme dwells on research findings and statistics, it may alienate and bore, if it attempts to personalise a story, it may become superficial, and if it tries to present information in a lively and attention-grabbing style, it may only contribute further to the creation of a soundbite culture.

## Note

[1] I would like to thank those who helped me organise the focus groups, those whom I interviewed, and most importantly, those who participated in the groups themselves.

## References

Achbar, Mark (ed.) (1994) *Manufacturing Consent. Noam Chomsky and the Media.* Montréal: Black Rose Books.

Ad hoc Commission on Referendum Information (1995) *A Statement of the Case AGAINST the Proposed Amendment to Article 41.3.2⁰ of the Constitution/A Statement of the Case IN FAVOUR OF the Proposed Amendment to Article 41.3.2⁰ of the Constitution.* Dublin: Ad hoc Commission on Referendum Information.

Carey, Martha Ann (1994) 'The Group Effect in Focus Groups: Planning, Implementing, and Interpreting Focus Group Research', pp. 225–41 in Janice M. Morse (ed.) *Critical Issues in Qualitative Research Methods.* London: Sage.

Coghlan, Denis (1995) 'Coalition Starts Real Campaign as Nailbiting Countdown Begins', *The Irish Times*, 21 November.

Coghlan, Denis (1996) 'Divorce Referendum Day Survey Gives Unprecedented Breakdown of Voters', *The Irish Times*, 5 January.

Coulter, Carol (1995a) 'Campaigners Stalk Wavering Voters as Poll Deadline Nears', *The Irish Times*, 28 October.

Coulter, Carol (1995b) 'Government Owes Yes Victory to Voluntary Groups', *The Irish Times*, 27 November.

Dillon, Michele (1993) *Debating Divorce. Moral Conflict in Ireland*. Lexington: University Press of Kentucky.

FitzGerald, Garret (1995) 'Why Ireland Only Just Voted for Divorce', *The Guardian*, 27 November.

Girvin, Brian (1987) 'The Divorce Referendum in the Republic. June 1986', *Irish Political Studies*, II: 93–9.

Government Information (1995) *The Referendum on Divorce. Some Questions and Answers*. Dublin: Government Information.

Gripsrud, Jostein (1995) *The Dynasty Years. Hollywood Television and Critical Media Studies*. London: Routledge.

Hallin, Daniel C. (1992) 'Sound Bite News: Television Coverage of Elections, 1968–1988', *Journal of Communication*, 42(2): 5–24.

Hamilton, Mark (1994) *The Case Against Divorce*. Dublin: Lir Press.

Höijer, Birgitta (1990) 'Reliability, Validity and Generalizability. Three Questions for Qualitative Reception Research', *Nordicom Review*, (1): 15–20.

Hornsby-Smith, Michael P. and Christopher T. Whelan (1994) 'Religious and Moral Values', pp. 7–44 in Christopher T. Whelan (ed.), *Values and Social Change in Ireland*. Dublin: Gill & Macmillan.

Inglis, Tom (1987) *Moral Monopoly. The Catholic Church in Modern Irish Society*. Dublin: Gill & Macmillan.

Irish Council for Civil Liberties (1995) *The Case for Divorce in the 1990s. A Study of the Arguments*. Dublin: Irish Council for Civil Liberties.

Jensen, Klaus Bruhn (1986) *Making Sense of the News*. Århus: University Press.

Jensen, Klaus Bruhn (1987) 'Qualitative Audience Research: Toward an Integrative Approach to Reception', *Critical Studies in Mass Communication*, (4): 21–36.

Jensen, Klaus Bruhn (1988) 'Answering the Question: What is Reception Analysis?', *Nordicom Review*, (9): 3–5.

Jensen, Klaus Bruhn (1990) 'The Politics of Polysemy: Television News, Everyday Consciousness and Political Action', *Media, Culture and Society*, (12): 57–77.

Jensen, Klaus Bruhn (1991) 'Reception Analysis: Mass Communication as the Social Production of Meaning', pp. 135–48 in Klaus Bruhn Jensen and Nicholas W. Jankowski (eds), *A Handbook of Qualitative Methodologies for Mass Communication Research*. London: Routledge.

Jensen, Klaus Bruhn and Karl Erik Rosengren (1990) 'Five Traditions in Search of the Audience', *European Journal of Communication*, (5): 207–38.

Jones, Jack (1995) 'Divorce Battle Has Yet to be Won or Lost as Waverers Wait for Guidance', *The Irish Times*, 8 November.

Lewis, Justin (1991) *The Ideological Octopus. An Exploration of Television and its Audience*. London: Routledge.

Liebes, Tamar and Rivka Ribak (1991) 'A Mother's Battle Against TV News: A Case Study of Political Socialization', *Discourse & Society*, 2(2): 203–22.

Little, John A. (1995) *The Ban on Divorce*. Mullingar: Ennel Press.

Livingstone, Sonia M. and Peter K. Lunt (1992) 'Expert and Lay Participation in Television Debates: An Exploration of Audience Discussion Programmes', *European Journal of Communication*, (7): 9–35.

Livingstone, Sonia and Peter Lunt (1994) *Talk on Television. Audience Participation and Public Debate*. London: Routledge.

Lunt, Peter and Sonia Livingstone (1996) 'Rethinking the Focus Group in Media and Communications Research', *Journal of Communication*, 46(2): 79–98.

Morgan, David L. (1988) *Focus Groups as Qualitative Research*. London: Sage.

O'Brien, Mags (ed.) (1995) *Divorce? Facing the Issues of Marital Breakdown*. Dublin: Basement Press.

Office of the Minister for Equality and Law Reform (1995a) *Divorce Referendum. Your Questions Answered*. Dublin: Office of the Minister for Equality and Law Reform.

Office of the Minister for Equality and Law Reform (1995b) *24 Things You Should Know for November 24*. Dublin: Office of the Minister for Equality and Law Reform.

O'Reilly, Emily (1992) *Masterminds of the Right*. Dublin: Attic Press.

O'Toole, Fintan (1995) 'Two Cheers for the Referendum', *The Irish Times*, 25 November.

Pollak, Andy (1995) 'Smyth Affair Damaged Standing of Church', *The Irish Times*, 2 March.

Prendiville, Patricia (1988) 'Divorce in Ireland. An Analysis of the Referendum to Amend the Constitution, June 1986', *Women's Studies International Forum*, 11(4): 355–63.

Robinson, John P. and Mark R. Levy (1986) *The Main Source. Learning From Television*. London: Sage.

Sarantakos, Sotirios (1993) *Social Research*. Basingstoke: Macmillan.

Schrøder, Kim Christian (1994) 'Audience Semiotics, Interpretive Communities and the 'Ethnographic Turn' in Media Research', *Media, Culture and Society*, 16(2): 337–47.

Simon, Roger (1982) *Gramsci's Political Thought. An Introduction*. London: Lawrence & Wishart.

Stationery Office (1992) *Marital Breakdown. A Review and Proposed Changes*. Dublin: Stationery Office.

Ward, Peter (1993) *Divorce in Ireland: Who Should Bear the Cost?* Cork: Cork University Press.


Film:

Wintonick, Peter and Mark Achbar (dirs) (1992) *Manufacturing Consent. Noam Chomsky and the Media*. London: Connoisseur Video.

## SECTION FIVE
## CONSTRUCTING MEDIA AUDIENCES

# 10

# A History of Irish Language Broadcasting: National Ideology, Commercial Interest and Minority Rights

## *Iarfhlaith Watson*

This chapter examines the development of Irish language broadcasting over the past 80 years. I follow Irish broadcasting from the early years of radio, through the emergence of television and of a separate Irish language radio station, to the development of a separate Irish language television station. In analysing these developments, particular emphasis is placed on investigating the ideological perspectives which have informed broadcasters and broadcasting policy makers regarding the audience for Irish language programmes. I will argue that, at the outset of Irish radio in the 1920s, the audience was primarily seen as the whole nation, with radio contributing to building a national and distinctive cultural project within which the Irish language was seen as an essential part. From the 1950s onwards the audience as a market for advertisers came to challenge this national project and to undermine commitment to Irish language programming.

At the present time the audience for Irish language programmes is seen in terms of three interrelated perspectives. The first emphasises national cultural distinctiveness; the second points out how the international televisual market-place and the economics of broadcasting may support or undermine this cultural project; while the third emphasises the rights of Irish language speakers. These three potentially antagonistic perspectives were, and continue to be, particularly evident in the debate on the establishment of a separate Irish language television station – Teilifís na Gaeilge (TnaG). This debate will be looked at in detail. Finally, the launch of TnaG, on 31 October 1996, and the types of programmes broadcast are discussed. The ensuing debate over TnaG's ratings is assessed and the linguistic and technical disadvantages associated with being a separate Irish language channel are outlined. In conclusion, it is argued that in its attempts to satisfy all three perspectives TnaG falls short.

# Radio Éireann: The Audience and National Ideology

The language policy which was adopted by the government in the early 1920s was directly influenced by the work of the Gaelic League in its attempt to revive the Irish language. The government's policy was to assign the Irish language to a significant place in the new state. One of its 'principal cultural aims [was] to revive Irish in English-speaking Ireland . . .' (Fennell 1980: 33). The reason for this cultural policy was that the Irish language was perceived to be a central prop of Irish identity. This belief has continued to be held by a majority of Irish people up to the present. Tovey, Hannan and Abramson (1989: iii) claim that 'it is the widespread use of our own language that provides the most effective basis for any valid claims to membership of a distinctive peoplehood', while the CLAR (Committee on Irish Language Attitudes Research) survey, carried out in 1973, found that Irish people regard the Irish language as a 'validator of our cultural distinctiveness' (Advisory Planning Committee, 1986: 61) and this was reaffirmed by the Institiúid Teangeolaíochta Éireann (ITÉ: Ó Riagáin and Ó Gliasáin, 1994) in 1983 and 1993. Broadcasting in Ireland has thus been a tool used by the state in this attempt to create a culturally distinct nation.

The Civil War ended in May 1923 and as early as November 1923 the Postmaster-General (J. J. Walsh) had prepared a White Paper on broadcasting. In the following months there were debates about whether or not an independent company should run Irish broadcasting for profit, but finally on 28 March 1924 it was declared that the Post Office would run it. Gorham (1967: 12) points out that

> . . . in making the case for having an Irish broadcasting station at all, he [the Postmaster-General] said: 'We . . . claim that this nation has set out on a separate existence. That existence not only covers its political life, but also its social and cultural life, and I take it to be a part of the fight which this nation has made during the last six or seven years that this separate entity should not only be gripped but developed to the utmost until this country is properly set on its feet as an independent, self-thinking, self-supporting nation in every respect . . . Any kind of Irish station is better than no Irish station at all.

The Postmaster-General also pointed to the negative effect on the restoration of the Irish language if Irish people could only hear British broadcasts (see also Kelly 1992).

In the first few years after independence there was no national broadcasting, but even before national transmission proper began, financial considerations (which were to be a continual problem) were pitted against national aims. First to be broadcast was 2RN (understood to mean 'to Erin'), which began in Dublin on 1 January 1926 and could be received as far away as Tipperary, with the right receiver, but for most radios the range was about 25 miles. The opening speech was made by Douglas Hyde, in which he said that 'a nation is made from inside itself, it is made first of all by its language . . .' (quoted in

Gorham 1967: 24). But, as has always been the case with Irish broadcasting, and especially with Irish language broadcasting, 2RN's budget was severely limited and its finances strictly controlled, illustrating at this early stage the tension between the ideal of creating a nation and the practicalities of economy.

A national channel using a more powerful transmitter had been discussed during the second half of the 1920s, but was eventually established in the early 1930s (Radio Áth Luain). The first broadcasting from this channel was earlier than planned in order to broadcast the Eucharistic Congress held in Dublin in June 1932. Ireland, to quote O'Dowd (1991: 33), was becoming a 'Catholic corporatist order'. The Irish language was not the sole marker of national distinctiveness, Catholicism also played a central role. In its attempts to create a nation the government emphasised what distinguished Irish people, in general, from others, specifically the English. This distinctiveness involved speaking a different language (Irish), having different religious beliefs and practices (Catholicism), playing different sports (hurling, gaelic football etc.) and even having a different socio-economic structure built around a rural agricultural society. This concept of the nation was reflected in broadcasting, in particular through the inclusion of religious, sporting and Irish language programmes on radio.[1]

Gorham (1967: 136–40) describes the variety of programmes broadcast during the Second World War years. Music (80 per cent of the total in the 1920s, 67 per cent of the total in the 1930s (Cathcart 1984: 47)) and news were central from the beginning, but there were also sports and school programmes. The most popular programme was *Question Time* at the weekend and its partner-programme, *Information Please*, in the mid-week. Austin Clarke (the poet) ran a poetry competition; there was also a ballad series and plays were broadcast regularly. On Sunday nights there were charity appeals and most Sundays there was mass. Some other programmes in English were *Scrapbook for Women*, *Radio Digest* and *Round the Fire*. Nearly all these programmes had their counterpart in the Irish language e.g. *Nuacht* and *Treimhseachán Teann* as well as talks and discussion programmes, poetry readings and plays, children's programmes and Irish language learners' programmes *Is Your Irish Rusty?* and *Listen and Learn*. 'However, the Irish side of the programmes suffered from two lasting shortages – of material and of reaction from the audience' (Gorham, 1967: 139). Indeed low audience levels have been a continued problem for broadcasting in the Irish language during its 70 years from 2RN in 1926 to the present.

## Radio Telefís Éireann: The Audience and Commercial Interest

During the late 1950s the government sponsored a shift away from the protectionist rural agricultural socio-economic structure to a more market-driven economy, a more 'modern' society. O'Dowd (1992: 33) argues that this was part of an ideological shift launched and supported by certain academics, economists, civil servants and politicians during this period and has persisted in the decades since.

During this period of modernization plans were progressing to establish television broadcasting in Ireland. From 1953 onward RÉ was considering the factors involved in establishing an Irish television service. As with radio in the 1920s, there was talk of television being a commercial venture. On 6 November 1957 the Minister for Posts and Telegraphs (Neil T. Blaney) declared that Ireland would have television and that it would be 'largely commercial in character' and that proposals would be considered. The first proposal was made by Gael-Linn (an Irish language organization). However, on 7 August 1959 the Minister for Posts and Telegraphs (Michael Hilliard) announced that television (and radio) would be operated by a semi-state board (the RTÉ Authority) funded by licence fees and advertising. The legislation necessary to establish the Authority was passed on 6 April 1960. The establishment of the RTÉ Authority marked the gradual distancing of broadcasting from the direct influence of the state. It also marked the increased influence of commercial over national interest.

It seemed from the beginning of RTÉ that ratings would be a major factor influencing which programmes would be broadcast. The first Director General of RTÉ, an American, Edward Roth, was appointed in November 1960, to serve for a period of two years. In mid-November 1960 Roth gave a press conference at which he maintained that viewership figures would determine which programmes should be broadcast. This viewpoint has continued with the use of TAM and Nielsen to quantify audience levels and marks a shift away from creating a nation toward market considerations. Although the earlier ideology continued to be reflected in the types of programmes broadcast on television (e.g. *Beirt Eile*, a traditional music and dance programme, the *Angelus* etc.), the 'new' ideology, which seemed to favour a market-driven society, was reflected in allowing the market, through ratings, to influence choices regarding the types of programmes that were broadcast (Doolan *et al.*, 1969).

The primary method used by RTÉ to visualise the audience is through ratings. These indicate that RTÉ 1 is more popular than Network 2, that certain times of the day are more popular than others, that certain programmes are more popular than others and that popular programmes can increase the ratings for adjacent programmes, i.e. there is a 'piggy-back' audience (Quill, 1994: 14) who watch a few minutes at the end of a programme before the programme they intend watching commences, and a 'follow-through audience' who watch programmes after the programme they had tuned-in to watch. The aim of using ratings is not only to provide programmes which are enjoyed by a large number of people, it is moreover an attempt to provide advertisers with a large number of consumers and consequently maximise profits within the statutory limits on advertising time. This takes the market into consideration and marks a shift of emphasis from the goals of creating a nation through promoting cultural distinctiveness.

For some types of programmes, such as Irish language programmes, achieving high ratings is difficult. Barbrook (1992: 209–10) has argued that 'the need to win mass audiences marginalised previously revered types of programmes, such as broadcasts in the Irish language'. Nonetheless, the Irish language continued to hold an important role. This was reflected in the Broadcasting Authority Act (1960), Article 17 which stated that:

> In performing its functions, the Authority shall bear constantly in mind the national aims of restoring the Irish language and preserving and developing the national culture and shall endeavour to promote the attainment of these aims.

However, according to Gorham the politicians and 'practical men' did not value Radio Éireann's work for the national culture and would have preferred high listening figures from continuous mass entertainment. In relation to the period of the early 1960s when the Authority took over he noted that 'such guidance as came down from above was to the effect that Radio Éireann programmes ought to be brightened and popularised; Irish language broadcasts and 'long-haired' music were understood not to be highly valued' (1967: 315).

From the beginning there were problems providing Irish-made programmes, let alone programmes in the Irish language. The viewers were provided with a diet of foreign programmes (usually around 60 per cent), mostly American (Doolan *et al.*[2] 1969: 20 and 24). This was mainly because of financial constraints.

The essence of the market forces which came to act upon RTÉ was the need to generate advertising revenue. On RTÉ this was reflected in reliance on advertising.[3] A central programming goal was thus to attract large audiences for advertising purposes. The result was that the majority was catered for to the neglect of the minority, and 'previously revered types of programmes' (Barbrook 1992: 209–10) supported by the ideology of national distinctiveness were marginalised.

Market-driven television is superficially egalitarian because the viewers are seen to 'get what they want'. However, the international television programmes market is in itself highly inegalitarian. Fundamentally, the cost of providing Irish-made programmes is far more than buying American-made programmes (on average ten times more per hour), because the American market is large enough to provide the finances and advertising revenue necessary to produce high quality programmes for the US market and then sell them abroad at a 'competitive' (i.e. lower) price.

Beyond the constraints imposed by the small size of the Irish television market and resulting financial resources, is the neglect of minorities, if programming is determined by ratings. If programmes are broadcast only because of high ratings, programmes such as Irish language programmes, which might not provide the required ratings might not be broadcast. Thoreau (1995: 3) argued against the rule of majority in his *Civil Disobedience* in 1849:

> After all, the practical reason why, when the power is once in the hands of the people, a majority are permitted, and for a long period continue, to rule, is not because they are most likely to be in the right, nor because it seems fairest to the minority, but because they are physically the strongest. But a government in which the majority rule in all cases cannot be based on justice, even as far as men understand it.

If the majority 'rule in all cases' with respect to the programmes broadcast on RTÉ, minorities, such as Irish speakers, would be neglected.

Irish language programmes suffered as a result of the converging, unifying and levelling force of the market. Doolan, Dowling and Quinn (1969: 295), who worked in RTÉ in its early years claimed that:

> Because of the neglect from which Irish language programmes have suffered for years, Irish-speaking directors in the station do not wish to be associated with them. Whoever is in charge of an Irish language programme understands that it will be broadcast at an unfavourable time and that the facilities and finances available to a comparable English language programme will not be made available to it . . . (Author's translation from Irish).

Ratings caused major change in Irish language broadcasting. Because of the emphasis on viewership, programmes with large audiences became prized, while Irish language programmes which had previously been revered became not merely marginalised, as Barbrook (1992: 209–10) claims, but minoritised. The Irish language became a minority issue rather than a national issue. Programmes in Irish became a matter of minority rights rather than nation building.

## Raidió na Gaeltachta: The Audience and Minority Rights

In 1969 Gluaiseacht ar son Cearta Sibhialta na Gaeltachta, a civil rights group, began demonstrations in Galway, demanding rights for people in the Gaeltacht. One example was a demonstration against the production of an episode of *Quicksilver* (a television quiz show) in English in a Gaeltacht area. This movement reflected the broader civil rights movements of the time. It recognised that the Irish language was a minority issue and that speakers of the language were a minority group. The group set up their own illegal radio station – Saor Raidió Chonamara. Although the authorities closed down the station, demands for an Irish language station continued. Raidió na Gaeltachta (RnaG – the Irish language Gaeltacht station) was initiated as a result of demands for an Irish language service. Although there were questions in the Dáil about an Irish language station, the Director General of RTÉ (Tom Hardiman) bypassed the need for authorisation from the Oireachtas (Irish Parliament) in 1970 by deciding to set it up within RTÉ.

The linking of nationalism with the Irish language was especially clear during the civil rights movement, when many people felt it was a wing of the IRA or at least a manifestation of nationalism (Browne 1992: 416–17). In relation to RnaG, the language was again directly linked to nationalism when 'certain Dáil members were opposed to what they saw as . . . a divisive service . . . divisive because Irish speakers "had a different agenda", allegedly favouring more radical action to reunite Ireland' (Browne 1992: 417–8). RnaG began broadcasting in April 1972 and was nationwide within a few years. Criticisms of RnaG continued from some RTÉ officials and politicians who could not understand much Irish and felt if it was in Irish it had something to do with the IRA (see Browne 1992: 427).

RTÉ hired seven people to run RnaG (six teachers and one businessman). They were located in the Gaeltacht in the hope that this would reinforce the aim of RnaG – to serve the Gaeltacht. This aim suited a minority rights policy, but at the same time some people in RTÉ and some politicians felt that RnaG should be maintained strictly within the Gaeltacht, thus attempting to restrict the Irish language to the minority, rather than allowing it to be a national issue and to continue to be directly associated with an ideology of national distinctiveness. 'RnaG staff determined from the outset that the service would not limit itself to mirroring everyday life in the Gaeltacht, although there were RTÉ officials who thought that it should' (Browne, 1992: 423–4; see also Ó Glaisne, 1982: 220). This is illustrated by RnaG's attempts to use Irish speakers throughout the world as correspondents and RTÉ's attempts to restrict RnaG's news to what RTÉ supplied.

Although RnaG has managed to some degree to reflect a more national and international lifeworld[4] and to show that the Irish language can be used to discuss the modern world, a major criticism has been that it reflects too much of the local and 'old fashioned' lifeworld which the younger population of the Gaeltacht find irrelevant and unreal for their life. While RnaG is a Gaeltacht station, the young people in the Gaeltacht, according to one Gaeltacht activist (Donncha Ó hÉallaithe), are as urban as young people in the rest of Ireland (Gogan 1996: 16). As a Gaeltacht station, RnaG seems to do quite well in terms of listenership (although research is infrequent). A survey carried out by sociology students from University College Galway in 1979 found that 36 per cent of all Gaeltacht people listened to RnaG 'yesterday' (Fahy, 1980: 57); and a study carried out by the MRBI (Market Research Bureau of Ireland) in November 1988 found that RnaG had a 43 per cent share of the adult listeners in the Gaeltacht. The preliminary findings of the research carried out by the ITÉ (Ó Riagáin and Ó Gliasáin 1994) suggested that RnaG has succeeded in attracting a relatively large national audience: 15 per cent of the national population listened to RnaG in 1983 and in 1993 (this 15 per cent consists of four per cent who listened daily or a few times a week and 11 per cent who listened less often). This figure is quite high when taking into account, firstly, that it is fundamentally a Gaeltacht station and, secondly, that the ITÉ report claims that only 11 per cent of the population have fluent or near-fluent ability in the Irish language. This figure also provides the context within which ratings for Irish language television programmes can be assessed.

## Teilifís na Gaeilge: Minority Rights, National Distinctiveness and Market Realities

A discourse of rights regarding Irish speakers developed throughout the 1970s and 1980s. This can be seen in two reports on Irish language broadcasting written during this period. The first was that of the Advisory Committee on Irish Language Broadcasting appointed by the RTÉ Authority in 1977.[5] The committee claimed that broadcasts in the Irish language were a personal right, that there were a large number of Irish speakers and that a large majority of the population agreed with the use of Irish on television and radio, thus implying a potentially large viewership. The committee recommended that in order to improve the situation of Irish language broadcasting RTÉ should provide a full and varied range of programmes in Irish. The report of this group was never published and their recommendations were not implemented.

A second report was that of the Working Group on Irish Language Television Broadcasting (1987). This was set up in 1986 by the Ministers for the Gaeltacht and for Communications, and contained members from both these departments, RTÉ and Bord na Gaeilge. In their report they reproduced some of the arguments addressed to them by Irish language groups, in particular the latter's emphasis on the cultural distinctiveness of the Irish language and their claim 'that television impacts on the formation of attitudes and outlooks, and that we are at present being influenced greatly by programmes from abroad, and by the English language' (Working Group on Irish Language Television Broadcasting, 1987: 13). They made similar recommendations to those made by the 1977 committee but argued that there should be a 'graduated approach towards improving Irish language programmes on television', accompanied by completion dates. A full range of Irish language programmes, according to the Group, would consist of news and current affairs, magazine programmes, films and soundtracks in Irish, sport, bilingual programmes, educational programmes, learners' programmes, features, drama and religious programmes. Although children's programmes were not mentioned in this range, the Group emphasised their importance and included them in their 'graduated approach'. However, as can be seen from Figure 1 below, there was no increase in the percentage of programmes in Irish between 1985 and 1995. The percentage has remained at two per cent. The continual decline of Irish language programmes as a percentage of the total, first on radio and then on television, since the 1940s can also be noted.

Figure 1: The Percentage of Total Broadcasting Time on Radio (RÉ) 1935–55 and Television (RTÉ) 1965–95 given to Irish Language Programmes.

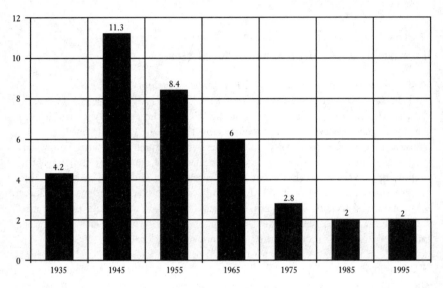

Programmes in Irish were originally broadcast on RTÉ 1, but 'with the advent of RTÉ 2 it was feared by certain groups that Irish language programmes might be relegated to the less popular second channel' (O'Connor 1983: 5) which had been set up to broadcast mainly foreign programmes. During the 1980s there was a gradual transfer to RTÉ 2/Network 2 and this has been regarded as causing a decline in the audience of these programmes. The attempts to improve the situation of Irish language broadcasting were in vain and during this period Irish language programmes were increasingly relegated to RTÉ 2/Network 2.

Primarily, the options that were open to improving Irish language television broadcasting, as seen by the Working Group (1987) and Irish language groups, were: that RTÉ assign a definite block of time on one channel for broadcasting through Irish; a second option was that more Irish programmes be assimilated into RTÉ's schedule and spread across both channels; the final option was to establish a separate Irish language channel. However, RTÉ did not support any of these suggestions (Working Group on Irish Language Television Broadcasting 1987: 4–5). The Working Group was also not in favour of a separate Irish language channel for fear of ghettoising the language and felt it would be better to improve the state of Irish on RTÉ.

RTÉ continued to regard Irish language programmes as unpopular and claimed in response to the Green Paper on Broadcasting (1995) that:

while the Survey figures quoted in the Green Paper may indeed indicate a growth in favour of the language and, out of that, a perceived growth in the need for more and better programmes in Irish, the fact is that this does not translate into any growth in audiences for such programmes when they are transmitted (RTÉ, 1995: 28).

One may raise the question as to whether RTÉ fully taps the potential audience for Irish language programmes on RTÉ 1 and Network 2 – *Cúrsaí Ealaíona* outstrips its English language equivalent, *Black Box*, and Irish language children's programmes such as *Dinín* and *Scéalaíocht Janosch*, which were broadcast on *The Den* achieved audiences of 250,000 (Gogan, 1996: 14). They continue to visualise the audience for Irish language programmes as a special interest group and broadcast current affairs and arts programmes (and virtually no other type of programme) which deal primarily with Irish language issues, while Irish speakers (and viewers of Irish language programmes generally) are as diverse in their interests as non-Irish speakers: thus 'gaeilgoirí are seen as a group with special minority rights, and as constituting a specialist listenership group' (Kelly and Rolston, 1995: 575). They have a limited concept of the lifeworld of Irish speakers, visualising it stereotypically. They also visualise the audience as small and make no effort to attract a larger audience, thus creating a self-fulfilling prophecy: they broadcast cheap, special interest, talking-heads programmes on Network 2, thereby ensuring a small audience and reinforcing audience perception of Irish language programmes.

Demands for a separate Irish language television channel were made regularly and range back as far as the late 1950s, when Gael Linn proposed to establish and operate Ireland's television channel. By the end of the 1960s Doolan, Dowling and Quinn (1969), who had been working in RTÉ, suggested having a Gaeltacht television channel. Bord na Gaeilge published a plan for improving the situation of Irish in which they recommended that an Irish language television service for the Gaeltacht be established (Bord na Gaeilge 1983: 5). The recommendation to establish a separate channel did not imply a preference for such, but for many it was viewed as the only available choice under the circumstances.

In 1980 Coiste ar son Teilifís Gaeltas was instituted by Irish language activists. They started by setting up a short-lived pirate television station. Subsequently, in 1987, Meitheal Oibre ar son Teilifís Gaeltachta was set up, which also involved people from the Gaeltacht. The group broadcast illegally from Ros Muc, County Galway in November 1987 and in December 1988. FNT (Feachtas Náisiúnta Teilifíse) was set up early in 1989 as an umbrella pressure group. They demanded that a station be set up for the Gaeltacht and all the country. This marked a shift from demands for a Gaeltacht community-type channel to demands for a national channel.

The establishment of the separate Irish language channel, Teilifís na Gaeilge (TnaG), may be the result of pressure from FNT or may be due to the interests of individual ministers such as Máire Geoghegan-Quinn (as Minister for Communications, 1991–3) and then Michael D. Higgins (as Minister for Arts, Culture and the Gaeltacht, 1993–97). However, what has made the channel acceptable is, firstly, that the language still holds a position within an ideology of national distinctiveness and the majority of the population still favours Irish language policies.[6] Secondly, most Irish speakers have been dissatisfied with RTÉ and have given up hope that RTÉ could provide an adequate service within the existing channels. Thirdly, insofar as the ideology of minority rights and EU policy is concerned, providing a separate Irish language channel conforms to EU principles of decentralisation, diversity and minority rights.

Most of the arguments in favour of the establishment of a separate Irish language channel were premised on a minority rights philosophy. Both the Fianna Fáil–Labour coalition (Fianna Fáil and The Labour Party, 1993: 5) and the Fine Gael–Labour–Democratic Left coalition (Fine Gael, The Labour Party and Democratic Left, 1994: 84) presented TnaG as a service through Irish for the Irish speaking and Gaeltacht community. TnaG also accepted this viewpoint in their response to the 1995 Green Paper on Broadcasting (TnaG, 1995b: 12) and in their apologetic *Cén Fáth TnaG?*: 'The Irish language community has a right to a comprehensive television service in their own language' (TnaG, 1995a) (Author's translation from Irish). However, it may also have the consequence of ghettoising the Irish language. Although RTÉ will still be required to broadcast Irish language programmes and to produce one hour per day for the new Irish language channel, the importance of Irish on the central stage of RTÉ's two national channels will be diminished. The audience for Irish language programmes may thus be a minority, both on TnaG and on RTÉ, and this represents a change from the previous ideological situation which was to attempt to reach everybody even with 'cúpla focal'.

Paradoxically, although political groups and TnaG itself may regard Irish language television as a right, the determining influence of the market may leave the minority to support itself. Achieving success within the market involves enticing an audience. This means providing programmes which are attractive. The primary principle of attractive programming is quality and one of the principal requirements for achieving quality is finance. RTÉ was told by the Minister for Arts, Culture and the Gaeltacht that it is required to provide one hour per day of programming to TnaG (included in this is news) and that IR£5,000,000 per annum should be enough to do this. This expenditure is equal to an average of over IR£13,500 per hour: RTÉ's average expenditure on independent productions is over IR£20,000 per hour (ITV spends about six times as much). TnaG was provided with IR£10,000,000 from the exchequer, from which TnaG is expected to provide two hours per day, this averages at IR£13,500 per hour. However, through a policy of repeats (i.e. providing an average of only one 'original' hour per day) TnaG claimed that its average expenditure on commissioning programmes is similar to RTÉ's at around IR£20,000 per hour. Ó Ciardha (Information Editor for TnaG) has commented:

> . . . our average figure is average, about the same figure that RTÉ has, twenty-one, twenty-three thousand pounds in total. Of course the small size of our service places huge constraints on our ability to do work on large dramas, large films (. . .) constraints which the BBC doesn't have (. . .) [for example] the Welsh channel, S4C, has a budget at least seven times as big as the budget we have. Now, they broadcast a small number more hours than we do but the average budget per hour . . . the cost per hour is at least twice as big as ours, it depends on how much you have but, I mean, it is true to say we have little money (Interview with the author. Author's translation from Irish).

TnaG should have the option of supplementing its finances through selling airtime outside the three-hour schedule and through advertising within the schedule. Achieving the maximum finances from advertising requires maximising the audience. Therefore, if TnaG wants to provide an attractive schedule it may be necessary to appeal to a wider audience than the minority Irish speakers.

It seems that TnaG envisions their viewers to include the population of the whole island of Ireland rather than focusing on the Irish speaking minority. Ó Ciardha makes this point clearly:

> We are a television service and we regard the whole country . . . island as our viewers, it happens that the programmes will be broadcast in Irish, of course it also happens that subtitles in English will be available on teletext for all recorded programmes, therefore we are not . . . restricting ourselves to those who speak and understand the Irish language. Also there are different ways to make a schedule more attractive even if it is in a minority language. For example, we have a whole television channel, and we have permission, and we have the resources, to use the spare time of the channel to broadcast programmes of the type that will attract a big audience, to attract people to the channel and thus to the Irish language service which will be part of the channel. That's one thing. The second point (. . .) on this island a few hundred thousand people is not a bad audience at all, certainly some of the programmes with the biggest resources and publicity on RTÉ at the moment have a very small audience.

He also recognises that the economics of broadcasting does not always require large audiences:

> . . . it is not the size of the audience which is most important to advertisers, for example, but the standard of expenditure and income which people have, the people who have the income to spend (Interview with the author. Author's translation from Irish).

TnaG, although being established as a minority channel seeks to maximise its audience to include people with little or no Irish as well as Irish speakers, mainly because of market forces and to a lesser degree in an attempt to follow the ideology of national distinctiveness. TnaG has carried out market research to provide a clearer picture of the audience, and visualise the six to fourteen-year-old audience as being central (with programmes such as *Boisiní* and *Cabúm*).

This seems to be a manifestation of the policy of preserving the language through concentrating on young people (as most Irish language organisations do) rather than simply providing an Irish language television service.

## TnaG Comes on Air: Programme Schedule and Audience Rating

TnaG began broadcasting on 31 October 1996. While press coverage of the launch and media response to the programmes, which were broadcast in the following months, appeared to be more positive than had been prior to broadcasting, ratings were a contentious issue. On Sunday 1 December 1996 several newspapers (e.g. *Sunday World* 1 December 1996) printed articles which presented the Nielsen ratings for TnaG. TnaG had not even attracted half of one per cent of the population on average; this meant that TnaG did not even achieve an average of 13,000 viewers and this figure was actually as low as 6,000 viewers or less (i.e. 0.22 per cent, *The Irish Times* 5 February 1997). Ó Ciardha (1997) argued that Nielsen had a panel of over 600 families which had been selected before TnaG began broadcasting and that their data was flawed both because there was no information on how many of these families could receive TnaG and because of inaccuracy due to a three per cent standard error. TnaG was subsequently unwilling to release figures.

TnaG commissioned Lansdowne Market Research in December 1996 to carry out research, from which they released only a vague summary of the main findings. From the relatively imprecise figures releasesd by TnaG, 90 per cent had heard of TnaG. A little over half could receive it, the primary reason for not receiving was technical difficulties outside Dublin, while in Dublin the primary reason was lack of interest and hence not bothering to tune TnaG in. From the Lansdowne survey, it appears that one in seven had at some point watched TnaG over the previous six weeks. As we know from Ó Riagáin and Ó Gliasáin's (1994: 12) research 12 per cent said they were regular (at least once a week) viewers of Irish language programmes on RTÉ (28 per cent were less regular viewers). It would appear that TnaG faces a major challenge in achieving a similar level of viewership.

Cathal Goan, director of TnaG, expected that TnaG should attract an average daily audience of 100,000 viewers (three per cent) within six months. He pointed to the fact that RTÉ 2 had initially attracted an average audience of only seven per cent. He added that 'we know that the figures have been disappointing and that we have a struggle in front of us. But, number one, we've had transmission difficulties and, number two, we are a new service' (*The Irish Times* 5 February 1997). He also mentioned that the most successful programme one Sunday was a children's programme called *Hiúdaí* which attracted 35,000 viewers. However, compared with programmes broadcast on *The Den* (regular afternoon children's programmes on Network 2) which achieved audiences of 250,000 (Gogan 1996: 14) this is quite small.

For TnaG to achieve the ratings RTÉ have achieved for Irish language programmes such as *Ros na Rún*, it would be necessary to increase the audience massively. However, as Network 2 has a lower average audience than RTÉ 1 for Irish language programmes, one could expect TnaG to have a smaller audience still, particularly when one considers that programmes on RTÉ 1 and Network 2 are intensively cross-promoted whereas TnaG programmes are not. Furthermore carry-over audiences from earlier popular programmes to the following less popular one are known to increase ratings for the latter significantly. Also, when one considers that while the dedicated Welsh language channel S4C has been successful (with a budget of around IR£70,000,000), Gàidhlig programmes, which are broadcast on mainly English language channels in Scotland, have been relatively more successful. Thus one could expect Irish language programmes on a dedicated Irish language channel, such as TnaG, to have less viewers than the same programmes on mainly English language channels, such as RTÉ. A positive factor is that, as Ó Ciardha has argued, it is the spending power of the viewers which matters to advertisers. The Lansdowne research found that TnaG had greatest appeal for the 'upmarket, educated with school-going children'. Thus TnaG may not find it necessary to achieve the same ratings as RTÉ to be financially viable.

With regard to the schedule, TnaG began by broadcasting around five hours a day or thirty hours a week of Irish language programmes (with at least four hours of repeats every week), 20 or 30 minutes in the early afternoon for young children, two hours from 5.00 until 7.00 for older children and teenagers, and two and a half hours from 8.00 until 10.30 in the evening for adults, with an emphasis on young people aged 14 to mid-thirties (Gogan, 1996: 15 and *The Irish Times*, 17 April 1996). There were also broadcasts in English: *Dáil Éireann: Question Time* in the afternoon, Tuesday to Thursday, and *EuroNews*, the European Broadcasting Union's news programme, in the early evening Monday to Friday, which supported the channel's public service obligation. In Irish, they offered a full range of programmes from soaps to news. There was an emphasis on drama, with a comedy series called *C. U. Burns* and a soap opera called *Ros na Rún*, which was commissioned from independent producers EO Teilifis and Tyrone Productions at a cost of IR£2,500,000 or 25 per cent of TnaG's annual budget, suggesting that it was to be a centre-piece on the new channel. As Cathal Goan (Head of TnaG) said:

> But we're clear about one thing. We, the staff and the authority, believe that we must have something as an anchor in this schedule and there's no better way to do that than to provide a credible drama. *Ros na Rún* proved, while it was on RTÉ for that short period, that it can be done. Our hearts are in it because we believe that this will be an enticement for people in the middle of the schedule (*The Irish Times* 17 April 1996) (Author's translation from Irish).

*Ros na Rún* was broadcast for twenty minutes four times a week with an omnibus edition on Saturdays. *Ros na Rún* also had been piloted on RTÉ 1 at Christmas 1992 and compared favourably with even the most popular, well-established English language soap operas on RTÉ at the time (see Figure 2) and was expected to achieve high ratings on TnaG as well.[7] In Scotland, the Gàidhlig soap opera *Machair* (which TnaG showed – undubbed) has had up to 500,000 viewers (*The Irish Times,* 3 November 1993), even though there are only around 50,000 Gàidhlig speakers. It was hoped that *Ros na Rún* would attract viewers with varying abilities of Irish from fluency to 'cúpla focal'. There were subtitles in English available on teletext, which meant that the programmes were accessible to people with little or no Irish, thus widening the potential audience. The aim, therefore, was not only to serve the minority Irish speaking community, as TnaG would attempt to attract a large audience irrespective of their ability to speak Irish (and the Lansdowne research commissioned by TnaG in December 1996 indicated that 70 per cent of TnaG's viewers did not have a good Irish language ability). Although achieving a large audience serves the ideology of cultural and national distinctiveness, it seems that the force behind the decision to attract a large audience is the market, survival depends on attracting a large enough audience to provide some degree of financial viability through advertising. TnaG's aim was to receive IR£2,000,000 in advertising revenue during its first year of broadcasting (*The Irish Times,* 28 April 1996). Overall, because TnaG is subject to market forces and a limited budget it must appeal to an audience larger than that provided by the Irish speaking community.

Figure 2: Average Number of Viewers of Ros na Rún and other Soap Operas on RTÉ 1 and Network 2 (28/12/92–3/1/93).

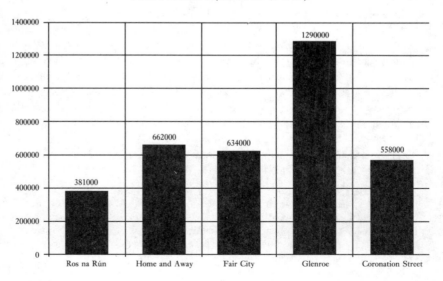

# Summary and Conclusion

During the first few decades of radio broadcasting in Ireland the listeners were primarily seen as a homogeneous whole, with radio contributing to building a national and distinctive cultural project within which the Irish language was seen as an essential part. With the advent of Irish television, the audience began to be regarded as a commodity for advertisers, challenging this national project and undermining commitment to Irish language programming. In the past few decades broadcasts in the Irish language have become minoritised and a minority rights perspective has emerged.

The perspective of national cultural distinctiveness is a reflection of the cultural nationalism which emerged in Ireland in the last century and has permeated broadcasting since independence. Within this perspective the restoration of the Irish language is seen as a national goal and broadcasting programmes in the Irish language as an important method for achieving this goal. In the early period of radio broadcasting this perspective emphasised the moulding of audiences in the national interest.

The second perspective points out how the international televisual marketplace and the economics of broadcasting may support or undermine the restoration of the Irish language. This perspective has always existed in Irish broadcasting but has gained prominence since the 1950s. Within this perspective the reality of the market compels the broadcaster to perceive the audience as a commodity and to broadcast programmes which are expected to attract a large audience and therefore produce more advertising revenue. Irish language television programmes have been viewed by RTÉ as attracting a small minority Irish speaking audience, whereas TnaG has attempted to attract a large audience (both Irish speaking and non-Irish speaking) to Irish language programmes.

The third perspective emphasises the rights of Irish language speakers. This is a more 'modern' perspective and has been gaining influence in Ireland since the 1950s and especially since Ireland joined the EU. This perspective is viewed as being neo-liberal, pluralistic and central to the modernisation of Ireland. However, this may be pseudo-pluralistic because power is not fragmented amongst a plurality of groups and most minorities are powerless. Minorities must have resources (both material and ideological) and organise and lobby to secure their rights (such as the right to be informed through one's own language).

These three potentially antagonistic perspectives were, and continue to be, particularly evident in the debate on the establishment of a separate Irish language television station – TnaG is acceptable within the minority rights  perspective, however, the market is allowed free reign. TnaG provides popularised programmes, emphasises drama and provides English language subtitles in an attempt to attract as large an audience as possible to entice advertisers. While this does not, strictly speaking, provide a service for the minority Irish speakers, it is acceptable both within the perspective of national cultural distinctiveness as an attempt to broadcast Irish to the whole nation and within the perspective of the international televisual market-place where the market rules. While RTÉ neglected Irish language programming because of the market, TnaG is forced to structure the schedule around market forces in providing Irish language programmes.

While RTÉ has been accused of providing programmes which fail to attract a large audience, TnaG can expect and indeed has achieved even smaller audiences. TnaG began with several disadvantages: firstly, technical problems meant that perhaps as much as 40 per cent of the population did not receive its broadcasts; secondly, financial contraints resulted in limited funding for production and the necessity to repeat programmes to fill the schedule; thirdly, the problem of being the third channel and in practice likely to receive lower ratings than RTÉ 1 and Network 2; fourthly, and in common with Irish language programmes on RTÉ, linguistic problems which resulted in a lower potential audience and the added expense of dubbing programmes. Bearing all these disadvantages in mind the Nielsen ratings of 0.22 per cent, which TnaG received initially, were nonetheless meagre. Although this rating has managed to reach around one per cent at least once, if TnaG is to remain ideologically acceptable it must achieve its aim of three or four per cent average daily audience.

## Notes

[1]   During the 1930s there was also an expectation that an Irish language channel might be established. In 1935 T. J. Kiernan was appointed Director of the radio station. He encouraged the formation of a committee in each county to which he would offer broadcasting access. The first committee formed was in Galway, where they hoped access would result in the establishment of some kind of Irish language station. When this was not forthcoming the committee lapsed. This was the first prospect for a separate Irish language broadcasting channel.

[2]   Doolan *et al.*'s (1969) *Sit Down and be Counted* makes a good companion volume for Gorham's (1967) *Forty Years of Irish Broadcasting*.

[3]   RTÉ Income (in millions of pounds)

|  | 1964 | 1965 | 1966 | 1967 | 1968 |
|---|---|---|---|---|---|
| Licence Fee | 1.258 | 1.458 | 1.612 | 1.680 | 1.926 |
| Advertising | 1.178 | 1.736 | 1.984 | 2.293 | 2.628 |

SOURCE: RTÉ ANNUAL REPORTS

[4]   Lifeworld, or *Lebenswelt*, is the 'everyday world' of 'everyday people'.

[5]   This report was not published, but, its findings are reported by the Working Group on Irish Language Television Broadcasting (1987).

[6]   Three quarters (75 per cent) of the population agree that the government should support the use of Irish on TV and three quarters (78 per cent) agree that the government should support Irish language organisations (Ó Riagáin and Ó Gliasáin, 1994: 30).

[7]   Initially figures were not available for *Ros na Rún* viewership on TnaG, because TnaG did not accept Nielsen's research and did not supply them with a programme log.

# References

Advisory Planning Committee (1986) *The Irish Language in a Changing Society: Shaping the Future.* Dublin: Bord na Gaeilge.

Barbrook, Richard (1992) 'Broadcasting and National Identity in Ireland', *Media, Culture and Society* 14: 203–27.

Bord na Gaeilge (1983) *Action Plan for Irish 1983–1986.* Dublin: Bord na Gaeilge.

Browne, Donald R. (1992) 'Radio na Gaeltachta: Swan Song or Preserver', *European Journal of Communications* 7.

Cathcart, Rex (1984) 'Broadcasting – The Early Decades', in B. Farrell (ed.) *Communications and Community in Ireland.* Dublin: Mercier Press.

CLAR (1975) *Committee on Irish Language Attitude Research Report.* Dublin: Government Stationery Office.

Cottle, Simon (1993) 'Producer-Driven Television?', *Media, Culture and Society* 17: 159–66.

Department of Arts, Culture and the Gaeltacht (1995) *Active or Passive? Broadcasting in the Future Tense: Green Paper on Broadcasting.* Dublin: Government Stationery Office.

Doolan, Lelia, Jack Dowling and Bob Quinn (1969) *Sit Down and be Counted: The Cultural Evolution of a Television Station.* Dublin: Wellington Publishers.

Fahy, Tony (1980) 'Listenership up 10 Per Cent', *Irish Broadcasting Review*, 8: 56–7.

Fennell, Desmond (1980) 'Can a Shrinking Linguistic Minority be Saved? Lessons from the Irish Experience', in E. Haugen *et al.* (eds) *Minority Languages Today.* Edinburgh: Edinburgh University Press.

Fianna Fáil and The Labour Party (1993) *Programme for Partnership Government 1993–1997: Fostering our Language, Culture and Heritage: Expanding Biligualism in Irish Society: Guidelines for Action Programmes in the State Sector.*

Fine Gael, The Labour Party and Democratic Left (1994) *A Government of Renewal: A Policy Agreement Between Fine Gael, The Labour Party and Democratic Left.*

Gogan, Johnny (1996) 'Ar Aghaidh Linn', *Film Ireland*, April/May.

Gorham, Maurice (1967) *Forty Years of Broadcasting.* Dublin: RTÉ.

Kelly, Mary (1992) 'The Media and National Identity in Ireland', pp. 75–89 in P. Clancy *et al.* (eds), *Ireland and Poland: Comparative Perspectives.* Dublin: Department of Sociology, University College Dublin.

Kelly, Mary and Bill Rolston (1995) 'Broadcasting in Ireland: Issues of National Identity and Censorship', pp. 563–92 in P. Clancy *et al.* (eds) *Irish Society: Sociological Perspectives.* Dublin: Institute of Public Administration.

Ó Ciardha, Pádhraic (1996) Personal Interview with the author 19 February 1996.

Ó Ciardha, Pádhraic (1997) Personal Interview with the author 3 February 1997.

O'Connor, Barbara (1983) *Irish Language Media: Discussion Document.* Dublin: Bord na Gaeilge.

O'Dowd, Liam (1992) 'State Legitimacy and Nationalism in Ireland', pp. 25–48 in P. Clancy *et al.* (eds) *Ireland and Poland: Comparative Perspectives.* Dublin: Department of Sociology, University College Dublin.

Ó Glaisne, Roibeard (1992) *Raidió na Gaeltachta.* Indreabháin: Cló Cois Fharraige.

Ó Riagáin, Pádraig and Mícheál Ó Gliasáin (1994) *National Survey on Languages 1993: Preliminary Report.* Dublin: ITÉ.

Quill, Tríona (1994) 'Television and the Irish Language', *Irish Communications Review* 4: 6–17.

RTÉ (1995) *RTÉ Response to the Government's Green Paper on Broadcasting.* Dublin: RTÉ.

Thoreau, Henry David (1995 orig. 1849) *Civil Disobedience.* London: Penguin.

TnaG (1995a) *Cén Fáth TnaG*. Dublin: TnaG.

TnaG (1995b) *Páipéar Glas an Rialtais ar Chraolachán: Freagra Theilifís na Gaeilge*. Dublin: TnaG.

Tovey, Hillary, Damien Hannan and Hal Abramson (1989) *Why Irish? Irish Identity and the Irish Language*. Dublin: Bord na Gaeilge.

Watson, Iarfhlaith (1996) 'The Irish Language and Television: National Identity, Preservation, Restoration and Minority Rights', *British Journal of Sociology* 47(2): 255–74.

Working Group on Irish Language Television Broadcasting (1987) *Report to the Ministers for the Gaeltacht and Communications*. Dublin: Government Stationery Office.

# 11

# The Theatre of Reassurance? *Glenroe*, Its Audience and the Coverage of Social Problems

## *Eoin Devereux*

Recent analysis of the Irish print and broadcast media indicates that the coverage of poverty and other social problems is largely absent from the newspaper pages and airwaves (Kelly, 1984; Gibbons, 1984a; Ruddy, 1987; Devereux, 1994). This chapter asks whether fictional television in the form of soap opera provides more or less space for the coverage of poverty themes. It takes the view that although analyses of media content on the visibility or invisibility of poverty are important, there is also something to be gained by attempting to understand more about the production of media messages and specifically in trying to learn about the perspectives of those who create media messages. This chapter is concerned therefore with how the *Glenroe* audience is constructed by those who are involved in the making of the series and its implications for the coverage of poverty and social problems. This analysis is seen as an essential prerequisite to any future work which might want to explore the views of audience members.

Drawing on material gathered from a larger study of poverty coverage on Radio Telefís Éireann's (RTÉ) news, current affairs, telethon and television drama programmes, this chapter examines the perceptions of those involved in the making of the drama serial *Glenroe* in terms of their expectations about audience interest in poverty and other social problems. The chapter is based upon data gathered using semi-structured interviews with those involved in the 1992–93 series of *Glenroe*. There are three sections to the chapter. Firstly, the history and background to Glenroe is outlined with specific reference to O'Connor's (1990) study on audience response to the programme. Secondly, the views of those involved in the making of the series are examined. I explore the creation of *Glenroe* drawing on interviews with some of the programme's directors, scriptwriters and actors. In particular, I discuss the programme's perceived remit; its concentration on characters rather than on issues and the views of programme personnel vis-à-vis audience interest in poverty stories. Apart from some notable exceptions within current affairs television, the creators of *Glenroe* conform to the wider institutional shyness of challenging the television audience vis-à-vis poverty and social problems. Thirdly, I consider the limitations and possibilities within the TV drama genre for the exploration and coverage of poverty and other social issues by comparing *Glenroe* to Channel 4's *Brookside*. Just how *Glenroe* deals with stories about the Travelling community is also examined in the chapter's final section. (A synopsis of storylines about the unemployed and Travellers is to be found in the chapter's appendix, p. 246.)

## *Glenroe*: Background, History and Audience Response

*Glenroe* is an RTÉ-produced weekly TV drama serial. (see also Sheehan 1987, 1993) First broadcast in 1983, the programme had completed its tenth series of 34 episodes in May 1993, which forms the basis of the discussion in this chapter. The programme's lineage may be traced to the RTÉ mini-series *Bracken*, which bridged the gap between the long running serial *The Riordans* and *Glenroe*. Set in County Wicklow, supposedly about 30 miles from Dublin, the programme is concerned with the inhabitants of the village of *Glenroe*, in which a mixture of rural and urban people live.

All three programmes have had the same creator in Wesley Burrowes and all three have been highly successful in terms of levels of viewership. *Glenroe* regularly attracts 1.5 million viewers to its 8.30 p.m. Sunday evening slot, and, for example, in its eight series, it pushed *The Late Late Show* into second place as the top rating programme on RTÉ. The average viewership of *Glenroe* during its 1992–93 season was 1,234,000 (39 per cent of the potential total audience) for the Sunday broadcast (20.30 to 21.00).

Given its positioning in RTÉ's programming schedule, and in terms of the types of issues explored in the series, the programme is clearly intended for what its makers describe as 'family' viewing. Controversial issues of a political nature such as Northern Ireland or even political corruption at local or national political level are never mentioned. Likewise, there is no debate on sexuality, even though there is a strong melodramatic emphasis in the series, which takes relations between the (usually married) sexes as their theme.

The series is dominated by the rural middle class of farmers and professionals (farmers, shopkeepers, auctioneers, publicans, but the other ends of the social spectrum are also represented (the ascendancy and the Travelling community). Class divisions, however, are not seen as barriers to interaction between the characters. The programme places a strong emphasis on the possibility of good relations between different social groupings based on a shared membership of the Glenroe community. The programme concentrates on the lives of two related families, the Byrnes (Dinny, Miley and Biddy) and the Morans (Dick and Mary) with other families and individuals getting coverage as a result of their interactions with the Byrnes and Morans. In common with other TV drama serials, there is a strong 'human interest' dimension to the programme with a great deal of emphasis on marital infidelity, failed love affairs and personal crises.

The formula of the programme is based on a series of contrasts, strong characterisation and humour. As Silj (1988:94) noted, drawing on O'Connor's research, 'The plot and characters revolve around the axis of the traditional versus the modern, the rural versus the urban'. The mixed rural and urban population of the series allows for these contrasts to be explored and in many ways the storylines of the programme present an interesting cultural mirror, representing in dramatic form some of what is actually happening in a rapidly changing society like Ireland.

According to a study of audience response to *Glenroe*, the programme's strengths were seen to be its humour and characterisation. O'Connor (1990:9) found that 'This humour was regarded as peculiarly Irish and was distinguished from other kinds of humour in a number of ways. It was perceived as being both subtle and clever.' An example from previous episodes might be when Dinny decided to go into the free-range egg business. He in fact was buying the eggs secretly from a supermarket and covering them in chicken dung and fooling his buyers. O'Connor's research indicated that the viewership of *Glenroe* were also attracted to the series because of its strong characterisation. Dinny, Miley and Biddy were the most popular figures with the audience and particular mention was given to the humorous exchanges between these characters. Other characters in this series were dismissed because of their lack of humour. As one of O'Connor's (1990:10) sample group told her: 'Dick Moran and the rest of you forget because they are too serious . . . where you are only watching for . . . the amusing parts . . . you dismiss them really when they come in . . . they are just the many people to keep it going'.

These findings are of importance in terms of our interest in how *Glenroe* either ignores or addresses social problems. The audience research carried out by O'Connor (1990:103-4) suggested that *Glenroe's* emphasis on humour was to the detriment of its coverage of social problems:

> . . . it is no coincidence that our audience research has shown that the age groups with which this serial is least popular are the younger ones. Young people criticise the stress on humour, feeling that in the end this produces a lightweight programme, inferior to British serials, particularly *Brookside*, which is regarded as far more attentive to social problems.

This is an interesting comment, in that two British serials, *Emmerdale* which is very similar in structure to *Glenroe*, and the urban based *Brookside*, have both dealt with contentious social problems, such as homelessness and unemployment. Newer soaps such as *Brookside, Eastenders* and to a lesser extent *Fair City* have evidently incorporated a social dimension into their storylines. This may be partially explained in terms of the desires of their creators to set their programmes apart from more traditional soaps such as *Coronation Street* or *Glenroe.* In the case of *Brookside* in particular, the producers clearly have a definite educative agenda in terms of challenging and informing their audience about a wide range of issues such as unemployment, AIDS and sexual identity. In the context of RTÉ's own soap output, *Glenroe's* rival programme *Fair City*, has in its 1996 series, begun to examine public attitudes towards gay men in a sustained way. In contrast to *Glenroe, Brookside* and to a lesser extent *Fair City* have managed with some success to balance character development with the coverage of social issues. They have shown that it is possible to combine entertainment with educative realism within a soap opera. In the following section I turn from examining audience expectations of *Glenroe* to explore the viewpoints of those who make the series.

## A View From Inside *Glenroe*: The Theatre of Reassurance

From the perspective of those who are involved in the creation of *Glenroe*, the programme is seen as having the core function of entertaining its audience. Character development is central to this process and social issues are included only if they have a dramatic potential. This point of view represents an interesting shift in the making of RTÉ's TV drama in that *Glenroe's* parent programme, *The Riordans*, had a remit which was to educate the rural population in terms of modern agricultural techniques, but also, more importantly, it was conceded to me by the creator of both *Glenroe* and *The Riordans* that the latter programme deliberately sought out social issues to investigate. Sheehan (1993:3) similarly in a critique of *Glenroe's* failure to deal with social issues argued that the creator of *Glenroe's* hands were '. . . raw from grasping nettles, as he had done in *The Riordans*, and that in his view *Glenroe* would be "not about issues, but about people and their relationships".'

The evident change of heart by the programme's creator has led to a significant alteration in the ways in which the role of TV drama is seen within the *Glenroe* camp. The formula for *Glenroe* is seen as being character driven rather than story or issue centred. One senior member of the production team told me that as a rule the stories or social issues always come from the characters. If and when some social issue emerges from the character development which the writer is attempting to create then it is dealt with, but only in terms of the character's development and not vice versa. Indeed, the programme's creator held the view that those few characters who were evidently poor were to be defined by the programme's writers and producers as characters first who in turn happen to be Travellers or unemployed. In addition to this belief that characters come first and not issues is a clear antipathy towards being seen as a programme which is preaching to its audience.

There is general agreement amongst the makers of *Glenroe* as to the programme's remit. The dominant view is that *Glenroe* is a realistic serialised drama and not a soap opera. Such an assertion is based on their assessment of the programme's quality in terms of both its production values and dramatic content. However, the extent to which the programme is 'realistic' is constrained by the premise that the programme should primarily be entertaining and only reflect reality in the words of one scriptwriter 'at a safe distance'.

Another person involved in the making of the series saw their relationship with the audience as one of collusion in that the programme makers believed that they had to 'look after their audience' by entertaining them and not attempting to be didactic. There are two potential problem areas here in that *Glenroe*'s makers assume that (a) the audience is a monolith; and (b) they know what the audience wants.

Built into this set of assumptions about what 'the audience' want is the view that audience expectations centre on being entertained in a comforting way. Indeed in terms of those audience members who are poor, the programme's creator held the view that he did not have the right to pontificate to them. Adding that '. . . entertaining them [the poor] has its own value. To be able to escape into this world once a week where everything is predictable and controlled in the hands of a writer and a production team is important in its own right.'

He saw the programme as being allowed to be as experimental or as socially conscientious as it liked, but it must never '. . . preach a gospel that will reflect one or other situation'. This notion that the programme is free from having an ideological position is a stance which may be questioned. The certainty with which those involved in making the programme speak about the tastes of their audience may also be questioned. The notion that a programme like *Glenroe* can tell stories about the Travellers or the unemployed without being ideological is not something which I accept. *Glenroe*'s limited account of the lives of some of those who make up the Irish poor conforms to the more general shortcomings in RTÉ's portrayal of poverty, which is a result of the fact that the television station reproduces a predominantly liberal framework in its coverage of poverty and other issues. In either its refusal to acknowledge the existence of the unequal social structure or in the often circumscribed ways in which it tells poverty stories it is patently ideological. It is ideological because it helps to maintain unequal power relationships through either the refusal to challenge the basis of such relationships or indeed to suggest possible alternatives. It is also ideological because it treats inequality in a 'taken for granted' fashion and thus contributes to the reification of poverty and inequality (see Thompson, 1990).

One of the programme's scriptwriters told me '. . . people don't expect it to be a gritty realistic programme . . . when we have done realistic stories, we wonder how far you can go with a story on a Sunday night?' Thus the location of the programme in what is seen as 'family' viewing time (8.30 p.m. Sunday) is seen by its makers as being a constraint on the parameters of *Glenroe*. Added to this is the issue of programme ratings. There is an evident pressure on the makers of *Glenroe* to keep the programme at the top of the TAM ratings list. In the words of one of the production team the most important issue for the makers of *Glenroe* is 'getting re-elected'. Thus the dominant view is that given the programme's success (in ratings terms) to date there is no need to change what is already a tremendously successful programme.

The apparent reticence amongst the makers of *Glenroe* to cover certain social issues in a more realistic way is symptomatic of a wider institutional inability to cover these themes. *Glenroe* is not alone in its fears of alienating sections of the audience. My wider fieldwork within RTÉ television would suggest that the reticence of programme makers takes on two main forms. Programme makers within current affairs television were concerned about alienating the poorer sections of their audience by reminding them of their poverty. As I have documented elsewhere (see Devereux 1996b), those engaged in current affairs television were self-conscious about the apparent tension between the comfortable, middle-class culture of RTÉ and the hinterlands of unemployment and poverty outside of the broadcasting organisation. During a planning meeting for a proposed programme on long-term unemployment one reporter summed up her position saying that if the suggested programme was '. . . just another unemployment programme' she imagined that many unemployed viewers would '. . . just switch off and go down to the video shop and take out *Lethal Weapon 4*'.

Even where programmes must allude to poverty or other social problems a concern about the expectations of middle-class audience members may serve to delimit the parameters of coverage. A film producer working on the 1992 *People in Need* Telethon consequently resorted to the use of symbolisation in his film-making. One of his appeal segments which dealt with the work of the hospice movement showed images of two women – one middle class, the other a Traveller – both of whom were waiting to die. In filming the Traveller woman's story, the producer selected a well-known symbol of Traveller culture – the trailer or caravan. He filmed it from a distance showing it at the end of a road. He viewed this as a way of illustrating the fact that this Traveller was not only dying of cancer, but was also in poverty, living at the side of the road. He very deliberately chose to articulate his messages about the Travellers at this symbolic level rather than using any stated verbal message. What is interesting is that in researching this piece of film, he learnt from the nurse who was caring for the woman, that when she died, true to Traveller culture, there was every possibility that the caravan and the woman's bed would be burnt in a funeral pyre.

The producer intentionally omitted this element of the story because he felt, whether it was true or not, it would feed the distorted views of Traveller culture which many middle-class viewers might hold. Thus he consciously used a symbol to give the audience a particular message about the Travelling community (i.e. they are poor) while at the same time attempting to avoid the possibility of invoking a negative reaction towards those who are invariably written off by many as the Devil's poor, by excluding any reference to how their culture might be misinterpreted and blamed for causing some of their hardships (see Devereux, 1996a).

There are others however within RTÉ who take a very different stance vis-à-vis the audience (see Devereux 1996b). The attempts by the maker of the *Tuesday File* documentary *Are You Sitting Comfortably?* to unnerve RTÉ's middle-class audience stand in sharp contrast to the cosy and comforting images produced in fictional and telethon television which only unveil the safer aspects of poverty. According to the programme's producer *Are You Sitting Comfortably?* was a documentary which was '. . . designed to do something dangerous . . . it was designed to make people uncomfortable.' Based on a phrase used by the programme's subject (Fr Peter McVerry) in which he saw Irish society as being divided between the comfortable and the struggling, the programme's title and content were intended to make audience members sit up and think. The producer said that 'The intention was to fling it at the audience and say "You there! Are you sitting comfortably? And if so, should you be thinking about what is going on around you, and why are you sitting comfortably when others aren't?"'

## Formal and Informal Practices

In terms of the making of *Glenroe*, my fieldwork revealed a number of interesting features. While formal procedures are observed there are also a number of informal practices which govern the production of the series. The formal production process is overseen by four meetings each year which review the development of the programme's characters. Some discussion takes place on the storylines which are about to be written, but attention is also given to the views of the audience panels who scrutinise programme content over a series. They may be asked to examine specific storylines to assess whether or not they are realistic or to evaluate the performance of a character recently introduced to the series. In recent times the audience panels indicated some disquiet about the absence of young people from the programme and the subsequent introduction of several younger characters and storylines which dealt with drugs experimentation and rape in the 1995–96 series would seem to indicate that their views held sway.

In addition to these considerations some thought is given to the various appeals which come from charities and voluntary organisations who want *Glenroe* to build in their particular cause into the programme's storylines. The groups which are successful will find either mention of their cause in the drama's dialogue or, at the very least, their poster may be situated on the wall of the local pub. In the 1996 series, the Third World charity Bóthar received several mentions by the programme's characters and one of the programme's storylines revolved around a charity concert in aid of their work.

It was noted to me by one of *Glenroe's* scriptwriters that arguments over the portrayal of particular characters took place at some of these meetings. The person in question wished to portray the Travelling community in, as he saw it, a more realistic light, but was disallowed from doing so because the majority of the programme team wanted the series to be comforting for its audience. The programme has in his view '. . . political correctness hanging around its neck' and therefore cannot explore issues in a realistic way. In the case of another storyline concerning the paternity of Carmel O'Hagan's son, the storyline was changed at one of these meetings because of the worry of antagonising the audience who held Miley Byrne's character in high regard. Another storyline on the exclusion of both Travellers and the disabled from the programme again saw division amongst the production team over the inclusion of this story. The debate centred on whether this was just an issue-based story or whether it would in fact help with the development of the two characters concerned. The programme's creator was opposed to covering this issue because in his words '. . . everything with me is the story and the relationship of the characters'. In his estimation there was nowhere you could bring the story afterwards and it contributed little if anything to character development. Although the issue was included in the programme, it in fact quickly disappeared from the programme's storyboards which allow us to conclude that the dissenting views of the programme's creator eventually held sway.

But it is the more informal production practices which are perhaps of greater interest. One source told me that in the making of the series if ever in scripts there arose elements which were, for example, anti-Traveller, the actors would change either the script or characterisation in a subtle way as they did not wish to be associated with the viewpoint being expressed.[1] Despite the later objections which might arise from a scriptwriter, the producer would allow these changes to be made because of the pressures of production and the possible delays in shooting the next episode if a rewrite were required.

In terms of the portrayal of the Travelling community a further informal practice has evolved. One of *Glenroe's* secondary characters is in real life a member of the Travelling community and is to the forefront of a public campaign to establish the recognition of Travellers as an ethnic minority. In the making of *Glenroe*, scripts which concern the Travellers are referred to the actor to check for their reliability in terms of both cultural practices and the language patterns which Travellers might use.

This practice of checking with this actor as to the correctness of the script is in turn replicated by many of the other cast members. He has in turn attempted (with limited success) to influence the programme's agenda in terms of Travellers issues. At the beginning of the 1992–93 series, the actor got in contact with the writers and producers of *Glenroe* to see if they would include more Traveller issues. He wanted his character's child to die because of the high rates of infant mortality amongst Travellers. According to him this story was rejected by the programme because they '. . . couldn't inflict it on the nation'. In this instance what was perceived by the programme makers as constituting 'good entertainment' and as contributing to character development won the day.

## Irish Fictional Television and Social Problems – Limitations and Possibilities

*Glenroe* is evidently popular with a large proportion of the viewing audience. There are, however, a number of limitations within the programme's formula which militate against the coverage of social problem issues in any in-depth way. *Glenroe* does not provide enough room for the examination of social problems. However the genre does offer the possibility for such an examination, for example, this is done in Channel 4's *Brookside* (see Geraghty, 1983, 1991). If *Glenroe* were to cover social problems such as unemployment or poverty in an in-depth and realistic way in the future, this would involve the programme taking risks in terms of not only the storylines themselves but also in terms of challenging some of its audience.

At present, the programme's formula which emphasises characterisation, entertainment, familism and communitarianism marginalises its treatment of poverty and social problems. The programme's over-emphasis on the lives and experiences of the rural middle class as its choice of central characters ensures that *Glenroe's* plots and storylines only occasionally touch upon problems of a social kind. When it does address these, invariably they are (temporarily) resolved by the actions of the community, individuals or families. Kindness, philanthrophy and good deeds are stressed over and above causes or lasting solutions.

The makers of *Glenroe* defend their failure to deal with social problems by stressing that their interests lie in developing characters and not issues. An obvious and fundamental problem with this perspective is that the programme does have some characters who are poor but who are relegated to the sidelines.

The programme concentrates on developing its middle class and relatively comfortably-off characters to the detriment of any other character development. Is this because this type of character development is of a safer kind? The evidence from *Glenroe* and other soaps would seem to confirm this to be the case (see Rose, 1979 and Greenberg, 1982). Buerkel-Rothfuss and Mayes (1981) suggested that soap operas in the US did not explore the contentious issues of poverty and inequality because their main concern was with the middle class and *Glenroe* would appear to conform to this pattern.

## God's Poor? *Glenroe's* Coverage of the Travelling Community and Other Social Issues     + 3.

*Glenroe's* treatment of the Travelling community is an example of how Irish fictional television chooses to aestheticise the poverty of a group of people demonised by most settled people. A paper by Davis *et al.* (1984) showed that the majority of the settled population exhibited negative attitudes towards the Travelling community: 62 per cent said they were untrustworthy, 75 per cent said they were careless, 68 per cent claimed that they were noisy. This research was in agreement with MacGreil's (1977) study of Irish prejudice and intolerance. In that work, 70 per cent of the sample interviewed said that they would not marry a Traveller, with the majority (62 per cent) saying that Travellers were not socially acceptable.

Glenroe has in fact converted the Travelling community into the deserving or God's poor (see Golding and Middleton, 1982). Through the main Traveller character Blackie Connors, the programme has managed to balance some instruction of its audience about Traveller ways, with an acute shyness in showing the harsher side of the Traveller experience. This is achieved by locating the Traveller character outside of the main action of the series, and by constructing Blackie Connors as one of what Thomas and Callanan (1982) refer to as the happy poor. This abstraction of the Travellers from their cultural and material context renders significant aspects of their lives invisible. Blackie Connors is a Traveller of a safe kind. He is settled, involved in community affairs and can hold his own in the humour stakes. These characteristics are the ones that are stressed repeatedly by the programme which only occasionally acknowledges the difficulties which Blackie and other Travellers experience. (See also Appendix p. 246 below.)

With the exception of Blackie Connors, the Travelling community portrayed in *Glenroe* are minor characters of incidental importance. Blackie Connors himself has a well developed character, yet we generally only see him in the context of stories which affect the better known characters such as Miley or Dinny Byrne. Much of the coverage which Blackie Connors receives serves as a humorous device for the programme. In the real world, Travellers experience racism on a daily basis of the most irrational kind such as being refused service in shops and public houses. Yet Blackie's identity as a Traveller is often the source of joking and humorous exchange, which symbolise his social and cultural acceptability rather than prejudice towards him.

There is a further aspect to the overall structure of *Glenroe* in its narration of stories about the Travelling community. I refer here to the tendency of the programme to raise a potentially controversial issue, begin to give it coverage and then very quickly drop the story out of sight never to be seen again. The issue of whether Travellers or the disabled are more likely to be excluded was considered in the 1992–93 series. This story had great potential as an eye-opener for the audience. Yet when the competition between David Brennan and Blackie took place to see who was more likely to be excluded, the result was a draw. We only saw them being excluded from two pubs and then the story simply disappeared, never being referred to again.

One reading of this phenomenon might be that the issues are explored only briefly to allow further development of the characters and to provide the possibility of greater coverage in further episodes of the series or the following series. My own view is that the tendency of programmes like *Glenroe* to short-change stories about the unemployed or Travellers is based on a shyness of concentrating on potentially controversial social issues. It is interesting that this programme does at least attempt to raise questions about our attitudes to the unemployed, the disabled or the Travelling community, yet somewhere along the line it falls short of giving these stories the full and thorough coverage which they deserve.

The programme is dominated by the twin ideologies of familism and communitarianism (see Gibbons, 1984b). Problems, whether individual or collective, are never seen as social problems. They are not solved by social or structural solutions. Thus, all problems which are to be resolved in this fictional setting are sorted out by individuals, families or the community of Glenroe. Typically, these problems, whether individual or collective, are ones which affect the Byrnes or the Morans thus allowing for a concentration on how the rural middle class experience and deal with personal, business or community difficulties. Their problems are given prominence above all others. The dominant message of the programme is that certain families and the community have the capacity to deal with problems whose causes often lie beyond the confines of Glenroe. Those who exist outside of the community such as the long-term unemployed – personified by Carmel and Damian O'Hagan – and those who are representative of the undeserving poor are left to their own devices. In the 1992–93 series of *Glenroe*, the O'Hagans' story represented an interesting narrative about unemployment and the unemployed. They are outsiders in the community and are treated with distrust by the locals. Their story is one of pain and hardship while other couples beset by hard times are saved by magic wand solutions. Carmel and Damian, however, are viewed with suspicion and hostility. Their right to assistance is questioned by many of the programme's characters and particular reference is made to the notion that they are 'sponging' off the state's social welfare system. *Glenroe* presents both

Damian and Carmel as examples of the Devil's poor. They are treated with indifference, hostility and suspicion. They are branded scroungers without question. Damian's character is of particular interest in that despite his obvious desire to work (he asks nearly every person in the village for employment) he is treated with distrust and references are made to whether he is light-fingered or prone to drinking too much. There are echoes of the immoral poor in terms of the attitudes of Glenroe's citizens (with the exception of Miley) to Damian and Carmel.

The Travellers (or more accurately a single Traveller) are deemed to be part of the Glenroe community and thus some of their problems of exclusion and poverty have been dealt with through community effort and the effort of individual families. The poor, when they are visible, are constructed as the 'other' of the middle-class audience. This type of coverage is constructed in such a way as to allow for the re-affirmation of the comfortable, showing them to be actively doing something about the weaker members of society. In Propp's (1928) terms, they are the heroes of this narrative convention, cast in the role of saviours of the victimised poor. Economic relations between the poor and the powerful become human relations. In *Glenroe* class relations become community relations. While selective examples of poverty and inequality are alluded to in *Glenroe* the focus is on how the more powerful groups in the community can respond to the individual needs of the poor. The status quo is not interfered with and no reference is made to either the class structure or the probable causes of poverty. There are parallels between Scannell's (1980) account of BBC's coverage of unemployment and the way in which RTÉ television approaches the issue of poverty. Scannell (1980:17) examined how the BBC covered unemployment between 1930 and 1935. He argued that:

> The construction of this discourse, its mode of address, its positioning of the audience as middle-class like itself, its exclusion of the unemployed, its conceal-ments and evasions, its transformation of the problem into the politics of the parish pump, and an exercise in good neighbourliness should all be noted.

Both position their discourse in terms of a middle-class audience and draw upon narratives which effectively conceal the true nature of the problem, while also managing to legitimise voluntarist solutions.

There is very little middle ground amongst researchers when it comes to the question of the importance of soap opera. More specifically, when it comes to examining how soaps explore social, as opposed to strictly personal problems, the field is split between those who are critical of the capacity of soaps to deal with social problems at all (Mayet, 1984) and those who feel that it is well within the capability of this type of television programme to educate, inform as well as challenge its audience. Livingstone (1988:56) argued that British soaps were responsible, realistic and educative:

. . . those who make soap operas appear to have specific social awareness – raising aims with respect to contemporary social, moral and political issues. For example, Jack Barton, former producer of Crossroads, says that 'With some of the more serious social comments we've made and issues we have dealt with, in each case they were very carefully thought out and researched, and they have positive results to the community.

For its part, *Glenroe* is naturalistic in style and educative in terms of certain usually personal issues. Typically, the programme has devoted its energies with some success to exploring problems which are non-threatening to the status quo. What are viewed by the programme as being problems of a personal kind are explored and usually given a satisfactory treatment. That is to say the experience of the individual, the cause of the particular problem and its resolution by the community or other agent takes place. Problems of a social or structural kind are less likely to be explored and if they are, less emphasis is given to their resolution.

In terms of the possibilities which exist within this genre for the exploration of problems which go beyond the personal or the individual, there are pointers which *Glenroe* might take from other soaps in this regard. A possible shift in emphasis in the programme's formula would be interesting, but not without some risk. *Coronation Street*, also a soap of the old school, attempted with little success to do this in the 1970s. Glaessner (1990) noted that *Coronation Street's* shift to doing tougher storylines dealing with welfare fraud for example was a provocative move by the programme. However, audience figures dropped significantly and the appointment of a new producer saw a return to the more traditional diet of lighter stories and humour. The reconstituted *Coronation Street* saw its role as being 'in the business of entertaining, not offending'.

A more recent lesson could be learnt from the makers of *Brookside*. Realistic in style, with an emphasis on social class, the programme deals with issues which are social as well as personal. The disappearance of community, the decline and fall of the trade union movement, inequality of employment opportunity in regional terms, the personal and social havoc caused by unemployment (most notably in the Corkhill family) and the activities of drug pushers and illegal moneylenders are just some of the many themes which this programme has examined over its 12-year history.

It is quite clear in watching the serial that there are greater forces at work outside of Brookside Close such as the declining British capitalist economic system or a political philosophy such as Thatcherism, which is the ultimate cause of the problems which the programme's characters experience at a personal level. Unlike *Glenroe* we know who votes for what political party and about the varying political philosophies which the characters hold. The 1996 series for example made reference to the existence of Arthur Scargill's Socialist Labour Party. The programme appears to be issue as well as character-driven and indeed the reappearance of certain issues such as the increasing difficulties encountered by trade union activists would suggest that the programme's stories mainly come from the issues and not just the characters as in *Glenroe*. In addition to this, there is evidence that the programme has consciously taken on specific issues with which it will deal in a much deeper fashion over a long period of time. The addition to the Farnham family of a baby with Down's Syndrome makes it clear that *Brookside* intends to deal with public as well as personal attitudes to mental handicap over a sustained period. Thus the issue can be dealt with in a more comprehensive manner than is usual in soap opera.

Yet in spite of the fact that *Brookside* is more engaged in dealing with issues of a social or personal nature, it does not ignore the more usual soap opera ingredients of humour and entertainment. In terms of its linguistic style specifically, the programme draws upon Liverpudlian or Scouse patterns of working-class speech which is characterised in the main by the use of irony, puns and nicknames. The dole office in *Brookside* is 'The Soc', unemployed people are 'Dolies', poor people are 'Povs'. Male characters will refer to other male characters as 'soft lad' i.e. mad. It is therefore possible to balance the perceived audience demands to entertain as well as deal with social issues which affect the lives of audience members.

## Conclusion

This chapter suggests that the apparent invisibility of poverty and other social problems on television must begin with an understanding of the perspectives of those who create such programmes. The limitations and possibilities of *Glenroe* are due to the kinds of decisions made amongst the programme makers. There is no reason other than perhaps an ideological one preventing the series from placing either a Traveller or unemployed character at the centre of the programme. My fieldwork experience indicates to me, however, that there is very little commitment amongst the programme makers towards developing these kinds of characters.

In many respects *Glenroe* is a victim of its own success in that given its constant placing at the summit of the TAM ratings, it is tied into a formula which offers very little by way of space for the consideration of a wider scope of individual and social problems. In the longer term the programme's makers may have to entertain the idea of moving beyond the humour/characterisation formula in order to make the programme more relevant to the rapidly changing society in which it is being made. As this chapter suggests, the fact that the programme does not attract younger viewers is a factor which will have to be addressed.

The premise upon which *Glenroe* is based – that the audience want to be entertained and not challenged – is one which has to be questioned. The apparent failure of factual television to cover social problem issues in a critical way has created the opportunity for these questions to be explored in a fictional setting (see Devereux, 1996c). There are many interesting stories to be told about the poor which are full of dramatic potential. Does anybody in *Glenroe* have to deal with a difficult social welfare officer? Are there women who worry about feeding and clothing their children? Does anybody return to school through an adult education course? How would any of these characters feel about 'The system'? Other than the occasional reference to Traveller issues, what about the attitudes of the programme's middle-class characters to the underclass or poor?

The assumptions that the lives of the poor are neither of interest to the audience nor the most suitable subject matter for factual or fictional television should be questioned. The success and ensuing debate about the BBC/RTÉ co-production of Roddy Doyles's *Family* is proof that audiences are interested in the lives of the marginalised.[2] Audience reaction to *Family*, whether positive or negative, gave a clear signal to RTÉ that there is a hunger amongst many audience members for realistic drama which examines the harsher side of Irish life.

This chapter has taken the view the most obvious starting point in doing this kind of analysis is that of beginning with the ways in which programme makers construct audience tastes and pleasures. Such a position does not rule out the importance of exploring actual audience tastes and pleasures. There is a great need for future research to examine audience expectations about factual and fictional television. Only then will there be the possibility of examining the perspectives of both programme makers and audiences to see whether or not their perspectives converge.

# Appendix

## Synopsis of unemployed and Traveller characters in the 1992–93 series of *Glenroe*.

### Blackie Connors

The Traveller Blackie Connors is a firmly established character in the series *Glenroe*. Having overcome the hostility of some of the locals in an earlier series, he is now broadly accepted by the community at large. We see Blackie moving with ease in the community, being on friendly terms with Miley Byrne the farmer and shopkeeper, George Manning the representative of the ascendancy and Dick Moran the auctioneer. Blackie is a member of the Neighbourhood Watch committee which in real life and in the fictional world of Glenroe is a community crime alert network. He is a regular in the local pub – The Molly Malone. Such a portrayal is of particular interest in that Travellers in Irish society are regularly refused entry to pubs and are also mistakenly and unjustly branded by many as being petty thieves. Blackie Connors is an easy going, friendly and sometimes humorous man all of which have helped in his integration into the community. Blackie has been to the forefront of the campaign to get better conditions for the local Travellers (whom we only ever see fleetingly) in the form of permanent accommodation in houses. In the 1992–93 series of *Glenroe* the storylines which affect Blackie dealt with the issues of Traveller integration, Traveller patriarchy, and the hostilities and prejudices experienced by Travellers in their attempts to socialise or find work.

### Carmel and Damian O'Hagan

In the first seven episodes of *Glenroe* the programme deals with the experiences of an unemployed couple Carmel and Damian O'Hagan. Both are Irish emigrants who have decided to return to Glenroe in search of work. Damian is portrayed as having a 'difficult' character while Carmel is generally viewed with a mixture of distrust and sympathy. The couple's attempts to get work are thwarted by everybody in the village (with the exception of Miley Byrne). Both Carmel and Damian, however, persevere in their search for employment. Carmel temporarily replaces Biddy Byrne in the vegetable shop while Damian does a number of odd jobs in the village. When Damian eventually gets an evening's work in the local pub, it ends with him having an argument with the proprietor's son. He leaves the pub in anger and is later found dead, having been killed in a hit and run car accident. This leaves Carmel a widow and sets the scene for a major storyline concerning infidelity between Carmel and Miley in the later episodes of the series.

## Notes

1   The actors who play the main characters in *Glenroe* have in real life a high public
    visibility in terms of specific causes. It is fair to assume that at least some members
    of the viewing public do not distinguish between the fictional characters and the
    actors themselves.
2   The second episode of *Family* attracted 1.2 million viewers to RTÉ 1.

## References

Ang, I. (1982) *Watching Dallas*. London: Methuen.
Buerkel-Rothfuss, N:L. and S. Mayes (1981) 'Soap Opera Viewing: The Cultivation
    Effect', *European Journal of Communication*, Summer: 108–15
Davis, E.E., J.W. Grube and M. Morgan (1984) *Attitudes Towards Poverty and Related
    Social Issues in Ireland*. ESRI Paper No. 117. Dublin: ESRI.
Devereux, E. (1994) 'Devils and Angels: The Rise of Irish Charity Television', *Irish
    Communications Review*, 4.
Devereux, E. (1996a) 'The Codes and Conventions of Irish Current Affairs Television:
    A Production Based Approach', *Irish Journal of Sociology*, 5.
Devereux, E. (1996b) 'Good Causes, God's Poor and Telethon Television', *Media,
    Culture and Society*, 18 (1): 47–68.
Devereux, E (1996c) 'Devils and Angels: The Ideological Construction of Poverty
    Stories on RTÉ Television', unpublished PhD thesis, School of Communications,
    Dublin City University.
Geraghty, C. (1983) 'Brookside – No Common Ground' *Screen*, 24 (4–5).
Geraghty, C. (1991) *Women and Soap Opera*. London: Polity.
Gibbons, L. (1984a) 'Catherine The Great's Villages', *Ian Hart Memorial Lectures*,
    Dublin: Simon Community.
Gibbons, L. (1984b) 'From Kitchen Sink to Soap', in M. McLoone and M. McMahon
    (eds) *Television and Irish Society*. Dublin: RTÉ/IFI.
Glaessner, V. (1990) 'Gendered Fictions', in A. Goodwin and G. Whannel (eds)
    *Understanding Television*. London: Routledge.
Golding, P. and S. Middleton (1982) *Images of Welfare, Press and Public Attitudes to
    Poverty*. Oxford: Blackwell.
Greenberg, B. (1982) 'The Soaps: What's on and Who Cares?', *Journal of Broadcasting*,
    26: 519–35.
Kelly, M. (1984) 'The Poor Aren't News', *Ian Hart Memorial Lectures*. Dublin: Simon
    Community.
Livingstone, S.M. (1988) 'Why People Watch Soap Opera: An Analysis of the
    Explanations of British Viewers', *European Journal of Communication*, 3: 55–80.
Mayet, G. (1984) 'Poverty and The Media', in S. Buxton (eds) *Social Action Through
    Television*. London: Thames TV Mimeograph.
MacGreil, M. (1977) *Prejudice and Tolerance in Ireland*. Dublin: College of Industrial
    Relations.
O'Connor, B. (1990) *Soap and Sensibility: Audience Response to Dallas and Glenroe*.
    Dublin: RTÉ.
Propp, V. (1928) *Morphology of The Folktale*. Texas: University of Texas Press.
Radio Telefis Éireann (1993) TAM Survey. Dublin: Audience Research Department
    RTÉ.
Rose, B. (1979) 'Thickening The Plot', *Journal of Communication*, 29 (Autumn): 85–8.

Ruddy, C. (1987) 'Media Coverage of The Poor in Ireland', Unpublished BA thesis, Dublin City University.

Scannell, P. (1980) 'The Social Eye of Television 1946–1955', *Media, Culture and Society*, 1: 97–106.

Sheehan, H. (1985) 'Is Television Drama Ideological?', *The Crane Bag*, 9 (1).

Sheehan, H. (1987) *Irish Television Drama: A Society and its Stories*. Dublin: RTÉ.

Sheehan, H. (1993) 'Biddy, Bella and The Big Issues of The Day' Paper presented to the *Imagining Ireland Conference: Soap Opera and Social Order, Glenroe, Fair City and Contemporary Ireland*. 13 October 1993 Irish Film Centre.

Silj, A. (1988) *East of Dallas*. London: BFI Publishing.

Thomas, S. and B.P. Callanan (1982) 'Allocating Happiness: TV Families and Social Class', *Journal of Communication*, 32 (3): 184–90.

Thompson, J. B. (1990) *Ideology and Modern Culture*. Cambridge: Polity.

12

# Children and Television Pleasure

*Margaret Gunning*

Traditionally, both research and public debate about children and television have been preoccupied with identifying the allegedly harmful effects of viewing. As Brigid Watt (1994:11) says 'the topic of children and television is one which has generated years of public anxiety, decades of academic concern and what seems like an eternity of social, and political hand wringing'. The decades of research have produced volumes of writings which have approached the topic of children and television from many angles, working within the traditions of psychology, sociology and media studies. The approaches have variously concentrated on the stimulus, through the adoption of a variety of methods from the 'direct effects' method to content analyses using quantitative and qualitative perspectives (Schramm, 1954, 1964; Himmelweit *et al.*, 1958; Bandura *et al.*, 1963; Bandura 1965). There have also been concentrations on the intervening variables through analysis of cognitive processing, social milieu and levels of viewing time (Gerbner and Gross, 1976; Winn, 1977; Wartella, 1979; Dorr 1986). The audience itself has not been ignored but studied through 'uses and gratifications', ethnographic and empirical methodologies, in an attempt to discover not 'what the media do to the people' but rather 'what people do with the media' (Katz and Foulkes, 1962). An overview of the research indicates that the concern has almost exclusively been with the negative effects of television. Whether the emphasis has been on children's behaviour, their mental development or their attitudes and beliefs, the role of television is predominantly presumed to be harmful. As Buckingham (1993: 9) emphasises 'What is often ignored here is the question of why children might choose to watch television in the first place, and the pleasure they might experience in doing so'.

Much of this research has been based on two presumptions, firstly that watching television is bad for children and secondly, that children are powerless in the face of this powerful medium. Some notable exceptions have included a significant work on children and television by Hodge and Tripp (1986). They adopted a broad-based approach drawing on the traditions of sociology, psychology, semiotics and linguistics to challenge the notion of children as 'TV zombies' and succeeded admirably in demystifying the process. Palmer (1986: 167) suggested that while children's interaction with television was purposeful, they were also a 'lively' audience, whose interactions ranged from 'intent viewing' to the monitoring of programmes 'by sight or sound while they spent most of their time on some other activity'. Another exception is found in the work of David Buckingham (1993) who, in a close analysis of children's talk about television, took into account children's own perceptions of the medium and acknowledged their powers.

This chapter is based on research conducted in 1995, which focused on an audience of Dublin schoolchildren. It hoped to follow in the tradition of the exceptions through focusing on the pleasures of the medium of television, rather than focusing on its negative aspects. The research approached the subject of television pleasure for children from two angles; psychoanalytic theory drawing on the methods used in *Screen* theory; and audience research using ethnographic methods. As Freudian theory regards the fundamental motivation of all human behaviour as the avoidance of pain and the gaining of pleasure, explained as the pleasure principle, and the central concern of the research being pleasure, it seemed an obvious tradition to turn to as a starting point. It has been pointed out by Hay (1993: 370) that:

> Psychoanalytic theory adds to narrative and semiotic criticism a recognition that more is going on when one watches television than simply the production of 'meanings' or 'readings', that television criticism also needs to explain how the audience's pleasures have just as much to do with fantasy and the unconscious.

Psychoanalytic theory has been drawn on in *Screen* theory, which is based on the work of Jacques Lacan (1977) rather than Freud. Lacan was credited with reinterpreting Freud in the context of structural linguistics, demonstrating an alliance between language, the unconscious, parents, the Symbolic order and cultural relations (Flitterman Lewis, 1993:208). In *Screen* theory the emphasis was primarily on the psychic dynamics of film spectatorship with the act of viewing defined in terms of psychoanalytic processes such as scopophilia, voyeurism and fetishism (Mulvey, 1976; Caughie, 1981; Metz, 1982). Through exploring these phenomena, *Screen* theory sought to define the ways in which a film text produces the subjectivity of the spectator, by constructing 'subject positions' from which it is to be read. *Screen* theory has been criticised from many angles (Garnham, 1974; Harvey, 1978; Lovell, 1980; Gallop, 1982) but perhaps the most damaging limitation from the point of view of audience research was its exclusive emphasis on texts and a 'reading off' of inferred audience responses and subject positions from the surface of the text. Nevertheless this exclusive emphasis allowed the development of a sophisticated and well thought out framework which recognised that different structures demand different responses from the audience. It must be acknowledged that a simple transference of *Screen* theory to the study of children's television was not possible because of the differences between film spectatorship and television viewing in terms of conditions of viewing, text, and the 'mental machinery of spectatorship' (Ellis, 1982). Cinema and television are two completely distinct media in relation to their textual systems and in the manner in which the viewer engages with them. Therefore there can be no simple exchange of method from one medium to the other. Rather, certain aspects of psychoanalytic film theory were used in a close analysis of the texts.

The second focus of the study was on the audience's responses to two particular programmes chosen by them as favourites, *Den TV* and *Baywatch*. This aspect of the research employed ethnographic methods in an effort to gain an 'ethnographic understanding', '. . . a form of interpretative knowing that purports to increase our sensitivity to the particular details of the ways in which actual people deal with television in their everyday lives' (Ang, 1991: 165).

As the actual people being focused on in this instance were children, the developmental theories of Piaget (1975) were turned to in order to gain an insight into the stages of cognitive development at which children of these ages would be expected to operate.

## Audience Profile

The 100 children who took part in the research were attending the same school, situated in a predominantly working–class area of Dublin. Two different age groups were involved, 50 children aged eight and nine years from third class, and 50 children aged eleven and twelve years from fifth class, with an equal balance between boys and girls.

The younger group, according to Piaget's (1975) stages of development, are in the process of acquiring a number of intellectual capacities that are in effect transformational operations, equivalent to such operations as the passive transformation in language. By nine years of age children are rather adept at reading television programmes designed for them (Hodge and Tripp 1986:71). They decode programmes using essentially the same grammar as adults, a grammar comprised of four components defined as:

> . . . a set of rules which produce a system of options (paradigms), a set of rules for combining these options into structures (syntagms), and changes to and permutations of these options and combinations (transformations), together with ways of situating messages in relation to an ostensible reality (modality) (Hodge and Tripp, 1986: 43).

Children of this age have a capacity to make classifications or recognise paradigms, and an ability to recognise interactions between the different classifications. It is in relation to transformations, or the ability to recognise changes and permutations in the paradigms and syntagms, that there are gaps in their understanding. This means that their facilities for abstraction, extrapolation, criticism and comprehension of complex structures are not fully developed but are in the process of being learned. According to Freud's stages of psychosexual development children of this age are in the latency period, with the superego, established in the Oedipus complex of the phallic stage, continuing to develop. In this stage demands are being made on the child's behaviours through schooling and other social interactions outside the family to adapt to the institutions of society.

The eleven and twelve year olds are at the start of adolescence and are moving from the stage of 'concrete operations' on to Piaget's fourth stage of development, 'formal operations'. This stage allows for more formal transformations, multiple successive transformations, the abstract, and hypothetical logical thought that distinguishes the scientist. However, these children are just moving into this stage, a level of development not fully realised by all normal persons (Watson and Johnson-Laird, 1977). In regard to their television viewing this group operate at a higher level of sophistication than the younger group, and are able to cope with structures of some scale and complexity (Hodge and Tripp, 1986:92). Following Freud's stages of psychosexual development (Thomas, 1992:150), these pre-adolescents are moving towards puberty, or the genital stage, where the components of the sexual instinct come together in adult sexuality.

The children in the school were familiar with the researcher who was working as a teacher in the school, but did not teach these particular children. Initially a questionnaire was administered to the children asking them to list their three favourite programmes. They nominated a total of 66 programmes showing a wide range of tastes of which a quarter were considered adult programmes rather than programmes specifically produced for children. The favourites for each age group were:

*Favourites for 8 and 9 year olds (Boys and Girls)*

| | |
|---|---|
| *Den TV* | Network 2 |
| *Home and Away* | Network 2 |
| *Saved by the Bell* | Children's Channel |
| *California Dreams* | Children's Channel |
| *Casper* | Children's Channel |

*Favourites for 11 and 12 year olds (Boys and Girls)*

| | |
|---|---|
| *Baywatch* | UTV |
| *Simpsons* | Sky 1 |
| *Quantum Leap* | Sky 1 |
| *Saved by the Bell* | Children's Channel |
| *Home and Away* | Network 2 |

Two focus groups were formed for each age group with the eight and nine year olds discussing *Den TV* and the eleven and twelve year olds talking about *Baywatch*. All of the children in these focus groups had specifically nominated the programmes being discussed in the initial questionnaire. The focus groups were composed of a mix of boys and girls with five children in each group. The discussion was based on the children's home viewing and did not refer to a particular episode of the programme. Conversation was initiated by the researcher through asking a number of open-ended questions, for example, tell me about a 'good bit' in the programme, describe your favourite character, with whom do you watch the programme? Is the programme like real life? Could these things happen here? The children were allowed to lead the conversation as much as possible, with the researcher asking questions, where necessary, to clarify issues or bring the conversation back on course. The duration of the discussions varied from 30 to 45 minutes and took place in an informally arranged seating area of the classroom while the other class members were engaged in written assignments.

## Mode of Address

Both television programmes were examined to see if there was a spatial coherence which locks the viewer into the text, or if the imaginary space which has been constructed is one which excludes the viewer and engages a different type of participation. This involved looking at the programmes in the first instance in terms of mode of address; whether the programmes directly address the viewer or unfold in a manner which effectively ignores their audience. According to film theory, the spectator's ability to construct a mentally continuous time and space out of fragments is based on a 'suturing' of looks, a structured relay of glances (1) from the filmmaker towards the scene observed by the camera; (2) between the characters within the fiction; and (3) across the visual field from spectator to screen. These glances tie the fiction together and bind the spectator to the film (Mulvey, 1976:17). Central to the process of tying the three looks together are the shot/reverse shot and the point-of-view shot. Shot/reverse shot sequences are frequently used in conversation scenes, where, by looking from the position of the character, the spectator is allowed to see who the character is talking to or listening to. A reverse shot taken from behind or closely beside the second character reveals the first character. In point-of-view shots the spectator is placed in the character's visual position and views the world of the film through his/her eyes during that shot. The programmes were assessed to find if it is possible for the viewer of television also to become an invisible mediator between the interplay of looks and a fictive participant in the fantasy of the programme.

Primary identification in relation to cinema refers to a 'unifying presence' at the site of spectatorship with the viewing subject locked into a relationship with the text (Metz, 1982). This type of identification involves the ability of the subject of fantasy to occupy a variety of roles, continually sliding, doubling and exchanging numerous fictive positions. Secondary identifications are usually provided for by means of some form of identification with the characters and their motives or actions, ensuring a sense of connection with the characters and enabling a slippage from fictive to real in order to solidify the connections between the character's world and the world of the viewer. The programmes were viewed assessing the opportunities for identification, both primary and secondary.

Within the programmes, devices were sought which engage the children's voyeuristic tendencies. Freud's theory of voyeurism is concerned with the power of looking, an instinct which centres on the desire to see the private and forbidden, modified by other factors as the child matures, in particular the constitution of the ego, but continuing as the erotic basis for the pleasure in looking at another person as object. Viewing the programmes involved finding the position of the viewer, and seeking techniques used to emphasise the act of looking

## Den TV

*Den TV* could be considered to be the backbone of children's television presentations on Network 2. Presented by Ray Darcy in the company of Dustin and Soky (puppets), it is shown on Monday to Friday of each week from 3pm to 6pm. *Den TV* is a strong bonding device linking together a variety of children's programmes including cartoons, studio games and magazine programmes. As initial discussion with the children indicated that the main attraction in the 'seamless flow' is found in the sections featuring Ray Darcy and his co-presenters, their interactions were the focus of analysis. They are much more than continuity announcers, being the hosts of a variety of regular slots, all of which encourage and allow children's participation either directly in the studio or indirectly through competitions, birthday slots, etc.

The setting for the interactions is a studio which includes a control desk behind which Ray sits, with the puppets moving freely in the space in front of and, to a lesser extent, behind the desk. To the left of the control desk a suspended television monitor displays videos and the sequence of programmes. The presenters frequently talk to the cameraman, laugh at fluffed cues, leave and return to the studio space and make derogatory comments about the flow of programmes. The focus in *Den TV* is on sound rather than image. It is in the verbal exchanges that much of the humour is found, with the viewer's attention frequently hailed through shouting which indicates that a particularly exciting happening is about to occur. The viewer is outside the scene looking in but becomes part of the space through participation. In a sense the studio is the children's space in which their presence is welcome. It is an actual physical space rather than an imaginary one. The presenters and children are sharing an experience which is happening now – the televisual mode of viewing.

However, there is a type of imaginary space in the sense that the children are invited to collude with Ray in the pretence that the puppets are real persons. They have histories, jobs, houses and very individual characteristics which all add to their realness. The imaginary space is one that allows for interactions with these puppets as real individuals and perhaps depends on the level of modality, or sense of reality brought to it. There are opportunities provided for identification with these well developed personalities.

Ray is the voice of reason who tries to keep order and is therefore the possessor of the ideological (Parent) meanings. The puppets carry the subversive (Child) meanings, being anarchic and saying the sort of 'rude' things frequently forbidden by parents. The struggle between the Parent and Child meanings is central to the interactions between the presenters, but in matters of importance the subversive voice becomes silenced and the ideological message is strengthened with both Ray and the puppets expressing caution or concern. An example of this occurred when a discussion arose on the use of safety helmets when cycling. Both Ray and the puppets agreed on the advantages and benefits of their use and advised the audience to wear them.

*Den TV* is an unlikely text to be subjected to analysis drawing on psychoanalytic criticism since there is no apparent narrative, or dependence on point-of-view and reverse-shot structures, and the direct mode of address is used. The only way that voyeuristic tendencies are indulged is in the sense of children being positioned as eavesdroppers (Messenger Davies, 1995: 29), being present at a social gathering where many of the jokes and references are not fully understood. Perhaps this, and the opportunities for identification, explain some of its attraction.

## Baywatch

*Baywatch* is a foreign import produced by the Baywatch Production Company, a Californian corporation. The location is a beach in California where the central characters are employed as lifeguards. The episode which was analysed consisted of two parallel stories, with one theme concentrating on the weekend activities of two of the female lifeguards, CJ and Stephanie; and the other featuring a male lifeguard Mitch and his son Hobie in their quest for a housekeeper. The episode fell into eleven segments, with two commercial breaks, and equal time given to both stories which intertwined only in the first sequence when Mitch and Stephanie discussed their forthcoming weekend.

*Baywatch* employs an indirect mode of address with the happenings on the screen unfolding with the presupposition of the viewer's engagement. A distinctive technique used in the construction of the imaginary space is a focus on image rather than sound. Two of the sequences unfolded to the accompaniment of a musical soundtrack. These sequences do not merely provide musical interludes but are crucial to the advancement of the narrative and are effectively filmic rather than televisual.

In *Baywatch* the filmmaker uses a variety of shot set-ups. Reverse shot structures were used in some conversation scenes, particularly those involving the romantic duos, allowing the viewer an insight into the potential relationships. The point-of-view shot was also used to good effect when Mitch's first view of the 'drop dead gorgeous' housekeeper Elkie becomes the viewer's first view also. The point-of-view shot was also used in an interesting way in the underwater scenes when the look of the camera becomes the look of one of the divers allowing the viewer to see the underwater world as they see it. Therefore, it appears that in *Baywatch* the look of the viewer is manipulated through the use of a variety of camera shots. In order for the viewer to become the invisible mediator who is a fictive participant in the fantasy, there is a dependence on a suturing which enables a smooth link from shot to shot (Caughie, 1981). These smooth links are there within each sequence, but the viewer's participation is necessarily short-lived owing to the fragmentation of the programme.

There are opportunities for identification provided in the motives and actions of the characters. The particular episode viewed focused on four central characters presented as polar opposites in terms of personal characteristics. CJ is dependent, trusting, fatalistic and helpless while Stephanie is independent, cautious, determined and resourceful. Mitch is adult, judgmental, orderly and methodical while Hobie is a child, nonjudgmental, slovenly and impulsive. There was an interesting interplay in the father/son relationship, with the child on two occasions expressing the Parent ideology and the adult asked to accommodate it. An example of this occurred when Mitch returned home from work and chastised Hobie for not having started to clean up or prepare dinner. The child pointed out that his role was not as wife, but that he should be allowed to do 'kid's stuff and not all this cooking and laundry'. Mitch was forced to admit that Hobie was right and the momentum for the storyline was put into action. Allowing the child to express the parent message perhaps makes the ideological message more palatable to the child viewer.

In *Baywatch* the techniques used guarantee exploitation of the viewer's voyeuristic instincts. There is an emphasis on image rather than sound and a manipulation of the viewer's look. The location of the programme allows maximum exposure of a variety of bodies, both male and female, all confined to the 'age of maximum sexuality' (Fiske, 1987:227), and to physical types that conform to the patriarchal sense of attractiveness for women, and men. From the initial title sequence, which shows a series of glimpses of bodies, a lure is provided for the voyeur to continue to watch as the voyeuristic instincts may be further stimulated and satisfied. With the emphasis on the look, the image and the body being so strong, it was ironic that Hobie, again expressing the Parent ideology, persuaded his father to hire the housekeeper by saying: 'All my life you've taught me not to judge people by their looks . . . that's what you're doing now . . . you can't base employment practices on looks . . . that's job discrimination'.

## Analysis of Children's Talk

### Child and Parent Voice

In the interpretation of children talking it is important to recognise that there are a number of 'selves' which can be identified (Hodge and Tripp, 1986: 47). Freud showed that some messages have a composite form as though the finally presented form is a fusion of meanings that come from different aspects of the psyche. Freud labelled the three selves id, ego, and superego. The meanings of the id are closest to those of an infantile self, while superego meanings come from an introjected parent figure, and the ego meanings represent the individual's sense of reality. Berne (1968) labelled the three selves Child (id), Adult (ego) and Parent (superego). In any exchange messages may be transmitted or received on behalf of more than one 'self'. The messages may be contradictory or simultaneous, and either fused in one medium or code or distributed among verbal and non-verbal codes.

Hodge and Tripp used an integration of the theories of Freud and Berne and deduced that television meanings could be classified as 'Parent' (moralistic, ideological meanings), 'Adult' (information) and 'Child' (subversive, pleasurable meanings) with those meanings layered together, not necessarily integrated. The child viewer may respond to ideological meanings by incorporating them (Parent response), subverting them (Child response) or treating them as information (Adult response). Labov (1972) provided a useful framework which helped develop a way of distinguishing the different selves in the flow of children's discourse. The characteristics of energy, falling intonation and the presence of laughter tend to go together typically marking a child's perspective.

In discussing *Den TV*, recounting their favourite incidents, and acting out the good bits, the eight and nine-year-old children spoke in a very uninhibited way about their emotional engagement with television. After an initial use of the Parent voice, the children for the most part used the Child voice. Much of the conversation consisted on the retelling of favourite parts, incidents that were usually followed by shared laughter. Interruptions by the interviewer meant that there was a reversal to the Parent voice, but this was only temporary:

| | |
|---|---|
| Angela: | Dustin's always singing and he burps and he farts on it. |
| GF: | Do you like when he does that? |
| All: | No, teacher. |
| Fiona: | Yeah! One day when he burped and I said 'excuse me' and he said 'excuse me' after me . . . |

The interactions of the younger focus groups were marked by the presence of laughter and uncontainable energy denoting the use of the Child voice.

The eleven and twelve year olds who discussed *Baywatch* were more inhibited initially than the younger group. Perhaps because of socialisation they were more aware of the appropriate selection from the register of selves to choose in the interview situation. In retelling some of the 'good bits' the children were hesitant and anxious to get the story right:

> Michael:   Matt captured a robber and the robber's brother came after him with his girlfriend . . . and they captured Matt to threaten him to see where his brother was and they were threatening to poison him and all with a gun . . . Matt was tied and he had a knife underneath the rope and the gun was sitting on a press and he grabbed it and put it to the girl's head and he said 'if you (move) I'll shoot her' . . . so the man went away and then the rest of the rescue squad came and helped and they were just arrested.
>
> Emma:   Mitch was having dinner with this girl and she locked him down in the cellar and the tide was coming in . . . she handcuffed him to a pipe and the tide was coming in and they nearly drowned. ( ) the girl had a twin and she came and she rescued them.
>
> Barry:   I saw it when Mitch's . . . when someone . . . I think it was Mitch's brother came and something happened to his son and Matt and Pamela Anderson had to rescue . . . he jumped off something . . .
>
> Scott:   He jumped off the bridge into the water, was it? . . . and he started going under the bridge 'cause it was too dangerous and they all rescued him.

Within the group there was a certain amount of collaboration involved in retelling the stories, a factor that indicated the importance of the narrative to the children. It was interesting that all of the excerpts ended with 'and they rescued them', emphasising the children's enjoyment of the build up of suspense followed by the resolution of the problem enabling narrative closure. These extracts were conveyed in the Parent voice, but the eleven and twelve year olds used the Child voice in discussing their favourite characters:

> John:   Pamela Anderson, I like her . . . what she looks like (shared laughter).
> Emer:   Matt . . . because . . . same as John.
> Matthew:   Pamela Anderson, 'cause she's a very good actor.
> John:   Very good actor! (all laugh again).

The presence of laughter, a level of embarrassment and energy marked this extract, which contrasted greatly with their laborious retelling of the narrative. Here the children were engaging the Child voice, and these interactions showed higher levels of enjoyment.

## Subversive and Ideological Meanings

It has been argued that of the two kinds of meaning, ideological and subversive, the emotional charge and attraction of a programme is invested in the subversive meanings (Hodge and Tripp, 1986:61). Therefore it appears that the pleasure found within a programme should be found in the subversive (Child) meanings. Another indicator which was taken into account together with a use of the Child voice was the exhibition of a level of embarrassment, which is experienced at the point of conflict between the conventional and the subversive, between the dominant and the subordinate, between top-down and bottom-up power (Fiske, 1989:64). The pleasure of liberating repressed or subordinate meanings can never be expressed freely, but only in conflict with those forces that seek to repress or subordinate them. Therefore a level of embarrassment indicates that pleasures have been engaged which are subversive and run counter to ideological notions.

When talking about *Den TV* the children showed great enjoyment of the subversive meanings:

Fiona:    Dustin was at the back, right, and he started singing and stuff and Ray says 'shut up' and then he (Dustin) came out and he says 'No' and then he started singing again . . . and then he started jumping up and down and all . . . then Ray says 'shut up' again and Dustin says 'you shut up' and he started jumping up and down again . . .

David:    They're always bashing each other . . . here they are behind Ray's control box, you know, going 'Psphew, Psphew, Psphew!' throwing each other on the ground . . . then Ted comes back in 'Psphew, Psphew, Psphew!' (All laugh together) . . . then he gets up and Dustin gets the hammer, the saw as he calls it, but the hammer as it is supposed to be, and he throws him out . . .

Colm:    Ray's Mam doesn't like Dustin 'cause he always has his Doc Martens up on the coffee table. (all laugh).

The children liked when Dustin answered Ray back, was rude and quarrelsome. They took pleasure in the silliness and repeated actions.

Another extract which showed an interesting way of accommodating the subversive versus ideological meanings referred to the predecessors of the current puppets:

Michael:    Yeah, last year at Christmas they went over, right? and do you know what happened? Zag brought them over and it was Zag's chocolate pudding, Zag's this and Zag's that . . . and Soky says 'I didn't come over here to do nothing, I'm not able to do anything' . . . but Zag wouldn't stop and Zig rang Santa.

In this interaction Zag, by refusing to share with his guests, was engaging in child-like egotistical behaviour. Zig carried the ideological message that sharing is necessary, and resolved the problem by dealing with it in a way that allowed the accommodation of the ideological notion through the use of a subversive technique, and rang Santa. Michael took pleasure in seeing the subversive behaviour censored, but the ideological message was imparted in a way that was understandable from a child-like perspective.

In talking about *Baywatch* some of the ideological notions mentioned by the children in the eleven and twelve year old age group included bravery, physical fitness, fearlessness, romance, honesty, masculinity and femininity.

Most of these structures were conveyed in the Parent mode, used in the retelling of the narratives, and were therefore unlikely to explain the children's emotional involvement with the programme. An extract which involved much embarrassment and laughter is more likely to illustrate their engagement with the subversive meanings:

GF:     Can you imagine meeting people like the people on *Baywatch*?
All:     (shared laughter, no response)
GF:     How would you feel?
Scott:   Embarrassed, totally embarrassed . . . I'd want to jump.
Emma:   Totally embarrassed.
Ian:     They're famous and you're just an ordinary person.
Scott:   I'll be famous when I grow up!

Here the children not only admitted that they would be embarrassed but exhibited a high level of embarrassment, manifested in the shared laughter, blushing, and expelling of breath. In this interaction the ideological meaning which is being subverted can only be understood inferentially. Further discussion which concentrated on the physical appearance of the actors seemed to suggest that much of the attraction of the programme and the pleasure experienced by the children was found in the admiration of the human form. Therefore the Adult meaning which is being suppressed appears to be the notion of the expression of sexuality.

## Modality

Modality refers to the reality attributed to a message. The perceived reality of television depends both on the characteristics of the text and on the comparison between the text and reality, or more accurately, what the viewer believes reality to be. Using semiotics, Hodge and Tripp (1986, 104–29) identified some of the modality markers of a text, that is, the formal and contextual cues which increase the transformational distance between the image and its referent, and thereby indicate that it has been consciously constructed. Nevertheless, they argue that these internal markers may not be recognised, and that viewers also use external criteria based on their experiences or beliefs about the world. Because these external markers are culturally and socially specific they are likely to be quite diverse.

The markers of modality which were sought within the children's discourse included both internal and external cues. Internal markers of modality refer to the forms and conventions of television and may include references to the narrative structure or a recognition of genre, and references to the technical processes used in the production process. Methods of media production are the most salient criteria of reality for eight and nine year olds. External markers of modality refer to comparisons made with the social experiences of the viewer, and a criterion which tests the programme for psychological plausibility. These media-external criteria are more important for older children (Hodge and Tripp, 1986:126), due to their increased social experience and more highly developed critical faculties.

In discussing *Den TV* the eight and nine year olds made references to internal markers of modality; stage, control box, studio, camera and commercial breaks were mentioned. When questioned on how the characters were created they responded that they did not really know:

> Mary: No, I don't really know . . . I was looking at this show and Ray, yeah Ray, was letting us know how they did it and all . . . there was this show and they introduced him and then he told us how they did it . . . what it was like years ago . . .

Whether Mary knew how the effects were created or not was difficult to ascertain from this extract. She distanced 'how the show was done' by saying that this was 'years ago', and gave no indication of the information imparted in this programme. When the question was rephrased a different response was elicited:

> GF: Where did they come from?
> Anthony: Ian Dempsey went up in a space ship, he claimed to, like you know, he didn't definitely do it . . . he went up and he had it all arranged . . . he changed the studio around and came back and there's Zig and Zag in the spaceship.

This extract showed that Anthony knew that the invention of Zig and Zag was a story. His use of the words 'claimed to', and the doubt of 'he didn't definitely do it' indicate that he was aware of the fictional nature of the puppets' existence.

The children made references to appearances made by Dustin and Soky on other programmes and media:

> Michael: The night of the Toy Show Gay Byrne had 200 guards outside the door so that Dustin wouldn't get in . . .
> Mary: Yeah! He had 200 guards and everybody had water pistols . . .
> Ann: They were identified in the *Evening Herald* . . .

This type of exposure seemed to give the characters high modality in the children's view. The children were also asked directly if Zig and Zag were real:

> Fiona: Yeah! I think they're real.
> Anthony: They're puppets.
> GF: Could you meet them on the street?
> Anthony: No, we couldn't.

| Fiona: | No, 'cause they're famous! |
|---|---|
| GF: | Could you visit them in their house? |
| Colm: | No, no . . . cause there'd be gardai and police officers. |
| Anthony: | They don't have gardai in England, do they? |

Each child seemed to apply a different criterion in the assessment of the modality of the characters. Anthony maintained his position by first of all saying that they were puppets and impossible to visit, and then attempted to deflate the others notions of reality by introducing the query; 'they don't have gardai in England, do they?' Fiona used different criteria, regarding the puppets as real, but was herself removed from them because of their fame. Modality for these children is certainly not a fixed property of the message, but something that is in the process of negotiation. Even among this relatively homogenous group in terms of age, social background and experience, very different criteria, internal and external cues, were used to inform their modality judgements.

A large proportion of the discussion time regarding *Baywatch* referred to issues of modality. The children used both internal and external markers in the discourse. Internal markers which made specific reference to the technical processes involved in television production were mentioned; 'good actors', convincing acting, camera effects and make-up.

| Emma: | Yeah, but it's just actors doing it. |
|---|---|
| Michael: | They would happen but it's not real . . . they're just actors doing it. |
| Scott: | That's just a swimming pool. |
| Sinéad: | It doesn't really look like a swimming pool in the show, 'cause when the cameras go under the water you can't see real clear. |

The eleven and twelve-year-old children were quite sure that the scenes were constructed but assigned a high modality to the narrative. In another extract they showed a greater willingness to suspend their disbelief:

| GF: | Where would you meet them? |
|---|---|
| Michael: | Down at the sea. |
| Scott: | In their house. |
| Michael: | You could try to drown yourself and then they'd come over and rescue you . . . |

Here, instead of pointing out that *Baywatch* was constructed using actors, the children seemed to attribute a high modality, and appeared to believe that the Rescue Squad actually existed on a beach somewhere. Perhaps their lack of social experience of Californian life is what affected their judgements:

| Emer: | Yeah, maybe it is when it's sunny and all. |
|---|---|
| John: | Yeah, it could happen over in America where it's always sunny . . . |
| Matthew: | I don't know, maybe . . . |

External markers were also used in the deconstruction of the physiques of the children's favourite characters. They compared the actor's looks to their own criteria of what normal people look like, and decided that certain enhancements were used to good effect.

| | |
|---|---|
| Scott: | That's the way she looks . . . that's the way she looks . . . her figure. |
| Emma: | I'd say they put make-up on her, her tan . . . |
| GF: | What makes her look good? |
| Scott: | Her plastic surgeon . . . |
| GF: | Did she have plastic surgery? |
| Scott: | Yeah! For here . . . (points to chest) |

Rather than negotiating the modality Scott appeared to respond to the challenge to state what his peers were indirectly trying to say, and made a direct reference to Pamela Anderson's physique which was an indirect sexual reference.

The children of this older group attached low modality to *Baywatch* and used both internal and external markers of modality to arrive at their judgements. One of their greatest pleasures was in the deconstruction of the programme in terms of the set and the physical make-up of the characters. However, their modality judgements in relation to narrative credibility were not as consistent as their judgements in relation to the constructed nature of the programme, with the children showing a reluctance to commit themselves, as social experience in relation to American lifestyles was not within their cultural range.

## Conscious and Unconscious Pleasures

The children's discourse was examined for actual mentions of the particular aspects of the programmes which gave them pleasure. It was expected that they would indicate what they liked about the programmes, either directly or inferentially, through the retelling of their favourite parts and talking about their favourite characters. The aspects of both programmes which were verbally indicated by the children as pleasurable were considered the conscious pleasures and relate to the less intense, more everyday type of pleasure which is governed by the reality principle and is therefore socially acceptable. In relation to *Den TV* the pleasures which the children mentioned were found in the humour, with the characters described as 'funny', 'mad', 'weird' and 'crazy'. The wide exposure of the puppets on other media seemed to add to their enjoyment. The conscious pleasures of *Baywatch* were clearly concerned with the narrative structure of the programme. The children indicated that they enjoyed the build-up of suspense followed by the solution of the problem guaranteeing narrative closure. A preoccupation with the looks of the characters was also a central pleasure, acknowledged by the children throughout the discourse:

| | |
|---|---|
| Emma: | I like Matt . . . what he looks like. |
| Michael: | He's a great actor . . . whenever he gets caught you'd swear like he was really captured and the way they rescue him and the way he rescues other people. |

GF:        That's the big guy, isn't it?
Emma:      Yeah, he's big and real good looking.

In this extract Emma focused on Matt's appearance while Michael was impressed by his acting ability and his bravery and valour. Interestingly both boys and girls indicated that they took pleasure in the looks of the actors, with the boys' attention focused on Pamela Anderson and the girls' focused on Matt. Throughout the discussions the children consistently used Pamela Anderson's real name rather than the name of the character she portrays in the series, CJ, a factor which could be attributed to the breadth of her fame, or the sense of admiration attached to her.

The children's talk was also analysed to discover pleasures which may be more intense, and are linked to the pleasure principle. As these are unconscious pleasures they are difficult to interpret, but, as already indicated, within any message there are levels of meaning which can be related to the id, ego and superego. The id is the level at which the pleasure principle operates, and is the level of meaning indicated by the use of the Child voice. These pleasures were considered as the unconscious pleasures. During the course of the conversations about *Den TV* many of the children made attempts to imitate the character's voices and actions. They mimicked the puppets and re-enacted scenes which often meant being two characters at once. With regard to children talking about their favourite television programmes, this type of imitation could be considered to be unconscious, as they automatically and unselfconsciously slipped into the imitation mode and actually 'became' the characters, without giving any indication of being aware of the difference between talking about the characters and actually imitating them. The unconscious pleasure which may be inferred from this type of interaction is that of identification. In their discourse the children consistently identified with the subversive meanings, and where ideological meanings were acknowledged, the pleasure was found in their subversion. The unconscious pleasures of *Baywatch*, indicated in the extracts where the eleven and twelve year olds engaged the Child voice and manifested high levels of embarrassment, appeared to be related to the pleasure of looking at and enjoying the human physical shape. In a sense this was also a conscious pleasure, because the children acknowledged it, but the unconscious pleasure, which can only be inferred, may be the erotic pleasure found in looking at another person as object, explained in Freud's theory of voyeurism. In *Baywatch* the invitation was extended to participate in the fictive space developing the narrative along a fantasy in which the desire to see more is continually being stimulated. This desire is only partially satisfied ensuring the reproduction of desire. The desire to see more is central to the engagement of voyeuristic pleasure, but because of the fragmentation of the fictive space and the division of the narrative into a number of sequences the engagement of voyeuristic pleasures in relation to *Baywatch* is dispersed.

# Conclusions

The programmes which were chosen by these particular children as favourites, *Den TV* and *Baywatch* are successful in that they are chosen from among a wide range of programmes. It has been argued that in order for a fictional work to hold attention and to be experienced as psychologically convincing it must be consistent with the ways in which the unconscious processes operate (Urwin, 1995:131). The analysis of the texts, in conjunction with an analysis of the children's discourse, illustrated that the most salient pleasure was found in those aspects of the text which linked to unconscious processes. *Den TV*'s attraction was found in the expression of the struggle between the Parent and Child selves in the individual. The pleasure that was highlighted by the children identified with this struggle, which links to the psychical apparatus of the id, ego and superego. In relation to *Baywatch* the most salient pleasure was also one which engaged with unconscious processes. The combination of techniques, use of point-of-view and reverse shot structures, a focus on image rather than sound, and an effect that was filmic rather than televisual invited the engagement of a pleasure that is voyeuristic in nature. The most salient pleasure indicated by the children both verbally and non-verbally, was the act of looking, a pleasure which is linked to voyeuristic instincts, and therefore consistent with ways in which unconscious processes operate.

The relationship between the salient pleasures of the programmes and the unconscious processes to which they relate, could be attributed to the text, as a particular response to a particular programme. It could also be suggested, somewhat tentatively, that the most intense pleasure indicated by the children is related to the stage of psychosexual development at which they are operating. Children aged eight and nine are in the latency stage of development when the energies are devoted to the learning of skills, both social and intellectual (Thomas, 1992:148). It is a time of learning to adapt to the rules and mores of society and culture, an accommodation which also takes place at the unconscious level in the resolution of demands between the id, ego and superego, but not without some conflict. The attraction of *Den TV* was found in the expression of the conflict between the different selves, and was therefore related to their stage of psychosexual development.

The older group of children are in the process of emerging from the latency stage and are moving towards the genital stage, where the component sexual instincts become organised into adult sexuality (Thomas, 1992:149). They are less centrally concerned with the demands of society and the accommodation of them within the different selves, as sexuality becomes the focus. The unconscious processes which *Baywatch* engaged appeared to link to the voyeuristic instinct, an instinct which is manifested in the sexual desire to look. The children of this age group were captivated by the aspect of the programme which emphasised sexuality, which indicates their stage of psychosexual development.

At first glance the engagement of the children's unconscious processes might seem to indicate that they are helpless victims who are malleable and gullible in response to the messages of television. Talking with the children illustrated that this was far from being the case, and revealed that the relationship between children and television is far more empowering. From the analysis of the two programmes in terms of text and responses to the text, it appears that the pleasures experienced by the children are to some extent bound by the text. In both cases the children found pleasure in responding in the way that the text demanded. However the pleasures indicated by the children were not all text-determined. With the younger group they used all the critical powers within their grasp to come to terms with the modality debate. A pleasure found outside the text was an enjoyment of the high level of exposure granted to the puppets on other programmes and media. Perhaps this conspiracy of fantasy legitimates the children's pleasure in the characters, and allows a social approval of their participation in the fiction. The critical processes of the older group of children were more developed as they found pleasure in the deconstruction of the programme and its characters, a factor which could not be described as text-determined. The children showed an ability to play around with the messages of the medium, whether in the form of playful imitation, or in the exhibition of their powers as critics in the destruction of its artificiality.

Talking with children about the pleasures they find in television was worthwhile in that it highlighted the factors which produced pleasure and revealed some variables which intervene in their relationship with the medium. This research was limited in that it focused on a set of responses elicited from a particular set of children in response to the particular texts, and as such provided a snap-shot perspective from which generalisations cannot be drawn. However its value lies in dispelling the notion, 'debilitating in its pessimism' (Fiske, 1989:105), of children's manipulation at the hands of a powerful medium over which they have little control. Instead it reinforced the notion that children's perspectives must be taken into account in the debate on children and television, and that their voices deserve to be heard.

# References

Allen, R.C. (1993) *Channels of Discourse, Reassembled*. London: Routledge.

Ang, I. (1991) *Desperately Seeking the Audience*. London: Routledge.

Bandura, A., Ross, D., and Ross, S.A. (1963) 'Imitation of film-mediated aggressive models', *Journal of Abnormal and Social Psychology*, 67: 601–7.

Bandura, A. (1965) 'Influence of models' reinforcement contingencies on the acquisition of initiative responses', *Journal of Personality and Social Psychology*, 1: 589–95.

Bazalgette, C. and Buckingham, D. (eds) (1995) *In Front of the Children: Screen Entertainment and Young Audiences*. London: British Film Institute.

Berne, E. (1968) *Games People Play: The Psychology of Human Relationships*. Harmondsworth: Penguin.

Buckingham, D. (1993) *Children Talking Television: The Making of Television Literacy.* London: Falmer Press.

Caughie, J. (1981) 'Rhetoric, Pleasure and Art Television: Dreams of Leaving', *Screen,* 22 (4): 9–31.

Dorr, A. (1986) *Television and Children: A special medium for a special audience.* Beverly Hills: Sage.

Ellis, J. (1982) *Visible Fictions.* London: Routledge.

Fiske, J. (1987) *Television Culture.* London: Methuen.

Fiske, J (1989) *Understanding Popular Culture.* London: Routledge.

Flitterman Lewis, S. (1993) 'Psychoanalysis, Film and Television', in R.C. Allen (ed.) *Channels of Discourse, Reassembled.* London: Routledge.

Freud, S. (1933) 'New Introductory Lectures on Psychoanalysis', in J Strachey (ed.) *Standard Edition,* Vol. 22.

Gallop, J. (1982) *Feminism and Psychoanalysis: The Daughter's Seduction.* London: Macmillan.

Garnham, N. (1974) 'Subjectivity, Ideology, Class and Historical Realism', *Screen,* 20 (1): 121–33

Gerbner, G. and Gross, L. (1976) 'Living with Television: The Violence Profile', *Journal of Communication:* 26 (2).

Harvey, S. (1978) *May '68 and Film Theory.* London: British Film Institute.

Hay, J. (1993) 'Afterword', in R.C. Allen, *Channels of Discourse, Reassembled.* London: Routledge.

Himmelweit, H.T., Oppenheim, A.N., and Vince, P. (1958) *Television and the Child.* London: Oxford University Press.

Hodge, B. and D. Tripp (1986) *Children and Television: A Semiotic Approach.* Cambridge: Polity.

Katz, E. and D. Foulkes (1962) 'Use of Mass Media as Escape: Clarification of a Concept', *Public Opinion Quarterly,* 26: 377–88.

Labov, W. (1972) 'The Logic of Non-Standard English', in P.P. Giglioli (ed.) *Language and Social Context.* Harmondsworth: Penguin.

Lacan, J. (1977) *The Four Fundamentals of Psychoanalysis.* London: Hogarth Press.

Lovell, T. (1980) *Pictures of Reality.* London: British Film Institute.

Messenger Davies, M. (1995) 'Babes 'n the Hood: Pre-school Television and its Audiences in the United States and Britain', in C. Bazalgette and D. Buckingham, *In Front of the Children: Screen Entertainment and Young Audiences.* London: British Film Institute.

Metz, C. (1982) *The Imaginary Signifier.* Bloomington: Indiana University Press.

Mulvey, L. (1976) 'Visual Pleasure and Narrative Cinema', *Screen,* 16 (3): 6–18.

Palmer, P. (1986) *The Lively Audience: A Study of Children Around the TV Set.* Sydney: Allen and Unwin.

Piaget, J. (1975) 'The Stages of Intellectual Development of the Child', in P. Mussen, J. Linger and J. Kagen (eds) *Basic and Contemporary Issues in Developmental Psychology.* New York: Harper and Row.

Schramm, W. (1954). *The Process and Effect of Mass Communication.* Urbana, Ill.: University of Illinois Press.

Schramm, W. (1964) *The Effects of TV on Children and Adolescents.* New York: UNESCO.

Strachey, J. (ed.) (1953–66) *The Standard Edition of the Complete Psychological Works of Sigmund Freud.* Vols. 1–24. London: Hogarth Press.

Thomas, K. (1992) 'Psychodynamics: The Freudian Approach', in *Introduction to Psychology.* Milton Keynes: Open University Press.

Urwin, C. (1995) 'Turtle Power: Illusion and Imagination in Children's Play', in C. Bazalgette and D. Buckingham (eds) *In Front of The Children: Screen Entertainment and Young Audiences*. London: British Film Institute.

Wartella, E. (ed.) (1979) *Children Communicating*. Beverly Hills: Sage.

Watson, P.C. and Johnson-Laird, P.N. (eds) (1977) *Thinking: Readings in Cognitive Science*. Cambridge: Cambridge University Press.

Watt, B. (1994) 'TV Lies About Us in our Infancy', *Media Educational Journal*, 16: 11–16.

Winn, M. (1977) *The Plug-in Drug*. New York: Viking Press.

# Key to Transcription Symbols for Verbatim Quotations

| | |
|---|---|
| . . . | (At the beginning of the quote) – not the beginning of the speaker's statement |
| . . . | (At the end of the quote) – not the end of the speaker's statement or speaker interrupted |
| . . . | (During the quote) – speaker pauses |
| (. . .) | Passage edited out |
| [( )] | Phatic communication, e.g. [(mm)] or [(yeah)] by others, while speaker continues |
| ( ) | Unclear as to what was being said |
| (word) | Possible hearing |
| [ ] | Author's clarification of what is being spoken about |
| GF | Group facilitator |
| I | Interviewer |
| / | New speaker |

# List of Contributors

Helen Byrne is a teacher in Coláiste na Maighdine, Presentation Secondary School, Waterford.

Eoin Devereux is a lecturer in the Department of Government and Society, University of Limerick.

Margaret Gunning is a teacher in Cnoc Mhuire Senior School, Killinarden, Tallaght, Co. Dublin.

Mary J. Kelly is a statutory lecturer in Sociology at University College Dublin.

David Miller is a member of the Stirling Media Research Institute, Scotland.

Paul Nolan is Director of the Workers' Educational Association, Belfast.

Barbara O'Connor is a lecturer in the School of Communications, Dublin City University

Brian O'Neill is a lecturer in the Communications Department, Dublin Institute of Technology.

Sara O'Sullivan is a Faculty of Arts fellow in the Department of Sociology, University College Dublin.

Stephen Ryan is a lecturer in the Communications Department, Dublin Institute of Technology.

Iarfhlaith Watson is a postgraduate student in the Department of Sociology, University College Dublin.

Raymond Watson is Group Editor of Flagship Newspapers, Belfast.

# Index

Religion

Class, gender, ethnicity